Introductory Statistics Using SPSS

For Mildred & Helen

Introductory Statistics Using SPSS

Herschel Knapp

University of California, Los Angeles

Los Angeles | London | New Delhi
Singapore | Washington DC

Los Angeles | London | New Delhi
Singapore | Washington DC

FOR INFORMATION:

SAGE Publications, Inc.
2455 Teller Road
Thousand Oaks, California 91320
E-mail: order@sagepub.com

SAGE Publications Ltd.
1 Oliver's Yard
55 City Road
London EC1Y 1SP
United Kingdom

SAGE Publications India Pvt. Ltd.
B 1/I 1 Mohan Cooperative Industrial Area
Mathura Road, New Delhi 110 044
India

SAGE Publications Asia-Pacific Pte. Ltd.
3 Church Street
#10-04 Samsung Hub
Singapore 049483

Acquisitions Editor: Helen Salmon
Assistant Editor: Katie Guarino
Editorial Assistant: Kaitlin Coghill
Production Editor: Libby Larson
Copy Editor: Gillian Dickens
Typesetter: C&M Digitals (P) Ltd.
Proofreader: A. J. Sobczak
Indexer: Will Ragsdale
Cover Designer: Edgar Abarca
Marketing Manager: Nicole Elliott

Printed in the United States of America

Library of Congress Cataloging-in-Publication Data

Knapp, Herschel.
Introductory statistics using SPSS / Herschel Knapp, University of California, Los Angeles.

pages cm
Includes index.

ISBN 978-1-4522-7769-1 (pbk.)
ISBN 978-1-4833-1310-8 (web pdf)

1. SPSS for Windows. 2. Social sciences—Statistical methods—Computer programs. I. Title.

HA32.K59 2014
005.5´5—dc23   2013024090

This book is printed on acid-free paper.

13 14 15 16 17 10 9 8 7 6 5 4 3 2 1

Brief Contents

Detailed Contents

2. Sampling

3. Working in SPSS

PART II—STATISTICAL PROCESSES

4. Descriptive Statistics

Preface

Somewhere, something incredible is waiting to be known.

—Carl Sagan

OVERVIEW OF BOOK

This book covers the statistical functions used most frequently in social science publications; this should not be considered a complete compendium of useful statistics, however, since in other technological fields that you are likely already familiar with (e.g., word processing, spreadsheet, presentation software, etc.), you have probably discovered that the "90/10 rule" applies: *You can get 90% of your work done using only 10% of the functions.* For example, if you were to thoroughly explore each submenu of your word processor, you would likely discover more than 100 functions and options; however, in terms of actual productivity, 90% of the time, you are probably using only about 10% of them to get your work done (e.g., save, load, copy, delete, paste, font, tab, center, print, spell check). Back to statistics: If you can master the statistical processes contained in this text, it is expected that this will arm you with what you need to effectively analyze the majority of your own data and confidently interpret the statistical publications of others.

This is not a book about abstract statistical theory or the derivation of statistical formulas; rather, this is a book about *applied* statistics. There are no formulas to memorize in this text. This book is designed to provide you with practical answers to the following questions: (1) *If I have this kind of data, what statistical test should I use?* (2) *How do I set up the data?* (3) *What parameters should I specify when ordering the test?* and (4) *How do I interpret the results?*

In terms of performing the actual statistical calculations, we will be using SPSS, a sophisticated statistical processing software package. This facilitates speed and accuracy when it comes to producing statistical results in the form of tables and graphs, but SPSS is not an automatic program. In the same way that your word processor does not write your papers for you, SPSS does not know what you want done with your data until you tell it. Fortunately, those instructions are issued through clear menus. Your job will be to learn what statistical procedure suits which circumstance, to configure the data properly, to order the appropriate tests, and to mindfully interpret the output reports.

ORGANIZATION

This book is organized into four parts:

Part I—Statistical Principles

These chapters provide the basis for understanding the statistical concepts and SPSS fundamentals that will be addressed in further detail in Part II.

Chapter 1—Research Principles

Chapter 2—Sampling

Chapter 3—Working in SPSS

Part II—Statistical Processes

These chapters contain the actual statistical procedures used to analyze data.

Chapter 4—Descriptive Statistics

Chapter 5—*t* Test

Chapter 6—ANOVA

Chapter 7—Paired *t* Test

Chapter 8—Correlation and Regression

Chapter 9—Chi-Square

After you have completed Chapters 4 through 9, the following table will help you navigate this book to efficiently select the statistical test(s) best suited to your (data) situation. For now, it is advised that you skip this table, as it contains statistical terminology that will be covered thoroughly in the chapters that follow.

Overview of Statistical Functions

Chapter	Statistical Function	When to Use	Results
4	Descriptive statistics	Any continuous or categorical variable	Generates a summary of a variable using figures and graphs
5	*t* Test	Two groups with continuous variables	Indicates if there is a statistically significant difference between the two groups (G_1:G_2)
6	ANOVA	Similar to the *t* test, except it is used when there are more than two groups	Similar to the *t* test, except it compares all pairs of groups (G_1:G_2, G_1:G_3, G_2:G_3)
7	Paired *t* test	Compare pretest to posttest (continuous variables within one group)	Indicates if there is a statistically significant difference between the pretest and posttest
8	Correlation and regression	Two continuous variables for each subject/record	Indicates the strength and direction of the relationship between two variables
9	Chi-square	Two categorical variables	Indicates if there is a statistically significant difference between two categories

Part III—Data Handling

This chapter provides useful data handling techniques and SPSS tips and tricks to facilitate efficient processing.

Chapter 10—Supplemental SPSS Operations

Part IV—Solutions to Odd-Numbered Exercises

This section provides fully developed solutions to the odd-numbered exercises for each chapter.

DOWNLOADABLE LEARNING RESOURCES

In Part II, Exercises 1 through 5 have the codebook (description of each variable) and corresponding data sets printed in the book. This will provide you with essential practice in setting up SPSS data sets from the ground up. Mastering this skill will enable you to analyze data from other sources. For convenience, larger data sets for Exercises 6 through 10 are available for download.

The website for this book is **www.sagepub.com/knapp,** which contains the following resources:

SPSS data sets for each example

SPSS data sets for Part II, Exercises 6 through 10

SPSS files for Part III

SPSS tutorial videos

RESOURCES FOR INSTRUCTORS

Password-protected instructor resources are available on the website for this book at **www.sagepub.com/knapp** and include:

Editable, chapter-specific PowerPoint slides

Solutions to even-numbered in-text questions

Sample course syllabi for semester and quarter courses

SPSS tutorial videos

SPSS data sets for all examples and exercises

MARGIN ICONS

This text includes icons to help you navigate (back) to critical points:

Icon   **Meaning**

 Pretest Checklist—*Instructions to check that the data meet the criteria necessary to run a statistical test*

 Test Run—*Procedures and parameters for running the statistical test*

 Results—*Interpreting the output from the* ***Test Run***

 Hypothesis Resolution—*Determining the outcome based on the* ***Results***

 Documenting Results—*Write-up based on* ***Hypothesis Resolution***

 Key Point—*Important fact*

 Reminder—*Critical point to remember*

 Technical Tip—*Helpful data-processing technique*

 Formula—*Useful formula that SPSS does not perform but can be easily processed on any calculator*

 Refer-Back—*This point will be referenced on future pages (think of this as a bookmark)*

Acknowledgments

SAGE and the author acknowledge and thank the following reviewers whose feedback contributed to the development of this text:

Patricia F. Pearce, University of Alabama at Birmingham

Brenda K. Vollman, Loyola University New Orleans

Holly Johnson, University of Ottawa

Jamail D. Carter, Azusa Pacific University; Barstow Community College; United States University

Timothy G. Ford, University of Louisiana at Monroe

Bruce H. Wade, Spelman College

Jo Brocato, California State University, Long Beach

Ellen P. McCann, George Mason University

Martha Vungkhanching, California State University, Fresno

Matthew Costello, University of Nebraska, Lincoln

Dazhi Yang, Boise State University

We also gratefully acknowledge the contribution of Dean Cameron, whose cartoons enliven this book.

About the Author

Herschel Knapp, PhD, MSSW, has 20 years of experience as a social science researcher; for seven of those years he provided project management for innovative implementations designed to improve the quality of patient care throughout the Veterans Health Administration via multisite, health science implementations. In addition to full-time work at the VA, he teaches masters-level courses at the University of California, Los Angeles and California State University, Los Angeles. Dr. Knapp has served as the lead statistician on a longitudinal cancer research project and managed the program evaluation metrics for a multisite, nonprofit children's center. His clinical work includes emergency/trauma therapy in hospital settings. The author of over 30 articles in peer-reviewed health science journals, he is also the author of *Therapeutic Communication: Developing Professional Skills, Second Edition* (SAGE, 2014) and *Introduction to Social Work Practice: A Practical Workbook* (SAGE, 2010). Dr. Knapp is currently involved in developing and implementing innovative telehealth systems, utilizing videoconferencing technology to facilitate optimal healthcare service delivery to remote patients, and to coordinate specialty consultations among healthcare providers.

PART I

Statistical Principles

I want the numbers to tell me a story.

—Anonymous

Research Principles

This'll get things started.

- Research Questions
- Control and Experimental Groups
- Rationale for Random Assignment
- Hypothesis Formulation
- Reading Statistical Outcomes
- Accept/Reject Hypothesis
- Levels of Measure
- Types of Variables

The scientific mind does not so much provide the right answers as ask the right questions.

—Claude Levi-Strauss

LEARNING OBJECTIVES

Upon completing this chapter, you will be able to:

- Identify various forms of research questions
- Differentiate between *control* and *experimental* groups
- Comprehend the rationale for random assignment
- Understand the basis for hypothesis formulation
- Understand the fundamentals of reading statistical outcomes
- Appropriately accept/reject hypotheses based on statistical outcomes
- Understand the four levels of measure
- Determine the variable type: *categorical* or *continuous*

OVERVIEW

This chapter introduces statistical concepts that will be used throughout this book. Applying statistics involves more than just processing tables of numbers; it involves being curious and assembling mindful questions in an attempt to better understand what is going on in a setting. As you will see, statistics extends far beyond simple averages and headcounts. Just as a toolbox contains a variety of tools to accomplish a variety of diverse tasks (e.g., screwdriver to place or remove screws, saw to cut materials, etc.), there are a variety of statistical tests, each suited to address a different type of research question.

RESEARCH QUESTIONS

A statistician colleague of mine once said, "I want the numbers to tell me a story." Those nine words elegantly describe the mission of statistics. Naturally, the story depends on the nature of the statistical question. Some statistical questions render descriptive (summary) statistics, such as: How many minors visit a public park on weekends? How many cars cross this bridge per day? What is the average age of students at a school? How many accidents have occurred at this intersection? What percentage of people in a geographical region has a particular disease? What is the average income per household in a community? What percentage of students graduates from high school? Attempting to comprehend such figures simply by inspecting them visually may work for a few dozen numbers, but visual inspection of these figures would not be feasible if there were hundreds or even thousands of numbers to consider. To get a reasonable idea of the nature of these numbers, we can mathematically and graphically summarize them and thereby better understand any amount of figures using *descriptive statistics,* as detailed in Chapter 4.

Another form of research question involves comparisons; often this takes the form of an experimental outcome. Some questions may involve comparisons of scores between two groups, such as: In a fourth-grade class, do girls or boys do better on math tests? Do smokers sleep more than nonsmokers? Do students whose parents are teachers have better test scores than students whose parents are not teachers? In a two-group clinical trial, one group was given a new drug to lower blood pressure, and the other group was given a placebo; is there a statistically significant difference between the blood pressure levels of these two groups? These sorts of questions, involving the scores from two groups, are answered using the *t* test, which is covered in Chapter 5.

Research questions and their corresponding designs may involve several groups. For example, in a district with four elementary schools, each uses a different method for teaching spelling; is there a statistically significant difference between spelling scores from one school to another? Another example would be a clinical trial aimed at discovering the optimal dosage of a new sleeping pill; Group 1 gets a placebo, Group 2 gets the drug at a 10-mg dose, and Group 3 gets the drug at a 15-mg dose; is there a statistically significant difference between the groups in terms of number of hours of sleep per night? Questions involving analyzing the scores from more than two groups are processed using analysis of variance (ANOVA), which is covered in Chapter 6.

Some research questions involve assessing the effectiveness of a treatment by administering a pretest, then the treatment, then a posttest to determine if the group's scores improved after the treatment. For example, suppose it is expected that brighter lighting may enhance mood. To test for this, the researcher administers a mood survey under normal lighting to a group, which renders a score (e.g., 0 = very depressed, 10 = very happy). Next, the lighting is brightened, after which that group is asked to reanswer the mood test. The question is: According to the pretest and posttest scores, did the group's mood (score) increase significantly after the lighting was changed? Consider another example: Suppose it is expected that physical exercise enhances math scores. To test this, a fourth-grade teacher administers a multiplication test to each student. Next, the students are taken out to the playground to run to the far fence and back three times, after which the students immediately return to the classroom to take another multiplication test. The question is: Is there a statistically significant difference between the test scores *before and after* the physical activity? Questions involving before-and-after scores within a group are processed with the paired *t* test, which is covered in Chapter 7.

Another kind of research question may seek to understand the (co)relation between two variables. For example: What is the relationship between the number of homework hours per week and grade point average (GPA)? We might expect that as homework hours go up, GPA would go up as well. Similarly, we might ask: What is the relationship between exercise and weight (if exercise goes up, does weight go down)? What is the relationship between mood and hours of sleep per night (when mood is low, do people sleep less)? Questions involving the correlation between two scores are processed using *correlation* and *regression,* which are covered in Chapter 8.

Research questions may also involve comparisons between categories. For example: Is there a difference in ice cream preferences (chocolate, strawberry, vanilla) based on gender (male, female)—in other words, does gender have any bearing on ice cream flavor selection? We could also investigate questions such as: Does the marital status of the parents (divorced, not divorced) have any bearing on the child's graduation from high school (graduated, not graduated)? Questions involving comparisons among categories are processed using *chi-square* (*chi* is pronounced *k-eye*), which is covered in Chapter 9.

As you can see, even at this introductory level, a variety of statistical questions can be asked and answered. An important part of knowing which statistical test to reach for involves understanding the nature of the question and the type of data at hand.

CONTROL AND EXPERIMENTAL GROUPS

Even if you are new to statistics, you have probably heard of *control* and *experimental* groups. To understand the rationale for using this two-group system, consider an investigation that uses an experimental group *only*. For prompt comprehension, we will begin with a silly example and then move on to a more real-world example.

Example 1: The Acme Company has just released a new Monster Spray, guaranteed to keep scary nighttime monsters from invading the bedroom all night. Clinical trials involved issuing canisters of Monster Spray to 100 households; participants are instructed to administer the Monster Spray every night for 1 month as directed and to journal the number of scary nighttime monsters encountered each night. At the end of the month, the data were gathered and processed, and based on statistical analysis, it was revealed that zero monsters were encountered in these test households—hence, the Acme Company marketing department proudly announces that scientific studies prove that Monster Spray is safe and effective in warding off scary nighttime monsters from bedrooms.

Naturally, the question stands, "Can we really attribute the absence of monsters to the use of Monster Spray?" In this single-group study design, we have no way of knowing how many monsters would have invaded had the Monster Spray not been used. To assess the effectiveness of Monster Spray in a more rigorous manner, we introduce a control group. Control groups typically get no level of treatment, or sometimes a placebo, wherein members of the control group are given something that appears to be a treatment but actually has no therapeutic properties (e.g., a sugar pill). A placebo is often preferable to administering absolutely no treatment because expectations can influence outcomes; to clarify—if participants are given a placebo but believe that they have been given a viable treatment designed to relieve their symptoms, some will begin to feel better through mechanisms that we do not fully understand. From a statistical standpoint, we could test the level of symptom relief experienced by individuals in the control group compared with those in the experimental group. To call this treatment effective, we would need to see that the experimental group statistically significantly outperforms the control group in terms of symptom relief.

Getting back to our Monster Spray example, consider an enhanced design for the experiment: 100 Monster Spray bottles are loaded with the newly formulated Monster Repellant, and another 100 Monster Spray bottles are loaded with distilled water. Let us also assume that the actual Monster Spray is indistinguishable from water—it produces a clear, light, unscented mist. The bottles are then distributed to 200 households, but the participants are not told which compound is in their spray bottle (the actual Monster Spray or the distilled water); participants are instructed to use the Monster Spray nightly for 1 month and to record the number of creepy nighttime monster invasions in the journal for each night. At the end of the month, the journals are collected, the data are entered and processed, and we discover that there were zero monster invasions in the experimental group (which got the actual Monster Repellant compound), which concurs with the initial trial. We also learn that there were zero monster invasions in the control group (which got the distilled water). Even without advanced statistical skills, it is becoming clear that the Monster Spray did not outperform the water—hence, we would more confidently doubt our initial conclusions that the absence of monsters is attributable to the use of Monster Spray; this experiment shows that there would have been zero monsters anyway.

Now that you have the basic rationale for using an experimental group coupled with a separate control group, consider a second, more realistic example.

Example 2: Suppose you conducted a one-group study and collected information only on people who received a flu shot, and you discover that 95% of those individuals remained healthy throughout the entire flu season. In isolation, this 95% finding seems fairly impressive. Now consider an enhanced design, where in addition to surveying people who *had the flu shot,* you also gather data on those who *did not have a flu shot,* and you discover that 95% of those who did not get a flu shot remained healthy throughout the flu season as well. Now suddenly that flu shot is starting to look considerably less impressive. Having the second group (the control group) gives you a baseline to compare with the experimental group. Intuitively, to determine the effectiveness of an intervention, you are looking for *substantial differences in the performance between the two groups*—is there a significant difference between the results of those in the experimental group compared with the control group? The statistical tests detailed in Chapters 5 through 9 focus on different types of procedures for evaluating the difference(s) between groups (experimental vs. control) to help determine the effect of the intervention–whether the experimental group significantly outperformed the control group.

RATIONALE FOR RANDOM ASSIGNMENT

Understanding the utility of randomly assigning subjects to experimental/control groups is best explained by example. Dr. Zinn and Dr. Zorders have come up with Z-Math, a revolutionary system for teaching multiplication. The Z-Math package is shipped out to schools in a local district to determine if it is more effective than the current teaching method. The instructions specify that each fourth-grade class should be divided in half and routed to separate rooms, with students in one room receiving the Z-Math teaching and students in the other room getting their regular math lesson. At the end, both groups are administered a multiplication test, with the results of both groups compared. The question is: *How should the class be divided into two groups?* This is not such a simple question. If the classroom is divided into boys and girls, this may influence the outcome; gender may be a relevant factor in math skills—if by chance we send the gender with stronger math skills to receive the Z-Math intervention, this may serve to inflate those scores. Alternatively, suppose we decided to slice the class in half by seating—this introduces a different potential confound; what if the half who sits near the front of the classroom are naturally more attentive than those who sit in the back half of the classroom? Again, this grouping method may confound the findings of the study. Finally, suppose the teacher splits the class by age; this presents yet another potential confound—maybe older students are able to perform math better than younger students. In addition, it is unwise to allow subjects to self-select which group they want to be in; it may be that more proficient math students, or students who take their studies more seriously, may systemically opt for the Z-Math group, thereby potentially influencing the outcome.

Through this simple example, it should be clear that the act of selectively assigning subjects to (control/experimental) groups can unintentionally affect the outcome of a study; it is for this reason that we often opt for *random assignment* to assemble such groups. In this example, the Z-Math instructions may specify that a coin flip be used to assign students to each of the two groups: Heads assigns a student to Z-Math, and tails assigns a student to the usual math teaching method. This random assignment method ultimately means that regardless of factors such as gender, seating position, age, math proficiency, and academic motivation, each student will have an equal (50/50) chance of being assigned to either group. The process of random assignment will generally result in roughly the same proportion of math-smart students, the same proportion of front- and back-of-the-room students, and the same proportion of older and younger students being assigned to each group. If done properly, random assignment helps to cancel out factors endemic in subjects that may have otherwise tipped the findings one way or another.

HYPOTHESIS FORMULATION

Everyone has heard of the word *hypothesis;* hypotheses simply spell out each of the anticipated possible outcomes of an experiment. In simplest terms, before we embark on the experiment, we need one hypothesis that states that nothing notable happened (because sometimes experiments fail). This would be the null hypothesis (H_0), basically meaning that the experiment had a null effect—nothing notable happened.

Another possibility is that something notable did happen (the experiment worked), so we would need an alternate hypothesis that accounts for this (H_1).

Continuing with the above example involving Z-Math, we first construct the null hypothesis (H_0); as expected, the null hypothesis states that the experiment produced null results—basically, the experimental group (the group that got Z-Math) and the control group (the group that got regular math) performed about the same; essentially, that would mean Z-Math was no more effective than the traditional math lesson. The test hypothesis (H_1) is phrased indicating that the experimental (Z-Math) group outperformed the control (regular math lesson) group. Hypotheses are typically written in this fashion:

H_0: Z-Math and regular math teaching methods produced equivalent test results.

H_1: Z-Math produced higher test results compared with regular teaching methods.

When the results are in, we would then know which hypothesis to reject and which to accept; from there, we can document and discuss our findings.

In cases involving more test factors or groups, additional hypotheses (e.g., H_2, H_3, H_4, etc.) can be rendered; this will be demonstrated in Chapter 6—ANOVA.

Remember: In simplest terms, the statistics that we will be processing are designed to answer the question: *Do the members of the experimental group (that get the innovative treatment) significantly outperform the members of the control group (who get no treatment, a placebo, or treatment as usual)?* As such, the hypotheses need to reflect each possible outcome. In this simple example, we can anticipate two possible outcomes: H_0 states that there is *no* significant difference between the experimental group and the control group, suggesting that *the treatment was ineffective.* On the other hand, we need another hypothesis that anticipates that the treatment will significantly outperform the control condition; as such, H_1 states that there *is* a significant difference in the outcomes between the experimental and control conditions, suggesting that *the treatment was effective.* The outcome of the statistical test will point us to which hypothesis to keep and which to reject.

READING STATISTICAL OUTCOMES

Statistical tests vary substantially in terms of the types of research questions each are designed to address, the format of the source data, their respective equations, and the content of their results, which can include figures, tables, and graphs. Although there are some similarities in reading statistical outcomes (e.g., means, alpha [α] level, p value), these concepts are best explained in the context of working examples; as such, discussion of how to read statistical outcomes will be thoroughly explained as each emerges in Chapters 4 through 9.

ACCEPT/REJECT HYPOTHESIS

As is the case with reading statistical outcomes, the decision to accept or reject a hypothesis depends on the nature of the test and, of course, the results: the alpha (α) level, p value, and, in some cases, the means. Just as with reading statistical outcomes, instructions for accepting/rejecting hypotheses for each test are best discussed in the context of actual working examples; these concepts will be covered in Chapters 5 through 9.

LEVELS OF MEASURE

Selecting the proper statistical test partly depends on the type of variables that are involved. There are four levels of measurement: nominal, ordinal, interval, and ratio.

Nominal

Nominal variables (also known as *discrete* or *categorical* variables) are used to represent categories that defy ordering. For example, suppose you wish to code ice cream flavor preference, and there are three choices: chocolate, strawberry, and vanilla. There is really no way to put these in any order; for coding and computing purposes, we could assign 1 = chocolate, 2 = strawberry, and 3 = vanilla. Since order does not matter among nominal variables, these flavors could have just as well been coded 1 = vanilla, 2 = chocolate, and 3 = strawberry. Nominal variables may be used to represent categorical variables such as gender (1 = female, 2 = male), agreement (1 = yes, 2 = no), religion (1 = atheist, 2 = Buddhist, 3 = Catholic, 4 = Hindu, 5 = Jewish, 6 = Taoist, etc.), or marital status (1 = single, 2 = married, 3 = separated, 4 = divorced, 5 = widow/widower). Since the numbers are arbitrarily assigned to labels within a category, it would be inappropriate to perform traditional arithmetic calculations on such numbers. For example, it would be foolish to compute the average *marital status* (e.g., would 1.5 indicate a *single married* person?). The same principle applies to other nominal variables such as religion or gender. There are, however, appropriate statistical operations for processing nominal variables that will be discussed in Chapter 4—descriptive statistics. In terms of statistical tests, nominal variables are considered categorical.

Ordinal

Ordinal variables are similar to nominal variables in that numbers are assigned to represent items within a category. Whereas nominal variables have no real rank order to them (e.g., chocolate, strawberry, vanilla), the values in an ordinal variable *can* be placed in a ranked order. For example, there is an order to educational degrees (1 = high school diploma, 2 = associate's degree, 3 = bachelor's degree, 4 = master's degree, 5 = doctorate degree). Other examples of ordinal variables include military rank (1 = private, 2 = corporal, 3 = sergeant, etc.) and meals (1 = breakfast, 2 = brunch, 3 = lunch, 4 = dinner, 5 = late-night snack). In terms of statistical tests, ordinal variables are considered categorical variables.

Interval

Interval variables consist of numbers that have equal spacing between them, such as numbers on a number line, ranging from $-\infty$ to $+\infty$; the distance between 1 and 2 is the same as the distance between 2 and 3, which is the same as the distance between 3 and 4, and so on. Some additional examples of interval variables are bank account balance (which could be negative) and time (seconds, minutes, hours, days, etc.). Interval variables are considered continuous variables.

Ratio

Ratio variables are similar to interval variables, except that interval variables can have negative values, whereas ratio variables cannot be less than zero. Such variables include measurements such as weight, distance, income, calories, academic grades (F = 0 . . . A = 4), number of pets, number of siblings, or number of members in a group. Ratio variables are considered continuous variables.

TYPES OF VARIABLES

When it comes to statistical processing, basically, variables fall into two types: categorical and continuous. Comprehending the types of variables involved in a data set or research design is essential when it comes to properly selecting, configuring, and running statistical tests as detailed in Part II.

Categorical

Categorical variables involve assigning a number to an item in a category; the sequence of the category may be irrelevant, as in *nominal* variables, wherein gender has no inherent order and hence could be coded 1 = female, 2 = male or 1 = male, 2 = female. *Ordinal* variables are also considered categorical; unlike nominal variables, ordinal variables *do* have an inherent order to them, which should be preserved in the coding sequence, such as 1 = breakfast, 2 = lunch, and 3 = dinner.

Continuous

Continuous variables contain the kinds of numbers that you are accustomed to dealing with. Continuous variables are *interval*- and *ratio*-type variables. Unlike categorical variables, wherein numbers are assigned to represent categories, continuous variables contain values that can stand up to actual arithmetic processing. For example, consider the variable age; it is possible to compute the average (mean) age for a list of ages.

Key Concepts

- Research question
- Control group
- Experimental group
- Random assignment
- Hypotheses
- Statistical outcomes
- Accepting/rejecting hypotheses
- Level of data (nominal, ordinal, interval, and ratio)
- Types of data (categorical and continuous)

Practice Exercises

Each of the following exercises describes the basis for an experiment that would render data that could be processed statistically.

1. It is expected that aerobic square dancing during the 30-minute recess at an elementary school will help fight childhood obesity.
   a. State the research question
   b. Identify the control and experimental group(s)
   c. Explain how you would randomly assign participants to groups
   d. State the hypotheses (H_0 and H_1)
   e. Discuss the criteria for accepting/rejecting the hypotheses

2. Recent findings suggest that nursing home residents may experience fewer depressive symptoms when they participate in pet therapy with certified dogs for 30 minutes per day.
   a. State the research question
   b. Identify the control and experimental group(s)
   c. Explain how you would randomly assign participants to groups
   d. State the hypotheses (H_0 and H_1)
   e. Discuss the criteria for accepting/rejecting the hypotheses

3. A chain of retail stores has been experiencing substantial cash shortages in cashier balances across 10 of their stores. The company is considering installing cashier security cameras.

   a. State the research question
   b. Identify the control and experimental group(s)
   c. Explain how you would randomly assign participants to groups
   d. State the hypotheses (H_0 and H_1)
   e. Discuss the criteria for accepting/rejecting the hypotheses

4. Anytown Community wants to determine if implementing a neighborhood watch program will reduce vandalism incidents.

   a. State the research question
   b. Identify the control and experimental group(s)
   c. Explain how you would randomly assign participants to groups
   d. State the hypotheses (H_0 and H_1)
   e. Discuss the criteria for accepting/rejecting the hypotheses

5. Employees at Acme Industries, consisting of four separate buildings, are chronically late. An executive is considering implementing a *get out of Friday free* lottery; each day an employee is on time, he or she gets one token entered into the weekly lottery.

   a. State the research question
   b. Identify the control and experimental group(s)
   c. Explain how you would randomly assign participants to groups
   d. State the hypotheses (H_0 and H_1)
   e. Discuss the criteria for accepting/rejecting the hypotheses

6. The Acme Herbal Tea Company advertises that their product is "the tea that relaxes."

   a. State the research question
   b. Identify the control and experimental group(s)
   c. Explain how you would randomly assign participants to groups
   d. State the hypotheses (H_0 and H_1)
   e. Discuss the criteria for accepting/rejecting the hypotheses

7. Professor Madrigal has a theory that singing improves memory.

   a. State the research question
   b. Identify the control and experimental group(s)
   c. Explain how you would randomly assign participants to groups
   d. State the hypotheses (H_0 and H_1)
   e. Discuss the criteria for accepting/rejecting the hypotheses

8. Mr. Reed believes that providing assorted colored pens will prompt his students to write longer essays.

   a. State the research question
   b. Identify the control and experimental group(s)

c. Explain how you would randomly assign participants to groups

d. State the hypotheses (H_0 and H_1)

e. Discuss the criteria for accepting/rejecting the hypotheses

9. Ms. Fractal wants to determine if working with flashcards helps students learn the multiplication table.

   a. State the research question

   b. Identify the control and experimental group(s)

   c. Explain how you would randomly assign participants to groups

   d. State the hypotheses (H_0 and H_1)

   e. Discuss the criteria for accepting/rejecting the hypotheses

10. A manager at the Acme Company Call Center wants to see if running a classic movie on a big screen (with the sound off) will increase the number of calls processed per hour.

   a. State the research question

   b. Identify the control and experimental group(s)

   c. Explain how you would randomly assign participants to groups

   d. State the hypotheses (H_0 and H_1)

   e. Discuss the criteria for accepting/rejecting the hypotheses

C H A P T E R   2

Sampling

Who needs the whole **population** when a **sample** will do nicely?

- Rationale for Sampling
- Sampling Terminology
- Representative Sample
- Probability Sampling
- Nonprobability Sampling
- Sampling Bias

Ya gots to work with what you gots to work with.

—Stevie Wonder

LEARNING OBJECTIVES

Upon completing this chapter, you will be able to:

- Comprehend the rationale for sampling: time, cost, feasibility, and extrapolation
- Understand essential sampling terminology: population, sample frame, and sample
- Derive a representative sample to facilitate external validity
- Select an appropriate method to conduct probability sampling: simple random sampling, systemic sampling, stratified sampling, disproportionate sampling, proportionate sampling, or area sampling
- Select an appropriate method to conduct nonprobability sampling: convenience sampling, snowball sampling, quota sampling, or purposive sampling
- Understand techniques for detecting and reducing sample bias

OVERVIEW

Statistics is about processing numbers in a way to produce concise, readily consumable information. One statistic that you are probably already familiar with is the average. Suppose you wanted to know the average age of students in a classroom; the task would be fairly simple—you could ask each person to write down his or her age on a slip of paper and then proceed with the calculations. In the relatively small setting of a classroom, it is possible to promptly gather the data on *everyone,* but what if you wanted to know the age of *all enrolled students* or *all students in a community?* Now the mission becomes more time-consuming, complex, and probably expensive. Instead of trying to gather data on *everyone,* as in the U.S. census survey, another option is to gather a *sample.* Gathering a sample of a population is quicker, easier, and more cost-effective than gathering data on everyone, and if done properly, the findings from your sample can provide you with quality information about the overall population.

You may not realize it, but critical decisions are made based on samples all the time. Laboratories process thousands of blood samples every day. On the basis of the small amount of blood contained in the test tube, a qualified health care professional can make determinations about the overall health status of the patient from whom the blood was drawn. Think about that for a moment: A few CCs (cubic centimeters) of blood are sufficient to carry out the tests to make quality determinations; the laboratory did not need to drain the entire blood supply from the patient, which would be time-consuming, complicated, expensive, and totally impractical—it would kill the patient. Just as a small sample of blood is sufficient to represent the status of the entire blood supply, proper sampling enables us to gather a small and manageable bundle of data from a population of interest, statistically process that data, and reasonably comprehend the larger population from which it was drawn.

RATIONALE FOR SAMPLING

Moving beyond the realm of a statistics course, statistics takes place in the real world to answer real-world questions. As with most things in the real world, gathering data involves the utilization of scarce resources; key concerns involve the time, cost, and feasibility associated with gathering quality data. With these very real constraints in mind, it is a relief to know that it is not necessary to gather *all* the data available; in fact, it is rare that a statistical data set consists of figures from the entire population (such as the U.S. census). Typically, we proceed with a viable sample and extrapolate what we need to know to better comprehend the larger population from which that sample was drawn. Let us take a closer look at each of these terms.

Time

Some consider time to be the most valuable asset; time cannot be manufactured or stored—it can only be used. Time spent doing one thing means that other things must wait. Spending an exorbitant amount of time gathering data from an entire population precludes the accomplishment of other vital activities. For example, suppose you are interested in people's opinions (yea/nay) regarding the death penalty for a paper that you are drafting for a course. Every minute you spend gathering data postpones your ability to proceed with the completion of the paper, and that paper has a firm due date. In addition, there are other demands competing for your time (e.g., other courses, work, family, friends, rest, recreation, etc.). Sampling reduces the amount of time involved in data gathering, enabling you to statistically process the data and proceed with the completion of the project within the allotted time.

Another aspect of time is that some (statistical) answers are time sensitive. Political pollsters must use sampling to gather information in a prompt fashion, hence leaving sufficient time to interpret the findings and fine-tune campaign strategies prior to the election; they simply do not have time to poll all registered voters—a well-drawn sample is sufficient.

Cost

Not all data are readily available (for free). Some statistical data may be derived from experiments or interviews, which involves multiple costs, including a recruitment advertising budget, paying staff to screen and process participants, providing reasonable financial compensation to study participants, facility expenses, and so on. Surveys are not free either; expenses may include photocopying, postage, website implementation charges, telephone equipment, and financial compensation to study participants and staff. Considering the costs associated with data collection, one can see the rationale for resorting to sampling as opposed to attempting to gather data from an entire population.

Feasibility

Data gathering takes place in the real world—hence, real-world constraints must be reckoned with when embarking on such research. Due to time and budgetary constraints, it is seldom feasible or necessary to gather data on a population-wide basis; sampling is a viable option. In the example involving the blood sample, clearly it is neither necessary nor feasible to submit the patient's entire blood supply to the lab for testing—quality determinations can be made based on well-drawn samples. In addition, if a research project focuses on a large population (e.g., all students in a school district) or a population spanning a large geographical region, it may not be feasible to gather data on that many people—hence, sampling makes sense.

Extrapolation

It turns out that by sampling properly, it is unnecessary to gather data on an entire population to achieve a reasonable comprehension of it. Extrapolation involves using sampling methods and sampling statistics to analyze the sample of data that was drawn from the population. If done properly, such findings help us to (better) understand not only the smaller (sample) group but also the larger group from which it was drawn.

SAMPLING TERMINOLOGY

As in any scientific endeavor, the realm of sampling has its own language and methods. The following terms and types of sampling will help you comprehend the kinds of sampling that you may encounter in scientific literature and provide you with viable options for carrying out your own studies. We will begin with the largest realm (the population) and work our way down to the smallest (the sample).

Population

The *population* is the entire realm of people (or items) that could be measured or counted. A population is not simply all people on the planet; the researcher specifies the population, which consists of the entire domain of interest. For example, the population may be defined as all students who are currently enrolled at a specified campus. Additional examples of populations could be all people who reside in a city, all people who belong to a club, all people who are registered voters in an election district, or all people who work for a company. As you might have surmised, the key word here is *all*.

Sample Frame

If the population that you are interested in is relatively small (e.g., the 5 people visiting the public park, the 16 people who are members of a club, etc.), then gathering data from the entire population is potentially doable. More often, the population is larger than you can reasonably accommodate, or you may be unable to attain a complete list of the entire population that you are interested in (e.g., all students enrolled in a school, every registered voter in an election district, etc.). The *sample frame,* sometimes referred to as the *sampling frame,* is the part of a population that you *could* potentially access. For example, Acme University publishes a list of student names and e-mail IDs in the form of a downloadable report on the school's public website. If this list included every single student enrolled, it would represent the entire population of the school; however, students have the privilege to opt out of this list, meaning that each student can go to his or her online profile and check a box to include or exclude his or her name and e-mail ID from this public roster. Suppose the total population of the university consists of 30,000 enrolled students, and 70% chose to have their name appear on this list; this would mean that the sample frame, the list from which you could potentially select subjects, consists of 21,000 students (30,000 × .70).

Sample

A *sample* is a portion of individuals selected from the sample frame. Certainly 21,000 is considerably less that 30,000, but that may still be an unwieldy amount for your purposes. Consider that your investigation involves conducting a 1-hour interview with participants and that each participant will be compensated $10 for his or her time; the subject fee budget for this study would be $210,000, and assuming you conducted back-to-back interviews for 8 hours a day, 7 days a week, you would have your data set in a little over 7 years. Considering the constraints mentioned earlier (time, cost, and feasibility), you can probably already see where this is going: (1) Is a $210,000 budget for subjects really feasible? (2) Do you really have 7 years to gather your findings? (3) Most of the students on this list will not be students 7 years from now. (4) After students graduate, their e-mail IDs may change. In this case, accessing the entire sample frame is untenable, but the sample frame is still useful; instead of attempting to recruit the 21,000 students, you may choose to gather information from a subset of 100 students from this sample frame. These 100 students will constitute the *sample*. Selecting a sample of 100 students from the sample frame of 21,000 means that your subject fee budget is reduced from $210,000 to $1,000, and instead of taking more than 7 years to gather the data, using the same interviewing schedule, you would have your complete data set in less than 2 weeks. In terms of feasibility, sampling is clearly the way to go. As for *how* to select that sample of 100 students from among the sample frame of 21,000, there are a variety of techniques covered in the sections on probability sampling and nonprobability sampling.

Just to recap, you can think of the population, sample frame, and sample as a hierarchy:

The *population* is the entire realm of those in a specified set (e.g., every person who lives in a city, all members of an organization or club, all students enrolled on a campus).

The *sample frame* is the list of those who could be potentially accessed from a population.

The *sample* is the sublist of those selected from the sample frame who you will (attempt to) gather data from.

REPRESENTATIVE SAMPLE

You may not realize it, but you already understand the notion of a *representative sample*. Suppose you are at a cheese tasting party, and the host brings out a large wheel of cheese from Acme Dairy. You are served a small morsel of the cheese and, based on that, decide if you like it enough to buy a hunk of it or not. The assumption that you are perhaps unknowingly making is that the whole rest of that big cheese wheel will be exactly like the tiny sample that you tasted. You are presuming that the bottom part of the cheese is not harder, that the other side of the cheese is not sharper, that the middle part of the cheese is not runnier, and so on. Essentially, you are assuming that the sample of cheese that you tasted is representative of the flavor and consistency of the whole wheel of cheese. This is what a representative sample is all about: The small sample that you drew is proportionally representative of the overall population (or big cheese) from which it was taken. Often, it is the goal of researchers to select a representative sample, thereby facilitating *external validity*—meaning that what you discover about the sample can be viably generalized to the overall population from which the sample was drawn.

Sampling is often about gathering a manageable set of data so that you can learn something about the larger population through statistical analysis. The question remains:

How do you get from the population, to the sample frame, to the actual representative sample? Depending on the nature of the information that you are seeking and the availability of viable participants/data, you may opt to employ probability sampling or non-probability sampling methods.

PROBABILITY SAMPLING

You can think of *probability sampling* as equal-opportunity sampling, meaning that each potential element (person/data record) has the same chance of being selected for your sample. There are several ways of conducting probability sampling.

Simple Random Sampling

Simple random sampling begins with gathering the largest sample frame possible and then assigning sequential numbers to the items (1, 2, 3, . . ., 1,000). For this example, let us assume that there are 1,000 items on this list and you want to recruit 30 participants; you could use SPSS to generate 30 random numbers ranging from 1 to 1,000. It is not essential that you perform this SPSS procedure at this time; Chapter 10 (Supplemental SPSS Operations) has a section that provides step-by-step instructions for generating random numbers to your specifications.

Systemic Sampling

Systemic sampling uses a simple periodic selection process to derive the sample. Suppose you had a list of 1,000 (numbered) records and you decide that your target sample size will be 10 items. Begin by dividing the total number of records by the target sample size (1,000 ÷ 10 = 100); the solution (100) is the "*k*" or *skip term*. Next, you need to identify the start point; this will be a random number between 1 and *k;* for this example, suppose the randomly derived start point number is 71. The selection process begins with item 71 and then skips ahead *k* (100) items at a time to select the next item(s) in the sample, which would be the following 10 items: 71, 171, 271, 371, 471, 571, 671, 771, 871, and 971.

Stratified Sampling

The sampling techniques described so far have used the entire sample frame from which to draw the sample. Suppose you want to specifically control for the number of females and males in your sample; stratified sampling would ensure that your sample is balanced by gender. To draw a *stratified sample* based on gender, divide your sample frame into two lists (strata): female and male. Next, decide on the number of items (*n*) that you would like each list to consist of and use simple random sampling or systemic sampling to make selections from each list. In this case, stratified sampling enables you to process the exact number of females and males you wish to involve in your study as opposed to leaving those counts to chance.

Disproportionate/Proportionate Sampling

Within stratified sampling, you can further specify if you want to work with a *disproportionate* or *proportionate sample*. Continuing with the gender stratification example, suppose you wished to conduct a student survey on a campus, and the student population consists of 60% females and 40% males. For simplicity, the sample frame consists of 10,000 records: 6,000 females and 4,000 males. The target sample size is 100.

The first step is to split the sample frame into two strata (lists): female and male. You then have the option to draw a disproportionate sample or a proportionate sample. To draw a disproportionate sample, you would randomly select 50% from the female stratum and the other 50% from the male stratum.

Alternatively, if you wanted to gather a proportionate sample, which might better represent the known gender proportions of this campus, then you would randomly select 60% of your sample from the female stratum and 40% from the male stratum.

The examples above used a two-stratum structure (gender: female, male), but you may introduce any number of strata. For example, you may wish to process figures pertaining not only to gender (female, male) but also to class ranking (freshman, sophomore, junior, senior), which would involve eight strata (lists) to randomly select from, as shown in Table 2.1.

Although there are no fixed limits when it comes to the number of strata that you can establish, practicality is an issue: Every stratum that you specify divides the data into smaller groups. When it comes to processing statistics, the solidity of the statistical tests can be compromised if the sample size within the stratum becomes too low.

If you encounter a stratum that has a particularly low count, this could compromise the power (solidity) of the statistical processes. Generally speaking, statistical results are

Table 2.1 Eight Strata Derived From Two Levels of Gender (Female, Male) and Four Levels of Class Ranking (Freshman, Sophomore, Junior, Senior)

Stratum	Group	
1	Female	Freshman
2	Female	Sophomore
3	Female	Junior
4	Female	Senior
5	Male	Freshman
6	Male	Sophomore
7	Male	Junior
8	Male	Senior

considered more robust when they are derived from larger samples. When the sample sizes for one or more strata are low because they are *proportionally* low, it may be appropriate to opt for disproportionate sampling to help increase the number of data elements in such lacking strata. For instance, a data set consisting of four strata that would naturally render *proportions* of 38%, 36%, 18%, and 8% could be rebalanced using disproportionate sampling to compensate for the low 8% stratum, resulting in groups with 25% in each stratum.

Area Sampling

Area sampling, also referred to as *cluster sampling* or *multistage cluster sampling,* is typically used when it comes to gathering samples from a geographical region or when a sample frame is not available. Since the characteristics of neighborhoods and their residents can vary substantially from block to block, this form of sampling is useful when it comes to appropriately capturing data spanning a geographical area.

This multistage process begins with acquiring a sample frame containing a list of domestic addresses within a given geographical domain. This example involves the city of Anytown, which consists of a population of about 60,000 people spanning 500 residential blocks. Your goal is to gather a sample of data from 1,000 households. Begin by building the *block* strata, which will consist of 500 strata (block 1, block 2, block 3 . . . block 500). Each stratum contains the addresses of each dwelling on that block. Next, randomly select *n* number of blocks (strata) and sample everyone from the selected blocks or select a randomly selected subset from those previously selected blocks, enough to meet your target sample.

For clarity, this example presumed uniform population density across the 500 blocks of Anytown—that each block contains about the same number of dwellings and about the same number of people living in each dwelling. Naturally, prior to selecting the sample, it would be wise to statistically check this assumption and consider adjusting the sampling proportions to best represent the residents of Anytown. For example, if it is found that 5% of the residents of Anytown live on one block, then it would be appropriate to draw 5% of the overall sample from that single block.

NONPROBABILITY SAMPLING

In probability sampling, each item in the sample frame has an equal chance of being selected when it comes to being included in the sample. In nonprobability sampling, either the sample frame does not exist or the researcher does not consider it relevant to the investigation at hand.

As you might expect, since the elements that will constitute the sample are not randomly drawn from a sample frame, which would be drawn from the overall population, *external validity* (the ability to viably generalize your sample findings to the overall population) is the first casualty of nonprobability sampling. Whatever is learned from a nonprobability sample, informative as it may be, cannot be generalized to the overall population; the proportions would be off, and since we do not know the size or characteristics of the source population, we would have no way of computing by how much they are off. Still, much can be learned from nonprobability sampling.

Convenience Sampling

Convenience sampling, sometimes referred to as *availability sampling,* is exactly what it sounds like; the researcher recruits whoever is relevant to the line of investigation and readily accessible. For example, suppose a student researcher has limited time to conduct a survey detailing students' opinions of the campus computer labs (e.g., questions regarding wait times, quality of equipment, skillfulness of attendants, recommendations, etc.). This researcher has a scheduled break on Tuesdays from 10:00 to 11:00 a.m. The researcher logs onto the school's enrollment system and selects courses that meet on Tuesdays from 10:00 to 11:00 a.m., with more than 200 students per class. The researcher then contacts each instructor, requesting permission to speak for one minute at the end of class to offer students the opportunity to partake in this computer lab online survey. For classes wherein the instructor consents, the researcher visits the class and provides a briefing of the project and instructions for taking the online survey.

In terms of external validity, clearly this survey was not designed to characterize the overall student population in terms of computer lab experience; instead, it was designed to provide the computer labs with some valuable ideas as to how they may improve their services.

Snowball Sampling

The term *snowball sampling* comes from the (cartoon) notion that if you roll a small snowball downhill from the top of a mountain, it will pick up more snow as it goes, ultimately building into a massive snowball. Actually, when it comes to snowball sampling, it might be more apt to think of the proverb: "Birds of a feather flock together."

Snowball sampling is useful when participants are scarce or difficult to readily identify. For example, suppose you are conducting a study of people who use a wheelchair, and by luck, you find someone in a wheelchair who is willing to participate in your study. After administering your survey/experiment, you courteously ask this person if he or she knows of anyone else who uses a wheelchair who might be interested in taking this survey. You would then follow up with these referrals and progressively ask each following participant for his or her list of referrals, and so on—hence, the sample *snowballs* up. Referrals may lead to *direct sources* (e.g., their friends, family, colleagues, etc.) or *indirect sources* (e.g., wheelchair repair shop, wheelchair accessory website, rehab center, etc.).

Unlike the wheelchair example, the sample that you are interested in may need to be drawn from an *invisible* or *hidden* population. This does not mean that these individuals are literally invisible or in hiding; it merely means that the feature(s) that you are interested in is not readily observable. For instance, such individuals may be invisible in that upon casual observation, they simply possess no identifying characteristics that would suggest that they meet your research criteria (e.g., single parent, bisexual, dyslexic, ballroom dancer, etc.). Alternatively, some individuals deliberately hide the fact that they would meet the criteria for your research because revealing such information could have legal consequences (e.g., illegal aliens, involvement in criminal activities, etc.) or be embarrassing (e.g., peculiar obsessions, fetishes, unpopular belief systems, uncommon interests, etc.).

In any case, if you are fortunate enough to find one such person and are able to establish a professional rapport with a genuine nonthreatening and nonjudgmental demeanor, snowball sampling may lead you to other suitable subjects.

Quota Sampling

Quota sampling is typically used when a prompt response is needed from the population. In quota sampling, one or several attributes are identified and quotas are set for each. For example, a researcher is conducting exit polls, asking voters how they just voted on selected issues. The researcher has specified the following quotas: 30 females and 30 males. Once the quotas are met for a gender, no further data will be collected for that gender. Suppose after the first hour, the researcher has gathered exit polling data on 10 females and 30 males; the researcher would stop attempting to gather data from males, even if they actively volunteered it, since that quota has been satisfied. The researcher would continue efforts to gather data from an additional 20 female voters, at which point the researcher could (immediately) process the findings.

Purposive Sampling

Purposive sampling is used when potential subjects must possess a (complex) set of specific characteristics. For example, suppose a researcher is interested in the effects that a particular drug has on patients undergoing radiation therapy. To be a viable participant in this study, each individual must meet *all* of the following criteria: (1) between 18 and 65 years old, (2) diagnosed with cancer, (3) set to begin radiation therapy, (4) undergoing a course of radiation therapy that consists of three to five treatments, (5) willing to take the experimental drug (or placebo), *and* (6) not using any nonprescribed medications.

Purposive sampling may involve one or several criteria for subject selection. In this case, *all* six criteria must be met in order for an individual to be a potential subject. Clearly, it would be virtually impossible to encounter individuals who meet all of these criteria simply by chance, as would be used in probability sampling. As you have likely surmised by now, each time an additional criterion is added in purposive sampling, the potential subject pool shrinks.

SAMPLING BIAS

Sampling bias occurs, perhaps unintentionally, when participants with certain characteristics are more likely to be selected. Such bias can corrupt the external validity of the findings. Depending on the methods used to identify potential participants or gather the sample, sampling bias is a concern. For example, while it may seem reasonable to administer a survey via the Internet, this method would preclude individuals who are not computer savvy or do not have access to the Internet.

Recruitment location can also introduce survey bias; imagine the bias your data would be subject to if you were to post recruitment flyers (only) in a women's locker room, a sports bar, the lobby of a technology company, a liquor store in an impoverished neighborhood, and so forth. Such strategies would clearly be inappropriate unless you are deliberately seeking to sample and comprehend individuals endemic to those domains.

It may not be possible to completely control for sample bias in every situation, but awareness of this potential confound can be helpful when considering the credibility of the research of others and in designing and implementing your own investigations.

Key Concepts

- Rationale for sampling (time, cost, feasibility, extrapolation)
- Population
- Sample frame
- Sample
- Representative sample
- External validity
- Probability sampling
  - Simple random sampling
  - Systematic sampling
  - Stratified sampling
  - Area sampling
- Nonprobability sampling
  - Availability sampling
  - Snowball sampling
  - Quota sampling
  - Purposive sampling
- Sample bias

Practice Exercises

1. Explain the rationale for sampling in terms of
   a. Time
   b. Cost

    c. Feasibility

    d. Extrapolation

2. Define the following terms and provide an example for each:

    a. Population

    b. Sample frame

    c. Sample

    d. Representative sample

3. A school is considering building a new library, which would involve a 1% tuition increase and take 2 years to complete. The school has selected you to conduct a survey of students to gather opinions regarding funding the new library. You will use simple *random sampling*.

    a. Define the population

    b. Define the sample frame

    c. Explain how you would select the sample

    d. Explain how you would gather the data

4. An Internet provider has commissioned you to conduct a customer satisfaction survey, providing you with a list of all its subscribers containing their name, phone number, and e-mail ID. You will use *systematic sampling*.

    a. Define the population

    b. Define the sample frame

    c. Explain how you would select the sample

    d. Explain how you would gather the data

5. A public library wants to determine the research needs of children and adults who access the reference section. You will use *stratified sampling*.

    a. Define the population

    b. Define the sample frame

    c. Explain how you would select the sample

    d. Explain how you would gather the data

6. Prior to building a factory in Cityville, Acme Corporation wants to conduct a survey of the residents. They provide you with a list of the addresses covering the 300 blocks of Cityville. You will use *area sampling*.

    a. Define the population

    b. Define the sample frame

    c. Explain how you would select the sample

    d. Explain how you would gather the data

7. An amusement park wants to assess how much money its patrons intend to spend at the park today (aside from the price of admission). You will use *availability sampling*.

    a. Explain how you would select the sample

    b. Explain how you would gather the data

8. A learning lab has commissioned you to administer a survey of people with dyslexia. You will use *snowball sampling*.

   a. Explain how you would select the sample
   b. Explain how you would gather the data

9. Acme Bus Company has selected you to conduct a survey of their riders. They want data on 50 minors (younger than 18 years) and 100 adults (18 years or older). You will use *quota sampling*.

   a. Explain how you would select the sample
   b. Explain how you would gather the data

10. A community tutorial program is recruiting students to participate in free tutoring. Students must live within the school district, be younger than 18 years, and be available 3 days a week from 3:30 to 5:00 p.m. You will use *purposive sampling*.

    a. Explain how you would select the sample
    b. Explain how you would gather the data

Working in SPSS

We can get **SPSS** to do all the hard work for us.

- Data View
- Variable View
- Codebook
- Saving Data Files

Computers are useless. They can only give you answers.

—Pablo Picasso

LEARNING OBJECTIVES

Upon completing this chapter, you will be able to:

- Operate within the two primary views in SPSS: Variable View and Data View
- Establish or modify variable definitions on the Variable View screen: name, type, width, decimals, label, values, missing, columns, align, measure, and role
- Use the value label icon to alternate between numeric and label displays
- Interpret and use a codebook to configure variables in SPSS
- Enter data into SPSS
- Save and identify SPSS data files

DIGITAL LEARNING RESOURCES

The tutorial video and data sets for this chapter are at **www.sagepub.com/knapp**

- SPSS setup video
- SPSS files

OVERVIEW

Based on what you have read thus far, you have probably figured out that when it comes to statistics, larger sample sizes facilitate more robust statistical findings. Appropriately large sample sizes are also important when it comes to gathering a *representative sample,* which helps when it comes to generalizing the findings from your sample to the overall population from which it was drawn (*external validity*).

Processing large samples can involve hundreds or thousands of calculations. For most statistical formulas, the mathematical complexity does not go beyond simple algebra, however; such formulas typically involve multiple mathematical operations on each record. Attempting to process such data by hand would be inefficient in two ways: (1) It would be very time-consuming, and (2) accuracy would be compromised. Performing a set of calculations on a lengthy data set is bound to produce some errors along the way. Even if each mathematical operation was correct, the data would be vulnerable to cumulative rounding error.

With the advent of affordable, powerful computers and menu-driven statistical programs, it is now possible to accurately perform a variety of statistical analyses in a matter of seconds. This chapter will provide you with what you need to know to get started using SPSS.

SPSS, which originally stood for "Statistical Program for the Social Sciences," has gone through some substantial evolution over time; some versions are now referred to as PASW—"Predictive Analytics Software." For the remainder of the text, the term *SPSS* will be used. Regardless of the name, the SPSS functionality of the statistics covered in this text has remained relatively stable across the evolution of the software.

TWO VIEWS: VARIABLE VIEW AND DATA VIEW

SPSS is laid out as two main screens: the *Variable View,* which is used for establishing the characteristics of each variable, and the *Data View,* which contains the gathered data. We will begin with the Variable View.

Variable View

The Variable View provides a screen for you to systematically set up the variables that will contain your data. This is where you will assign the name and characteristics of each variable that you will be including in the data set. To access the Variable View screen, click on the tab at the bottom of the screen that says *Variable View,* as shown in Figure 3.1.

Basically, for each variable, you are telling SPSS the name of the variable and the kind of data it will contain (e.g., regular numbers, dates, text, etc.), along with some other properties (parameters). Once you have established each variable in the Variable View screen, you can proceed to enter the data that you have gathered on the Data View screen, which resembles a traditional spreadsheet.

The Variable View screen has 11 properties that you can set for each variable. Some versions of SPSS may have a different amount of properties; you should be able to proceed nonetheless. Naturally, you will use care when establishing variables on the Variable View screen, but there is no need to be nervous; even after you have entered data on the Data View screen, you can always return to the Variable View screen and make changes (e.g., include more variables, delete variables, and, to some extent, reconfigure the properties of existing variables).

Figure 3.1　SPSS Variable View Screen

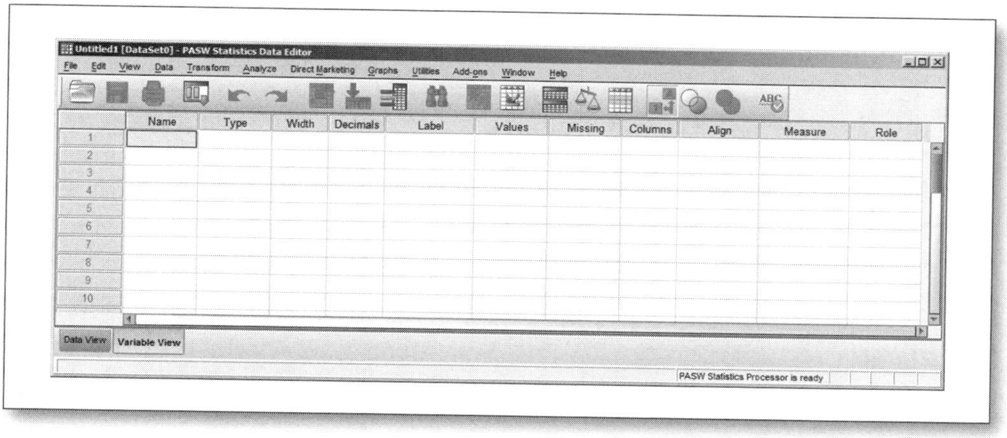

The cursor is positioned in the *Name* column for the first variable; this is where the data definition process begins.

Name

Each variable needs a unique name. The name can contain up to 64 letters and numbers; the first character must be a letter. Some older versions of SPSS allow only eight characters for variable names, so you may need to be imaginative when it comes to assigning briefer variable names. Spaces are not allowed in the variable name, but you can use the underscore (_) character instead. For your own convenience, try to assign meaningful names (e.g., age, date_of_birth, first_name, last_name, gender, gpa, question01, question02, question03, etc.). It is okay if you are unable to assign a perfect variable name; this will be discussed in more detail when we look at the *Label* property.

The cursor is positioned in the first cell for the first variable. We will build a database containing two variables: gender and age. Begin by entering *gender* in row 1 under *Name*. When you press Enter, notice that SPSS automatically enters default values for all of the remaining properties except for label. Each of these properties can be changed, but we will accept the automatic defaults for some.

Type

The system needs to know what *type* of data the variable will contain. The system assigns the default type as a numeric variable with a width of eight integer digits and two decimal digits (which you can change), meaning that this variable will accommodate a number such as 12345678.12 (Figure 3.2).

Figure 3.2   SPSS Variable Type Window

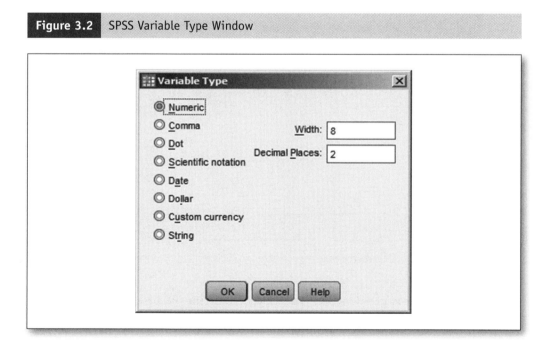

To access the menu shown in Figure 3.2, click on the *Type* cell for that variable. The options for variable type are fairly self-explanatory except for *String*; a *string* variable contains nonmathematical data (e.g., name, note, comment, memo, etc.). A string variable is useful for data that contain alphanumeric characters (letters, numbers, punctuation, or a mixture of letters and numbers), such as an ID code, an address, or a name (e.g., APB-373, 852 S. Bedford Street, Dusty Jones, etc.); if your data are not a date or a numeric value, then select *String* type. Obviously, it is not possible to perform mathematical or statistical operations on string variables.

Width

The *Width* property is the same as the *Width* parameter on the *Variable Type* menu (Figure 3.2).

Decimals

The *Decimals* property is the same as the *Decimals* parameter on the *Variable Type* menu (Figure 3.2).

Label

If the *Label* property is left blank, SPSS will use the variable *name* in all output reports; otherwise, it will use whatever you specify as the label. For example, suppose the name of the variable is *dob,* but in your reports, you want it to display as *Date of Birth;* in that case, simply enter *Date of Birth* in the *Label* property. Notice that the *Label* can contain spaces, but the *Name* cannot.

Values

The *Values* property provides a powerful instrument for assigning meaningful names to the values (numbers) contained in categorical variables. For example, *gender* is a nominal variable consisting of two categories (1 = female, 2 = male). When it comes to nominal variables, SPSS handles categories as numbers (1, 2) as opposed to the textual names (female, male). The *Values* property allows you to assign the textual name to each category number, so even though you will code *gender* using 1s and 2s, the output reports will exhibit these 1s and 2s as *female* and *male*. Here is how it works:

In the *Name* column, create a variable called *gender;* accept all the default values, except change the *Decimals* property to *0.*

Click on the *Values* cell for *gender;* this will bring up the *Value Labels* menu (Figure 3.3).

Assign the values one at a time; begin by entering *1* in *Value* and *female* in *Label,* then click *Add.*

Do the same for the second category: Enter *2* in *Value* and *male* in *Label,* then click *Add.*

To finalize these designations, click *OK.*

You will see the utility of this labeling system when you enter data on the Data View screen and when you run your first reports.

| Figure 3.3 | SPSS Variable Labels Window |

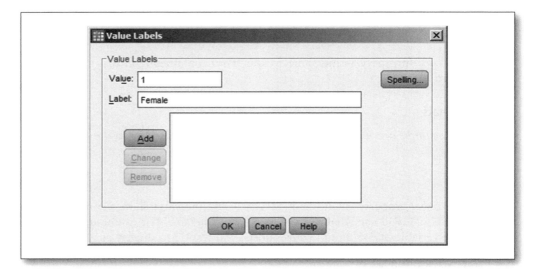

Missing

Sometimes, when the source data are either erroneous or missing, the cell is simply left blank, in which case, the *Missing* property can remain blank as well. Other times, the erroneous or missing data are represented by special codes; a common convention is to code erroneous data as 888, and missing data are represented as 999—this conveys that a blank cell is not an oversight. Consider the variable *age;* if the data contained an erroneous entry (e.g., "I'm a kid"), or if the entry were left blank, the corresponding 888 or 999 codes would radically throw off the statistical (age) calculations. The *Missing* property enables us to specify such codes (888 and 999) that we want SPSS to ignore so that they will not be processed in the statistical calculations. Here is how it works:

Create a variable with the name *age;* accept all the default values, except change the *Decimals* property to *0.*

Click on the Select *Discrete missing values* and enter *888* and *999* (Figure 3.4).

If you need to indicate more than three such values, you may opt for the *Range plus one optional discrete missing value* function, which would enable you to specify a range of values (e.g., *Low: 888, High: 999*—meaning that all values from 888 through 999 inclusive will be omitted from all statistical analysis for that variable). In addition, you can specify one additional value (e.g., *Discrete value: −1*).

To finalize these designations, click *OK.*

The numbers 888 and 999 have been generally adopted as special values since they are visually easy to recognize in a data set. Also, if these special values are not properly

| Figure 3.4 | SPSS Missing Values Window |

designated as erroneous/missing values, statistical clues will begin to emerge, such as a report indicating a mean age of 347 or a maximum height of 999 inches or centimeters. Such extreme results alert you to check that the missing/erroneous designations have been properly specified for a variable.

Columns

The *Columns* property allows you to change the column width on the Data View screen; you can specify how many characters wide you want that column to be.

Align

The *Align* property lets you specify how you want the variable to be presented on the Data View screen and in the output reports. Typically, *Right* alignment is used for numeric data and *Left* alignment is used for string data or categorical variables with data labels assigned to them. *Center* is also an option.

Measure

The *Measure* property pertains to the four levels of measures (*nominal, ordinal, interval,* and *ratio*) covered in the level of measure section in Chapter 1. For variables that contain *continuous* variables, select *Scale*. For the *categorical* variables, which may contain value labels, select *Nominal*.

Role

Some versions of SPSS have the *Role* property; do not panic if the version that you are using does not include this property—we will not be using it in this text. *Role* enables you to define how the variable will be used in the statistical processes. If your version of the software includes the *Role* property, just use the default setting: *Input*.

Use SPSS to set up the Variable View screen to establish the *gender* and *age* variables as shown in Figure 3.5.

Figure 3.5	SPSS Variable View Screen

Data View

Now that the properties for each variable have been established on the Variable View screen, the next step is to enter the actual data. To switch to the data entry mode, click on the *Data View* tab at the bottom of the screen.

As you enter the data in Table 3.1 into the Data View screen, notice that for the *gender* variable, you can access the pull-down menu in each cell to select *female* or *male*. Alternatively, you can enter the corresponding numbers that you defined: 1 for *female* or 2 for *male*. Notice that SPSS will not allow you to type the words *female* or *male* in the *gender* field; you will need to enter a number (in this case, 1 or 2) or use the pull-down menu feature for this variable. The Data View screen should resemble Figure 3.6.

Value Labels Icon

When it comes to viewing your data, there will be times when you will want to see the value labels (e.g., *female, male*) and other times when you will want to see the source numbers (e.g., 1, 2). To toggle this display back and forth, from numbers to text (and back), click on the *Value Labels* icon (with the *1 A* on it), as shown in Figure 3.7.

Table 3.1		Gender and Age Source Data							

Male	24	Male	30	Female	22	Male	26	Female	25
Male	25	Male	25	Male	25	Male	25	Female	25
Male	31	Female	26	Male	25	Female	24	Female	22
Female	19	Male	27	Female	24	Male	29	Male	22
Female	27	Male	24	Female	23	Male	23	Female	20
Male	20	Female	25	Male	25	Female	21	Female	22
Male	28	Male	24	Female	19	Female	22	Male	18
Female	23	Female	26	Female	23	Female	21	Female	18
Male	26	Female	23	Female	28	Female	24	Female	23
Male	24	Male	22	Female	24	Male	26	Female	27

Figure 3.6	Data View Screen With Data Entered

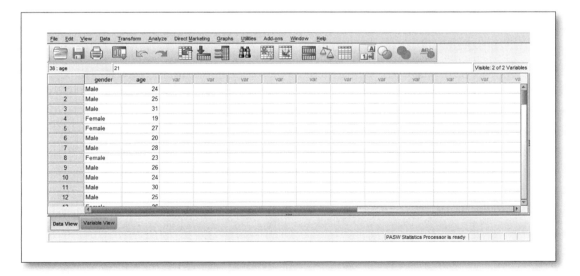

Codebook

For learning purposes, the two-variable data set used in this chapter is admittedly simple. Even so, without being told that for the variable *gender,* 1 stands for female and 2 stands for male, this coding scheme would lead to confusion. Designations such as 1 = female

Figure 3.7	The Value Labels Icon, Alternating the Display of Categorical Variables From Text to Numeric Display (and Back)

and 2 = male and other characteristics of each variable in a data set are traditionally contained in the *codebook,* which is the companion to the data set. The codebook is written by the person who develops the experiment or survey; it provides a list and a description of each variable contained in a data set. This is particularly valuable in data sets that contain numerous variables with arcane names. For example, suppose you came across a variable named *q105* and it contained dates. Without the codebook, we would have no idea what any of this means; we would not know how this variable was gathered or be able to assign any meaning to these dates (e.g., birth date, graduation date, anniversaries, date of arrest, date admitted to a hospital, etc.); if you do not know the story of a variable, that variable is virtually useless. Although there is no standard form for codebooks, a quality codebook should indicate the information essential to understanding each variable in the data set. Continuing with the *q105* example, a reasonable codebook entry for this variable might look like this:

Variable: q105 (Question 105)

Question: When did you graduate high school?

Type: Date

Format: MM/DD/YY

For our simple two-variable database detailed in Table 3.1, the codebook would look like this:

Variable: gender

Question: What is your gender?

Type: Numeric (1 = Female, 2 = Male)

Format: 1 integer, 0 decimal

Error: 888

Missing: 999

Variable: age

Question: How old are you?

Type: Numeric

Format: 3 integer, 0 decimal

Error: 888

Missing: 999

Saving Data Files

The 50-record database that you entered earlier will be used in Chapter 4; to save the file, click on the *Save this document* icon as shown in Figure 3.8. Use the file name *Chapter 03 – Example 01 – Descriptives;* SPSS automatically appends the *.sav* extension (suffix) to the filename. The file on your system will be listed as *Chapter 03 – Example 01 – Descriptives.sav.*

Figure 3.8   The *Save this document* Icon

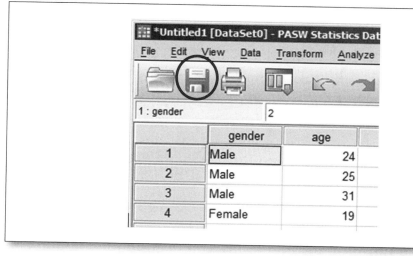

Key Concepts

Variable View	Align
Name	Measure
Type	Role
Width	Data View
Decimals	*Value Labels* icon
Label	Codebook
Values	Saving data files
Missing	*Save this document* icon
Columns	.sav files

Practice Exercises

Use the provided codebook in each exercise to establish the variables on the Variable View screen, and then enter the data on the Data View screen.

To check your work, produce a variable list; click on *Analyze, Reports, Codebook,* as shown in Figure 3.9.

Figure 3.9 Ordering a List of All Variables; Click on *Analyze, Reports, Codebook*

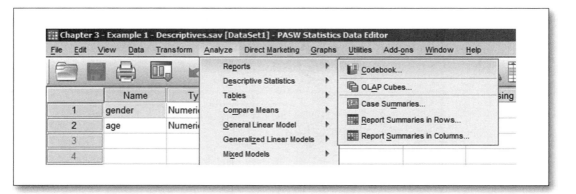

Next, select all the variables that you want to include in the codebook report; move the variables from the left *Variables* window to the right *Codebook Variables* window (using double-click, drag & drop, or the arrow button), then click OK, as shown in Figure 3.10.

Figure 3.10 Codebook Report Order Screen; Move Variables of Interest to Right (Codebook Variables) Window

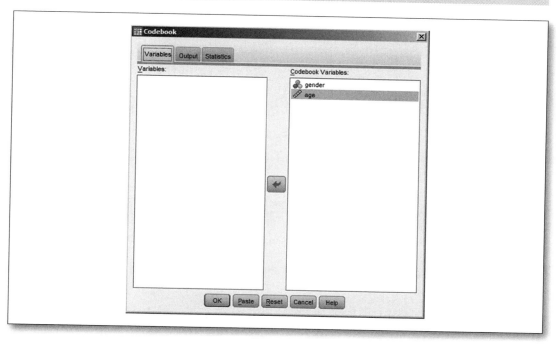

This will generate a Variable Information report showing the properties of all variables, as shown in Table 3.2.

Table 3.2 Codebook Report Displaying the Variable Properties

gender				
		Value	Count	Percent
Standard Attributes	Position	1		
	Label	<none>		
	Type	Numeric		
	Format	F8		
	Measurement	Nominal		
	Role	Input		
Valid Values	1	Female	27	54.0%
	2	Male	23	46.0%

(Continued)

Table 3.2   (Continued)

age		Value
Standard Attributes	Position	2
	Label	<none>
	Type	Numeric
	Format	F8
	Measurement	Scale
	Role	Input
N	Valid	50
	Missing	0
Central Tendency and Dispersion	Mean	23.96
	Standard Deviation	2.770
	Percentile 25	22.00
	Percentile 50	24.00
	Percentile 75	26.00

You can compare your Variable Information report with those in the solution section to check for accuracy.

After each exercise, clear out the data; click on *File, New, Data,* as shown in Figure 3.11.

Figure 3.11   Clearing the Data, Click on *File, New, Data*

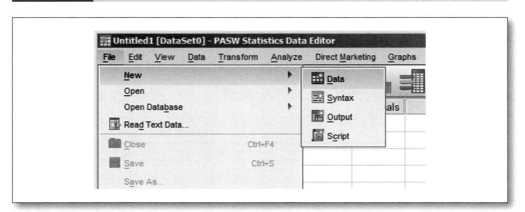

1. Codebook

   Variable: enrolled

   Question: Are you currently enrolled in school?

   Type: Numeric (1 = Yes, 2 = No)

Format: 1 integer, 0 decimal

Variable: units

Question: How many units are you taking?

Type: Numeric

Format: 2 integer, 0 decimal

Error: 888

Missing: 999

Variable: gpa

Question: What is your overall GPA?

Type: Numeric

Format: 1 integer, 2 decimal

Error: 888

Missing: 999

Data:

NOTE: Do not enter the data in the *Rec. #* column; this column corresponds to the leftmost column in SPSS, indicating the record (row) number.

Rec. #	enrolled	units	gpa
1	Yes	12	2.80
2	Yes	12	3.71
3	No	0	2.65
4	Yes	6	2.90
5	Yes	16	3.64

2. Codebook

Variable: id

Question: What is your ID number?

Type: String

Characters: 12

Variable: volunteer_hours

Question: How many hours per week are you willing to volunteer?

Type: Numeric

Format: 2 integer, 2 decimal

Data:

Rec. #	id	volunteer_hours
1	QF732	2.00
2	AL331	1.50
3	JW105	3.00
4	RK122	.50
5	DD987	4.00

3. Codebook

Variable: degree

Question: What is the highest degree you've completed?

Type: Numeric (1 = Associate's, 2 = Bachelor's, 3 = Master's, 4 = Doctorate)

Format: 1 integer, 0 decimal

Variable: pretest

Question: What was your pretest score?

Type: Numeric

Format: 3 integer, 0 decimal

Variable: posttest

Question: What was your posttest score?

Type: Numeric

Format: 3 integer, 0 decimal

Data:

Rec. #	degree	pretest	posttest
1	Associate's	22	29
2	Master's	31	48
3	Bachelor's	28	38
4	Bachelor's	25	34
5	Master's	30	46

4. Codebook

Variable:	employment_status
Question:	What is your current employment status?
Type:	Numeric (1 = Unemployed, 2 = Temporary, 3 = Part-time, 4 = Full-time)
Format:	1 integer, 0 decimal

Variable:	work_hours
Question:	In an average week, how many hours do you work?
Type:	Numeric
Format:	2 integer, 0 decimal

Variable:	sleep_hours
Question:	In an average day, how many hours do you sleep?
Type:	Numeric
Format:	2 integer, 2 decimal
Error:	888
Missing:	999

Data:

Rec. #	employment_status	work_hours	sleep_hours
1	Unemployed	0	10.00
2	Temporary	16	9.00
3	Full-time	40	7.50
4	Full-time	45	8.00
5	Part-time	20	7.00

5. Codebook

Variable: first_initial

Question: What is the first initial of your first name?

Type: String

Characters: 1

Variable: last_name

Question: What is your last name?

Type: String

Characters: 25

Variable: siblings

Question: How many siblings do you have?

Type: Numeric

Format: 2 integer, 0 decimal

Error: 888

Missing: 999

Variable: adopted

Question: Are you adopted?

Type: Numeric (1 = Yes, 2 = No)

Format: 2 integer, 0 decimal

Error: 888

Missing: 999

Data:

Rec. #	first_initial	last_name	siblings	adopted
1	J	Gower	0	No
2	D	Freeman	2	No
3	T	Rexx	3	No
4	P	Smith	2	Yes
5	V	Jones	1	No

6. Codebook

Variable: patient_id

Question: What is your patient ID number?

Type: Numeric

Format: 10 integer, 0 decimal

Variable: age

Question: How old are you?

Type: Numeric

Format: 2 integer, 0 decimal

Error: 888

Missing: 999

Variable: temperature

Question: What is your temperature (in Celsius)?

Type: Numeric

Format: 2 integer, 1 decimal

Error: 888

Missing: 999

Variable: flu_shot

Question: Have you had a flu shot this season?

Type: Numeric (1 = Yes; 2 = No, and I don't want one; 3 = Not yet, but I'd like one)

Format: 1 integer, 0 decimal

Error: 888

Missing: 999

Variable: rx

Question: What medications are you currently taking?

Type: String

Characters: 100

Data:

Rec. #	patient_id	age	temperature	flu_shot	rx
1	2136578099	22	37.0	Yes	
2	8189873094	46	37.2	No, and I don't want one	Multivitamin
3	2144538086	53	38.6	Not yet, but I want one	
4	8046628739	81	37.1	Yes	
5	5832986812	38	38.3	Yes	Xamine, Tutsocol

7. Codebook

Variable: passport

Question: Do you have a valid passport?

Type: Numeric (1 = Yes, 2 = No, 3 = Decline to answer)

Format: 1 integer, 0 decimal

Variable: fired

Question: Have you ever been fired from a job?

Type: Numeric (1 = Yes, 2 = No, 3 = Decline to answer)

Format: 1 integer, 0 decimal

Variable: er

Question: Have you ever been treated in an emergency room?

Type: Numeric (1 = Yes, 2 = No, 3 = Decline to answer)

Format: 1 integer, 0 decimal

Variable: dob

Question: What is your birth date?

Type: Date

Format: MM/DD/YYYY

Data:

Rec. #	passport	fired	er	dob
1	No	Decline to answer	No	01/23/1936
2	Yes	No	Yes	08/18/1928
3	Yes	No	No	03/01/1987
4	No	Yes	No	06/07/1974
5	No	No	Yes	11/30/2001

8. Codebook

Variable: dogs

Question: I like dogs.

Type: Numeric (1 = Strongly disagree, 2 = Disagree, 3 = Neutral, 4 = Agree, 5 = Strongly agree)

Format: 1 integer, 0 decimal

Variable: cats

Question: I like cats.

Type: Numeric (1 = Strongly disagree, 2 = Disagree, 3 = Neutral, 4 = Agree, 5 = Strongly agree)

Format: 1 integer, 0 decimal

Variable: pets

Question: How many pets do you currently have?

Type: Numeric

Format: 2 integer, 0 decimal

Data:

Rec. #	dogs	cats	pets
1	Strongly agree	Disagree	1
2	Agree	Strongly agree	0
3	Strongly agree	Neutral	0
4	Strongly agree	Strongly agree	2
5	Neutral	Strongly disagree	3

9. Codebook

Variable: blood_type

Question: What is your blood type (respond "?" if you don't know)?

Type: Numeric (1 = A–, 2 = A+, 3 = B–, 4 = B+, 5 = AB–, 6 = AB+, 7 = O–, 8 = O+, 9 = don't know)

Format: 1 integer, 0 decimal

Variable: gender

Question: What is your gender?

Type: Numeric (1 = Female, 2 = Male)

Format: 1 integer, 0 decimal

Variable: prior_donor

Question: Have you ever donated blood before?

Type: Numeric (1 = Yes, 2 = No)

Format: 1 integer, 0 decimal

Data:

Rec. #	blood_type	gender	prior_donor
1	B+	Female	Yes
2	?	Female	No
3	A−	Male	No
4	AB+	Male	No
5	O−	Male	Yes

10. Codebook

    Variable: entree_food

    Question: What entrée did you order?

    Type: Numeric (1 = Fish, 2 = Chicken, 3 = Beef, 4 = Vegetarian)

    Format: 1 integer, 0 decimal

    Variable: entree_quality

    Question: On a scale of 1 to 10 (10 being the best), how would you rate your meal?

    Type: Numeric

    Format: 2 integer, 0 decimal

    Variable: dessert

    Question: On a scale of 1 to 10, how would you rate your dessert (if you did not order a dessert, please mark "X")?

    Type: Numeric

    Format: 2 integer, 0 decimal

Missing: 999

HINT: Code "X" as 999

Data:

Rec. #	entree_food	entree_quality	dessert
1	Fish	9	X
2	Fish	8	9
3	Fish	9	X
4	Beef	10	8
5	Fish	7	10

PART II

Statistical Processes

C H A P T E R   4

Descriptive Statistics

Wanna summarize your variables? Run **descriptive statistics.**

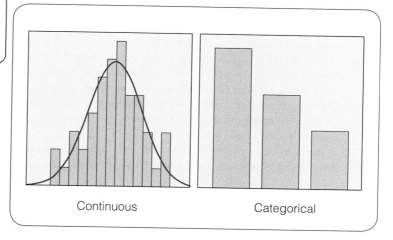

Continuous

Categorical

Whenever you can, count.

—Sir Francis Galton

LEARNING OBJECTIVES

Upon completing this chapter, you will be able to:

- Comprehend the meaning of each descriptive statistic: number (n), mean, median, mode, standard deviation, variance, minimum, maximum, and range
- Load an SPSS data file
- Order and interpret descriptive statistics for continuous variables: frequency statistics tables, histogram with normal curve, and skewed distribution
- Order and interpret descriptive statistics for categorical variables: frequency statistics table and bar chart
- Select records to process/rule out
- Select all records to process

DIGITAL LEARNING RESOURCES

The tutorial video and data sets for this chapter are at: **www.sagepub.com/knapp**

- Descriptive statistics—continuous video
- Descriptive statistics—categorical video
- SPSS files

OVERVIEW

Statistics is about making sense of data, which could consist of one or many groups and involve data sets of virtually any size. Take a look at the data set from Chapter 3 (Table 4.1); if someone were to ask you to describe this data set, you might say, "It looks like a list of about half women and half men, mostly in their 20s," which would not be wrong, but we can be more precise than that. This list consists of (only) 50 records and 100 data items, but how would you make a viable summary statement if the list consisted of 100, 1,000, or even 100,000 records? Such data would span multiple pages and defy cursory visual inspection.

To better comprehend the nature of a data set, we use *descriptive statistics,* sometimes referred to as *summary statistics*. Descriptive statistics enable us to concisely understand a data set of any size using a handful of figures and simple graphs that serve to concisely *describe* the contents of a variable.

Table 4.1	Data Set Containing 50 Records With Two Variables per Record: Gender and Age								
Male	24	Male	30	Female	22	Male	26	Female	25
Male	25	Male	25	Male	25	Male	25	Female	25
Male	31	Female	26	Male	25	Female	24	Female	22
Female	19	Male	27	Female	24	Male	29	Male	22
Female	27	Male	24	Female	23	Male	23	Female	20
Male	20	Female	25	Male	25	Female	21	Female	22
Male	28	Male	24	Female	19	Female	22	Male	18
Female	23	Female	26	Female	23	Female	21	Female	18
Male	26	Female	23	Female	28	Female	24	Female	23
Male	24	Male	22	Female	24	Male	26	Female	27

Continuous variables can be summarized using the nine descriptive statistics: *number (n), mean, median, mode, maximum, minimum, range, standard deviation,* and *variance.* Graphically, continuous variables can be depicted using a histogram (a special kind of bar chart) with a normal curve.

Categorical variables can be summarized using *number (n)* and *percent.* Graphically, categorical variables are depicted using a simple bar chart. You can see examples of a *histogram with a normal curve* for a continuous variable and a *bar chart* for a categorical variable on the first page of this chapter (next to the dog).

We will begin with an explanation of the nine summary statistics used to analyze continuous variables. For simplicity, we will work with a small data set—the first 10 ages drawn from the second column of Table 4.1: 24, 25, 31, 19, 27, 20, 28, 23, 26, and 24.

DESCRIPTIVE STATISTICS

Number (*n*)

The most basic descriptive statistic is the *number,* represented as the letter *n.* To compute the *n,* simply count the number of elements (numbers) in the sample; in this case, there are 10 elements—count them: 24 is the first, 25 is the second, 31 is the third . . . 24 (at the end) is the tenth, so *n* = 10.

The lowercase *n* is the number of elements in a *sample,* whereas the uppercase *N* is the number of elements in the (whole) *population.* Either way, *n* or *N* is an element count; SPSS output reports always use the capital *N.* Since it is rare to be processing a data set consisting of an entire population, it is considered good practice to use the lowercase *n* in your documentation, as such: *n*(age) = 10.

Mean

In statistical language, the *average* is referred to as the *mean.* The calculation for the *mean* is the same as the average: Add up all the elements and then divide that amount by the total number of elements (*n* = 10):

Mean(age) = (24 + 25 + 31 + 19 + 27 + 20 + 28 + 23 + 26 + 24) ÷ 10

Mean(age) = 247 ÷ 10

Mean(age) = 24.7

The mean can be written using the lowercase Greek letter μ (pronounced *m-you*) or as the variable with a horizontal bar over it—hence, the mean may be documented as such:

$$\mu(age) = 24.7$$

$$\overline{age} = 24.7$$

For consistency throughout the rest of this text, the mean will be documented using the μ(age) style.

Median

The *median* is the middle value of a variable. Think of the term *median* in terms of a street—the median is in the middle; it splits the street in half. To find the median, arrange the data in the variable from lowest to highest and then select the middle value(s).

When the *n* is even, as in the data set below (*n* = 10), there are two middle numbers: 24 and 25. The median is the mean of these two middle numbers:

$$19, 20, 23, 24, \boxed{24, 25} 26, 27, 28, 31$$

$$\text{Median(age)} = (24 + 25) \div 2$$

$$\text{Median(age)} = (49) \div 2$$

$$\text{Median(age)} = 24.5$$

When the *n* is odd, as in this small data set below (*n* = 5), there is (only) one middle number—hence, the median is simply the (one) middle number: 86.

$$6, 24, \boxed{86}, 91, 99$$

Mode

The *mode* is the most common number in the data set. Notice that *mode* and *most* share the first two letters. In this case, we see that each number in this data set is present only once, except for 24, which occurs twice, and hence the mode is 24.

$$19, 20, 23, \boxed{24, 24} 25, 26, 27, 28, 31$$

It is possible for a data set to have more than one mode; the example below has two modes: 24 and 31 since both have the most (there are two 24s and two 31s; all the other numbers appear just once). Such a variable would be referred to as *bimodal*—meaning two modes.

$$9, 20, 23, \boxed{24, 24} 25, 26, 27, 28, \boxed{31, 31}$$

Although it is relatively rare, a variable may have more than two modes, which would be referred to as *multimodal*.

When SPSS detects more than one mode within a variable, it only reports the lowest one and provides a footnote indicating that there is more than one mode.

The mean, median, and mode are referred to as *measures of central tendency,* as together they suggest the *center* point of the variable.

Standard Deviation

The *standard deviation* describes the dispersion of the data within a variable. The core of the standard deviation formula involves calculating the differences between each individual number in the data set and the mean.

If the data set consists of relatively middle-of-the-road numbers, which are only slightly lower or slightly higher than the mean, then this will result in a relatively low standard deviation, indicating that overall, the numbers do not *deviate* very far from the mean. Conversely, if the values in a data set are more diverse, meaning that the values deviate substantially further from the mean (lower lows and higher highs), this will increase the standard deviation.

We will begin with the 10-item sample of ages:

Data Set A: 19, 20, 23, 24, 24, 25, 26, 27, 28, 31

We know that the mean is 24.7, and we can see that the numbers in this data set do not stray too far from that mean. The standard deviation for this variable is 3.592; this would be written as SD(age) = 3.592. Now we will increase the diversity of these numbers; we will subtract 15 from the lowest number and add 15 to the highest number, thus forcing these numbers to deviate further from the mean, making for greater dispersion within the variable:

Data Set B: 4, 20, 23, 24, 24, 25, 26, 27, 28, 46

After making this adjustment, the standard deviation for Data Set B is 10.144, which is nearly three times as large as the standard deviation for Data Set A (3.592). What is going on? In Data Set A, the end values (19 and 31) were fairly close to the mean (24.7); there was only a 5.7 difference between 19 and the mean (24.7) and a 6.3 difference between 31 and the mean (24.7), but in Data Set B, we increased those differences by 15 (each); these numbers now deviate further from the mean, which is reflected in the higher standard deviation.

Another way to understand the standard deviation is to inspect the formula; we will discuss a selected portion of the standard deviation formula, but we will not process it manually.

The formula for the *sample standard deviation* is

$$SD_x = \sqrt{\frac{\sum(x - \mu_x)^2}{n_x - 1}}$$

but for now focus only on the $(x - \mu_x)$ term in the numerator. This expression says that for each value in the variable x (in this case, age), calculate the difference between that age value (x) and the mean age (μ_x). Very low and very high ages would deviate substantially from the mean, producing a larger difference; these differences accumulate in the numerator, which increases the value of the fraction, thus resulting in a higher standard deviation—there is more deviation from the mean. Graphically, this would be depicted as a wider, shorter bell curve on the histogram. Conversely, if the ages in this data set are all fairly close together, then computing the difference between each age and the mean age would produce relatively small(er) numbers accumulating in the numerator; the smaller the numerator, the smaller the value of the fraction. Such a data set would produce a smaller standard deviation—there is less deviation from the mean. Graphically, we would see a thinner, taller normal curve on the histogram.

Variance

The *variance* is simply the standard deviation squared. For example, we will compute the variance of age from the Data Set A:

$$\text{Variance(age)} = (\text{Standard Deviation(age)})^2$$

$$\text{Variance(age)} = (3.592)^2$$

$$\text{Variance(age)} = 3.592 \times 3.592$$

$$\text{Variance(age)} = 12.902$$

The variance is seldom included in statistical reports; it is primarily used as a term within other statistical formulas.

Minimum

The *minimum* is the smallest number in a variable. In the data set below, the minimum is 19.

⑲ 20, 23, 24, 24, 25, 26, 27, 28, 31

Maximum

The *maximum* is the largest number in a variable. In the data set below, the *maximum* is 31.

19, 20, 23, 24, 24, 25, 26, 27, 28, ㉛

Identifying the minimum and maximum values has some utility, but try not to bring inappropriate suppositions to your interpretation of such figures—bigger is not necessarily better. The meaning of the minimum and maximum values depends on the nature of the variable. For example, high bowling scores are considered good, but low golf scores are considered good, and high (or low) phone numbers or street addresses are considered neither good nor bad.

Range

The *range* is the span of the data set; the formula for the range is maximum − minimum. In the data set below, we would calculate: 31 − 19 = 12; the range is 12 (years).

⑲ 20, 23, 24, 24, 25, 26, 27, 28, ㉛

SPSS—LOADING AN SPSS DATA FILE

For clarity, the examples used thus far have involved only 10 data items. Now it is time to use SPSS to process descriptive statistics using the entire data set consisting of 50 records and both variables (gender and age).

Run SPSS.

Use the *Open Data Document* icon (Figure 4.1) to load the file that you created (and saved) in Chapter 3: *Chapter 03 – Example 01 – Descriptives.sav*.

| Figure 4.1 | *Open Data Document* Icon |

SPSS—Descriptive Statistics: Continuous Variables (Age)

There are two types of variables in this SPSS file: Age is a continuous variable, and gender is a categorical variable. In this section, we will process descriptive statistics for the continuous variable (age); later in this chapter, we will process the categorical variable (gender).

1. When the data have loaded, click on *Analyze, Descriptive Statistics, Frequencies* . . . (Figure 4.2).

Figure 4.2   Running a Descriptive Statistics Report: Click on *Analyze, Descriptive Statistics, Frequencies . . .*

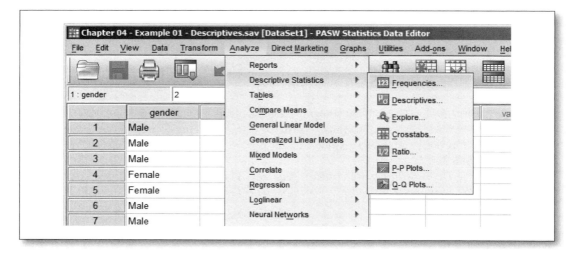

2. SPSS will then prompt you to select the variable(s) that you would like to process. Move the *age* variable to the *Variable(s)* window (Figure 4.3).

3. Click on the *Statistics . . .* button.

Figure 4.3   Move the Variable(s) to Be Analyzed (Age) From the Left Window to the Right *Variable(s)* Window

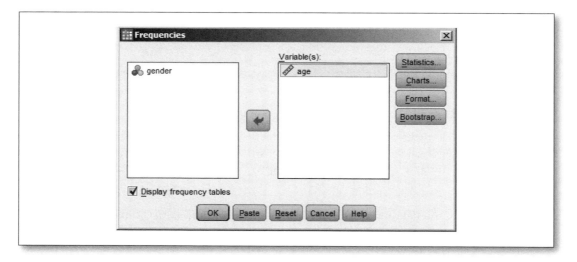

Figure 4.4 *Frequencies: Statistics* Order Screen

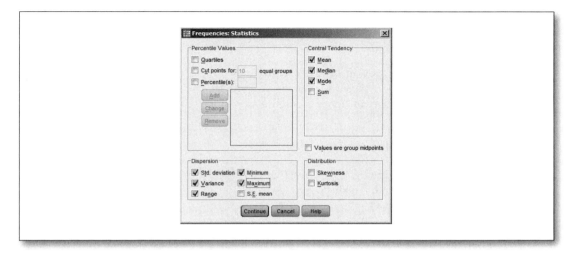

4. Select the descriptive statistics indicated by the checkboxes (Figure 4.4): *Mean, Median, Mode, Std. deviation, Variance, Range, Minimum,* and *Maximum.*

5. Click on the *Continue* button. This will take you back to the *Frequencies* screen (Figure 4.3).

Figure 4.5 Frequencies: Charts Order Screen; Select *Histograms* and *Show normal curve on histogram*

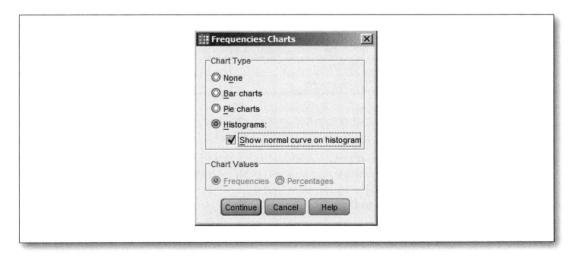

6. On the *Frequencies* screen (Figure 4.3), click on the *Charts* . . . button.

7. Select *Histograms* and *Show normal curve on histogram* (Figure 4.5).

8. Click on the *Continue* button. This will take you back to the *Frequencies* screen (Figure 4.3).

9. Click on the *OK* button on the *Frequencies* screen; this tells SPSS to process the *Frequencies* report based on the parameters that you just specified. SPSS should produce this report in under a minute (try to be patient).

Frequency Statistics Tables

The first part of the report is the Frequency Statistics table (Table 4.2), which shows the summary statistical results as discussed earlier.

Table 4.2 Frequency Statistics Table Showing Summary Statistics for Age

Statistics

age

N	Valid	50
	Missing	0
Mean		24.00
Median		24.00
Mode		25
Std. Deviation		2.857
Variance		8.163
Range		13
Minimum		18
Maximum		31

The second part of the report shows the frequency of each value in the age variable (Table 4.3). Focus on columns 1 and 2 of this table, which show that the numbers 18, 19, 20, and 21 each occur twice in the data set; 22 and 23 each occur six times; 24 occurs eight times; 25 occurs nine times; and so on.

Table 4.3	Frequency Statistics Table Showing the Frequency of Each Value in the Age Variable

age

		Frequency	Percent	Valid Percent	Cumulative Percent
Valid	18	2	4.0	4.0	4.0
	19	2	4.0	4.0	8.0
	20	2	4.0	4.0	12.0
	21	2	4.0	4.0	16.0
	22	6	12.0	12.0	28.0
	23	6	12.0	12.0	40.0
	24	8	16.0	16.0	56.0
	25	9	18.0	18.0	74.0
	26	5	10.0	10.0	84.0
	27	3	6.0	6.0	90.0
	28	2	4.0	4.0	94.0
	29	1	2.0	2.0	96.0
	30	1	2.0	2.0	98.0
	31	1	2.0	2.0	100.0
	Total	50	100.0	100.0	

Histogram With Normal Curve

The third part of this report is the histogram of the age variable. The *histogram* is simply a graphical representation of the frequency statistics. Basically, Figure 4.6 is a picture of the data in Table 4.3. Notice that the first four bars are each two units tall; this is because the first four numbers in the table (18, 19, 20, and 21) each occur two times in the data set. Notice that the tallest bar is nine units tall; this is because the number 25 occurs nine times in the data set.

In addition to understanding the nature of a variable via the descriptive statistics (mean, median, mode, etc.), the histogram provides further insight into the characteristics of a continuous variable—a picture is indeed worth a thousand words.

In addition to the bars, which constitute the histogram, it is also traditional to include a *normal curve*—sometimes referred to as a "bell curve" because of its shape. The normal curve is derived from the same source data as the bar chart; you can think of this normal curve as the smoothed-out version of the bar chart. More often than not, we see this sort of symmetrical distribution among continuous variables—most of the values are gathered

Figure 4.6 Histogram of the Age Variable

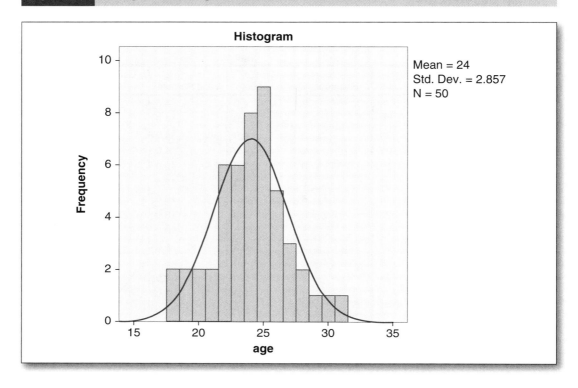

toward the middle, with the frequencies progressively dropping off as the values depart (negatively or positively) from the mean.

For example, if we were to measure the height of 100 randomly selected people, we would expect to find that most people are moderate height (which would constitute the tallness in the middle of the normal curve). We would also expect to find a few exceptionally short people and about the same amount of exceptionally tall people, which would account for the tapering off seen on the left and right tails of the normal curve. This phenomenon of the bell-shaped distribution is so common that it is referred to as a *normal distribution,* as represented by the normal curve. When assessing a histogram for *normality,* focus primarily on inspecting the normal curve for symmetry; if we were to slice the normal curve vertically down the middle, the left half of the normal curve should resemble a mirror image of the right half. When inspecting a histogram with a normal curve, we expect to see some variations/asymmetry among the heights of the bars.

Skewed Distribution

As with any rule, there are of course, exceptions; not all histograms produce normally shaped curves. Depending on the distribution of the data within the variable, the histogram may be *skewed,* meaning that the distribution is tilted, as shown in Figures 4.7 and 4.8.

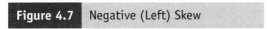

| **Figure 4.7** Negative (Left) Skew | **Figure 4.8** Positive (Right) Skew |

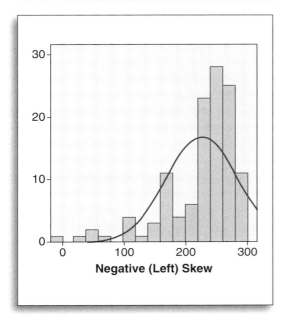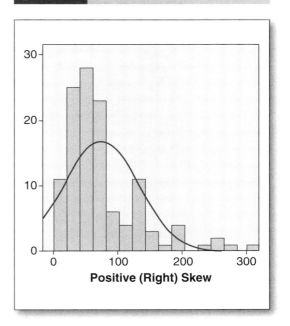

In Figure 4.7, we see that most of the data are on the right, between about 150 and 300, but there is a small scattering of lower values (under 100), forcing the left tail of the curve to be extended out. These few low values that substantially depart from the majority of the data are referred to as *outliers.* Typically, outliers become apparent when graphing the data. We would say that the histogram in Figure 4.7 has outliers to the left—hence, it is *skewed left,* or *negatively skewed.*

Outliers are not always negative. Figure 4.8, which is a virtual mirror image of Figure 4.7, shows outliers scattered to the right; this distribution would be referred to as being *skewed right,* or *positively skewed.* The notion of *normality* of the data distribution will be discussed further in Chapters 5, 6, 7, and 8.

SPSS—DESCRIPTIVE STATISTICS: CATEGORICAL VARIABLES (GENDER)

Descriptive statistics for categorical variables are derived using the same ordering screens as for continuous variables, except you will be specifying different options.

1. Click on *Analyze, Descriptive Statistics, Frequencies* . . . (Figure 4.9).

Figure 4.9   Running a Descriptive Statistics Report: Click on *Analyze, Descriptive Statistics, Frequencies . . .*

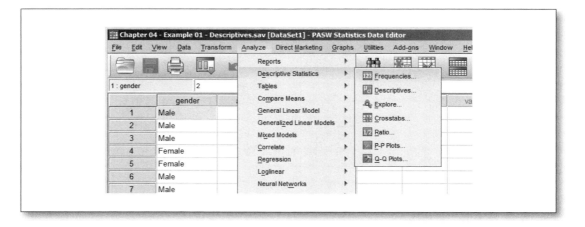

---

2. First, click on the *Reset* button; this will clear the parameters on the submenus that you specified when running the summary statistics for age.

3. Next, move the *gender* variable from the left window to the right *Variable(s)* window (Figure 4.10).

4. Click on the *Charts . . .* button.

Figure 4.10   Click on the *Reset* Button to Clear Prior Options, Then Move the Variable(s) to Be Analyzed (Gender) From the Left Window to the Right *Variable(s)* Window

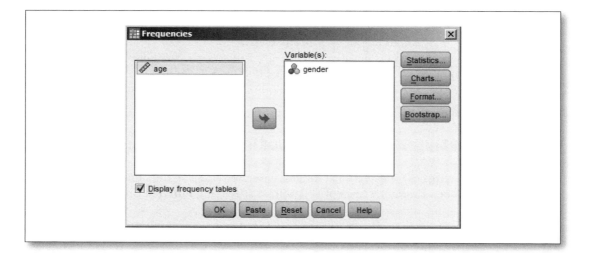

5. On the *Frequencies: Charts* menu, there are two viable options: *Bar charts* or *Pie charts* (Figure 4.11). In statistics, bar charts are used more often than pie charts. You can also choose to represent the numbers as frequencies (the actual counts) or percentages. For this example, select *Frequencies*.

NOTE: After running this analysis as specified, feel free to return to this menu to rerun this analysis using different settings (e.g., try selecting *Pie chart, Percentages*).

| **Figure 4.11** | *Frequencies: Charts* Order Screen; Select *Bar charts* and *Frequencies* |

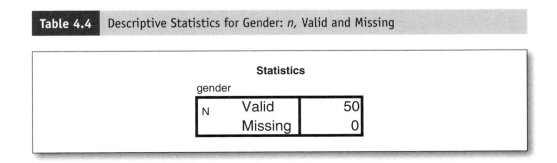

6. Click on the *Continue* button; this will return you to the *Frequencies* menu.

7. Click on the *OK* button on the *Frequencies* screen; this tells SPSS to process the *Frequencies* report based on the parameters that you just specified.

Frequency Statistics Tables

The first part of this frequency report shows the overall *n* (*N*)—the total number of entries (records) in the variable: 50 valid records and 0 missing as shown (Table 4.4).

| **Table 4.4** | Descriptive Statistics for Gender: *n*, Valid and Missing |

Statistics

gender

N	Valid	50
	Missing	0

The next part of the report provides more detailed information regarding the *n*, indicating the frequency (actual number) and percent for each category within the gender variable (female/male), as shown in Table 4.5. Incidentally, to calculate the percent, divide the frequency for the category by the (valid) *n*, so for female, it would be 27 ÷ 50 = .54 (54%).

Table 4.5 Descriptive Statistics for Gender: Frequency and Percent

		Frequency	Percent	Valid Percent	Cumulative Percent
Valid	Female	27	54.0	54.0	54.0
	Male	23	46.0	46.0	100.0
	Total	50	100.0	100.0	

gender

Bar Chart

Last, the report provides a bar chart representing the two gender categories (female/male) (Figure 4.12).

Figure 4.12 Bar Chart of the Gender Variable

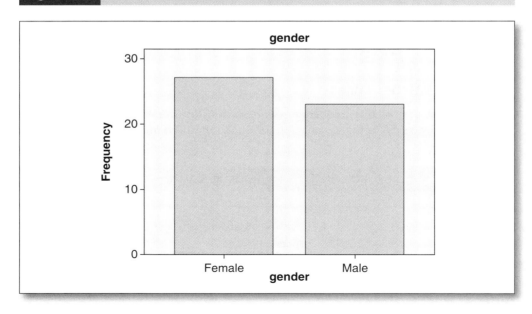

SPSS—DESCRIPTIVE STATISTICS: CONTINUOUS VARIABLE (AGE) SELECT BY CATEGORICAL VARIABLE (GENDER)—FEMALES ONLY

So far, we have processed the continuous variable, age, with both genders combined, but it is also possible to produce separate reports for females only and males only, showing the summary statistics and histograms for each. This technique not only satisfies curiosity about what is going on in each category but also will be essential for running the pretest checklist reports that will be covered in Chapters 5, 6, 7, and 8.

We will begin with processing the age summary statistics for females only, and then we will repeat the process but select data for males only. The *Select Case* option allows you to specify which cases (rows of data, also known as *records*) you would like to process; SPSS will temporarily ignore all other cases—they will not be included in any statistical computations until you choose to reselect them.

The following procedure will select only the cases where gender = 1 (female).

1. Click on the *Select Cases* icon (Figure 4.13).

Figure 4.13	The *Select Cases* Icon

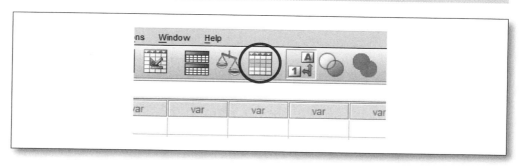

2. This will bring you to the *Select Cases* menu (Figure 4.14). The default Selection is *All cases*. Click on *If condition is satisfied,* then click on the *If . . .* button.

Figure 4.14	The *Select Cases* Screen (Top Only)

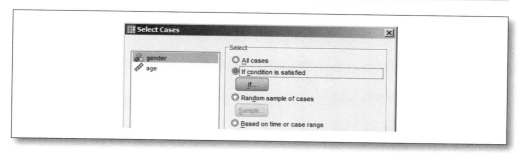

3. This will bring you to the *Select Cases: If* screen (Figure 4.15).

Figure 4.15   The *Select Cases: If* Screen (Top Only)

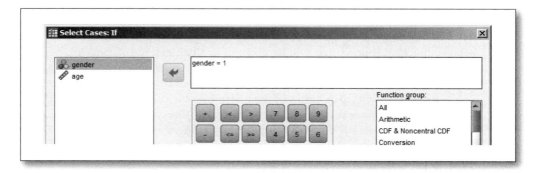

4. Remember: SPSS handles categorical variables as numbers; earlier, we had established that for the categorical variable gender, 1 = female and 2 = male. Since we want statistical reports on females only, we enter the inclusion criteria, gender = 1, in the big box at the top of the screen. Then click on the *Continue* button.

5. This will return you to the *Select Cases* screen. Click on the *OK* button, and the system will process your selection criteria.

Figure 4.16   The Data View Screen After *Select Cases* (Gender = 1) Has Been Executed (Section Only)

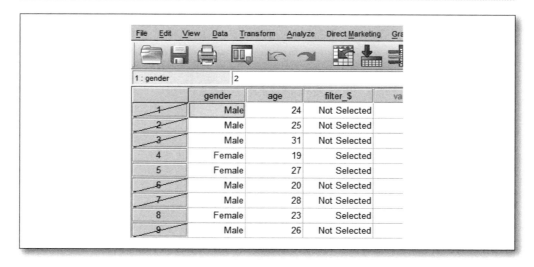

6. Switch back to the Data View screen. First, notice that the record (row) numbers for each male is slashed out (Figure 4.16). You can think of all the data in the slashed-out rows as being in a sort of penalty box—they are still part of the data set, but they cannot play. Slashed-out data will not be included in any statistical processing.

Also notice that SPSS has created the temporary variable *Filter_$* in the last column, which corresponds to the slashes in each row. If you click on the *Value Labels* icon or go to the Variable View screen, you will see that the *Filter_$* variable contains two categories: 0 = not selected and 1 = selected.

Since we selected only cases where gender = 1, this means that if we were to run the descriptive statistics report again, the summary statistics and histogram would reflect females only, as opposed to the earlier report which combined females and males.

7. At this time, rerun the analysis for the age variable. The resulting statistical report should resemble the data shown in Table 4.6.

Table 4.6	Frequency Statistics Table Showing Summary Statistics for Age for Females Only

Statistics

age

N	Valid	27
	Missing	0
Mean		23.19
Median		23.00
Mode		23
Std. Deviation		2.543
Variance		6.464
Range		10
Minimum		18
Maximum		28

8. Notice that the *N* has changed from 50, which included both females and males, to 27, which is females only. Compared with the first report, all other statistics have changed as well. Continuing our analysis of the females only, observe the frequency statistics (Table 4.7) and corresponding histogram (Figure 4.17).

| Table 4.7 | Frequency Statistics Table Showing the Frequency of Each Value in the Age Variable for Females Only |

age

		Frequency	Percent	Valid Percent	Cumulative Percent
Valid	18	1	3.7	3.7	3.7
	19	2	7.4	7.4	11.1
	20	1	3.7	3.7	14.8
	21	2	7.4	7.4	22.2
	22	4	14.8	14.8	37.0
	23	5	18.5	18.5	55.6
	24	4	14.8	14.8	70.4
	25	3	11.1	11.1	81.5
	26	2	7.4	7.4	88.9
	27	2	7.4	7.4	96.3
	28	1	3.7	3.7	100.0
	Total	27	100.0	100.0	

| Figure 4.17 | Histogram of the Age Variable for Females Only |

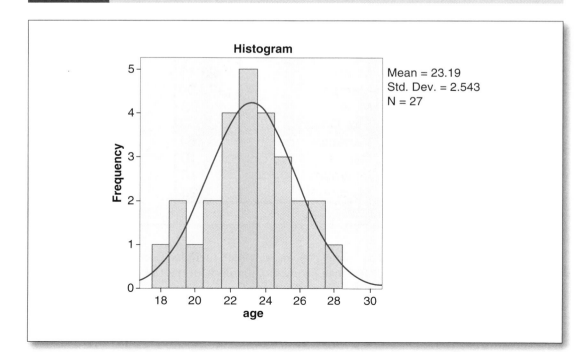

Histogram

Mean = 23.19
Std. Dev. = 2.543
N = 27

SPSS—DESCRIPTIVE STATISTICS: CONTINUOUS VARIABLE (AGE) SELECT BY CATEGORICAL VARIABLE (GENDER)—MALES ONLY

9. As you can see, there is a lot to be learned by selecting the data and examining statistics pertaining to females only. The next step is to run the same reports for males only.

10. Repeat the steps to order the descriptive statistics report, except when you get to Step 3, instead of specifying gender = 1, change that to gender = 2 (remember, we established gender as 1 = female and 2 = male).

11. Upon (re)running the data for males, notice that the slashes, *Filter_$*, and output reports all change to reflect males only (see Table 4.8, Table 4.9, and Figure 4.18).

| Table 4.8 | Frequency Statistics Table Showing Summary Statistics for Age for Males Only |

Statistics

age

N	Valid	23
	Missing	0
Mean		24.96
Median		25.00
Mode		25
Std. Deviation		2.962
Variance		8.771
Range		13
Minimum		18
Maximum		31

| Table 4.9 | Frequency Statistics Table Showing the Frequency of Each Value in the Age Variable for Males Only |

age

		Frequency	Percent	Valid Percent	Cumulative Percent
Valid	18	1	4.3	4.3	4.3
	20	1	4.3	4.3	8.7
	22	2	8.7	8.7	17.4
	23	1	4.3	4.3	21.7
	24	4	17.4	17.4	39.1
	25	6	26.1	26.1	65.2
	26	3	13.0	13.0	78.3
	27	1	4.3	4.3	82.6
	28	1	4.3	4.3	87.0
	29	1	4.3	4.3	91.3
	30	1	4.3	4.3	95.7
	31	1	4.3	4.3	100.0
	Total	23	100.0	100.0	

| Figure 4.18 | Histogram of the Age Variable for Males Only |

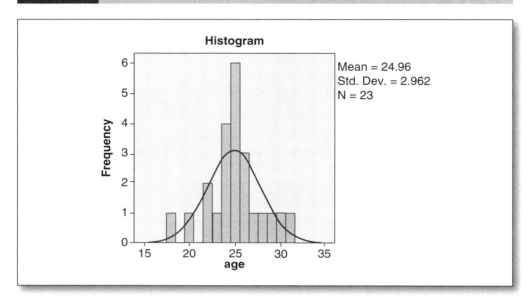

 ## SPSS—SELECTING ALL VARIABLES

At this point, we have run three sets of descriptive statistics on age: (1) all records, (2) females only, and (3) males only. Now, suppose we want to perform further analyses using the entire data set again. There are several ways to do this:

On the Data View screen, click on the column header *Filter_$* (which will highlight the whole column) and press the *Delete* key.

On the Variable View screen, click on the corresponding row number—in this case, row 3 (which will highlight the whole row)—and press the *Delete* key.

Click on the *Select Cases* icon, then click on the *All Cases* button. Finally, click on the *OK* button.

GOOD COMMON SENSE

The acronym GIGO (pronounced *gig-oh*) comes from the early days of computing; it stands for *garbage in, garbage out,* and it is just as valid today. Basically, it means that if you input junk data into a program, the output will be junk too.

Although SPSS is proficient at processing statistical data, keep in mind that the program has no real intelligence per se—it just pushes the numbers through the functions using the parameters that you specify. As such, it is up to you to make intelligent selections.

In the examples detailed in this chapter, we ordered a variety of statistical analyses on the *age* variable, which makes sense; knowing the mean age can be useful. Larger databases are likely to contain other numeric variables such as ID numbers, street addresses, phone numbers, serial numbers, license numbers, and so on. Technically, you could order SPSS to compute descriptive statistics on such variables; SPSS is not bright enough to know that computing the mean for a series of phone numbers makes no sense; SPSS (or any other statistical processing software) would mindlessly process the variable and provide you with an average phone number, which would be useless. In summary, it is up to you to proceed mindfully when using any such software.

Key Concepts

- Descriptive statistics
  - Number—*N*(variable) for population, *n*(variable) for sample
  - Mean—μ(variable) or $\overline{\text{variable}}$
  - Median
  - Mode
  - Standard deviation—*SD*(variable)
  - Variance
  - Minimum
  - Maximum
  - Range
- Loading SPSS data files
- Histogram
- Normal curve
- Skew
  - Negative (left) skew
  - Positive (right) skew
  - Outlier
- Bar chart
- Pie chart
- Select cases
- Good common sense

Practice Exercises

For Exercises 1 to 5:

- Configure SPSS per the specifications of the codebook.
- Enter the data set as shown in the table.
- Order descriptive statistics as indicated for each exercise.

For Exercises 6 to 10:

- Use the prepared SPSS data sets (download from **www.sagepub.com/knapp**).
- Load, process, and document your findings for each exercise.

1. A survey was conducted in Professor Lamm's class and Professor Milner's class. The question that students responded to is, "How many siblings do you have?"

   Codebook—set up SPSS to contain two variables:

   - *class* is a categorical variable (1 = Prof. Lamm, 2 = Prof. Milner)
   - *siblings* is a continuous variable (number of siblings)

   Data set—enter the data set:

Rec. #	class	siblings
1	Prof. Lamm	2
2	Prof. Lamm	1
3	Prof. Lamm	2
4	Prof. Lamm	0
5	Prof. Lamm	3
6	Prof. Lamm	1
7	Prof. Lamm	2
8	Prof. Lamm	2
9	Prof. Lamm	1
10	Prof. Lamm	2
11	Prof. Lamm	2
12	Prof. Lamm	1
13	Prof. Lamm	0
14	Prof. Lamm	2
15	Prof. Lamm	1
16	Prof. Lamm	1
17	Prof. Lamm	2
18	Prof. Lamm	1

19	Prof. Lamm	0
20	Prof. Lamm	1
21	Prof. Milner	2
22	Prof. Milner	3
23	Prof. Milner	2
24	Prof. Milner	1
25	Prof. Milner	0
26	Prof. Milner	0
27	Prof. Milner	1
28	Prof. Milner	1
29	Prof. Milner	1
30	Prof. Milner	2
31	Prof. Milner	1
32	Prof. Milner	3
33	Prof. Milner	1
34	Prof. Milner	2
35	Prof. Milner	2
36	Prof. Milner	4
37	Prof. Milner	3
38	Prof. Milner	1
39	Prof. Milner	1
40	Prof. Milner	3
41	Prof. Milner	2

a. Run descriptive statistics and a histogram with a normal curve for *siblings* for the whole data set.
b. Run descriptive statistics and a bar chart for *class* for the whole data set.
c. Run descriptive statistics and a histogram with a normal curve for *siblings* for members of Prof. Lamm's class only.
d. Run descriptive statistics and a histogram with a normal curve for *siblings* for members of Prof. Milner's class only.

2. While waiting in line to donate blood, donors were asked, "How many times have you donated before?" The researcher recorded their gender and number of prior donations.

Codebook—set up SPSS to contain two variables:

- *gender* is a categorical variable (1 = females, 2 = males).
- *donated* is a continuous variable (total number of blood donations given before today).

Data set—enter the data set:

Rec. #	gender	donated
1	Female	7
2	Male	4
3	Male	5
4	Female	4
5	Female	5
6	Male	3
7	Female	9
8	Female	2
9	Male	7
10	Female	1
11	Male	3
12	Female	5
13	Male	2
14	Female	3
15	Male	4
16	Female	0
17	Male	2

a. Run descriptive statistics and a histogram with a normal curve for *donated* for the whole data set.

b. Run descriptive statistics and a bar chart for *gender* for the whole data set.

   c. Run descriptive statistics and a histogram with a normal curve for *donated* for females only.

   d. Run descriptive statistics and a histogram with a normal curve for *donated* for males only.

3. You want to know if typing proficiency is associated with better spelling skills. You administer a spelling test consisting of 20 words to the students in a classroom. At the bottom of the sheet, there is a question: *Can you type accurately without looking at the keyboard?*

Codebook—set up SPSS to contain two variables:

- *looker* (1 = looks at keyboard, 2 = doesn't look at keyboard)
- *spelling* (score on spelling test)

Data set—enter the data set:

Rec. #	looker	spelling
1	Looks at keyboard	15
2	Looks at keyboard	14
3	Looks at keyboard	16
4	Doesn't look at keyboard	18
5	Looks at keyboard	16
6	Looks at keyboard	16
7	Doesn't look at keyboard	20
8	Looks at keyboard	12
9	Looks at keyboard	14
10	Looks at keyboard	15
11	Doesn't look at keyboard	19
12	Looks at keyboard	17
13	Looks at keyboard	13
14	Looks at keyboard	18
15	Doesn't look at keyboard	19
16	Doesn't look at keyboard	14
17	Doesn't look at keyboard	20
18	Looks at keyboard	16

19	Doesn't look at keyboard	13
20	Looks at keyboard	17
21	Looks at keyboard	18
22	Looks at keyboard	17

    a. Run descriptive statistics and a histogram with a normal curve for *spelling* for the whole data set.

    b. Run descriptive statistics and a bar chart for *looker* for the whole data set.

    c. Run descriptive statistics and a histogram with a normal curve for *spelling* for "looks at keyboard" only.

    d. Run descriptive statistics and a histogram with a normal curve for *spelling* for "doesn't look at keyboard" only.

4. You are interested in the length of time it takes for individuals to complete their transactions at an ATM. You use a stopwatch to record your unobtrusive observations and gather two pieces of information on each person: gender and the length of his or her ATM session (in seconds).

Codebook—set up SPSS to contain two variables:

- *gender* is a categorical variable (1 = female, 2 = male).
- *atmsec* is a continuous variable (number of seconds spent at ATM).

Data set—enter the data set:

Rec. #	gender	atmsec
1	Female	220
2	Male	164
3	Male	166
4	Female	165
5	Female	131
6	Male	95
7	Female	162
8	Female	140
9	Male	98
10	Female	107

11	Male	144
12	Male	185
13	Male	142
14	Female	179
15	Female	218
16	Female	163
17	Female	180
18	Male	142
19	Female	108
20	Male	138

a. Run descriptive statistics and a histogram with a normal curve for *atmsec* for the whole data set.

b. Run descriptive statistics and a bar chart for *gender* for the whole data set.

c. Run descriptive statistics and a histogram with a normal curve for *atmsec* for female only.

d. Run descriptive statistics and a histogram with a normal curve for *atmsec* for male only.

5. You are interested in finding out how many units students are enrolled in. You conduct a survey of 40 students and record two pieces of information: the degree (level) the student is working on (bachelor's, master's, doctorate) and total number of units they are taking this term.

Codebook—set up SPSS to contain two variables:

- *degree* is a categorical variable (1 = bachelor's, 2 = master's, 3 = doctorate).
- *units* is a continuous variable (current number of enrolled units).

Data set—enter the data set:

Rec. #	degree	units
1	Bachelor's	12
2	Bachelor's	12
3	Bachelor's	12

4	Bachelor's	12
5	Bachelor's	12
6	Bachelor's	15
7	Master's	12
8	Bachelor's	15
9	Bachelor's	12
10	Doctorate	12
11	Bachelor's	15
12	Master's	9
13	Bachelor's	12
14	Bachelor's	15
15	Master's	12
16	Bachelor's	12
17	Bachelor's	12
18	Bachelor's	9
19	Bachelor's	12
20	Bachelor's	12
21	Bachelor's	15
22	Bachelor's	9
23	Bachelor's	9
24	Master's	9
25	Bachelor's	12
26	Doctorate	15
27	Bachelor's	9
28	Bachelor's	15
29	Bachelor's	15
30	Bachelor's	15
31	Master's	15

32	Master's	9
33	Bachelor's	12
34	Bachelor's	9
35	Bachelor's	9
36	Bachelor's	12
37	Bachelor's	12
38	Bachelor's	12
39	Master's	6
40	Bachelor's	9

a. Run descriptive statistics and a histogram with a normal curve for *units* for the whole data set.
b. Run descriptive statistics and a bar chart for *degree* for the whole data set.
c. Run descriptive statistics and a histogram with a normal curve for *units* for Bachelor's degree only.
d. Run descriptive statistics and a histogram with a normal curve for *units* for Master's degree only.
e. Run descriptive statistics and a histogram with a normal curve for *units* for doctorate only.

6. You stand at a register in a hospital cafeteria; for each patron, you gather two pieces of information: professional role (nurse, doctor, other), as indicated on their badge, and the amount of their bill (as shown on the register).

Codebook—the SPSS file contains two variables:

- *profrole* (professional role) is a categorical variable (1 = nurse, 2 = doctor, 3 = other).
- *bill* is a continuous variable (total as shown on the register).

Data set—load *Chapter 04 – Exercise 06.sav.*

a. Run descriptive statistics and a histogram with a normal curve for *bill* for the whole data set.
b. Run descriptive statistics and a bar chart for *profrole* for the whole data set.
c. Run descriptive statistics and a histogram with a normal curve for *bill* for nurse only.
d. Run descriptive statistics and a histogram with a normal curve for *bill* for doctor only.

    e. Run descriptive statistics and a histogram with a normal curve for *bill* for other only.

7. You recruit a group of people who agree to report their total email counts (sent + received) for 30 days. Each participant also completed a survey regarding his or her employment status (full-time, part-time, unemployed).

    Codebook—the SPSS file contains two variables:

      • *employ* is a categorical variable (1 = full-time, 2 = part-time, 3 = unemployed).

      • *emails* is a continuous variable (total number of emails).

    Data set—load *Chapter 04 – Exercise 07.sav.*

    a. Run descriptive statistics and a histogram with a normal curve for *emails* for the whole data set.

    b. Run descriptive statistics and a bar chart for *employ* for the whole data set.

    c. Run descriptive statistics and a histogram with a normal curve for *emails* for full-time only.

    d. Run descriptive statistics and a histogram with a normal curve for *emails* for part-time only.

    e. Run descriptive statistics and a histogram with a normal curve for *emails* for unemployed only.

8. The members of an exercise walking group agree to partake in your study; you randomly give half of the group walking music in a major key, and the others are given walking music in a minor key. Each participant can walk as often and for as long as he or she likes. The participants will record and submit the total number of minutes that they walked in a week.

    Codebook—the SPSS file contains two variables:

      • *musickey* is a categorical variable (1 = major, 2 = minor).

      • *minwalk* is a continuous variable (total number of minutes walked).

    Data set—load *Chapter 04 – Exercise 08.sav.*

    a. Run descriptive statistics and a histogram with a normal curve for *minwalk* for the whole data set.

    b. Run descriptive statistics and a bar chart for *musickey* for the whole data set.

    c. Run descriptive statistics and a histogram with a normal curve for *minwalk* for major only.

    d. Run descriptive statistics and a histogram with a normal curve for *minwalk* for minor only.

9. The administrator of a two-ward hospital randomly selects one ward wherein the nurses will be assigned to tend to two patients each; nurses in the other ward will tend to four patients each. Over the course of a month, upon discharge, each patient will complete a nursing care satisfaction survey,

which renders a score ranging from 1 to 100 (1 = very unsatisfied . . .
100 = very satisfied).

Codebook—the SPSS file contains two variables:

- *ward* is a categorical variable (1 = 2 patients per nurse, 2 = 4 patients per nurse).
- *nsatisfy* is a continuous variable (patient's nurse satisfaction score).

Data set—load the data set: *Chapter 04 – Exercise 09.sav.*

a. Run descriptive statistics and a histogram with a normal curve for *nsatisfy* for the whole data set.
b. Run descriptive statistics and a bar chart for *ward* for the whole data set.
c. Run descriptive statistics and a histogram with normal curve for *nsatisfy* for the 2 patients per nurse ward only.
d. Run descriptive statistics and a histogram with a normal curve for *nsatisfy* for the 4 patients per nurse ward only.

10. To determine if dancing enhances mood, you recruit 100 people who are interested. You randomly select 50 and give them seven free dance lessons; the other 50 get no dance lessons. After the seventh class, you administer the Acme Happiness Scale Survey (AHSS) to all 100 individuals; this survey renders a score ranging from 1 to 30 (1 = extremely unhappy . . .
30 = extremely happy).

Codebook—the SPSS file contains two variables:

- *dance* is a categorical variable (1 = dancer, 2 = nondancer).
- *ahss* is a continuous variable (Acme Happiness Scale Survey score).

Data set—load the data set: *Chapter 04 – Exercise 10.sav.*

a. Run descriptive statistics and a histogram with a normal curve for *ahss* for the whole data set.
b. Run descriptive statistics and a bar chart for *dance* for the whole data set.
c. Run descriptive statistics and a histogram with a normal curve for *ahss* for the dancers only.
d. Run descriptive statistics and a histogram with a normal curve for *ahss* for the nondancers only.

C H A P T E R   5

t Test

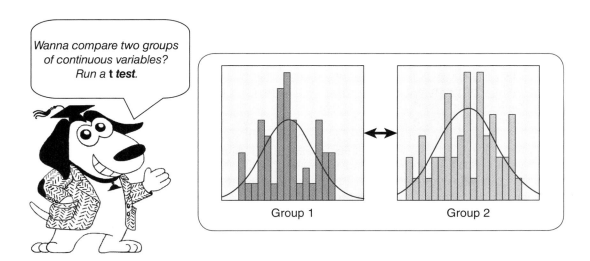

*Wanna compare two groups of continuous variables? Run a **t test**.*

Group 1   Group 2

The difference between a violin and a viola is that a viola burns longer.

—Victor Borge

LEARNING OBJECTIVES

Upon completing this chapter, you will be able to:

- Determine when it is appropriate to run a *t* test
- Verify that the data meet the criteria for *t* test processing: normality, homogeneity of variance, and *n*
- Order a *t* test with graphics
- Interpret the test results
- Comprehend the α level and *p* value
- Resolve the hypotheses
- Document the results in plain English
- Understand the implications of Type I and Type II errors
- Apply techniques for reducing the likelihood of committing Type I and Type II errors

DIGITAL LEARNING RESOURCES

The tutorial video and data sets for this chapter are at **www.sagepub.com/knapp**

- *t* Test pretest checklist video
- *t* Test run video
- SPSS files

OVERVIEW

NOTE: From here forward, the "μ" character will be used to symbolize the mean.

The *t* test is one of the most common and versatile statistical tests in the realm of experimental research and survey methodology. The *t* test is used when there are two groups, each of which renders a continuous variable for the outcome (e.g., height, age, weight, number of teeth, bank account balance, IQ score, score on a depression assessment instrument, blood pressure, test score, typing speed, etc.).

In the most basic experimental setting, the design consists of two groups: a control group, which gets a placebo or treatment as usual, and a treatment group, which gets the innovative intervention that is the focus of the study.

We can compute the mean for each group, and we would not expect the two means to be identical; they would likely be different. The *t* test answers the question, "Is there a statistically significant difference between μ(Control) and μ(Treatment)?" In other words, the result of the *t* test helps us to determine if one group *substantially* outperformed the other or if the differences between the means are essentially *incidental*.

EXAMPLE

Dr. Zinn and Dr. Zorders arranged to offer Z-Math, their innovative method for teaching students the multiplication table (1 × 1 . . . 10 × 10), to fourth graders at Pico Street School.

RESEARCH QUESTION

Does Z-Math outperform traditional multiplication educational methods?

GROUPS

The names of all 60 fourth graders at the school are written on slips of paper and placed into a hat. The principal randomly draws 30 names from the hat; these students will be assigned to the control group. The remaining 30 students will be assigned to the Z-Math group.

PROCEDURE

From 10:00 to 11:30 a.m., the usual time for the daily math lesson, the students in the control group will go to Room 14, where they will receive the regular math lesson (treatment as usual). The students in the Z-Math group will go to Room 8 for their Z-Math lesson. The students in the Z-Math group are instructed not to disclose the Z-Math method to the other students.

After 4 weeks, all 60 students will be given a test; they will have 10 minutes to write out the entire multiplication table with the solutions on a blank sheet of paper (e.g., $1 \times 1 = 1$, $1 \times 2 = 2 \ldots 10 \times 10 = 100$).

HYPOTHESES

H_0: There is no statistically significant difference in the test scores between the two groups.

H_1: The Z-Math group statistically significantly outperformed the math-as-usual group.

DATA SET

Use the following data set: *Chapter 05–Example 01–T Test.sav.*

PRETEST CHECKLIST

The statistical pretest checklist is akin to looking both ways before you cross the street; certainly you *could* cross the street without looking, but you would probably wind up in much better shape if you looked first. In terms of statistical tests, certainly you *could* run the statistical test without tending to the pretest checklist, but you may unknowingly wind up with misleading findings.

The formulas that compose each statistical test require that the source data meet a unique set of criteria in order for that test to operate properly. These criteria are referred to as *assumptions*—we *assume* that the data meet the criteria specified by the test at hand. Actually, we need to do more than just passively assume that the data are suitable for processing; we need to *actively assess* the source data before proceeding with the test.

When the tests on the pretest checklist (statistical assumptions) are satisfied, we can consider the statistical results relatively "robust." When one or more of the pretest checklist criteria are not satisfied, we still proceed with the analysis, but we would be a bit less confident in the solidity of our findings. In the interest of proper scientific ethics and the principles of full disclosure, it would be appropriate to mention any such (statistical) shortcomings when discussing the results. This notion pertains to the unique pretest checklists for the other tests covered in this text as well.

The pretest criteria for running a *t* test involve checking the data for (1) *normality*, (2) *homogeneity* (pronounced *hoe-moe-juh-nay-it-tea*) *of variance*, and (3) an *n* quota. SPSS is equipped to run all of these (pre)tests.

Pretest Checklist Criterion 1—Normality

Checking for *normality* involves producing a histogram with a normal curve for each of the two groups. In this instance, you would click on the *Select Cases* icon to select the records pertaining to the math-as-usual group; the selection criteria would be group = 1. Next, run a histogram (with normal curve) on the variable score. Then repeat the process for the Z-Math group (group = 2). For more details on this procedure, please refer to Chapter 4 ("SPSS—Descriptive Statistics: Continuous Variable (Age) Select by Categorical Variable (Gender)—Females Only"); see the star (★) icon on page **71**.

This will produce two histograms with normal curves—one for scores in the math-as-usual group and the other for the scores in the Z-Math group. The histograms should resemble the graphs shown in Figures 5.1 and 5.2.

As we read these two histograms, set aside the *X,Y* scales and the possible irregularities among the bars; our attention is focused on the shape of the *normal curve*. We are looking for *normality* (symmetry) in these two curves. Although the normal curve in Figure 5.1 is shorter and fatter than the normal curve in Figure 5.2; in terms of normality, this is not an issue. The critical thing to observe is that both normal curves are

Figure 5.1	Histogram of Score for G_1: Math-as-Usual Group

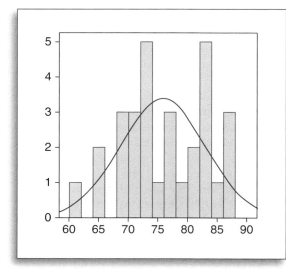

Figure 5.2	Histogram of Score for G_2: Z-Math Group

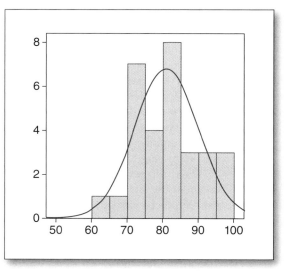

sufficiently symmetrical—in other words, if you sliced this curve vertically down the middle, the left side would resemble a mirror image of the right side; sometimes this normal curve is aptly referred to by its characteristic shape as a "bell curve." In this example, we see that both curves are symmetrical; there is no notable *skew* in either curve. Hence, we would say that the criteria of normality are satisfied for both the math-as-usual and the Z-Math groups.

Pretest Checklist Criterion 2—Homogeneity of Variance

Homogeneity pertains to *sameness;* the homogeneity of variance criteria involve checking that the variances of the two groups are not too different from each other. As a rule of thumb, homogeneity of variance is likely to be achieved if the variance from one group is not more than twice the variance of the other group. In this case, the variance (standard deviation squared) for score in the math-as-usual group is 49.84, and the variance for score in the Z-Math group is 77.96. Clearly, 77.96 is not more than twice the value of 49.84, so we would expect that the homogeneity of variance test would pass.

Take a look at Figures 5.3 and 5.4; these graphs are drawn from two theoretical data sets, both of which have three things in common: $n = 100$, mean = 50, and normal distributions. The most notable difference is the *spread* of the data—in Figure 5.3, the data ranges from 27 to 70, with a variance of 80 ($SD = 8.957$), whereas the data in Figure 5.4 have a much broader range, from 7 to 92, with a variance of 313 ($SD = 17.690$). As discussed in Chapter 4, as values deviate further from the mean, this increases the standard

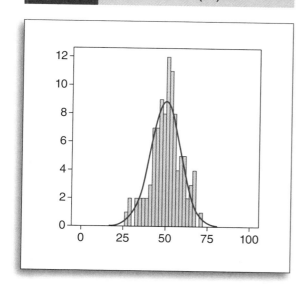

Figure 5.3   Smaller Variance (80)

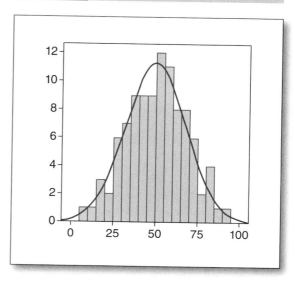

Figure 5.4   Larger Variance (313)

deviation. Since the variance = the standard deviation squared, the variance reflects these deviations in an even more pronounced way.

Considering that the variance from one data set (313) is more than double the variance from the other data set (80), we would expect the homogeneity of variance test to render a (p) value that is less than .05, indicating a statistically significant difference between the variances of these two variables and a violation of that criterion.

In SPSS, the homogeneity of variance test is an option selected during the actual run of the t test. If the homogeneity of variance test renders a significance (p) value that is greater than .05, then this suggests that there is no statistically significant difference between the variance from one group to the other group. This would mean that the data pass the homogeneity of variance test. The notion of the p value will be discussed in detail in the Results section in this chapter, when we examine the findings produced by the t test.

Pretest Checklist Criterion 3—n

Technically, you can process a t test with an n of any size in each group, but when the n is at least 30 in each group, the result of the t test is considered more robust. We will see the n reported for each group in the Results section, when we examine the findings produced by the t test.

 ## TEST RUN

To run a t test:

1. On the main screen, click on *Analyze, Compare Means, One-Way ANOVA . . .* (Figure 5.5).

Figure 5.5   Running a t Test

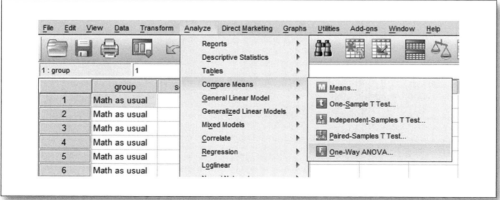

2. On the *One-Way ANOVA* menu, move the continuous variable that you wish to analyze (*score*) into the *Dependent List* window, and move the variable that contains the categorical variable that specifies the group (*group*) into the *Factor* window (Figure 5.6).

NOTE: SPSS does offer a *t* test menu screen, but the ANOVA order menu (below) is easier to load and produces an equivalent report. In addition, this same menu will be used to run ANOVA tests, which will be covered in Chapter 6; it is easier to learn one menu instead of two.

Figure 5.6   The One-Way ANOVA Menu

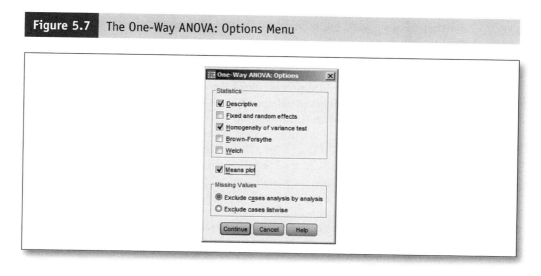

3. Click on the *Options . . .* button, and on the *One-Way ANOVA: Options* menu, check *Descriptive, Homogeneity of variance test,* and *Means plot,* then click on the *Continue* button (Figure 5.7).

Figure 5.7   The One-Way ANOVA: Options Menu

4. This will take you back to the *One-Way ANOVA* menu (Figure 5.6); click on the *OK* button, and the *t* test will process.

RESULTS

We will begin this section by completing the pretest checklist; we still need answers regarding the homogeneity of variance and the *n*s for each group. The last column of the homogeneity of variance table (Table 5.1) shows a significance (*p*) value of .433; since this is greater than the α level of .05, this tells us that there is no statistically significant difference between the variances in the score variable from the math-as-usual group compared with the score variable from the Z-Math group. We would conclude that the criteria of the homogeneity of variance have been satisfied.

Table 5.1	Homogeneity of Variance Test Results

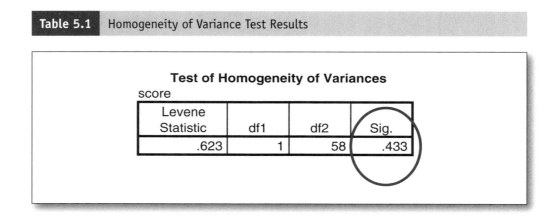

Test of Homogeneity of Variances
score

Levene Statistic	df1	df2	Sig.
.623	1	58	.433

Further details regarding these criteria will be discussed further, but before proceeding with any further interpretation of the results report, it is necessary to discuss two statistical concepts that pertain to the rest of the statistical tests contained in this text: *p* value and the alpha (α) level, both of which will be covered shortly.

As for the final item on the pretest checklist, the *n,* we can see from the second column in Table 5.2 that math as usual and Z-Math each has an *n* of 30. This satisfies the *n assumption,* stating that each group should have an *n* of at least 30.

At this point, you have probably noticed column 3 in Table 5.2, which shows that the mean score for the Z-Math group (80.97) is higher than the mean score for the math-as-usual group (75.77). You can also see these means plotted graphically (Figure 5.8). On the basis of these means, you may hastily conclude that the school should just adopt the Z-Math system since this group scored higher than the math-as-usual group, but in statistics, the world is not so simple.

Statisticians recognize and actively acknowledge that we do not live in a perfect world; no matter how hard we try to conduct quality investigations, the scientific process can

Table 5.2   Descriptive Statistics of Score for Math-as-Usual and Z-Math Groups

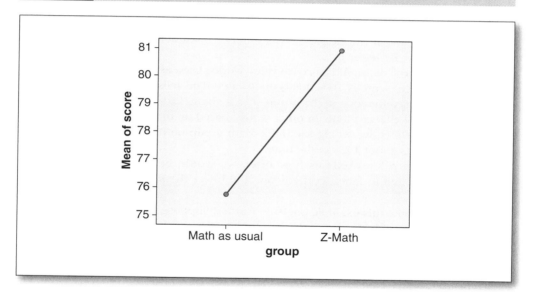

Descriptives

score

	N	Mean	Std. Deviation	Std. Error	95% Confidence Interval for Mean Lower Bound	95% Confidence Interval for Mean Upper Bound	Minimum	Maximum
Math as usual	30	75.77	7.060	1.289	73.13	78.40	61	87
Z-Math	30	80.97	8.830	1.612	77.67	84.26	62	99
Total	60	78.37	8.348	1.078	76.21	80.52	61	99

Figure 5.8   Means Plot of Math-as-Usual and Z-Math Groups

be a messy proposition littered with multiple *confounding variables*—conditions for which we cannot fully control or account for.

In our simple example, judging by the mean test scores of the two groups, it looks like the Z-Math group outperformed the math-as-usual group, and this may in fact turn out to be the case, but other factors may have contributed to the differences observed between the (mean) scores of these two groups. For example, maybe the random distribution process unexpectedly routed more math-smart students to the Z-Math group; maybe the class clown was routed to the math-as-usual group and created amusing distractions during the lessons or the test; maybe the members of the math-as-usual group held slumber parties where the Z-Math students were not invited, and there was very little slumber—this lack of sleep may have adversely affected their concentration levels; maybe the Z-Math group developed a sense of rivalry, which motivated them to work harder to try to outperform the other group; maybe the members of the math-as-usual group were displeased that they were not assigned to the Z-Math group and developed a negative attitude toward their math lessons. Any number of these or other things that we do not know about may have been going on over the course of this study.

As you can see, there is virtually no limit to the variety of *confounding variables* that could potentially influence the outcome of a study. Since we cannot fully account for or compensate for such confounds, we know we do not have a pure experimental setting. Hence, we do not speak of our statistical findings with *absolute certainty;* rather, we speak of *how much confidence* we have in our findings.

The key question in this case is, How certain can we be that the 5.2-point difference that we detected between the group means (μ(math as usual) = 75.77 and μ(Z-Math) = 80.97) is actually due to the superiority of the intervention (Z-Math) and not due to chance alone? In other words, we want a number that will tell us how likely we would detect this result (the 5.2-point difference in the means) if Z-Math was a sham—if it did nothing. This number is known as the significance level, represented by the letter p.

Here is how the significance (p) value works: Look at the last column of Table 5.3; the Sig.(nificance) score is .015; this is the p value. This tells us that we would expect to see the 5.2-point difference in the group scores about 1.5% of the time if it were occurring by (random) chance alone. In other words, based on the data gathered, if Z-Math in fact had a null effect, we would see the Z-Math group outperform the math-as-usual group by 5.2 points about 1.5% of the time.

Since the p level tells us how often we would be accepting the intervention as effective, when in fact it really is not, the lower the p level, the more significant the findings.

We will take this example one step further: Suppose the p level had been .001 in our study; this would tell us that there is (only) 1 chance in 1,000 that we would be seeing such results by chance alone (e.g., if Z-Math was completely ineffective), which would

Table 5.3   *t* Test Results Comparing Scores for Math-as-Usual and Z-Math Groups

ANOVA

score

	Sum of Squares	df	Mean Square	F	Sig.
Between Groups	405.600	1	405.600	6.347	.015
Within Groups	3706.333	58	63.902		
Total	4111.933	59			

lead us to wrongly believe that the differences in the scores that we are observing are likely attributable to the effectiveness of the intervention (Z-Math).

In the next section, we will see how we use the *p* value to determine which hypothesis to reject and which to accept.

HYPOTHESIS RESOLUTION

We need to have a way of using the *p* level to guide us in making decisions about our pending hypotheses:

H_0: There is no statistically significant difference in the test scores between the two groups.

H_1: The Z-Math group statistically significantly outperformed the math-as-usual group.

p Value

To do this, before we embark on our research process, we draw a somewhat arbitrary numerical line in the sand, known as the alpha (α) level. In social sciences, the α level is typically set to .05. Think of the α level as a sort of statistical significance threshold—any *p* value that is .05 or less is considered statistically significant—hence, we reject H_0, which states that there is no significant difference between the groups. If the *p* value is over .05, then the differences between the means are not considered statistically significant—hence, we do not reject H_0. This will guide us in making our decisions regarding the hypotheses.

> ### *p* Value Summary
>
> α = .05 (typical for social sciences)
>
> If $p \leq \alpha$, then there is a statistically significant difference; reject H_0.
>
> If $p > \alpha$, then there is no statistically significant difference; do not reject H_0.

Our investigation produced a *p* value of .015; since this is less than the α level (.05), we consider the differences detected between the groups statistically significant, and as such, we reject the null hypothesis (H_0), which states that there is no statistically significant difference between the groups, and opt for the alternate hypothesis (H_1), which states that the difference detected between the groups is attributable to the Z-Math intervention.

Alternatively, if our *p* value had been greater than .05 (e.g., .85), then we would have accepted the null hypothesis (H_0) and considered the differences observed an artifact of random chance; furthermore, we would have rejected the alternate hypothesis (H_1), which states that it was the intervention (Z-Math) that accounted for the differences observed between groups.

Another way of understanding the value of the p level is to consider running this experiment repeatedly. The p level of .05 tells us that if we were to run this study 100 times and, in reality, Z-Math had no effect (students in the Z-Math group achieved about the same scores as those in the math-as-usual group), then about 5% of the time, we would see the Z-Math group outperform the math-as-usual group just by chance alone and not because Z-Math is genuinely superior. So, as we encounter lower p levels, this suggests that the difference in the (mean) scores between groups was more likely due to the treatment and not simply attributable to random chance.

If the p level had been .85, then this tells us that if we ran this study 100 times, 85% of the time we would expect to see the Z-Math group outperform the math-as-usual group just by random chance and not because Z-Math is genuinely superior. Hence, the lower the p level, the less likely that random chance is responsible for producing the observed differences between the groups.

Furthermore, suppose we got the following results:

$$\mu(\text{Z-Math}) = 97$$

$$\mu(\text{Math as usual}) = 67$$

$$p = .01$$

Here is how we would interpret this: The Z-Math group outperformed the math-as-usual group by 30 points ($97 - 67 = 30$). The p level of .01 tells us that if we ran this experiment 100 times and Z-Math had a null effect (meaning, it did not really work), then we would see results like this just by random chance alone about 1% of the time. So, as the p level gets lower, we can have more confidence that the (30-point) difference observed between the groups is attributable to the treatment (Z-Math) and not merely an artifact of random chance.

With the principles of the p (significance) value and the α level in mind, it is time to revisit the results of the homogeneity of variance test (Table 5.4).

Table 5.4   Homogeneity of Variance Test Results (Same as Table 5.1)

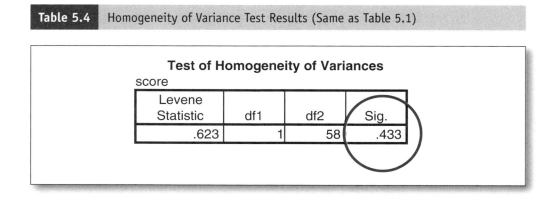

Test of Homogeneity of Variances

score

Levene Statistic	df1	df2	Sig.
.623	1	58	.433

The homogeneity of variance test checks to see that the variances of the groups involved are similar enough to each other. Remember: The variance is the standard deviation squared (*SD* scores derived from Table 5.2):

$$\text{Variance for math as usual} = 7.06^2 = \mathbf{49.84}$$

$$\text{Variance for Z-Math} = 8.83^2 = \mathbf{77.96}$$

The homogeneity of variance test compared 49.84 with 77.96 and computed a Sig.(nifi-cance) score (*p* value) of .433, which is greater than the α level of .05. This tells us that there is no statistically significant difference between these two variances, meaning that the vari-ances are similar enough to say that the homogeneity of variance criteria are satisfied.

DOCUMENT RESULTS

Although it is essential to comprehend the meaning of key values in the statistical reports, it would be inappropriate to simply present the figures in a results section with-out providing a concise narrative. While all figures below are technically correct, try to avoid documenting your findings as such.

Accurate but Inappropriate Numerical Statistical Abstract

Math as usual: *n* = 30, μ = 75.77, *SD* = 7.06

Z-Math: *n* = 30, μ = 80.97, *SD* = 8.83

p = .015, α = .05, therefore, use Z-Math

While the above data may be useful in assembling a table, it is important that you become proficient at translating your methodology and numerical findings into a brief textual abstract detailing the story of the study specifying the research question, along with an overview of how you got from the research question to the results.

Appropriate Verbose Statistical Abstract

A group of 60 fourth graders were randomly assigned to one of two groups to determine if Z-Math was superior to traditional teaching methods when it comes to learning the multi-plication table.

After 1 month, students in the Z-Math group learned an average of 80.97% of the mul-tiplication table, significantly outperforming students taught using traditional methods, who, on average, learned 75.77% of the multiplication table (*p* = .015, α = .05).

In addition to the full manuscript, scientific journals also require authors to submit an abstract that tells the overall story of the study and key findings; usually the limit for the abstract is about 200 words. While initially it can be a challenge to write technical information so concisely, this is a worthy skill to develop. The above abstract is under 100 words.

NOTE: In the example processed in this chapter, we saw that the *t* test assessed the means of the two groups and revealed that the mean for the treatment group (Z-Math) was statistically significantly higher than the mean for the control group (math as usual). As you will see in the exercises for this chapter, the *t* test is equally effective in detecting statistically significant differences when the mean of the treatment group is lower than the mean of the control group. For example, instead of the treatment (Z-Math) that is designed to increase a test score, in Exercise 1 in the Practice Exercises, the treatment (meditation) is designed to lower resting pulse rate. Remember: The *t* test is designed to simply detect statistically significant differences between the means of two groups; it does not matter which group mean is higher and which is lower.

TYPE I AND TYPE II ERRORS

The world is imperfect; despite all best efforts, errors can occur in virtually any realm no matter how careful you are. For starters, consider the two types of errors that can occur in a legal verdict:

- (Error 1) The court finds the defendant *not guilty* when, in fact, he or she actually *is* guilty.
- (Error 2) The court finds the defendant *guilty* when, in fact, he or she is actually *not* guilty.

These same two types of errors can happen in statistics:

- **Type I Error:** A Type I error (α error) occurs when the findings indicate that there is a statistically significant difference between two variables (or groups) when, in fact, on the whole, there actually is not, meaning that you would erroneously reject the null hypothesis. The consequence is that you would conclude the treatment was effective when, in fact, on the whole, it was not. This is connected with the *p* value; a *p* value of .05 means that there is a 5% chance that you have committed a Type I error—hence, the lower the *p* value, the less likely that you have committed a Type I error.

- **Type II Error:** A Type II error (β error) occurs when the findings indicate that there is no statistically significant difference between two variables (or groups) when, in fact, on the whole, there actually is, meaning that you would erroneously accept the null hypothesis. The consequence is that you would conclude the treatment was ineffective when, in fact, on the whole, it was. Sample size is inversely related to Type II errors—the higher the sample size, the lower the likelihood of committing a Type II error.

There is no formal metric that you can run that will tell you if you have a Type I or Type II error on hand; they are just characteristics endemic in the realm of statistical testing. The point to keep in mind is that even if a statistical test produces a statistically significant *p* level (e.g., *p* < .05), this does not mean that you have solid evidentiary *proof* of anything; at best, you have reduced uncertainty. Essentially, a *p* value of .05 means that if the effect of the treatment group were the same as the control group (null intervention), we would see this (anomalous) statistical outcome (where the treatment group outperforms the control group, just by chance) about 5% of the time. Since *p* never goes to zero, there is always some level of uncertainty in statistical findings.

Remember: Statistics is not about *proving* or *disproving* anything; statistics is about reducing uncertainty—there is always some margin of error, no matter how small. The notion of Type I and Type II errors pertains to all other tests covered in the chapters that follow.

GOOD COMMON SENSE

Clearly, it is essential that you comprehend key figures of the statistical reports that you order, but when it comes to using these findings to make decisions in the real world, other considerations must be taken into account.

For example, suppose you measured the results of a new treatment, wherein Group 1 was the control group (received no treatment) and Group 2 received the treatment. Your analysis revealed that on a 100-point scale, μ(Group 1) = 88.1, μ(Group 2) = 88.3, and *p* = .01. Your first reaction might be to leap to the conclusion that since *p* = .01, and this is less than the α level of .05, Group 2 statistically significantly outperformed Group 1, so we should adopt the treatment that was used for Group 2. Statistically speaking, you would be right, but consider some other real-world factors: Group 2 outperformed Group 1 by (only) .2 points; one might wonder if, in the real world, a .2-point difference is of any *practical* significance—can anyone really detect the difference between an outcome of 88.1 and 88.3?

Also, scarce resources may be an issue; the intervention used for Group 2 might have been very costly, time-consuming, labor intensive, or complex to carry out—it would be reasonable to consider if the cost, time, labor, and inconvenience involved are really worth the .2-point improvement.

Another concern might be the initial goal of the intervention: If the goal was to raise the score to at least 80, then clearly both groups achieved the desired effect—in this light, the innovative treatment would seem less worthy.

The lesson at hand is that when interpreting statistical findings, it is important that you not only tend to the numbers but also mindfully comprehend that those numbers are only a *part* of the picture when it comes to making *practical* decisions in the real world.

Key Concepts

- *t* Test
- Pretest checklist
  - Normality
  - Homogeneity of variance
  - *n*

- α
- *p*
- Hypothesis resolution
- Documenting results
- Good common sense
- Type I (α) error
- Type II (β) error

Practice Exercises

For Exercises 1 to 5:

- Configure SPSS per the specifications of the codebook.
- Enter Data Set A as shown in the table.
- Process and document your findings for Data Set A.
- Repeat each exercise using Data Set B (which will produce different results).
- Be sure to save the data sets since they will be used again in Chapter 6.

For Exercises 6 to 10:

- Use the prepared SPSS data sets (download from **www.sagepub.com/knapp**).
- Load, process, and document your findings for Data Set A.
- Repeat each exercise using Data Set B (which will produce different results).

1. You want to determine if meditation can reduce resting pulse rate. Participants were recruited and randomly assigned to one of two groups: Members of Group 1 (the control group) did not meditate; members of Group 2 (the treatment group) meditated for 30 minutes per day on Mondays, Wednesdays, and Fridays over the course of 2 weeks. At the end, you gathered the resting pulse rates for each participant.

   Codebook—set up SPSS to contain two variables:

   - *group* is a categorical variable (1 = no meditation, 2 = meditates 3 days).
   - *pulse* is a continuous variable (number of beats per minute).

   Data set—enter Data Set A.

   - Save Data Set A as *Chapter 05 – Exercise 01 A.sav;* it will be used again for Chapter 6, Exercise 1.

Data Set A		
Rec. #	group	pulse
1	1	104
2	1	108

Data Set B		
Rec. #	group	pulse
1	1	96
2	1	86

3	1	100
4	1	87
5	1	94
6	1	101
7	1	99
8	1	103
9	1	104
10	1	94
11	1	92
12	1	107
13	1	101
14	1	96
15	1	102
16	1	107
17	1	95
18	1	84
19	1	92
20	1	102
21	1	93
22	1	85
23	1	92
24	1	97
25	1	86
26	1	93
27	1	96
28	1	108
29	1	98
30	1	98
31	1	100
32	1	109
33	1	88
34	1	94
35	1	100
36	2	102

3	1	99
4	1	101
5	1	97
6	1	100
7	1	100
8	1	99
9	1	80
10	1	93
11	1	102
12	1	105
13	1	87
14	1	92
15	1	96
16	1	103
17	1	99
18	1	94
19	1	87
20	1	95
21	1	90
22	1	86
23	1	90
24	1	99
25	1	91
26	1	89
27	1	101
28	1	102
29	1	100
30	1	95
31	1	94
32	1	95
33	1	97
34	2	81
35	2	84
36	2	95

37	2	100	37	2	100
38	2	78	38	2	102
39	2	105	39	2	91
40	2	90	40	2	90
41	2	96	41	2	83
42	2	93	42	2	93
43	2	83	43	2	79
44	2	99	44	2	94
45	2	90	45	2	90
46	2	88	46	2	104
47	2	105	47	2	101
48	2	94	48	2	100
49	2	94	49	2	91
50	2	93	50	2	99
51	2	86	51	2	95
52	2	79	52	2	87
53	2	93	53	2	96
54	2	88	54	2	97
55	2	80	55	2	92
56	2	82	56	2	92
57	2	96	57	2	90
58	2	98	58	2	105
59	2	89	59	2	94
60	2	96	60	2	93
61	2	104	61	2	102
62	2	93	62	2	84
63	2	97	63	2	89
64	2	95	64	2	107
65	2	82	65	2	90
66	2	88	66	2	98
67	2	97	67	2	93
68	2	93	68	2	93
69	2	96			
70	2	85			

a. Write the hypotheses.

b. Run each criterion of the pretest checklist (normality, homogeneity of variance, and *n*) and discuss your findings.

c. Run the *t* test and document your findings (*ns*, means, and Sig. [*p* value]).

d. Write an abstract under 200 words detailing a summary of the study, the *t* test results, hypothesis resolution, and implications of your findings.

- Repeat this exercise using Data Set B.
- Save Data Set B as *Chapter 05 – Exercise 01 B.sav;* it will be used again for Chapter 6, Exercise 1.

2. You want to determine if pairing an incoming freshman with a sophomore in a protégé-mentor relationship will enhance the freshman's grade point average (GPA). You recruit sophomores who are willing to mentor a student in their major for their first term. You then recruit freshmen who are interested in having a mentor. Freshmen who apply to this program will be assigned to the mentor group (and will be designated a mentor) or to the control group (no mentor) on an alternating basis. Those in the mentor group are to meet in person once a week at a time of their choosing. All freshmen, in both groups, agree to submit their transcript at the conclusion of the term.

Codebook—set up SPSS to contain two variables:

- *group* is a categorical variable (1 = no mentor, 2 = in-person mentor).
- *gpa* is a continuous variable (the first-term GPA for each freshman).

Data set—enter Data Set A.

- Save Data Set A as *Chapter 05 – Exercise 02 A.sav;* it will be used again for Chapter 6, Exercise 2.

Data Set A		
Rec. #	group	gpa
1	1	2.76
2	1	3.14
3	1	2.32
4	1	2.12
5	1	2.93
6	1	2.89
7	1	3.15
8	1	2.87
9	1	2.85
10	1	2.22
11	1	2.45
12	1	2.38

Data Set B		
Rec. #	group	gpa
1	1	2.42
2	1	2.69
3	1	1.98
4	1	1.94
5	1	2.30
6	1	2.43
7	1	2.30
8	1	2.44
9	1	2.70
10	1	2.76
11	1	2.85
12	1	3.10

13	1	2.68	13	1	2.53
14	1	3.04	14	1	2.68
15	1	3.17	15	1	2.60
16	1	3.15	16	1	2.44
17	1	2.48	17	1	2.50
18	1	2.57	18	1	2.85
19	1	2.88	19	1	2.50
20	1	2.82	20	1	2.78
21	1	2.97	21	1	2.30
22	1	2.49	22	1	2.40
23	1	2.99	23	1	2.61
24	1	2.92	24	1	2.77
25	1	2.90	25	1	3.03
26	2	2.69	26	2	3.30
27	2	2.62	27	2	3.00
28	2	2.66	28	2	3.01
29	2	2.70	29	2	2.80
30	2	3.29	30	2	2.70
31	2	2.53	31	2	2.85
32	2	2.60	32	2	2.53
33	2	2.72	33	2	2.21
34	2	3.40	34	2	2.79
35	2	2.43	35	2	2.85
36	2	2.90	36	2	2.68
37	2	2.88	37	2	2.83
38	2	2.48	38	2	2.45
39	2	2.54	39	2	3.06
40	2	2.60	40	2	2.65
41	2	2.57	41	2	3.05
42	2	3.07	42	2	3.00
43	2	2.95	43	2	2.55
44	2	2.61	44	2	2.57
45	2	3.11	45	2	2.54
46	2	3.32	46	2	3.00
47	2	2.97	47	2	3.17
48	2	2.93	48	2	2.60
49	2	2.58	49	2	3.35
50	2	2.31	50	2	2.18

a. Write the hypotheses.
b. Run each criterion of the pretest checklist (normality, homogeneity of variance, and *n*) and discuss your findings.
c. Run the *t* test and document your findings (*ns*, means, and Sig. [*p* value]).
d. Write an abstract under 200 words detailing a summary of the study, the *t* test results, hypothesis resolution, and implications of your findings.

- Repeat this exercise using Data Set B.
- Save Data Set B as *Chapter 05 – Exercise 02 B.sav;* it will be used again for Chapter 6, Exercise 2.

3. The Acme Company claims that its new reading lamp increases reading speed; you want to test this. You will record how long (in seconds) it takes for subjects to read a 1,000-word essay. Half of the subjects will be randomly assigned to the control group; they will read the essay using regular room lighting. The other half of the subjects will read the same essay using the Acme reading lamp.

Codebook—set up SPSS to contain two variables:

- *group* is a categorical variable (1 = room lighting, 2 = Acme lamp).
- *seconds* is a continuous variable (the time it takes to read the essay).

Data set—enter Data Set A.

- Save Data Set A as *Chapter 05 – Exercise 03 A.sav;* it will be used again for Chapter 6, Exercise 3.

Data Set A		
Rec. #	group	seconds
1	1	411
2	1	442
3	1	438
4	1	432
5	1	374
6	1	378
7	1	431
8	1	509
9	1	436
10	1	429
11	1	436
12	1	400
13	1	502
14	1	413
15	1	432

Data Set B		
Rec. #	group	seconds
1	1	450
2	1	429
3	1	430
4	1	436
5	1	489
6	1	367
7	1	405
8	1	410
9	1	410
10	1	424
11	1	386
12	1	331
13	1	433
14	1	440
15	1	430

16	1	377		16	1	403
17	1	386		17	1	424
18	1	484		18	1	402
19	1	471		19	1	463
20	1	470		20	1	414
21	1	449		21	1	434
22	1	414		22	1	396
23	1	505		23	1	400
24	1	437		24	1	355
25	1	441		25	1	450
26	2	455		26	2	442
27	2	399		27	2	364
28	2	393		28	2	406
29	2	432		29	2	442
30	2	369		30	2	434
31	2	406		31	2	455
32	2	443		32	2	460
33	2	357		33	2	404
34	2	395		34	2	395
35	2	376		35	2	479
36	2	391		36	2	441
37	2	366		37	2	415
38	2	445		38	2	449
39	2	452		39	2	481
40	2	364		40	2	408
41	2	407		41	2	344
42	2	415		42	2	390
43	2	408		43	2	451
44	2	412		44	2	398
45	2	380		45	2	348
46	2	446		46	2	390
47	2	403		47	2	421
48	2	451		48	2	361
49	2	366		49	2	394
50	2	443		50	2	418
51	2	363				
52	2	424				
53	2	405				

a. Write the hypotheses.

b. Run each criterion of the pretest checklist (normality, homogeneity of variance, and *n*) and discuss your findings.

c. Run the *t* test and document your findings (*n*s, means, and Sig. [*p* value]).

d. Write an abstract under 200 words detailing a summary of the study, the *t* test results, hypothesis resolution, and implications of your findings.

- Repeat this exercise using Data Set B.
- Save Data Set B as *Chapter 05 – Exercise 03 B.sav;* it will be used again for Chapter 6, Exercise 3.

4. You want to determine if chocolate enhances mood. Subjects will be recruited and randomly assigned to one of two groups: Those in the control group will eat their regular diet, and those in the experimental group will also eat their usual meals and have one piece of chocolate at breakfast, lunch, and dinner over the course of a week. At the end of the week, all subjects (in both groups) will complete the Acme Mood Scale (1 = extremely bad mood . . . 100 = extremely good mood).

Codebook—set up SPSS to contain two variables:

- *group* is a categorical variable (1 = no chocolate, 2 = chocolate [1 per meal]).
- *mood* is a continuous variable (score on the Acme Mood Scale).

Data set—enter Data Set A.

- Save Data Set A as *Chapter 05 – Exercise 04 A.sav;* it will be used again for Chapter 6, Exercise 4.

Data Set A		
Rec. #	group	mood
1	1	71
2	1	74
3	1	73
4	1	73
5	1	67
6	1	67
7	1	73
8	1	82
9	1	73
10	1	73
11	1	74
12	1	70
13	1	81
14	1	71

Data Set B		
Rec. #	group	mood
1	1	98
2	1	71
3	1	93
4	1	83
5	1	84
6	1	69
7	1	72
8	1	63
9	1	76
10	1	76
11	1	78
12	1	78
13	1	85
14	1	68

15	1	73		15	1	74
16	1	60		16	1	79
17	1	63		17	1	71
18	1	78		18	1	72
19	1	77		19	1	80
20	1	77		20	1	85
21	1	75		21	1	74
22	1	71		22	1	72
23	1	81		23	1	78
24	1	74		24	1	83
25	1	74		25	1	74
26	2	72		26	1	82
27	2	78		27	1	96
28	2	75		28	1	93
29	2	77		29	2	78
30	2	69		30	2	82
31	2	81		31	2	69
32	2	83		32	2	84
33	2	78		33	2	84
34	2	69		34	2	86
35	2	74		35	2	67
36	2	80		36	2	75
37	2	78		37	2	75
38	2	81		38	2	74
39	2	80		39	2	74
40	2	74		40	2	89
41	2	73		41	2	96
42	2	83		42	2	71
43	2	78		43	2	79
44	2	77		44	2	79
45	2	79		45	2	75
46	2	83		46	2	71
47	2	75		47	2	79
48	2	67		48	2	85
49	2	73		49	2	88
50	2	80		50	2	83
				51	2	78

a. Write the hypotheses.

b. Run each criterion of the pretest checklist (normality, homogeneity of variance, and *n*) and discuss your findings.

c. Run the *t* test and document your findings (*ns*, means, and Sig. [*p* value]).

d. Write an abstract under 200 words detailing a summary of the study, the *t* test results, hypothesis resolution, and implications of your findings.

- Repeat this exercise using Data Set B.
- Save Data Set B as *Chapter 05 – Exercise 04 B.sav;* it will be used again for Chapter 6, Exercise 4.

5. You want to find out if music enhances problem solving. Subjects will be recruited and randomly assigned to one of two groups: Those in the control group will be given a standard 100-piece jigsaw puzzle to solve in a quiet room. Participants in the experimental group will be given the same puzzle to assemble, but instead of silence, there will be classical music playing at a soft volume (30 decibels [dB]) in the room. You will record the time it takes for each person to complete the puzzle.

Codebook—set up SPSS to contain two variables:

- *group* is a categorical variable (1 = no music, 2 = music at 30 dB).
- *seconds* is a continuous variable (how long it took to finish the puzzle).

Data set—enter Data Set A.

- Save Data Set A as *Chapter 05 – Exercise 05 A.sav;* it will be used again for Chapter 6, Exercise 5.

Data Set A		
Rec. #	group	seconds
1	1	541
2	1	565
3	1	604
4	1	612
5	1	590
6	1	614
7	1	578
8	1	564
9	1	640
10	1	609
11	1	564
12	1	627
13	1	634

Data Set B		
Rec. #	group	seconds
1	1	588
2	1	635
3	1	608
4	1	602
5	1	616
6	1	592
7	1	629
8	1	618
9	1	598
10	1	600
11	1	606
12	1	595
13	1	611

14	1	687		14	1	624
15	1	606		15	1	610
16	1	616		16	1	590
17	1	655		17	1	592
18	1	679		18	1	610
19	1	660		19	1	611
20	1	551		20	1	627
21	1	592		21	1	605
22	1	623		22	1	591
23	1	638		23	1	607
24	1	625		24	1	605
25	1	634		25	1	624
26	1	632		26	1	599
27	1	655		27	1	626
28	1	624		28	1	595
29	1	610		29	1	606
30	1	609		30	1	613
31	1	621		31	1	611
32	1	657		32	1	611
33	1	645		33	1	621
34	1	620		34	1	614
35	1	649		35	1	615
36	1	613		36	1	608
37	1	590		37	1	607
38	1	660		38	1	604
39	1	600		39	1	621
40	1	690		40	1	611
41	2	612		41	1	616
42	2	669		42	1	608
43	2	525		43	1	604
44	2	590		44	2	610
45	2	586		45	2	597
46	2	590		46	2	602
47	2	590		47	2	592
48	2	612		48	2	601
49	2	533		49	2	595

50	2	621	50	2	619
51	2	624	51	2	585
52	2	634	52	2	627
53	2	528	53	2	597
54	2	564	54	2	593
55	2	566	55	2	620
56	2	561	56	2	628
57	2	566	57	2	592
58	2	655	58	2	618
59	2	696	59	2	596
60	2	547	60	2	602
61	2	596	61	2	598
62	2	594	62	2	607
63	2	568	63	2	614
64	2	548	64	2	590
65	2	596	65	2	597
66	2	629	66	2	600
67	2	648	67	2	637
68	2	617	68	2	618
69	2	587	69	2	614
70	2	707	70	2	624
71	2	547	71	2	611
72	2	682	72	2	606
73	2	620	73	2	619
74	2	622	74	2	609
75	2	534	75	2	594
76	2	554	76	2	601
77	2	497	77	2	617
78	2	575	78	2	587
79	2	576	79	2	612
80	2	592	80	2	606
			81	2	614
			82	2	598

a. Write the hypotheses.
b. Run each criterion of the pretest checklist (normality, homogeneity of variance, and *n*) and discuss your findings.

      c. Run the *t* test and document your findings (*ns*, means, and Sig. [*p* value]).

      d. Write an abstract under 200 words detailing a summary of the study, the *t* test results, hypothesis resolution, and implications of your findings.

- Repeat this exercise using Data Set B.
- Save Data Set B as *Chapter 05 – Exercise 05 B.sav;* it will be used again for Chapter 6, Exercise 5.

6. You want to determine if watching a video of a comedy with a laugh track is more enjoyable than watching without it. Subjects will be recruited and randomly assigned to one of two groups: Those in the control group will watch the video without the laugh track, and those assigned to the treatment group will watch the same video with the sound(s) of a 50-person audience included in the soundtrack. Each participant will watch the video individually; no others will be present in the room. Immediately following the video, each participant will be asked to rate how enjoyable the show was on a scale of 1 to 5 (1 = not very enjoyable . . . 5 = very enjoyable).

    Codebook—set up SPSS to contain two variables:

- *group* is a categorical variable (1 = no laugh track, 2 = laugh track at 50).
- *enjoy* is a continuous variable (1 = not very enjoyable . . . 5 = very enjoyable).

    Data set—load *Chapter 05 – Exercise 06 A.sav.*

      a. Write the hypotheses.

      b. Run each criterion of the pretest checklist (normality, homogeneity of variance, and *n*) and discuss your findings.

      c. Run the *t* test and document your findings (*ns*, means, and Sig. [*p* value]).

      d. Write an abstract under 200 words detailing a summary of the study, the *t* test results, hypothesis resolution, and implications of your findings.

- Repeat this exercise using *Chapter 05 – Exercise 06 B.sav.*

7. In an effort to determine the effectiveness of light therapy to alleviate depression, you recruit a group of subjects who have been diagnosed as depressed. The subjects are randomly assigned to one of two groups: The control group will receive no light therapy, and the treatment group will get light therapy for 1 hour on even-numbered days over the course of 1 month, at which time, all participants will complete the Acme Mood Scale, consisting of 10 questions; this instrument renders a score between 1 and 100: 1 = extremely bad mood . . . 100 = extremely good mood.

    Codebook—the data set contains two variables:

- *group* is a categorical variable (1 = no light therapy, 2 = light therapy: even days).
- *mood* is a continuous variable (1 = extremely bad mood . . . 100 = extremely good mood).

Data set—load *Chapter 05 – Exercise 07 A.sav*.

   a. Write the hypotheses.

   b. Run each criterion of the pretest checklist (normality, homogeneity of variance, and *n*) and discuss your findings.

   c. Run the *t* test and document your findings (*ns*, means, and Sig. [*p* value]).

   d. Write an abstract under 200 words detailing a summary of the study, the *t* test results, hypothesis resolution, and implications of your findings.

     • Repeat this exercise using *Chapter 05 – Exercise 07 B.sav*.

8. It is thought that exercising early in the morning will provide better energy throughout the day. To test this idea, subjects are recruited and randomly assigned to two groups: For 30 days, members of the experimental group will walk from 7:00 to 7:30 a.m., Monday through Friday; members of the control group will do no walking. At the conclusion of the study, each subject will answer the 10 questions on the Acme End-of-the-Day Energy Scale. This instrument produces a score between 1 and 100 (1 = extremely low energy . . . 100 = extremely high energy).

Codebook—the data set contain two variables:

   • *group* is a categorical variable (1 = no walking, 2 = walking: 30 minutes).

   • *energy* is a continuous variable (1 = extremely low energy . . . 100 = extremely high energy).

Data set—load *Chapter 05 – Exercise 08 A.sav*.

   a. Write the hypotheses.

   b. Run each criterion of the pretest checklist (normality, homogeneity of variance, and *n*) and discuss your findings.

   c. Run the *t* test and document your findings (*ns*, means, and Sig. [*p* value]).

   d. Write an abstract under 200 words detailing a summary of the study, the *t* test results, hypothesis resolution, and implications of your findings.

     • Repeat this exercise using *Chapter 05 – Exercise 08 B.sav*.

9. Clinicians at a nursing home facility want to see if giving residents a plant to tend to will help to lower depression. To test this idea, the residents are randomly assigned to two groups: Each member of the treatment group will be issued a small bamboo plant along with a card detailing care instructions; members of the control group will receive no plant. After 90 days, all participants will complete the Acme Depression Scale, a 10-question instrument that renders a score between 1 and 100 (1 = low depression . . . 100 = high depression).

Codebook—the data set contain two variables:

   • *group* is a categorical variable (1 = no plant, 2 = bamboo).

   • *depress* is a continuous variable (1 = low depression . . . 100 = high depression).

Data set—load *Chapter 05 – Exercise 09 A.sav*.

   a. Write the hypotheses.

   b. Run each criterion of the pretest checklist (normality, homogeneity of variance, and *n*) and discuss your findings.

   c. Run the *t* test and document your findings (*ns*, means, and Sig. [*p* value]).

   d. Write an abstract under 200 words detailing a summary of the study, the *t* test results, hypothesis resolution, and implications of your findings.

     • Repeat this exercise using *Chapter 05 – Exercise 09 B.sav*.

10. During flu season, the administrators at a walk-in health clinic want to determine if providing patients with a pamphlet will increase their receptivity to flu shots. Once escorted to the exam room, patients who had an odd-numbered service ticket were given a flu shot information pamphlet; patients with even tickets were given nothing. At the end of the day, the charts were reviewed and two entries were made in the database: total number of flu shots given to patients who received a pamphlet and total number of flu shots given to patients who were not given flu shot pamphlets.

Codebook—the data set contain two variables:

   • *group* is a categorical variable (1 = nothing, 2 = flu shot pamphlet).

   • *shots* is a continuous variable (number of flu shots given in a day [for each group]).

Data set—load *Chapter 05 – Exercise 10 A.sav*.

   a. Write the hypotheses.

   b. Run each criterion of the pretest checklist (normality, homogeneity of variance, and *n*) and discuss your findings.

   c. Run the *t* test and document your findings (*ns*, means, and Sig. [*p* value]).

   d. Write an abstract under 200 words detailing a summary of the study, the *t* test results, hypothesis resolution, and implications of your findings.

     • Repeat this exercise using *Chapter 05 – Exercise 10 B.sav*.

ANOVA

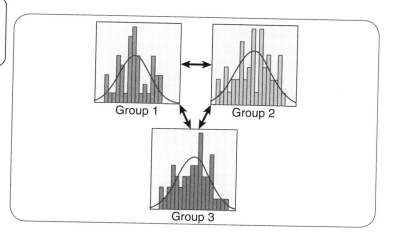

Three is a magic number.

—Bob Dorough

LEARNING OBJECTIVES

Upon completing this chapter, you will be able to:

- Determine when it is appropriate to run an ANOVA test
- Verify that the data meet the criteria for ANOVA processing: normality, homogeneity of variance, and n
- Order an ANOVA test with graphics
- Select an appropriate ANOVA post hoc test: Tukey or Sidak
- Derive results from the multiple comparisons table
- Compute a unique pairs formula
- Resolve the hypotheses
- Document the results in plain English

DIGITAL LEARNING RESOURCES

The tutorial video and data sets for this chapter are at **www.sagepub.com/knapp**

- ANOVA pretest checklist video
- ANOVA test run video
- SPSS files

OVERVIEW

The ANOVA (analysis of variance) test is similar to the *t* test, except whereas the *t* test compares *two* groups of continuous variables with each other, the ANOVA test can compare *three or more* groups.

The *t* test and ANOVA are so similar that this chapter will use the same example and the same exercises used in Chapter 5; the only difference is that the data sets have been enhanced to include a third or fourth group. If you are proficient with the *t* test, you are already more than halfway there to comprehending ANOVA. The only real differences between the *t* test and ANOVA are in ordering the test run and interpreting the test results; several other minor differences will be pointed out along the way.

That being said, let us go into the expanded example, drawn from Chapter 5, which involved Group 1 (math taught as usual), Group 2 (Z-Math), and now a third group: Group 3 (flashcards).

The ANOVA test will reveal which (if any) of these groups statistically significantly outperforms the others.

EXAMPLE

Dr. Zinn and Dr. Zorders arranged to offer Z-Math, their innovative method for teaching students the multiplication table ($1 \times 1 \ldots 10 \times 10$), to fourth graders at Sepulveda Street School. The principal is willing to try the Z-Math method, but she is also curious about how effective multiplication flashcards with a math coach might be.

RESEARCH QUESTION

Which is the best method for teaching multiplication: (1) the usual teaching method, (2) Z-Math, or (3) flashcards with a math coach?

GROUPS

The names of all 90 fourth graders at the school are written on slips of paper and placed in a hat. The principal randomly draws 30 names from the hat; these students will be assigned to the control group, the next 30 names drawn will be assigned to the Z-Math group, and the remaining 30 students will be assigned to the flashcard group.

PROCEDURE

From 10:00 to 11:30 a.m., the usual time for the daily math lesson, the students in the control group will go to Room 14, where they will receive the regular math lesson (treatment as usual). The students in the Z-Math group will go to Room 8 for their Z-Math lesson. Finally, the students in the flashcard group will go to Room 20, where each student will be paired with a community volunteer to work with the student using flashcards. The students in the Z-Math group are instructed not to disclose the Z-Math method to the other students, and the students in the flashcard group are instructed not to share their flashcards with other students.

After 4 weeks, all 90 students will be given a test; they will have 10 minutes to write out the entire multiplication table with the solutions on a blank sheet of paper (e.g., $1 \times 1 = 1$, $1 \times 2 = 2 \ldots 10 \times 10 = 100$).

HYPOTHESES

H_0: There is no statistically significant difference in the test scores among the three groups.

H_1: The Z-Math group outperforms the math-as-usual group.

H_2: The flashcards group outperforms the math-as-usual group.

H_3: The Z-Math group outperforms the flashcards group.

H_4: The flashcards outperforms the Z-Math group.

Notice that as more groups are introduced, more comparisons are possible, and hence the supplemental hypotheses: H_2 addresses the comparison between the math-as-usual and flashcards groups, and H_3 and H_4 involve comparing the Z-Math and flashcards groups. As there are more groups, there are more comparisons to analyze, which is what ANOVA is all about.

DATA SET

Use the following data set: *Chapter 06 – Example 01 – ANOVA.sav.*

Notice that this data set has 90 records; the first 60 records (rows) are the same as the *t* test example data set used in Chapter 5:

Records 1 to 30 are for Group 1: math as usual.

Records 31 to 60 are for Group 2: Z-Math.

Records 61 to 90 are new; they contain the data for Group 3: Flashcards.

NOTE: The data are grouped this way just for visual clarity; you do not need to load your data sequenced by group.

If you go to the Variable View and open the *Values* menu for *group,* you will see that the label *Flashcards* for the third group has been assigned to the value 3 (Figure 6.1).

Figure 6.1	Value Labels for a Three-Group ANOVA Analysis

PRETEST CHECKLIST

The statistical pretest checklist for the ANOVA is similar to the *t* test, except instead of processing *two* groups, you will process *three* or however many groups there are.

Pretest Checklist Criterion 1—Normality

Check for normality by inspecting the histogram with a normal curve for each of the three groups. Begin by using the *Select Cases* icon to select the records pertaining to the math-as-usual group; the selection criteria would be group = 1. Next, run a histogram (with normal curve) on the variable score. For more details on this procedure, please refer to Chapter 4 ("SPSS—Descriptive Statistics: Continuous Variable (Age) Select by Categorical Variable (Gender)—Females Only"); see the star (★) icon on page **71**.

Then repeat the process for the Z-Math group (group = 2), and finally, repeat the process a third time for the flashcards group (group = 3).

This will produce three histograms with normal curves—one for the scores in the math-as-usual group, a second for the scores in the Z-Math group, and a third for the scores in the flashcard group. The histograms should resemble the graphs shown in Figures 6.2, 6.3, and 6.4.

Figure 6.2	Histogram of Score for G_1: Math-as-Usual Group

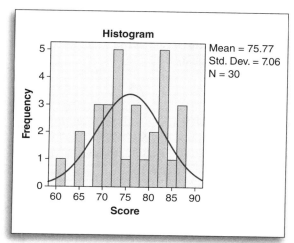

Figure 6.3	Histogram of Score for G_2: Z-Math Group

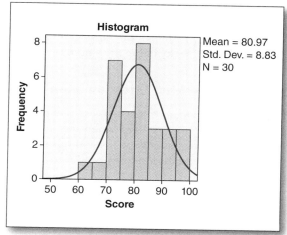

As we read these three histograms, our focus is on the *normality of the curve,* as opposed to the characteristics of the individual bars. Although each curve is unique in terms of height and width, we see that each is bell-shaped and shows good symmetry with no substantial *skewing.* On the basis of the inspection of these three figures, we would conclude that the criteria of *normality* are satisfied for all three groups.

Next, you need to (re)activate all records for further analysis; you can either delete the temporary variable *Filter_$* or click on the *Select Cases* icon and select the *All cases* button. For more details on this procedure, please refer to Chapter 4 ("SPSS—Selecting All Variables"); see the star (★) icon on page **76**.

Figure 6.4	Histogram of Score for G_3: Flashcards Group

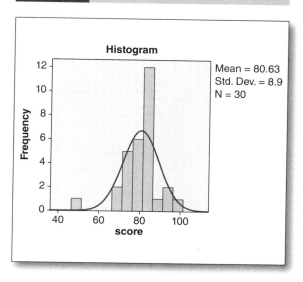

Pretest Checklist Criterion 2—Homogeneity of Variance

Since we process the ANOVA with the same menu as the *t* test, we will select the homogeneity of variance test when we order the ANOVA test and read the findings as part of the results. The homogeneity of variance rule of thumb for the ANOVA test is just like the *t* test: None of the groups should have a variance (standard deviation^2) that is more than twice the variance of any other group. In other words, if Group 1 had a variance of 20.1, Group 2 had a variance of 24.7, and Group 3 had a variance of 90.6, we would expect the homogeneity of variance criteria to fail since 90.6 is clearly more than twice as large as 20.1 or 24.7.

The results of the homogeneity of variance test will be discussed in the Results section when we examine the findings produced by the ANOVA test.

Pretest Checklist Criterion 3—*n*

Again, as with the *t* test, technically, you can run an ANOVA test with an *n* of any size in each group, but when the *n* is at least 30 in each group, the ANOVA is considered more robust. We will see the *n* reported for each group in the Results section when we examine the findings produced by the ANOVA test.

 ## TEST RUN

To run an ANOVA test (for the most part, this is *t* test déjà vu time):

1. On the main screen, click on *Analyze, Compare Means, One-Way ANOVA* . . . (Figure 6.5).

Figure 6.5   Running an ANOVA Test

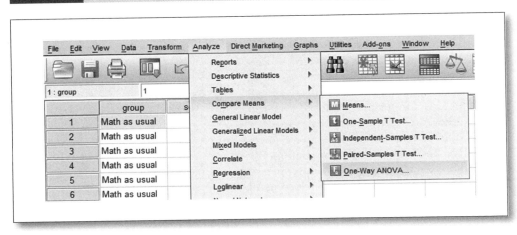

2. On the *One-Way ANOVA* menu, move the continuous variable that you wish to analyze (*score*) into the *Dependent List* window, and move the variable that contains the categorical variable that specifies the group (*group*) into the *Factor* window (Figure 6.6).

Figure 6.6 The One-Way ANOVA Menu

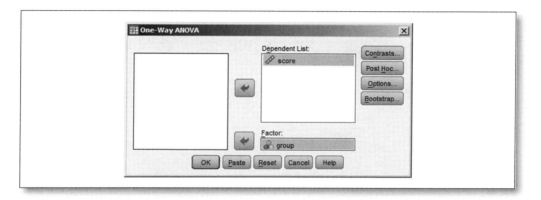

3. Click on the *Options . . .* button, and on the *One-Way ANOVA: Options* menu, check *Descriptive, Homogeneity of variance test,* and *Means plot,* then click on the *Continue* button (Figure 6.7).

Figure 6.7 The One-Way ANOVA: Options Menu

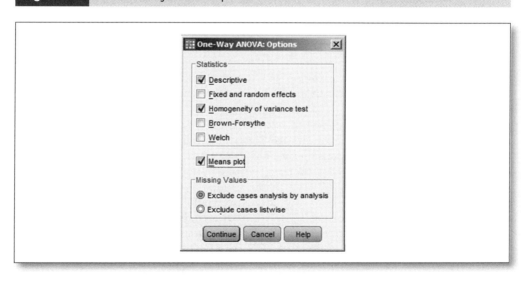

This will take you back to the *One-Way ANOVA* menu.

4. Click on the *Post Hoc . . .* button.

5. This will take you to the *One-Way ANOVA: Post Hoc Multiple Comparisons* menu (Figure 6.8).

Figure 6.8	The One-Way ANOVA: Options Menu

6. If you were to run the ANOVA test without selecting a post hoc test, then all it would return is a single p value; if that p is statistically significant, then that would tell you that somewhere among the groups processed, the mean for at least one group is statistically significantly different from the mean of at least one other group, but it would not tell you specifically which group is different from which. The post hoc test produces a table comparing the mean of each group with that of each other group, along with the p values for each pair of comparisons. This will become clearer in the Results section when we read the post hoc table.

As for which post hoc test to select, there are a lot of choices. To keep things simple, we will focus on only two options: *Tukey* and *Sidak*. Tukey is an appropriate selection when each group has the same ns; in this case, each group has an n of 30, so check the *Tukey* checkbox, then click on the *Continue* button (this will take you back to the *One-Way ANOVA* menu [Figure 6.6]). If the groups had different ns (e.g., $n(Group_1) = 40$, $n(Group_2) = 55$, $n(Group_3) = 36$), then you would select the *Sidak* post hoc test. If you do not know the ns for each group in advance, just select either *Tukey* or *Sidak* and observe the ns on the resulting report; if you guessed wrong, you can always go back and rerun the analysis using the appropriate post hoc test.

ANOVA Post Hoc Summary

- If all groups have the same *ns*, then select *Tukey*.
- If the groups have different *ns*, then select *Sidak*.

7. On the *One-Way ANOVA* menu (Figure 6.6), click on the *OK* button, and the *ANOVA* test will process.

RESULTS

Now that we have the results for the ANOVA test, we can complete the pretest checklist: We still need answers regarding the homogeneity of variance and the *ns* for each group. As we can see in Table 6.1, the homogeneity of variance test produced a significance (*p*) value of .752; since this is greater than the α level of .05, this tells us that there are no statistically significant differences among the variances of the score variable for the three groups analyzed. In other words, the variances for score are similar enough among the three groups: math as usual, Z-Math, and flashcards. We would conclude that the criteria of the homogeneity of variance have been satisfied.

Table 6.1   Homogeneity of Variance Test Results

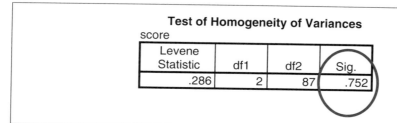

Test of Homogeneity of Variances
score

Levene Statistic	df1	df2	Sig.
.286	2	87	.752

As for the final item on the pretest checklist, the *n*, we can see from the second column in Table 6.2 that each group has an *n* of 30. This satisfies the *n assumption,* indicating that the ANOVA test becomes more robust when the *n* for each group is at least 30.

Next, we look at the ANOVA table (Table 6.3) and find a significance (*p*) value of .029; since this is less than the α level of .05, this tells us that there is a statistically significant difference between the (three) group means for score, but unlike reading the results of the *t* test, we are not done yet.

Table 6.2 Descriptive Statistics of Score for Math-as-Usual, Z-Math, and Flashcard Groups

Descriptives

score

	N	Mean	Std. Deviation	Std. Error	95% Confidence Interval for Mean Lower Bound	95% Confidence Interval for Mean Upper Bound	Minimum	Maximum
Math as usual	30	75.77	7.060	1.289	73.13	78.40	61	87
Z-Math	30	80.97	8.830	1.612	77.67	84.26	62	99
Flashcards	30	80.63	8.900	1.625	77.31	83.96	49	98
Total	90	79.12	8.554	.902	77.33	80.91	49	99

Table 6.3 ANOVA Test Results Comparing Score of Math-as-Usual, Z-Math, and Flashcards Groups

ANOVA

score

	Sum of Squares	df	Mean Square	F	Sig.
Between groups	508.356	2	254.178	3.684	.029
Within groups	6003.300	87	69.003		
Total	6511.656	89			

Remember that in the realm of the *t* test, only *two* groups are involved, so when it comes to interpreting the *p* value, there is no question as to which group is different from which—clearly, the mean from Group 1 is statistically significantly different from the mean of Group 2, but when there are three or more groups, we need more information as to which group is different from which; that is what the post hoc test answers.

Consider this: Suppose you have two kids, Ariel and Blake; you are in the living room, and someone calls out from the den, "The kids are fighting again!" Since there are only two kids, you immediately know that the fight involves Ariel and Blake. Now suppose you have three kids—Ariel, Blake, and Cary—and the voice calls out, "The kids are fighting again!" You can no longer simply know that the fight is between Ariel and Blake; you need more information. Instead of just one possibility, there are now three possible combinations of fighters:

Ariel vs. Blake

Ariel vs. Cary

Blake vs. Cary

Back to our example: The statistically significant *p* value observed in the ANOVA table (Table 6.3) tells us that there is a statistically significant difference in the score variable somewhere among the three groups ("The kids are fighting!"); the post hoc table will tell us precisely where that difference is coming from (which pair of kids is fighting).

This brings us to the (Tukey post hoc) multiple comparisons table (Table 6.4). As with the three kids fighting, in this three-group design, there are three possible pairs of comparisons that we can assess in terms of (mean) score for the groups.

Comparison 1—math as usual vs. Z-Math

Comparison 2—math as usual vs. flashcards

Comparison 3—Z-Math vs. flashcards

We will use Table 6.2 (descriptives) and Table 6.4 (multiple comparisons) to analyze the ANOVA test results. Table 6.2 lists the mean score for each of the three groups: μ(math as usual) = 75.77, μ(Z-Math) = 80.97, and μ(flashcards) = 80.63. We will assess each of the three pairwise score comparisons separately.

Comparison 1—Math as Usual vs. Z-Math

Table 6.4 first compares the mean score for the math-as-usual group with the mean score for the Z-Math group, which produces a Sig.(nificance) (p) of .045. Since the p is less than the .05 α level, this tells us that for score, there is a statistically significant difference between math as usual and Z-Math.

Table 6.4 ANOVA Post Hoc Multiple Comparisons Table

Multiple Comparisons

score
Tukey HSD

(I) group	(J) group	Mean Difference (I–J)	Std. Error	Sig.	95% Confidence Interval	
					Lower Bound	Upper Bound
Math as usual	Z-Math	−5.200*	2.145	.045	−10.31	−.09
	Flashcards	−4.867	2.145	.066	−9.98	.25
Z-Math	Math as usual	5.200*	2.145	.045	.09	10.31
	Flashcards	.333	2.145	.987	−4.78	5.45
Flashcards	Math as usual	4.867	2.145	.066	−.25	9.98
	Z-Math	−.333	2.145	.987	−5.45	4.78

*. The mean difference is significant at the .05 level.

Comparison 2—Math as Usual vs. Flashcards

The second score comparison in Table 6.5 is between math as usual and flashcards, which produces a Sig.(nificance) (p) of .066. Since the p is greater than the .05 α level, this tells us that for score, there is no statistically significant difference between math as usual and flashcards.

Table 6.5   ANOVA Post Hoc Multiple Comparisons Table

Multiple Comparisons

score
Tukey HSD

(I) group	(J) group	Mean Difference (I–J)	Std. Error	Sig.	95% Confidence Interval Lower Bound	Upper Bound
Math as usual	Z-Math	−5.200*	2.145	.045	−10.31	−.09
	Flashcards	−4.867	2.145	.066	−9.98	.25
Z-Math	Math as usual	5.200*	2.145	.045	.09	10.31
	Flashcards	.333	2.145	.987	−4.78	5.45
Flashcards	Math as usual	4.867	2.145	.066	−.25	9.98
	Z-Math	−.333	2.145	.987	−5.45	4.78

*. The mean difference is significant at the .05 level.

Comparison 3—Z-Math vs. Flashcards

The third score comparison in Table 6.6 is between Z-Math and flashcards, which produces a Sig.(nificance) (p) of .987. Since the p is greater than the .05 α level, this tells us that for score, there is no statistically significant difference between Z-Math and flashcards.

Table 6.6   ANOVA Post Hoc Multiple Comparisons Table

Multiple Comparisons

score
Tukey HSD

(I) group	(J) group	Mean Difference (I–J)	Std. Error	Sig.	95% Confidence Interval Lower Bound	Upper Bound
Math as usual	Z-Math	−5.200*	2.145	.045	−10.31	−.09
	Flashcards	−4.867	2.145	.066	−9.98	.25
Z-Math	Math as usual	5.200*	2.145	.045	.09	10.31
	Flashcards	.333	2.145	.987	−4.78	5.45
Flashcards	Math as usual	4.867	2.145	.066	−.25	9.98
	Z-Math	−.333	2.145	.987	−5.45	4.78

*. The mean difference is significant at the .05 level.

This concludes the analysis of the multiple comparisons (post hoc) table. You have probably noticed that we skipped analyzing half of the rows because there is a double redundancy among the figures in the Sig. column. This is the kind of double redundancy that you would expect to see in a typical two-dimensional table. For example, in a multiplication table, you would see two 32s in the table because 4 × 8 = 32 and 8 × 4 = 32. In the same sense, comparing math as usual with Z-Math renders the same p level (.45) as comparing Z-Math with math as usual (Table 6.7). As you would expect, the Sig. column in Table 6.8 also contains two .066 entries (math as usual vs.

flashcards and flashcards vs. math as usual) and two .987 entries (Z-Math vs. math as usual and math as usual vs. Z-Math).

Table 6.7 ANOVA Post Hoc Multiple Comparisons Table Containing Double-Redundant Sig. Figures

Multiple Comparisons

score
Tukey HSD

(I) group	(J) group	Mean Difference (I − J)	Std. Error	Sig.	95% Confidence Interval	
					Lower Bound	Upper Bound
Math as usual	Z-Math	−5.200*	2.145	.045	−10.31	−.09
	Flashcards	−4.867	2.145	.066	−9.98	.25
Z-Math	Math as usual	5.200*	2.145	.045	.09	10.31
	Flashcards	.333	2.145	.987	−4.78	5.45
Flashcards	Math as usual	4.867	2.145	.066	−.25	9.98
	Z-Math	−.333	2.145	.987	−5.45	4.78

*. The mean difference is significant at the .05 level.

The ANOVA test can process any number of groups, provided the pretest criteria are met. As the number of groups increases, the number of (multiple) comparisons increases as well (see Table 6.8).

Table 6.8 Increasing Groups Substantially Increases ANOVA Post Hoc Multiple Comparisons

2 Groups Renders 1 Comparison	3 Groups Renders 3 Comparisons	4 Groups Renders 6 Comparisons		
$G_1{:}G_2$	$G_1{:}G_2$ $G_2{:}G_3$	$G_1{:}G_2$	$G_2{:}G_3$	$G_3{:}G_4$
	$G_1{:}G_3$	$G_1{:}G_3$	$G_2{:}G_4$	
		$G_1{:}G_4$		

If you have a design that exceeds four groups, you can easily calculate the number of (unique) pairwise comparisons the post hoc test will produce:

Unique Pairs Formula

G = Number of groups

Number of ANOVA post hoc unique pairs $= G! \div (2 \times (G - 2)!)$

HYPOTHESIS RESOLUTION

To simplify the hypothesis resolution process, it is helpful to organize the findings in a table and use an asterisk to flag statistically significant difference(s) (Table 6.9).

NOTE: SPSS does not generate this table directly; you can assemble this table by gathering the means from the descriptives table (Table 6.2) and the p values from the Sig. column in the multiple comparisons table (Table 6.4).

Table 6.9	Results of ANOVA for Score	
Groups		p
μ(math as usual) = 75.77 vs. μ(Z-Math) = 80.97		.045*
μ(math as usual) = 75.77 vs. μ(flashcards) = 80.63		.066
μ(Z-Math) = 80.97 vs. μ(flashcards) = 80.63		.987

*Statistically significant difference(s) (α = .05).

With this summary assembled, we can make clear decisions about our pending hypotheses, which focus on determining if there is a better way to teach the multiplication tables. Resolving these hypotheses will tell us which hypotheses came true:

H_0: There is no statistically significant difference in the test scores among the three groups.

H_1: The Z-Math group outperforms the math-as-usual group.

H_2: The flashcards group outperforms the math-as-usual group.

H_3: The Z-Math group outperforms the flashcards group.

H_4: The flashcards group outperforms the Z-Math group.

Since there is a statistically significant difference between at least two groups, we would reject H_0.

The Z-Math group did outperform the math-as-usual group, and that difference is statistically significant, so we accept H_1.

The flashcards group did outperform the math-as-usual group, but that difference is not statistically significant, so we would reject H_2.

The Z-Math group did outperform the flashcards group, but that difference is not statistically significant, so we would reject H_3.

The flashcards group did not outperform the Z-Math group, but that difference is not statistically significant, so we would reject H_4.

DOCUMENT RESULTS

The data arranged in Table 6.10 could be used as a supplement in documenting the results of this study:

A group of 90 fourth graders was randomly assigned to one of three groups to determine which method of teaching the multiplication table is most effective: math as usual, Z-Math, or flashcards with a volunteer math coach.

After 1 month, students in the Z-Math group learned an average of 80.97% of the multiplication table, significantly outperforming students in the math-as-usual group; those who received math as usual learned an average of 75.77% of the multiplication table, and those who used flashcards learned an average of 80.63% (see Table 1).

Table 1	Results of ANOVA for Score

Groups	p
μ(math as usual) = 75.77 vs. μ(Z-Math) = 80.97	.045*
μ(math as usual) = 75.77 vs. μ(flashcards) = 80.63	.066
μ(Z-Math) = 80.97 vs. μ(flashcards) = 80.63	.987

*Statistically significant difference(s) ($\alpha = .05$).

Considering the above results report, you may feel compelled to comment that the .066 p level is approaching statistical significance. While the optimism may be commendable, this semantic error is a common mistake. The term *approaching* wrongly implies that the p level is a dynamic value—that it is somehow in motion and on its way to crossing the .05 finish line, but this is not at all the case. The .066 p value is a static variable, meaning that it is not in motion—the .066 p value is no more *approaching* .05 than it is *approaching* .07. Think of the .066 p value as parked; it is not going anywhere, in the same way that a parked car is neither approaching nor departing from the car parked in front of it, no matter how close those cars are parked to each other. At best, one could state that it (the .066 p value) is close to the .05 α level and that it would be interesting to consider monitoring this variable should this experiment be repeated at some future point.

Here is a simpler way to think about this: 2 + 2 = 4, and 4 is not approaching 3 or 5; it is just 4, and it is not drifting in any direction.

GOOD COMMON SENSE

When carrying the results of an ANOVA test into the real world, there are some practical considerations to take into account. Using this example, suppose the goal for this school district was to get multiplication test scores over 80%; the school principal may opt to set aside the p values and simply reference the mean scores rendered by Z-Math and flashcards, each of which exceeded 80%.

Cost-effectiveness may be another influential factor when it comes to applying these findings in the real world. Suppose it costs $75.00 per student to implement Z-Math but only $2.00 per student to provide each with a full set of multiplication flashcards. The principal of the school, who is responsible for the budget, may inspect the means and p values and make the following determination:

> According to the p value, Z-Math clearly outperformed math as usual, but there is no statistically significant difference ($p = .987$) between Z-Math ($\mu = 80.97$) and flashcards ($\mu = 80.63$). It would cost $6,750.00 ($75.00 \times 90$) to provide Z-Math to our 90 fourth graders, but it would only cost $180.00 to provide them with flashcards. The cost difference of $6,570.00 ($6,750.00 - $180 = $6,570.00$) is not worth the .34-point improvement ($80.97 - 80.63 = .34$) in multiplication test scores that would be gained by using Z-Math over flashcards. Also, after the students achieve 100% scores on their multiplication tests, the flashcards could be returned to the school and reused (repeatedly) for future fourth graders, thereby reducing future math education costs.

Another issue involves the capacity of the ANOVA model. Table 6.8 and the *combinations* formula (**Unique pairs = G! ÷ (2 × (G − 2)!)**) reveal that as more groups are included, the number of ANOVA post hoc paired comparisons increases substantially. A 5-group design would render 10 unique comparisons, 6 groups would render 15, and a 10-group design would render 45 unique comparisons along with their corresponding p values. While SPSS or any statistical software would have no problem processing these figures, there would be some real-world challenges to address. Consider the pretest criteria—in order for the results of an ANOVA test to be considered robust, there should be a minimum n of 30 per group. Hence, for a design involving 10 groups, this would require an overall n of at least 300. In addition, a 10-group study would render 45 unique pairwise comparisons in the ANOVA post hoc table, which, depending on the nature of the data, may be a bit unwieldy when it comes to interpretation and overall comprehension of the results.

Key Concepts

- ANOVA
- Pretest checklist
  - Normality
  - Homogeneity of variance
  - n

THE DOG BUZZ In the 19th century, street organ grinders and circus talent scouts discovered that the Bichon Frise, an intelligent and agile dog, could be trained to be an excellent performer. Today you might see glimmers of the breed's theatrical past when he runs from room to room, jumping off furniture in an amusing whirlwind of movement. Devotees call this entertaining performance the "Bichon Buzz."

TRUFFLES (BICHON FRISE)—EILEEN T. CHUA, QUEZON CITY, PHILIPPINES

Gyn appt. @ UTMC
Dr. Theresa Betts-Cohen
W 3-16   8:40am

- Post hoc tests
  - Tukey
  - Sidak
- Hypothesis resolution
- Documenting results
- Good common sense

Practice Exercises

For Exercises 1 to 5:

- If you saved the data sets from Chapter 5 (*Chapter 05 – Exercise 01 A.sav* through *Chapter 05 – Exercise 05 B.sav*), you will have less data entry to do; you will find that the data for Groups 1 and 2 from the exercises in Chapter 5 are the same as in this chapter. All you need to do is load the file(s) that you saved from the exercises in Chapter 5, enter the data from the table below pertaining to additional group(s) starting at the bottom of your loaded data set, and add the corresponding value label(s) (on the Variable View screen) to account for the new group(s).

NOTE: The data sets for Questions 3 and 5 involve four groups.

- After finalizing Data Set A, repeat the exercise using Data Set B, which will produce different findings.

For Exercises 6 to 10:

- Use the prepared SPSS data sets (download from **www.sagepub.com/knapp**).
- Load, process, and document your findings for Data Set A.
- Repeat each exercise using Data Set B (which will produce different results).

1. You want to determine if meditation can reduce resting pulse rate. Participants were recruited and randomly assigned to one of three groups: Members of Group 1 (the control group) will not meditate; members of Group 2 (the first treatment group) will meditate for 30 minutes per day on Mondays, Wednesdays, and Fridays over the course of 2 weeks; and members of Group 3 (the second treatment group) will meditate for 30 minutes a day 6 days a week, Monday through Saturday. At the end, you gathered the resting pulse rates for each participant.

   Codebook—set up SPSS to contain two variables:

   - *group* is a categorical variable (1 = no meditation, 2 = meditates 3 days, 3 = meditates 6 days).
   - *pulse* is a continuous variable (number of beats per minute).

Data set—enter Data Set A.

Data Set A				Data Set B		
Rec. #	group	pulse		Rec. #	group	pulse
1	1	104		1	1	96
2	1	108		2	1	86
3	1	100		3	1	99
4	1	87		4	1	101
5	1	94		5	1	97
6	1	101		6	1	100
7	1	99		7	1	100
8	1	103		8	1	99
9	1	104		9	1	80
10	1	94		10	1	93
11	1	92		11	1	102
12	1	107		12	1	105
13	1	101		13	1	87
14	1	96		14	1	92
15	1	102		15	1	96
16	1	107		16	1	103
17	1	95		17	1	99
18	1	84		18	1	94
19	1	92		19	1	87
20	1	102		20	1	95
21	1	93		21	1	90
22	1	85		22	1	86
23	1	92		23	1	90
24	1	97		24	1	99
25	1	86		25	1	91
26	1	93		26	1	89
27	1	96		27	1	101
28	1	108		28	1	102
29	1	98		29	1	100
30	1	98		30	1	95
31	1	100		31	1	94
32	1	109		32	1	95

33	1	88
34	1	94
35	1	100
36	2	102
37	2	100
38	2	78
39	2	105
40	2	90
41	2	96
42	2	93
43	2	83
44	2	99
45	2	90
46	2	88
47	2	105
48	2	94
49	2	94
50	2	93
51	2	86
52	2	79
53	2	93
54	2	88
55	2	80
56	2	82
57	2	96
58	2	98
59	2	89
60	2	96
61	2	104
62	2	93
63	2	97
64	2	95
65	2	82
66	2	88
67	2	97
68	2	93

33	1	97
34	2	81
35	2	84
36	2	95
37	2	100
38	2	102
39	2	91
40	2	90
41	2	83
42	2	93
43	2	79
44	2	94
45	2	90
46	2	104
47	2	101
48	2	100
49	2	91
50	2	99
51	2	95
52	2	87
53	2	96
54	2	97
55	2	92
56	2	92
57	2	90
58	2	105
59	2	94
60	2	93
61	2	102
62	2	84
63	2	89
64	2	107
65	2	90
66	2	98
67	2	93
68	2	93

69	2	96		69	3	92
70	2	85		70	3	87
71	3	91		71	3	98
72	3	93		72	3	82
73	3	87		73	3	97
74	3	77		74	3	91
75	3	95		75	3	88
76	3	95		76	3	95
77	3	103		77	3	93
78	3	89		78	3	91
79	3	93		79	3	94
80	3	89		80	3	100
81	3	99		81	3	104
82	3	92		82	3	104
83	3	95		83	3	85
84	3	89		84	3	100
85	3	89		85	3	100
86	3	82		86	3	102
87	3	106		87	3	79
88	3	90		88	3	97
89	3	81		89	3	83
90	3	95		90	3	86
91	3	94		91	3	92
92	3	96		92	3	93
93	3	100		93	3	90
94	3	95		94	3	82
95	3	95		95	3	88
96	3	84		96	3	100
97	3	83		97	3	91
98	3	79		98	3	93
99	3	87		99	3	96
100	3	98				
101	3	84				
102	3	99				
103	3	94				
104	3	96				
105	3	85				

     a. Write the hypotheses.

     b. Run each criterion of the pretest checklist (normality, homogeneity of variance, and n) and discuss your findings.

     c. Run the ANOVA test and document your findings (ns, means, and Sig. [p value]).

     d. Write an abstract under 200 words detailing a summary of the study, the ANOVA test results, hypothesis resolution, and implications of your findings.

- Repeat this exercise using Data Set B.

2. You want to determine if pairing an incoming freshman with a sophomore in a protégé-mentor relationship will enhance the freshman's grade point average (GPA). You recruit sophomores who are willing to mentor a student in their major for their first term. You then recruit freshmen who are interested in having a mentor. Freshmen who apply to this program will be sequentially assigned to one of three groups: Group 1 will be the control group (no mentor), Group 2 will be the in-person mentor group, and Group 3 will be the e-mentor group. Those in the in-person mentor group are to meet in person once a week at a time of their choosing, and those in the e-mentor group will communicate digitally at least once a week. All freshmen, in each group, agree to submit their transcript at the conclusion of the term.

Codebook—set up SPSS to contain two variables:

- *group* is a categorical variable (1 = no mentor, 2 = in-person mentor, 3 = e-mentor).
- *gpa* is a continuous variable (the first-term GPA for each freshman).

Data set—enter Data Set A.

Data Set A				Data Set B		
Rec. #	group	gpa		Rec. #	group	gpa
1	1	2.76		1	1	2.42
2	1	3.14		2	1	2.69
3	1	2.32		3	1	1.98
4	1	2.12		4	1	1.94
5	1	2.93		5	1	2.30
6	1	2.89		6	1	2.43
7	1	3.15		7	1	2.30
8	1	2.87		8	1	2.44
9	1	2.85		9	1	2.70
10	1	2.22		10	1	2.76
11	1	2.45		11	1	2.85
12	1	2.38		12	1	3.10

13	1	2.68	13	1	2.53
14	1	3.04	14	1	2.68
15	1	3.17	15	1	2.60
16	1	3.15	16	1	2.44
17	1	2.48	17	1	2.50
18	1	2.57	18	1	2.85
19	1	2.88	19	1	2.50
20	1	2.82	20	1	2.78
21	1	2.97	21	1	2.30
22	1	2.49	22	1	2.40
23	1	2.99	23	1	2.61
24	1	2.92	24	1	2.77
25	1	2.90	25	1	3.03
26	2	2.69	26	2	3.30
27	2	2.62	27	2	3.00
28	2	2.66	28	2	3.01
29	2	2.70	29	2	2.80
30	2	3.29	30	2	2.70
31	2	2.53	31	2	2.85
32	2	2.60	32	2	2.53
33	2	2.72	33	2	2.21
34	2	3.40	34	2	2.79
35	2	2.43	35	2	2.85
36	2	2.90	36	2	2.68
37	2	2.88	37	2	2.83
38	2	2.48	38	2	2.45
39	2	2.54	39	2	3.06
40	2	2.60	40	2	2.65
41	2	2.57	41	2	3.05
42	2	3.07	42	2	3.00
43	2	2.95	43	2	2.55
44	2	2.61	44	2	2.57
45	2	3.11	45	2	2.54
46	2	3.32	46	2	3.00
47	2	2.97	47	2	3.17
48	2	2.93	48	2	2.60

49	2	2.58		49	2	3.35
50	2	2.31		50	2	2.18
51	3	2.59		51	3	2.77
52	3	3.21		52	3	2.38
53	3	3.01		53	3	3.02
54	3	3.28		54	3	2.87
55	3	3.50		55	3	3.06
56	3	3.46		56	3	2.83
57	3	3.53		57	3	2.77
58	3	2.95		58	3	2.89
59	3	2.41		59	3	2.61
60	3	3.43		60	3	2.65
61	3	3.39		61	3	2.41
62	3	2.78		62	3	2.99
63	3	2.81		63	3	3.11
64	3	3.36		64	3	3.00
65	3	3.35		65	3	2.23
66	3	2.64		66	3	2.81
67	3	3.10		67	3	2.91
68	3	2.00		68	3	3.34
69	3	2.75		69	3	2.28
70	3	2.96		70	3	2.96
71	3	3.43		71	3	3.16
72	3	3.00		72	3	3.35
73	3	2.27		73	3	2.57
74	3	3.61		74	3	2.52
75	3	2.84		75	3	2.78

a. Write the hypotheses.

b. Run each criterion of the pretest checklist (normality, homogeneity of variance, and n) and discuss your findings.

c. Run the ANOVA test and document your findings (ns, means, and Sig. [p value]).

d. Write an abstract under 200 words detailing a summary of the study, the ANOVA test results, hypothesis resolution, and implications of your findings.

- Repeat this exercise using Data Set B.

3. The Acme Company claims that its new reading lamp increases reading speed; you want to test this. You will record how long (in seconds) it takes for participants to read a 1,000-word essay. Participants will be randomly assigned to one of four groups: Group 1 will be the control group; they will read the essay using regular room lighting. Those in Group 2 will read the essay using the Acme lamp. Those in Group 3 will read the essay using a generic reading lamp. Those in Group 4 will read the essay using a flashlight.

Codebook—set up SPSS to contain two variables:

- *group* is a categorical variable (1 = room lighting, 2 = Acme lamp, 3 = generic lamp, 4 = flashlight).
- *seconds* is a continuous variable (the time it takes to read the essay).

Data set—enter Data Set A.

Data Set A				Data Set B		
Rec. #	group	seconds		Rec. #	group	seconds
1	1	411		1	1	450
2	1	442		2	1	429
3	1	438		3	1	430
4	1	432		4	1	436
5	1	374		5	1	489
6	1	378		6	1	367
7	1	431		7	1	405
8	1	509		8	1	410
9	1	436		9	1	410
10	1	429		10	1	424
11	1	436		11	1	386
12	1	400		12	1	331
13	1	502		13	1	433
14	1	413		14	1	440
15	1	432		15	1	430
16	1	377		16	1	403
17	1	386		17	1	424
18	1	484		18	1	402
19	1	471		19	1	463
20	1	470		20	1	414
21	1	449		21	1	434

22	1	414		22	1	396
23	1	505		23	1	400
24	1	437		24	1	355
25	1	441		25	1	450
26	2	455		26	2	442
27	2	399		27	2	364
28	2	393		28	2	406
29	2	432		29	2	442
30	2	369		30	2	434
31	2	406		31	2	455
32	2	443		32	2	460
33	2	357		33	2	404
34	2	395		34	2	395
35	2	376		35	2	479
36	2	391		36	2	441
37	2	366		37	2	415
38	2	445		38	2	449
39	2	452		39	2	481
40	2	364		40	2	408
41	2	407		41	2	344
42	2	415		42	2	390
43	2	408		43	2	451
44	2	412		44	2	398
45	2	380		45	2	348
46	2	446		46	2	390
47	2	403		47	2	421
48	2	451		48	2	361
49	2	366		49	2	394
50	2	443		50	2	418
51	2	363		51	3	430
52	2	424		52	3	347
53	2	405		53	3	436
54	3	429		54	3	440
55	3	470		55	3	441
56	3	447		56	3	470
57	3	455		57	3	437

58	3	397		58	3	436
59	3	342		59	3	366
60	3	453		60	3	362
61	3	440		61	3	338
62	3	379		62	3	386
63	3	382		63	3	454
64	3	438		64	3	380
65	3	436		65	3	457
66	3	365		66	3	429
67	3	464		67	3	444
68	3	420		68	3	374
69	3	376		69	3	421
70	3	397		70	3	411
71	3	444		71	3	458
72	3	438		72	3	353
73	3	328		73	3	444
74	3	462		74	3	430
75	3	385		75	3	398
76	3	400		76	4	437
77	3	330		77	4	512
78	3	352		78	4	522
79	3	433		79	4	361
80	3	389		80	4	485
81	3	372		81	4	396
82	3	463		82	4	421
83	3	404		83	4	453
84	4	451		84	4	463
85	4	449		85	4	440
86	4	409		86	4	384
87	4	368		87	4	423
88	4	446		88	4	513
89	4	421		89	4	449
90	4	371		90	4	462
91	4	382		91	4	483
92	4	466		92	4	373

93	4	473		93	4	400
94	4	422		94	4	471
95	4	466		95	4	510
96	4	512		96	4	525
97	4	448		97	4	448
98	4	468		98	4	445
99	4	461		99	4	393
100	4	383		100	4	448
101	4	418				
102	4	467				
103	4	449				
104	4	461				
105	4	400				
106	4	489				
107	4	510				

a. Write the hypotheses.

b. Run each criterion of the pretest checklist (normality, homogeneity of variance, and *n*) and discuss your findings.

c. Run the ANOVA test and document your findings (*ns*, means, and Sig. [*p* value]).

d. Write an abstract under 200 words detailing a summary of the study, the ANOVA test results, hypothesis resolution, and implications of your findings.

- Repeat this exercise using Data Set B.

4. You want to determine if chocolate enhances mood. Subjects will be recruited and randomly assigned to one of three groups: Those in Group 1 will be the control group and will eat their regular diet. Those in Group 2 will eat their usual meals and have a piece of chocolate at breakfast, lunch, and dinner over the course of a week. Those in Group 3 will eat their meals as usual and have two pieces of chocolate at breakfast, lunch, and dinner over the course of a week. At the end of the week, all participants will complete the Acme Mood Scale (1 = extremely bad mood . . . 100 = extremely good mood).

Codebook—set up SPSS to contain two variables:

- *group* is a categorical variable (1 = no chocolate, 2 = chocolate [1 per meal], 3 = chocolate [2 per meal]).
- *mood* is a continuous variable (score on the Acme Mood Scale).

Data set—enter Data Set A.

Data Set A				Data Set B		
Rec. #	group	mood		Rec. #	group	mood
1	1	71		1	1	98
2	1	74		2	1	71
3	1	73		3	1	93
4	1	73		4	1	83
5	1	67		5	1	84
6	1	67		6	1	69
7	1	73		7	1	72
8	1	82		8	1	63
9	1	73		9	1	76
10	1	73		10	1	76
11	1	74		11	1	78
12	1	70		12	1	78
13	1	81		13	1	85
14	1	71		14	1	68
15	1	73		15	1	74
16	1	60		16	1	79
17	1	63		17	1	71
18	1	78		18	1	72
19	1	77		19	1	80
20	1	77		20	1	85
21	1	75		21	1	74
22	1	71		22	1	72
23	1	81		23	1	78
24	1	74		24	1	83
25	1	74		25	1	74
26	2	72		26	1	82
27	2	78		27	1	96
28	2	75		28	1	93
29	2	77		29	2	78
30	2	69		30	2	82
31	2	81		31	2	69
32	2	83		32	2	84
33	2	78		33	2	84

34	2	69
35	2	74
36	2	80
37	2	78
38	2	81
39	2	80
40	2	74
41	2	73
42	2	83
43	2	78
44	2	77
45	2	79
46	2	83
47	2	75
48	2	67
49	2	73
50	2	80
51	3	78
52	3	73
53	3	72
54	3	76
55	3	69
56	3	71
57	3	74
58	3	75
59	3	73
60	3	75
61	3	72
62	3	71
63	3	77
64	3	74
65	3	71
66	3	77
67	3	77
68	3	82
69	3	74
70	3	75

34	2	86
35	2	67
36	2	75
37	2	75
38	2	74
39	2	74
40	2	89
41	2	96
42	2	71
43	2	79
44	2	79
45	2	75
46	2	71
47	2	79
48	2	85
49	2	88
50	2	83
51	2	78
52	3	82
53	3	84
54	3	82
55	3	83
56	3	84
57	3	87
58	3	81
59	3	79
60	3	80
61	3	81
62	3	87
63	3	86
64	3	81
65	3	86
66	3	80
67	3	77
68	3	88
69	3	78
70	3	93

71	3	78
72	3	81
73	3	79
74	3	70
75	3	74

71	3	82
72	3	92
73	3	67
74	3	78
75	3	78
76	3	78
77	3	88
78	3	78

a. Write the hypotheses.
b. Run each criterion of the pretest checklist (normality, homogeneity of variance, and *n*) and discuss your findings.
c. Run the ANOVA test and document your findings (*ns*, means, and Sig. [*p* value]).
d. Write an abstract under 200 words detailing a summary of the study, the ANOVA test results, hypothesis resolution, and implications of your findings.

   • Repeat this exercise using Data Set B.

5. You want to find out if music enhances problem solving. Subjects will be recruited and randomly assigned to one of four groups: Those in Group 1 will serve as the control group and will be given a standard 100-piece jigsaw puzzle to solve in a quiet room. Participants in Group 2 will be given the same puzzle to assemble but instead of silence, there will be classical music playing at a soft volume (30 decibels [dB]) in the room. Participants in Group 3 will be given the same puzzle to assemble using the same classical music, but the music will be played at a moderate volume (60 dB). Participants in Group 4 will be given the same puzzle to assemble using the same classical music, but the music will be played at a loud volume (90 dB). You will record the time (in seconds) that it takes for each person to complete the puzzle.

Codebook—set up SPSS to contain two variables:
   • *group* is a categorical variable (1 = no music, 2 = music at 30 dB, 3 = music at 60 dB, 4 = music at 90 dB).
   • *seconds* is a continuous variable (how long it took to finish the puzzle).

Data set—enter Data Set A.

Data Set A		
Rec. #	group	seconds
1	1	541
2	1	565

Data Set B		
Rec. #	group	seconds
1	1	588
2	1	635

3	1	604	3	1	608
4	1	612	4	1	602
5	1	590	5	1	616
6	1	614	6	1	592
7	1	578	7	1	629
8	1	564	8	1	618
9	1	640	9	1	598
10	1	609	10	1	600
11	1	564	11	1	606
12	1	627	12	1	595
13	1	634	13	1	611
14	1	687	14	1	624
15	1	606	15	1	610
16	1	616	16	1	590
17	1	655	17	1	592
18	1	679	18	1	610
19	1	660	19	1	611
20	1	551	20	1	627
21	1	592	21	1	605
22	1	623	22	1	591
23	1	638	23	1	607
24	1	625	24	1	605
25	1	634	25	1	624
26	1	632	26	1	599
27	1	655	27	1	626
28	1	624	28	1	595
29	1	610	29	1	606
30	1	609	30	1	613
31	1	621	31	1	611
32	1	657	32	1	611
33	1	645	33	1	621
34	1	620	34	1	614
35	1	649	35	1	615
36	1	613	36	1	608
37	1	590	37	1	607
38	1	660	38	1	604
39	1	600	39	1	621

40	1	690		40	1	611
41	2	612		41	1	616
42	2	669		42	1	608
43	2	525		43	1	604
44	2	590		44	2	610
45	2	586		45	2	597
46	2	590		46	2	602
47	2	590		47	2	592
48	2	612		48	2	601
49	2	533		49	2	595
50	2	621		50	2	619
51	2	624		51	2	585
52	2	634		52	2	627
53	2	528		53	2	597
54	2	564		54	2	593
55	2	566		55	2	620
56	2	561		56	2	628
57	2	566		57	2	592
58	2	655		58	2	618
59	2	696		59	2	596
60	2	547		60	2	602
61	2	596		61	2	598
62	2	594		62	2	607
63	2	568		63	2	614
64	2	548		64	2	590
65	2	596		65	2	597
66	2	629		66	2	600
67	2	648		67	2	637
68	2	617		68	2	618
69	2	587		69	2	614
70	2	707		70	2	624
71	2	547		71	2	611
72	2	682		72	2	606
73	2	620		73	2	619
74	2	622		74	2	609
75	2	534		75	2	594

76	2	554		76	2	601
77	2	497		77	2	617
78	2	575		78	2	587
79	2	576		79	2	612
80	2	592		80	2	606
81	3	583		81	2	614
82	3	631		82	2	598
83	3	524		83	3	624
84	3	563		84	3	605
85	3	592		85	3	613
86	3	546		86	3	609
87	3	549		87	3	615
88	3	597		88	3	603
89	3	632		89	3	603
90	3	565		90	3	624
91	3	550		91	3	595
92	3	589		92	3	597
93	3	621		93	3	599
94	3	562		94	3	609
95	3	612		95	3	609
96	3	696		96	3	608
97	3	679		97	3	588
98	3	650		98	3	622
99	3	589		99	3	597
100	3	659		100	3	615
101	3	686		101	3	609
102	3	539		102	3	606
103	3	619		103	3	606
104	3	559		104	3	610
105	3	585		105	3	627
106	3	507		106	3	597
107	3	505		107	3	618
108	3	571		108	3	601
109	3	611		109	3	596
110	3	623		110	3	592
111	3	616		111	3	609

112	3	611	112	3	630
113	3	569	113	3	603
114	3	585	114	3	609
115	3	623	115	3	610
116	3	622	116	3	622
117	3	668	117	3	607
118	3	571	118	3	605
119	3	576	119	3	622
120	3	601	120	4	622
121	4	644	121	4	626
122	4	727	122	4	609
123	4	674	123	4	622
124	4	654	124	4	629
125	4	634	125	4	611
126	4	634	126	4	615
127	4	636	127	4	601
128	4	580	128	4	616
129	4	530	129	4	614
130	4	621	130	4	620
131	4	629	131	4	613
132	4	602	132	4	604
133	4	627	133	4	630
134	4	567	134	4	620
135	4	660	135	4	616
136	4	597	136	4	611
137	4	669	137	4	601
138	4	674	138	4	625
139	4	589	139	4	644
140	4	586	140	4	601
141	4	581	141	4	643
142	4	653	142	4	599
143	4	678	143	4	601
144	4	627	144	4	611
145	4	707	145	4	622
146	4	525	146	4	610
147	4	616	147	4	624

148	4	557
149	4	655
150	4	633
151	4	660
152	4	626
153	4	617
154	4	634
155	4	591
156	4	599
157	4	562
158	4	651
159	4	669
160	4	652

148	4	627
149	4	611
150	4	600
151	4	608
152	4	633
153	4	642

a. Write the hypotheses.
b. Run each criterion of the pretest checklist (normality, homogeneity of variance, and n) and discuss your findings.
c. Run the ANOVA test and document your findings (ns, means, and Sig. [p value]).
d. Write an abstract under 200 words detailing a summary of the study, the ANOVA test results, hypothesis resolution, and implications of your findings.

   • Repeat this exercise using Data Set B.

6. You want to determine if watching a video of a comedy with a laugh track enhances enjoyment. Subjects will be recruited and randomly assigned to one of three groups: Those in Group 1 (the control group) will watch the video without the laugh track, those assigned to Group 2 will watch the same video with the sound(s) of a 50-person audience included in the soundtrack, and those assigned to Group 3 will watch the same video with the sound(s) of a 100-person audience included in the soundtrack. Each participant will watch the video individually; no others will be present in the room. Immediately following the video, each participant will be asked to rate how enjoyable the show was on a scale of 1 to 5 (1 = not very enjoyable . . . 5 = very enjoyable).

Codebook—The data set contains two variables:

   • *group* is a categorical variable (1 = no laugh track, 2 = laugh track at 50, 3 = laugh track at 100).
   • *enjoy* is a continuous variable (1 = not very enjoyable . . . 5 = very enjoyable).

Data set—load *Chapter 06 – Exercise 06 A.sav.*

   a. Write the hypotheses.
   b. Run each criterion of the pretest checklist (normality, homogeneity of variance, and *n*) and discuss your findings.
   c. Run the ANOVA test and document your findings (*n*s, means, and Sig. [*p* value]).
   d. Write an abstract under 200 words detailing a summary of the study, the ANOVA test results, hypothesis resolution, and implications of your findings.

   • Repeat this exercise using *Chapter 06 – Exercise 06 B.sav.*

7. In an effort to determine the effectiveness of light therapy to alleviate depression, you recruit a group of subjects who have been diagnosed with depression. The subjects are randomly assigned to one of three groups: Group 1 will be the control group—members of this group will receive no light therapy. Members of Group 2 will get light therapy for 1 hour on even-numbered days over the course of 1 month. Members of Group 3 will get light therapy every day for 1 hour over the course of 1 month. After 1 month, all participants will complete the Acme Mood Scale, consisting of 10 questions; this instrument renders a score between 1 and 100 (1 = extremely bad mood . . . 100 = extremely good mood).

Codebook—the data set contains two variables:

   • *group* is a categorical variable (1 = no light therapy, 2 = light therapy: even days, 3 = light therapy: every day).
   • *mood* is a continuous variable (1 = extremely bad mood . . . 100 = extremely good mood).

Data set—load *Chapter 06 – Exercise 07 A.sav.*

   a. Write the hypotheses.
   b. Run each criterion of the pretest checklist (normality, homogeneity of variance, and *n*) and discuss your findings.
   c. Run the ANOVA test and document your findings (*n*s, means, and Sig. [*p* value]).
   d. Write an abstract under 200 words detailing a summary of the study, the ANOVA test results, hypothesis resolution, and implications of your findings.

   • Repeat this exercise using *Chapter 06 – Exercise 07 B.sav.*

8. It is thought that exercising early in the morning will provide better energy throughout the day. To test this idea, subjects are recruited and randomly assigned to one of three groups: Members of Group 1 will constitute the control group and not be assigned any walking. Members of Group 2 will walk from 7:00 to 7:30 a.m., Monday through Friday, over the course of 30 days. Members of Group 3 will walk from 7:00 to 8:00 a.m., Monday through Friday, over the course of 30 days. At the conclusion of the study,

each subject will answer the 10 questions on the Acme End-of-the-Day Energy Scale. This instrument produces a score between 1 and 100 (1 = extremely low energy . . . 100 = extremely high energy).

Codebook—the data set contains two variables:

- *group* is a categorical variable (1 = no walking, 2 = walking: 30 minutes, 3 = walking: 60 minutes).
- *energy* is a continuous variable (1 = extremely low energy . . . 100 = extremely high energy).

Data set—load *Chapter 06 – Exercise 08 A.sav.*

  a. Write the hypotheses.

  b. Run each criterion of the pretest checklist (normality, homogeneity of variance, and *n*) and discuss your findings.

  c. Run the ANOVA test and document your findings (*n*s, means, and Sig. [*p* value]).

  d. Write an abstract under 200 words detailing a summary of the study, the ANOVA test results, hypothesis resolution, and implications of your findings.

- Repeat this exercise using *Chapter 06 – Exercise 08 B.sav.*

9. Clinicians at a nursing home facility want to see if giving residents a plant to tend to will help lower depression. To test this idea, the residents are randomly assigned to one of three groups: Those assigned to Group 1 will serve as the control group and will not be given a plant. Members of Group 2 will be given a small bamboo plant along with a card detailing care instructions. Members of Group 3 will be given a small cactus along with a card detailing care instructions. After 90 days, all participants will complete the Acme Depression Scale, a 10-question instrument that renders a score between 1 and 100 (1 = low depression . . . 100 = high depression).

Codebook—the data set contains two variables:

- *group* is a categorical variable (1 = no plant, 2 = bamboo, 3 = cactus).
- *depress* is a continuous variable (1 = low depression . . . 100 = high depression).

Data set—load *Chapter 06 – Exercise 09 A.sav.*

  a. Write the hypotheses.

  b. Run each criterion of the pretest checklist (normality, homogeneity of variance, and *n*) and discuss your findings.

  c. Run the ANOVA test and document your findings (*n*s, means, and Sig. [*p* value]).

  d. Write an abstract under 200 words detailing a summary of the study, the ANOVA test results, hypothesis resolution, and implications of your findings.

- Repeat this exercise using *Chapter 06 – Exercise 09 B.sav.*

10. During flu season, the administrators at a walk-in health clinic want to determine if providing patients with a pamphlet or a video will increase their receptivity to flu shots. Each patient will be given a ticket at the check-in desk with a 1, 2, or 3 on it; the tickets will be issued in (repeating) sequence. Once escorted to the exam room, patients with a number 1 ticket will serve as control participants and will not be offered any flu shot informational material. Patients with a number 2 ticket will be given a flu shot information pamphlet. Patients with a number 3 ticket will be shown a brief video covering the same information as contained in the pamphlet. At the end of the day, the charts were reviewed and three entries were made in the database: total number of flu shots given to patients in Group 1, total number of flu shots given to patients in Group 2, and the total number of flu shots given to patients in Group 3.

    Codebook—the data set contains two variables:

    - *group* is a categorical variable (1 = nothing, 2 = flu shot pamphlet, 3 = flu shot video).
    - *shots* is a continuous variable (number of flu shots given in a day [for each group]).

    Data set—load *Chapter 06 – Exercise 10 A.sav*.

    a. Write the hypotheses.
    b. Run each criterion of the pretest checklist (normality, homogeneity of variance, and *n*) and discuss your findings.
    c. Run the ANOVA test and document your findings (*ns*, means, and Sig. [*p* value]).
    d. Write an abstract under 200 words detailing a summary of the study, the ANOVA test results, hypothesis resolution, and implications of your findings.

        - Repeat this exercise using *Chapter 06 – Exercise 10 B.sav*.

Paired *t* Test

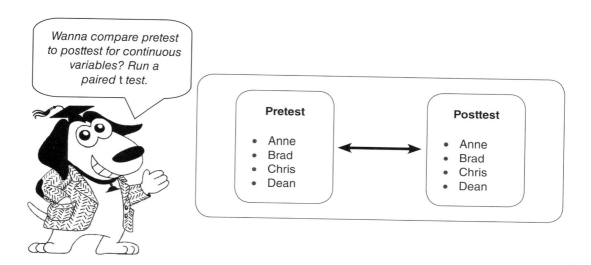

Things never happen the same way twice.

—C. S. Lewis

LEARNING OBJECTIVES

Upon completing this chapter, you will be able to:

- Determine when it is appropriate to run a paired *t* test
- Verify that the data meet the criteria for paired *t* test processing: normality of differences
- Order a paired *t* test
- Interpret test results
- Resolve the hypotheses
- Document the results in plain English
- Calculate and document the Δ% formula

DIGITAL LEARNING RESOURCES

The tutorial video and data sets for this chapter are at **www.sagepub.com/knapp**

- Paired *t* test pretest checklist video
- Paired *t* test run video
- SPSS files

OVERVIEW

The *t* test and ANOVA test were appropriate for conducting research using a classic experimental model, which involves random assignment of participants to a control group and at least one other (treatment) group. There will be times when such rigorous designs are not feasible due to limited resources (e.g., low *n*, limited staff, lack of facilities, budget constraints, etc.). The paired *t* test provides an alternate approach that can be used to test the effectiveness of an implementation using a single group that does not require a sizable *n*.

Pretest/Posttest Design

The design associated with the paired *t* test is typically referred to as a *pretest/posttest design,* also known as a *simple time-series design,* or *O-X-O design* (O = observation, X = treatment) (Figure 7.1).

This design consists of one group and three steps:

Step 1—Pretest: Begin by gathering a quantitative metric, and attach each participant's name or ID to the score. The score needs to be a continuous variable. This could be an existing score or a test that you administer. This will be the pretest score, sometimes referred to as the *baseline* score, indicating the level that each participant was at prior to exposing him or her to the *treatment*. Essentially, each subject acts as his or her own control group.

Figure 7.1   Pretest/Posttest Design

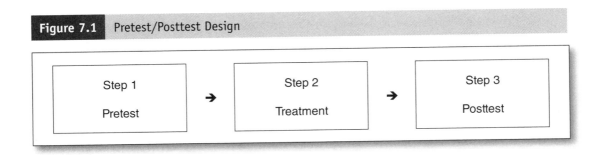

Step 2—Treatment: Execute the treatment (e.g., intervention, change in condition, training, etc.).

Step 3—Posttest: Administer the same test that was used in Step 1 (pretest), or gather the (same) metric and record the participant's name or ID with the score.

The paired *t* test analysis presents three critical pieces of information: (1) the mean pretest score, (2) the mean posttest score, and (3) the *p* value. If the *p* value is less than the specified α level (.05), then this indicates that there is a statistically significant difference between the pretest score and the posttest score, suggesting that the treatment made an impact.

EXAMPLE

Acme Industries has 10 people on its production staff. The supervisor is looking for an affordable way to boost productivity and is considering offering unlimited free coffee to the staff.

RESEARCH QUESTION

The question is: Will providing the staff with unlimited free coffee increase productivity?

GROUPS

As stated earlier, part of the utility of the paired *t* test is that it can function with just one group. The (one) group will consist of the 10 members of the production staff.

PROCEDURE

Step 1—Pretest: First, the manager will count the total number of units that each staff member processed last week; this will constitute the pretest score.

Step 2—Treatment: The manager will announce that the coffee machine has been set to free access; the staff can have as much coffee as they want at no charge.

Step 3—Posttest: At the end of the week, the manager will gather the total number of units that each staff member processed (that week); this will constitute the posttest score.

HYPOTHESES

H_0: Providing the staff with free coffee will have no impact on productivity.

H_1: Providing the staff with free coffee will enhance productivity.

DATA SET

Use the following data set: *Chapter 07 – Example 01 – Paired T Test.sav.*

PRETEST CHECKLIST

Pretest Checklist Criterion 1—Normality of Differences

To run a paired *t* test, you must satisfy only one pretest criterion: The difference between the *pretest* scores and the *posttest* scores must be normally distributed. This process involves two steps:

(1) We will have SPSS compute a new variable (*diff*), which will contain the *diff*erence between the pretest scores and the posttest scores (*diff* = posttest – pretest).

(2) We will run a histogram with a normal curve for *diff* and inspect the curve for normality.

Begin by selecting *Transform, Compute Variable* . . . (Figure 7.2).

Figure 7.2	*Select Transform, Compute Variable . . .*

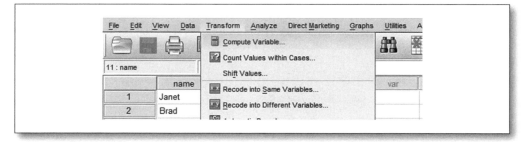

This will take you to the *Compute Variable* menu (Figure 7.3). Enter *diff* in the *Target Variable* box. Enter *posttest – pretest* in the *Numeric Expression* box. You can type in the variables *posttest* and *pretest*, double-click on them, or use the arrow key to copy them from the left box to the right box.

NOTE: For this test, you can enter *posttest – pretest* or *pretest – posttest;* either is fine.

Click the *OK* button to process this menu.
At this point, let us review the data on the Data View screen (Figure 7.4):

Column 1 contains the *name* of each staff member; this is a string (alphanumeric) variable.

Columns 2 and 3 contain the *pretest* and *posttest* scores for each staff member.

Figure 7.3   *Compute Variable* Menu

Column 4 contains the *diff* variable; this variable, as well as the data in it, was created as we specified on the *Compute Variable* menu (*diff = posttest – pretest*).

It is now time to generate the histogram with a normal curve for the *diff* variable. This is the same procedure used as part of the pretest checklist for the *t* test and ANOVA. For more details on this procedure, please refer to Chapter 4 ("SPSS—Descriptive Statistics: Continuous Variables (Age)"); see the star (★) icon on page **61**.

Figure 7.4   Data View

File Edit View Data Transform Analyze Direct Marketing Graphs Utilitie			
	name	pretest	posttest	diff
1	Janet	40	41	1.00
2	Brad	35	38	3.00
3	George	36	45	9.00
4	Jane	37	38	1.00
5	Michael	41	40	-1.00
6	Boris	37	41	4.00
7	Natasha	30	42	12.00
8	Harold	34	40	6.00
9	Maude	36	41	5.00
10	Rufus	38	35	-3.00
11				

Alternatively, the following steps will produce a histogram with a normal curve for *diff*:

1. From the main screen, select *Analyze / Descriptive Statistics / Frequencies . . .*; this will take you to the *Frequencies* menu.

2. On the *Frequencies* menu, move *diff* from the left window to the right (*Variables*) window.

3. Click on the *Charts . . .* button; this will take you to the *Charts* menu.

4. Click on the *Histograms* button, and check the *Show normal curve on histogram* checkbox.

5. Click on the *Continue* button; this will return you to the *Frequencies* menu.

6. Click on the *OK* button, and the system will produce a histogram with a normal curve for the *diff* variable (Figure 7.5).

Figure 7.5   Histogram With Normal Curve for *diff*

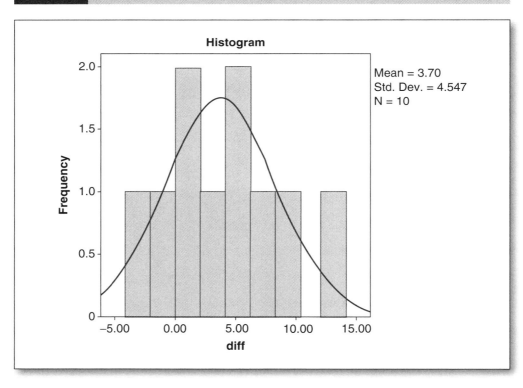

The normal curve for *diff* (Figure 7.5) presents as a reasonably symmetrical bell shape—hence, we would say that the difference between the pretest and posttest scores meets the criteria of normality.

TEST RUN

To run the paired *t* test, from the main screen, click on *Analyze, Compare Means, Paired-Samples T Test . . . .* This will take you to the paired-samples *t* test (Figure 7.6).

Figure 7.6	Histogram With a Normal Curve for *diff*

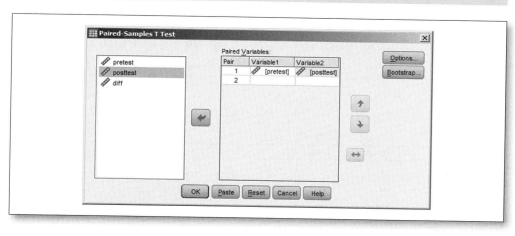

Copy the *pretest* variable from the left window to the right window (under *Variable1*), then copy the *posttest* variable from the left window to the right window (under *Variable2*), and then click on the *OK* button.

RESULTS

The results of the paired *t* test are read from two tables: The paired-samples statistics test (Table 7.1) reports the means for each group: μ(pretest) = 36.40 and μ(posttest) = 40.10. The table also shows the corresponding *n*s and standard deviations.

The paired-samples test (Table 7.2) focuses on the difference between the pretest and posttest scores. Column 2 shows that there is a (−)3.700-point difference between the means (36.40 − 40.10 = −3.700). The last column (Sig.) shows that the *p* value is .030 for this comparison; since .030 is less than the specified α level of .05, we would conclude that there is a statistically significant difference between the pretest and posttest scores.

Table 7.1	Paired Samples (Summary) Statistics for Pretest and Posttest

Paired-Samples Statistics

		Mean	N	Std. Deviation	Std. Error Mean
Pair 1	pretest	36.40	10	3.098	.980
	posttest	40.10	10	2.685	.849

Table 7.2	Paired Samples Test Results

Paired-Samples Test

		Paired Differences							
					95% Confidence Interval of the Difference				
		Mean	Std. Deviation	Std. Error Mean	Lower	Upper	t	df	Sig. (2-tailed)
Pair 1	pretest – posttest	–3.700	4.547	1.438	–6.953	–.447	–2.573	9	.030

HYPOTHESIS RESOLUTION

H_0: Providing the staff with free coffee will have no impact on productivity.

H_1: Providing the staff with free coffee will enhance productivity.

Since the p value (.030) is less than the specified α level (.05), this suggests that the 3.7-point increase in productivity (from 36.4 to 40.1) is statistically significant. In terms of the hypotheses, we would reject H_0 and not reject H_1.

DOCUMENT RESULTS

Since the paired t test is a fairly straightforward process, the documentation is typically concise:

We compared weekly productivity figures the week before and after implementing a free unlimited coffee program. Our 10 staff members processed an average of 3.7 additional cases per week with the coffee (up from 36.4 to 40.1), which is statistically significant (p = .03, α = .05).

Another useful way of documenting such change is the Δ% formula (Δ is the Greek letter delta, which symbolizes *change*). The Δ% formula is simple, yet expressive; you can run it on any calculator by plugging in two variables: the old value (pretest mean = 36.4) and the new value (posttest mean = 40.1) (Table 7.3).

Table 7.3   Δ% Formula Computes Change Percentage

Δ% Formula
Δ% = (New − Old) ÷ Old × 100
Δ% = (40.1 − 36.4) ÷ 36.4 × 100
Δ% = (3.7) ÷ 36.4 × 100
Δ% = .1016 ×100
Δ% = 10.16

In terms of documentation, you could include the Δ% = 10.16 as-is or express it verbosely: ". . . we observed a 10.16% increase in weekly productivity, from an average of 36.4 cases per week to 40.1."

GOOD COMMON SENSE

For simplicity, the example used in this chapter focused exclusively on *weekly productivity,* but you may opt to gather additional pre/post data (e.g., job satisfaction survey scores, attendance scores, minutes late, etc.) and conduct separate paired *t* tests on those metrics as well. Such findings may shed light on other relevant variables; since this intervention involves introducing free unlimited coffee, it may be wise to include additional pre/post metrics that gather data on other possibly relevant topics such as irritability, coworker relations, workplace satisfaction, and so on.

When opting for the pretest/posttest design and corresponding paired *t* test, the potential for historical confounds must be considered. In a classic experimental design, the control group and treatment group(s) are being processed during the same timeframe, but when using the paired *t* test, the pretest (control/baseline) data and posttest (treatment) data are collected at different time points. This time difference may involve minutes, hours, weeks, or even months, depending on the study design. During this time, history does not stand still; things outside your investigation can change over time either in the individual or in the environment (e.g., personal issues, sociopolitical events, season, etc.), which could potentially affect the pretest or posttest scores.

In addition, in some cases, there is a chance that participants may show improvement in the posttest, partly because they are familiar with it—they remember it from the pretest phase.

Key Concepts

- Paired *t* test
- Paired *t* test designs (synonyms):
  - Pretest/treatment/posttest
  - Pre/post design
  - Simple time-series design
  - O-X-O design
- Histogram with a normal curve
- Paired *t* test with multiple metrics
- Historical confound
- Δ%

Practice Exercises

1. The Acme Company produces Monster Spray, a pleasant fragrance that parents can use to help relax children who are afraid of nighttime monsters. A group of parents who use the spray has been recruited to find out how effective the spray is in calming monster-anxious children. Prior to spraying, the parent will ask the child to rate his or her anxiety on a 1 to 10 scale (1 = not afraid at all . . . 10 = very afraid); the parent will ask the same anxiety scale question after spraying. The parent will record both the *before* and *after* (spraying) numbers.

   Codebook—set up SPSS to contain three variables:

   - *ID* is an alphanumeric (string) variable (the participant's ID).
   - *pretest* is a continuous variable (level of anxiety before spraying).
   - *posttest* is a continuous variable (level of anxiety after spraying).

   Data set—enter Data Set A.

Data Set A			
Rec. #	*ID*	*pretest*	*posttest*
1	Jay	9	6
2	Reva	6	5
3	Bill	6	4
4	Sue	4	4
5	Marie	5	5
6	Ed	7	3

Data Set B			
Rec. #	*ID*	*pretest*	*posttest*
1	Claire	3	3
2	David	8	8
3	Marcia	8	8
4	Kyle	3	3
5	Tina	6	6
6	Stan	5	5

7	Megan	8	5
8	Justin	7	6
9	Dusty	7	3
10	Bob	6	1
11	Cole	9	3
12	Jon	7	4

7	Jeff	6	5
8	Bev	6	5
9	Greg	4	3
10	Chris	8	8

   a. Write the hypotheses.

   b. Run the criteria of the pretest checklist (normality for *posttest – pretest*) and discuss your findings.

   c. Run the paired *t* test and document your findings (means and Sig. [*p* value]).

   d. Write an abstract under 200 words detailing a summary of the study, the paired *t* test results, hypothesis resolution, and implications of your findings.

   • Repeat this exercise using Data Set B.

2. Prior to a Heart Health presentation, you administer a survey asking participants to indicate how many times they used the stairs (as opposed to the elevator) in the past week. A week after the lecture, you resurvey the attendees.

Codebook—set up SPSS to contain three variables:

   • *ID* is an alphanumeric (string) variable (the participant's ID).

   • *pretest* is a continuous variable (number of times per week the participant used the stairs before the lecture).

   • *posttest* is a continuous variable (number of times per week the participant used the stairs after the lecture).

Data set—enter Data Set A.

Data Set A			
Rec. #	ID	pretest	posttest
1	101	1	4
2	102	3	1
3	103	1	4
4	104	2	3
5	105	3	1
6	106	4	2
7	107	4	3

Data Set B			
Rec. #	ID	pretest	posttest
1	201	3	7
2	202	9	8
3	203	5	8
4	204	6	4
5	205	5	5
6	206	3	8
7	207	0	7

8	108	3	4
9	109	4	0
10	110	2	4
11	111	0	1
12	112	3	3
13	113	4	2
14	114	2	1
15	115	2	3
16	116	3	2

8	208	5	8
9	209	4	4
10	210	0	9
11	211	1	11
12	212	6	8
13	213	7	4
14	201	3	7

a. Write the hypotheses.

b. Run the criteria of the pretest checklist (normality for *posttest – pretest*) and discuss your findings.

c. Run the paired *t* test and document your findings (means and Sig. [*p* value]).

d. Write an abstract under 200 words detailing a summary of the study, the paired *t* test results, hypothesis resolution, and implications of your findings.

- Repeat this exercise using Data Set B.

3. An English teacher recognizes that students already know how to spell some of the words assigned for the weekly spelling test. This teacher wants to discover how many new words students learn. The usual assignment is 25 words per week. At the beginning of the month, the teacher administers a spelling test consisting of all 100 words that will be assigned over the month. The teacher then administers the same 100-word test at the end of the month.

Codebook—set up SPSS to contain three variables:

- *ID* is an alphanumeric (string) variable (the student's ID).
- *pretest* is a continuous variable (number of words spelled correctly on the test given at the beginning of the month).
- *posttest* is a continuous variable (number of words spelled correctly on the test given at the end of the month).

Data set—enter Data Set A.

Data Set A			
Rec. #	ID	pretest	posttest
1	A01	46	56
2	A02	72	78

Data Set B			
Rec. #	ID	pretest	posttest
1	B01	87	93
2	B02	82	86

3	A03	68	80
4	A04	68	56
5	A05	63	67
6	A06	54	70
7	A07	78	67
8	A08	59	68
9	A09	61	59
10	A10	76	78
11	A11	61	66
12	A12	59	79
13	A13	70	56
14	A14	52	78
15	A15	63	55
16	A16	73	72
17	A17	48	67
18	A18	59	74
19	A19	53	86
20	A20	58	79

3	B03	90	80
4	B04	86	85
5	B05	84	99
6	B06	94	85
7	B07	87	81
8	B08	87	84
9	B09	87	88
10	B10	83	86
11	B11	78	85
12	B12	86	87
13	B13	84	93
14	B14	79	88
15	B15	80	88
16	B16	89	89
17	B17	89	94
18	B18	84	82
19	B19	89	91
20	B20	94	89
21	B21	87	86
22	B22	89	88

a. Write the hypotheses.

b. Run the criteria of the pretest checklist (normality for *posttest – pretest*) and discuss your findings.

c. Run the paired *t* test and document your findings (means and Sig. [*p* value]).

d. Write an abstract under 200 words detailing a summary of the study, the paired *t* test results, hypothesis resolution, and implications of your findings.

 • Repeat this exercise using Data Set B.

4. The staff at a mental health clinic wants to determine if their current form of short-term therapy substantially reduces depression. Prior to treatment, each patient will be asked to complete the Acme Depression Inventory (ADI), which renders a score from 0 to 75 (0 = low depression . . . 75 = high depression). Patients will also be asked to complete the same instrument at the conclusion of their final appointment.

Codebook—set up SPSS to contain three variables:

- *ID* is an alphanumeric (string) variable (the patient's initials).
- *pretest* is a continuous variable (ADI score before therapy).
- *posttest* is a continuous variable (ADI score after therapy).

Data set—enter Data Set A.

Data Set A			
Rec. #	*ID*	*pretest*	*posttest*
1	CD	48	45
2	FM	37	31
3	DL	57	62
4	CC	59	54
5	HA	67	66
6	TH	51	46
7	MG	56	61
8	LM	51	48
9	KB	64	70
10	EC	54	48
11	KM	58	53
12	SM	50	46
13	MF	51	57
14	GA	42	41
15	BK	72	72
16	JB	53	49
17	JP	41	41
18	QT	58	54

Data Set B			
Rec. #	*ID*	*pretest*	*posttest*
1	PO	68	66
2	NT	70	65
3	YK	70	66
4	NA	69	65
5	PP	67	61
6	TB	69	66
7	SG	73	77
8	HC	69	68
9	SD	70	68
10	SB	71	67
11	DH	67	65
12	BC	68	67
13	AJ	70	71
14	TS	73	63
15	LI	73	73

a. Write the hypotheses.
b. Run the criteria of the pretest checklist (normality for *posttest – pretest*) and discuss your findings.
c. Run the paired *t* test and document your findings (means and Sig. [*p* value]).
d. Write an abstract under 200 words detailing a summary of the study, the paired *t* test results, hypothesis resolution, and implications of your findings.

- Repeat this exercise using Data Set B.

5. The staff of the Physical Education Department wants to know if providing a single 15-minute individual coaching session with an expert bowler will enhance students' bowling scores. Each participant will bowl one game, during which time the coach will unobtrusively observe his or her bowling style. Then, the coach provides the 15-minute coaching session. Finally, the student bowls a second game. The scores from both games are recorded.

Codebook—set up SPSS to contain three variables:

- *ID* is an alphanumeric (string) variable (the bowler's first name).
- *pretest* is a continuous variable (score from first game).
- *posttest* is a continuous variable (score from second game).

Data set—enter Data Set A.

Data Set A			
Rec. #	ID	pretest	posttest
1	Bob	134	134
2	Lori	148	154
3	Pete	161	159
4	Mike	144	160
5	Rob	132	148
6	Marty	166	170
7	Don	158	157
8	Peggy	175	171
9	Marie	146	151
10	Jim	150	159
11	John A.	152	160
12	Dale	142	155
13	Kate	187	195
14	John E.	136	149
15	Elaine	143	144

Data Set B			
Rec. #	ID	pretest	posttest
1	Jake	71	72
2	Jon	74	75
3	Chad	73	75
4	Lynn	73	79
5	Stuart	72	66
6	Todd	70	74
7	Duncan	67	76
8	Sue	80	77

a. Write the hypotheses.
b. Run the criteria of the pretest checklist (normality for *posttest − pretest*) and discuss your findings.

    c. Run the paired *t* test and document your findings (means and Sig. [*p* value]).

    d. Write an abstract under 200 words detailing a summary of the study, the paired *t* test results, hypothesis resolution, and implications of your findings.

- Repeat this exercise using Data Set B.

6. The administrators of a school want to determine if issuing students laptop computers will enhance their grades. At the beginning of the academic term, each student in a class was issued a laptop computer. At the end of the term, the grade point average (GPA) for each student was gathered at two time points: the GPA for the term before issuing the laptop and the current GPA.

Codebook—the data set contains three variables:

- *ID* is an alphanumeric (string) variable (the student's ID).
- *pretest* is a continuous variable (GPA for term before issuing computers).
- *posttest* is a continuous variable (GPA for term after issuing computers).

Data set—load *Chapter 07 – Exercise 06 A.sav.*

    a. Write the hypotheses.

    b. Run the criteria of the pretest checklist (normality for *posttest – pretest*) and discuss your findings.

    c. Run the paired *t* test and document your findings (means and Sig. [*p* value]).

    d. Write an abstract under 200 words detailing a summary of the study, the paired *t* test results, hypothesis resolution, and implications of your findings.

- Repeat this exercise using *Chapter 07 – Exercise 06 B.sav.*

7. Acme Brand allergy medicine claims that its product reduces allergy-related sneezing. To test this claim, you recruit a group of allergy sufferers who are not currently taking any medications for their allergies and ask them to count the number of times they sneeze per day. The next day, each participant takes the Acme allergy medicine in the morning as directed and keeps a (separate) sneeze tally for that day too.

Codebook—the data set contains three variables:

- *ID* is an alphanumeric (string) variable (the participant's ID).
- *pretest* is a continuous variable (number of sneezes per day before taking allergy medicine).
- *posttest* is a continuous variable (number of sneezes per day after taking allergy medicine).

Data set—load *Chapter 07 – Exercise 07 A.sav.*

    a. Write the hypotheses.

    b. Run the criteria of the pretest checklist (normality for *posttest – pretest*) and discuss your findings.

   c. Run the paired *t* test and document your findings (means and Sig. [*p* value]).

   d. Write an abstract under 200 words detailing a summary of the study, the paired *t* test results, hypothesis resolution, and implications of your findings.

- Repeat this exercise using *Chapter 07 – Exercise 07 B.sav.*

8. An herbalist interested in natural remedies wants to assess the effectiveness of the Tutsle root (a fictitious plant) in reducing fever. The investigator recruits a group of patients who have fever and records the temperature for each person. Next, each participant is given one cup of Tutsle root tea. An hour later, the investigator takes each participant's temperature again.

Codebook—the data set contains three variables:

- *ID* is an alphanumeric (string) variable (the participant's ID).
- *pretest* is a continuous variable (participant's temperature before drinking Tutsle root tea).
- *posttest* is a continuous variable (participant's temperature 1 hour after drinking Tutsle root tea).

Data set—load *Chapter 07 – Exercise 08 A.sav.*

   a. Write the hypotheses.

   b. Run the criteria of the pretest checklist (normality for *posttest – pretest*) and discuss your findings.

   c. Run the paired *t* test and document your findings (means and Sig. [*p* value]).

   d. Write an abstract under 200 words detailing a summary of the study, the paired *t* test results, hypothesis resolution, and implications of your findings.

- Repeat this exercise using *Chapter 07 – Exercise 08 B.sav.*

9. In an effort to discover ways to boost morale, an investigator wants to assess the effects that chocolate has on attitude. The researcher recruits a group of participants and has them complete the Acme Attitude Survey (AAS), which renders a score ranging from 0 to 100 (0 = very bad attitude . . . 100 = very good attitude). After gathering the (pre)tests, the researcher serves each participant a generous slice of chocolate fudge cake. One hour later, the researcher administers the AAS a second time.

Codebook—the data set contains three variables:

- *ID* is an alphanumeric (string) variable (the participant's ID).
- *pretest* is a continuous variable (AAS score before eating chocolate).
- *posttest* is a continuous variable (AAS score 1 hour after eating chocolate).

Data set—load *Chapter 07 – Exercise 09 A.sav.*

   a. Write the hypotheses.

   b. Run the criteria of the pretest checklist (normality for *posttest – pretest*) and discuss your findings.

      c. Run the paired *t* test and document your findings (means and Sig. [*p* value]).

      d. Write an abstract under 200 words detailing a summary of the study, the paired *t* test results, hypothesis resolution, and implications of your findings.

      • Repeat this exercise using *Chapter 07 – Exercise 09 B.sav.*

10. A political consultant wants to judge the impact of a speech. The consultant recruits a group of registered voters and asks them to indicate their voting intentions on a 1 to 7 scale (1 = absolutely will not vote for this candidate . . . 7 = absolutely will vote for this candidate). Next, the candidate delivers the speech. Finally, the consultant readministers the one-question survey to each participant.

Codebook—the data set contains three variables:

      • *ID* is an alphanumeric (string) variable (the participant's ID).

      • *pretest* is a continuous variable (voter's score before speech).

      • *posttest* is a continuous variable (voter's score after speech).

Data set—load *Chapter 07 – Exercise 10 A.sav.*

      a. Write the hypotheses.

      b. Run the criteria of the pretest checklist (normality for *posttest – pretest*) and discuss your findings.

      c. Run the paired *t* test and document your findings (means and Sig. [*p* value]).

      d. Write an abstract under 200 words detailing a summary of the study, the paired *t* test results, hypothesis resolution, and implications of your findings.

      • Repeat this exercise using *Chapter 07 – Exercise 10 B.sav.*

CHAPTER 8

Correlation and Regression

Wanna see the correlation between two continuous variables? Run a regression.

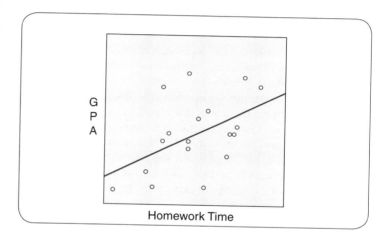

He who laughs most, learns best.

—John Cleese

LEARNING OBJECTIVES

Upon completing this chapter, you will be able to:

- Determine when it is appropriate to run regression and correlational analyses
- Interpret the direction and strength of a correlation
- Verify that the data meet the criteria for running regression and correlational analyses: normality, linearity, and homoscedasticity
- Order a regression analysis: correlation and scatterplot with regression line
- Interpret the test results
- Resolve the hypotheses
- Document the results in plain English
- Understand the criteria for causation: association/correlation, temporality, and nonspurious
- Differentiate between *correlation* and *causation*

DIGITAL LEARNING RESOURCES

The tutorial video and data sets for this chapter are at: www.sagepub.com/knapp

- Regression and correlation pretest checklist video
- Regression and correlation test run video
- SPSS files

OVERVIEW

Regression involves assessing the correlation between two variables. Before proceeding, let us deconstruct the word *correlation:* The prefix *co* means *two*—hence, correlation is about the relationship between two things. *Regression* is about assessing the correlation between two continuous variables.

Correlation involving two variables, sometimes referred to as *bivariate correlation,* is notated using the lowercase *r* and has a value between −1 and +1. Correlations have two primary attributes: direction and strength.

Direction is indicated by the sign of the *r* value: − or +. *Positive correlations* (*r* = 0 . . . +1) emerge when the two variables move in the same direction. For example, we would expect that low homework hours would correlate with low grade point average (GPA), just as we would expect that high homework hours would correlate with high GPA. *Negative correlations* (*r* = −1 . . . 0) emerge when the two variables move in different directions. For example, we would expect that high alcohol consumption would correlate with low GPA, just as we would expect that low alcohol consumption would correlate with high GPA (see Table 8.1).

Strength is indicated by the numeric value. A correlation wherein the *r* is close to 0 is considered weaker than those nearer to −1 or +1 (see Figure 8.1). Continuing with the prior example, we would expect to find a strong negative correlation between alcohol consumption and GPA (e.g., *r* = −.81); conversely, we would expect to find a strong positive correlation between homework hours and GPA (e.g., *r* = +.81). However, we would not expect that a variable such as height would have much to do with academic

Table 8.1 Correlation Direction Summary

Correlation (*r*) Direction Summary		
Correlation	*r*	Variable directions
Positive	0 . . . +1	X↑ Y↑ or X↓ Y↓
Negative	−1 . . . 0	X↑ Y↓ or X↓ Y↑

Figure 8.1   Correlation Strength Summary

Correlation (*r*) Strength Summary

−1   0   +1

Strong   Weak   Strong

performance, and hence we would expect to find a relatively weak correlation between height and GPA (e.g., *r* = +.02 or *r* = −.02).

The concepts of correlation *direction* and *strength* will become clearer as we examine the test results, specifically upon inspecting the graph of the scatterplot with the regression line in the Results section.

EXAMPLE

One might intuit that there is a correlation between the number of hours a student spends doing homework per week and his or her GPA. An instructor wants to investigate this.

RESEARCH QUESTION

Is there a statistically significant correlation between homework hours per week and GPA?

GROUPS

Bivariate regression/correlation involves only one group, but two different continuous variables are gathered for each participant: In this case, the variables are (1) homework hours per week and (2) GPA.

Notice that in correlation analysis, you can mix apples and oranges; homework hours is a measure of *time,* whereas GPA is a measure of *academic performance.* The only constraints in this respect are that the two metrics must both be continuous variables, and of course, the comparison needs to inherently make sense.

PROCEDURE

The instructor will record two values for each student for a week: total number of hours spent on homework (as reported by the student's parent) and the GPA for that week based on a multisubject test given on Friday afternoon.

HYPOTHESES

H_0: There is no correlation between homework hours and GPA

H_1: There is a positive correlation between homework hours and GPA.

H_2: There is a negative correlation between homework hours and GPA.

DATA SET

Use the following data set: *Chapter 08 – Example 01 – Correlation & Regression.sav*.

For clarity, notice that the *name* of each participant is coded to demonstrate that *homework hours* and *GPA* data are recorded for each subject.

PRETEST CHECKLIST

The pretest criteria for running a correlation/regression involve checking the data for (1) normality, (2) linearity, and (3) homoscedasticity (pronounced *hoe-moe-skuh-daz-tis-city*).

Pretest Checklist Criterion 1—Normality

The two variables involved in the correlation/regression each need to be inspected for normality. To do this, generate separate histograms with normal curves for *homework* and *gpa* (this is similar to the steps used to check for normality when using the *t* test and ANOVA).

For more details on this procedure, please refer to Chapter 4 ("SPSS—Descriptive Statistics: Continuous Variables (Age)"); see the star (★) icon on page **61**. Instead of processing *age,* load the two variables: *homework* and *gpa*. Alternatively, the following steps will produce a histogram with a normal curve for homework and GPA:

1. From the main screen, select *Analyze / Descriptive Statistics / Frequencies . . .* ; this will take you to the *Frequencies* menu.

2. On the *Frequencies* menu, move *homework* and *gpa* from the left window to the right (*Variables*) window. With the data in this configuration, you can order both histograms at the same time.

3. Click on the *Charts . . .* button; this will take you to the *Charts* menu.

4. Click on the *Histograms* button, and check the *Show normal curve on histogram* checkbox.

5. Click on the *Continue* button; this will return you to the *Frequencies* menu.

Figure 8.2	Histogram With a Normal Curve for Homework

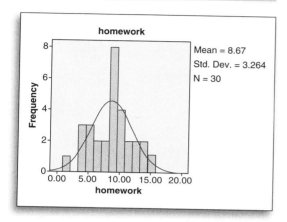

Figure 8.3	Histogram With a Normal Curve for GPA

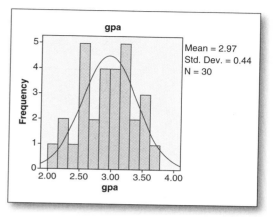

6. Click on the *OK* button, and the system will produce (two) histograms with normal curves for homework and GPA (Figures 8.2 and 8.3).

The curves on each histogram are reasonably symmetrically bell shaped; there is no notable skewing, and hence these criteria are satisfied.

Linearity and homoscedasticity are both graphical in nature; they are read off the scatterplot with the regression line. We will observe and discuss the findings for these two remaining criteria in the Results section.

 TEST RUN

The test run for correlation and regression is a two-part process; first we will process the correlation table, which will render the correlation value (*r*) and the corresponding *p* value. Next, we will order a *scatterplot,* which will provide a clear graph showing the paired points from both variables plotted on an *X, Y*-axes along with the *regression line,* sometimes referred to as a *trend line,* which can be thought of as the average pathway through the points.

Correlation

1. To run a correlation, starting from the main screen click on *Analyze* (Figure 8.4).

2. Click on *Correlate.*

3. Click on *Bivariate . . . ;* this will take you to the *Correlate* menu (Figure 8.5).

Figure 8.4 Accessing the *Correlation* Menu: *Analyze, Correlate, Bivariate . . .*

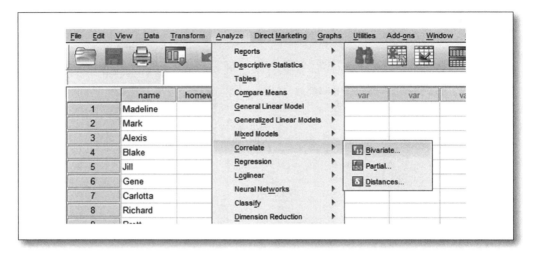

Figure 8.5 Accessing the *Correlation* Menu: *Analyze, Correlate, Bivariate . . .*

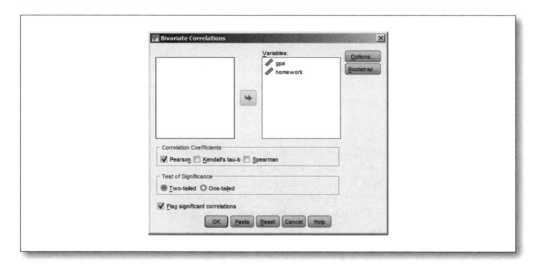

4. On the *Correlate* menu (Figure 8.5), move the GPA and homework variables from the left window to the right (*Variables*) window.

5. Click the *OK* button, and the correlation will process. For now, set aside the correlations table that is produced; we will interpret it in the Results section.

Scatterplot With Regression Line

NOTE: SPSS graphics processing menus tend to differ across versions. If these instructions do not fit your version of the software, use the *Help* menu to guide you to order a scatterplot with the regression line. Indicate that you want the *homework* variable on the *X*-axis and the *GPA* variable on the *Y*-axis.

6. To order a scatterplot with a regression line, from the main menu, click on *Graphs* (Figure 8.6).

7. Click on *Chart Builder . . . .* This will bring you to the *Chart Builder* menu (Figure 8.7).

Figure 8.6 Accessing the Chart Builder Menu: *Graphics, Chart Builder . . .*

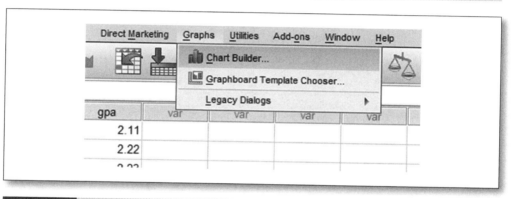

Figure 8.7 *Chart Builder* Menu

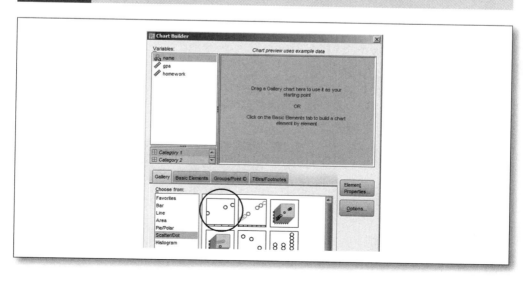

8. In the *Choose from:* list, click on *Scatter/Dot* (Figure 8.7).

9. Double-click on the (circled) first choice, or click and drag this icon to the *Chart preview uses example data* window.

10. Click and drag *homework* from the *Variables* window to the *X-Axis?* box (Figure 8.8).

11. Click and drag *gpa* from the *Variables* window to the *Y-Axis?* box.

12. Click on the *OK* button, and the system will produce the scatterplot.

Figure 8.8	*Chart Builder* Menu—Assign *homework* to X-axis and *gpa* to Y-axis

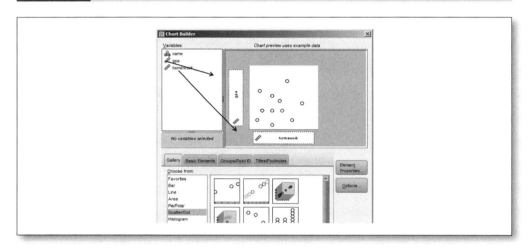

13. When the scatterplot emerges, you will need to order the regression line: In the *Output* window, double-click on the scatterplot. This will bring you to the *Chart Editor* (Figure 8.9).

Figure 8.9	*Chart Editor* Menu—Click on *Add Fit Line at Total* Icon to Include the Regression Line on the Scatterplot

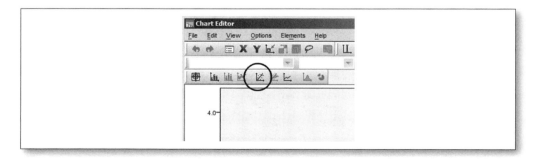

14. Click on the *Add Fit Line at Total* icon to include the regression line on the scatterplot.

15. When you see the regression line emerge on the scatterplot, close the *Chart Editor* and you will see that the regression line is now included on the scatterplot in the *Output* window.

RESULTS

In this section, we will begin by explaining the two elements present on the scatterplot: the points and the regression line. Next, we will finalize the two remaining pretest criteria (linearity and homoscedasticity), and finally, we will discuss the overall meaning of the scatterplot and correlation findings.

Scatterplot Points

The coordinates of each point on the scatterplot is derived from the two variables: homework and GPA for each record (individual).

Figure 8.10 Source Data for Scatterplot

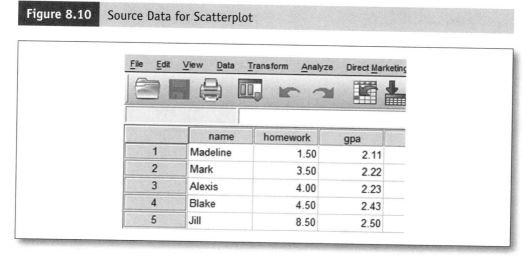

The first record of the data set shows that Madeline did homework for 1.5 hours and her GPA was 2.11 (Figure 8.10). When we ordered the histogram, we placed *homework* on the *X*-axis and *gpa* on the *Y*-axis—hence, Madeline's point on the scatterplot is at coordinates (1.50, 2.11), Mark's point on the scatterplot is at (3.50, 2.22), and so on.

Scatterplot Regression Line

The simplest way to conceive the regression line, without presenting the formula, is to think of it as the average straight-line pathway through the cloud of points, based on their positions. Just as the descriptive statistics provide a summary of a single variable, the regression line provides a sort of graphical summary of two variables—in this case, homework and GPA.

NOTE: We already covered Pretest Checklist Criterion 1—normality of distribution of the two variables, homework and GPA, via the histograms with normal curves; now we will assess the remaining pretest checklist criteria: (2) linearity and (3) homoscedasticity.

Pretest Checklist Criterion 2—Linearity

The points on the scatterplot should form a relatively straight line (Figure 8.11); the regression line should take a middle-of-the-road path through the cloud of points. If the overall shape of the points departs into some other shape(s) that is not conducive to drawing a straight (regression) line through (Figure 8.12), then this would constitute a violation of the linearity assumption.

Figure 8.11	Linearity Satisfied

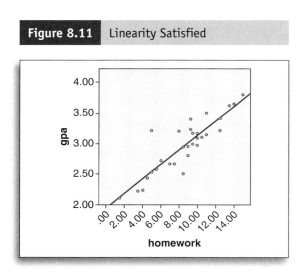

Figure 8.12	Linearity Violated

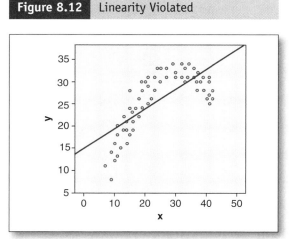

Pretest Checklist Criterion 3—Homoscedasticity

Homoscedasticity pertains to the *density* of the points along the regression line. The criterion of homoscedasticity is satisfied when the cloud of points is densest in the middle and tapers off at the ends (Figure 8.13). The rationale for this distribution of points on the scatterplot follows the same notion as the shape of the normal curve of the histogram— the majority of the values are gathered around the mean, which accounts for the height of the normal bell-shaped curve on the histogram, whereas the tapered tails signify that there are considerably fewer very low and very high values. The positions of the points on the scatterplot are derived from the same data that rendered the normally distributed histograms for the two variables (Figures 8.13 and 8.14), so it follows that the middle of the cloud should contain considerably more points (and be denser) than the ends.

| **Figure 8.13** | Homoscedasticity Satisfied |

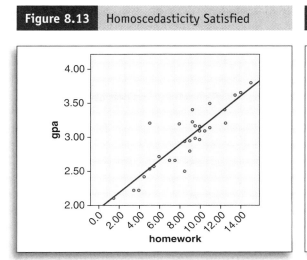

| **Figure 8.14** | Homoscedasticity Violated |

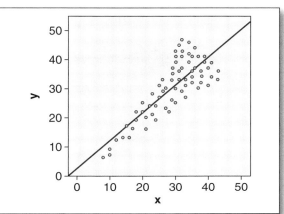

Correlation

Table 8.2 shows a positive correlation ($r = .881$) between homework and GPA, with a p value of .000. Actually, there is no such thing as a p value that equals zero; in this case, $p = .0000000001385$. When the p value is less than .01, it is typically notated as $p < .001$. Since the p value is less than the α level of .05, we would say that there is a statistically significant correlation between homework (hours) and GPA. The positive correlation ($r = .881$) pertains to the positive slope of the regression line.

| **Table 8.2** | Correlations Between Homework and GPA |

Correlations

		gpa	homework
gpa	Pearson Correlation	1	.881**
	Sig. (2-tailed)		.000
	N	30	30
homework	Pearson Correlation	.881**	1
	Sig. (2-tailed)	.000	
	N	30	30

**. Correlation is significant at the 0.01 level (2-tailed).

Notice that the correlations table is double-redundant; there are two .881s and two .000s in the table. This is because the correlation between homework and GPA is the same as the correlation between GPA and homework. A larger image of the corresponding graph (scatterplot with regression line) is shown in Figure 8.15.

Figure 8.15   Scatterplot With Regression Line for the Homework-GPA Correlation

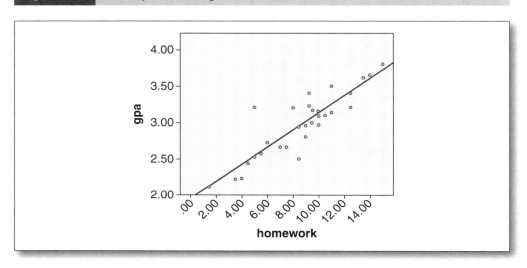

The points clearly plot the intersection between each student's homework hours and his or her corresponding GPA. The regression line can be thought of as the average pathway through the cloud of points, or a linear summary of the points.

Another way to think about this graph is to consider the regression line as a predictive pathway. For example, if you drew a vertical line from 8.00 on the homework (X) axis up, you would see that it would intersect the regression line at about 3.0 on the GPA (Y) axis. Since we know that this is a statistically significant correlation, we can use this chart as a viable predictor—we would predict that for a student who did homework for about 8 hours a week, we would expect to see a corresponding GPA of about 3.0.

HYPOTHESIS RESOLUTION

Since the correlation calculation produced a p ($p < .001$) that is less than the specified .05 α level, we would say that there is a statistically significant (positive) correlation between homework and GPA. As such, we would reject H_0 and H_2 but not reject H_1.

DOCUMENT RESULTS

We were interested in discovering if there was a correlation between the number of hours of homework a student did in a week and his or her GPA for that week. Correlation analysis revealed a strong positive correlation between these two variables ($r = .881$), which was statistically significant ($p < .001$) using an α level of .05.

GOOD COMMON SENSE

Even though a statistically significant, strong positive correlation was found between homework and GPA, it is presumptuous to simply claim that homework hours (and nothing else) *caused* the GPA. An underlying unaccounted-for factor that would not be revealed by correlation analysis may be responsible for affecting homework hours, which, in turn, may have affected GPA. For example, an adverse factor (e.g., household stress, health problem, adverse social issue, etc.) may be cutting into the student's ability to engage in longer homework hours; conversely, a pleasurable factor may be detracting from homework time (e.g., great social circle, multiple extracurricular activities, compelling videogames, etc.).

Alternatively, an overarching factor may affect both homework and GPA, such as an undiagnosed learning disability, depression, exhaustion, and so forth.

The point is that correlation, no matter what the *r* or the *p,* is just that—correlation; try to avoid jumping to conclusions regarding causation.

 ## Correlation vs. Causation

Correlation only means that two variables appear to move in a predictable fashion with respect to each other (e.g., when one goes up, the other goes up; when one goes down, the other goes down; or when one goes up, the other goes down), but keep in mind, this is not necessarily due to *causation,* which would involve the change in one variable *causing* the change in the other. To make the leap from correlation to causation, three criteria must be met: (1) association/correlation, (2) temporality (meaning timing), and (3) nonspurious (meaning authentic) (Table 8.3):

Admittedly, the criteria to claim causation are strict, but without this rigor, numerous spurious correlations could be wrongly attributed to causality, leading to inappropriate conclusions and potentially misguided interventions.

Table 8.3 Three Criteria for Satisfying Causality

Criteria	Rule	Example
1 Association/ correlation	Variables A and B must be empirically related; there must be a (scientific) logical relationship between A and B.	Taking a dose of aspirin lowers fever.
2 Temporality	A (cause [independent variable]) precedes B (effect [dependent variable]).	The person took aspirin, and *then* the fever went down, not the other way around.
3 Nonspurious	The relationship between A and B is not caused by other variable(s).	The drop in fever is not due to the room getting colder, submerging the person in an ice bath, or other factors.

For example, one might find a positive correlation between chocolate milk consumption and automobile theft—as chocolate milk sales go up, so do car thefts. Instead of concluding that chocolate milk causes people to steal cars or that car theft causes one to crave chocolate milk, anyone reasonable would continue their investigation and probably discover that *population* may be a variable worth consideration: In a town with a population of 2,000, we would find low chocolate milk sales and few car thefts, whereas in a city with a population of 2,000,000, chocolate milk sales and car thefts would both be considerably higher. In this case, we would be free to notice the positive correlation between chocolate milk consumption and car theft, but the causal criteria between these two variables clearly break down at all three levels.

Key Concepts

- Correlation
  - Strength
  - Direction
- Normality
- Linearity
- Homoscedasticity
- Bivariate correlation
- Scatterplot
- Regression
- *r*
- *p*
- Correlation vs. causation

Practice Exercises

1. An exercise advocate wants to determine the effect that walking rigorously has on weight loss. The researcher recruits participants to engage in a weeklong study. The researcher instructs participants to take a brisk walk as many days of the week as possible for as long as they can. Participants will record the following data: weight prior to engaging in the walking regimen, the amount of time walked each day, and their weight at the end of the week. Participants will submit their data to the researcher at the end of the week. The researcher will preprocess the data to derive the total number of hours walked (*walkhrs*) and the change in weight for each participant (*wtloss* = weight at the end of the week – weight at the beginning of the week).

   Codebook—set up SPSS to contain two variables:
   - *walkhrs* is a continuous variable (number of hours walked in a week).
   - *wtloss* is a continuous variable (number of pounds lost in a week).

Data set—enter Data Set A.

NOTE: In Data Set A, Record 3, notice that the weight loss (*wtloss*) is −1.00; this indicates that the participant *gained* 1 pound. Data Set B, Record 16 also signifies a half-pound weight *gain* for that participant.

Data Set A				Data Set B		
Rec. #	walkhrs	wtloss		Rec. #	walkhrs	wtloss
1	3.50	2.50		1	4.50	3.00
2	3.75	1.30		2	6.25	2.25
3	1.10	−1.00		3	5.75	1.25
4	2.50	2.60		4	4.50	0.75
5	2.00	0.00		5	6.25	1.75
6	4.75	1.60		6	11.00	0.75
7	6.25	1.30		7	8.25	3.50
8	6.75	0.50		8	5.00	0.00
9	6.25	2.60		9	4.75	1.75
10	4.25	0.70		10	4.25	0.50
11	2.50	0.20		11	9.25	2.00
12	8.50	3.10		12	6.75	2.00
13	8.25	2.80		13	1.25	1.50
14	4.00	1.30		14	7.00	2.00
15	4.00	0.50		15	5.00	2.00
16	7.25	2.70		16	4.00	−0.50
17	5.00	1.90		17	6.50	2.50
18	4.25	2.60		18	6.25	1.10

a. Write the hypotheses.
b. Run the criteria of the pretest checklist (normality [for both variables], linearity, homoscedasticity) and discuss your findings.
c. Run the bivariate correlation and the scatterplot with regression line and document your findings (r and Sig. [p value]).
d. Write an abstract under 200 words detailing a summary of the study, the bivariate correlation, hypothesis resolution, and implications of your findings.
   • Repeat this exercise using Data Set B.

2. A social scientist has noticed that people seem to be spending a lot of nonwork hours on computers and wants to determine if this may, in some way, be associated with social relationship satisfaction (satisfaction derived from interacting with others). To determine if there is a correlation between nonwork computer hours and social satisfaction, the scientist recruited a group of participants and asked them to indicate (about) how many nonwork hours they spend on the computer each week. Next, each participant was given the Acme Social Satisfaction Inventory (ASSI); this self-administered instrument renders a score between 0 and 80 (0 = very low social satisfaction . . . 80 = very high social satisfaction).

Codebook—set up SPSS to contain two variables:

- *comphrs* is a continuous variable (number of nonwork hours spent on computer per week).
- *assi* is a continuous variable (Acme Social Satisfaction Inventory).

Data set—enter Data Set A.

Data Set A		
Rec. #	comphrs	assi
1	23.00	51
2	6.00	31
3	25.00	35
4	21.50	53
5	26.75	56
6	13.50	61
7	9.00	56
8	16.75	65
9	29.00	96
10	16.00	42
11	18.00	67
12	15.00	54
13	9.25	67
14	23.50	52
15	20.25	83

Data Set B		
Rec. #	comphrs	assi
1	21.00	69
2	16.25	70
3	9.00	96
4	22.25	54
5	18.75	80
6	22.00	61
7	29.25	21
8	14.00	65
9	24.75	52
10	24.00	62
11	16.50	77
12	25.50	48
13	8.00	53
14	23.25	62
15	14.00	74

16	21.00	77
17	22.00	57
18	23.25	65
19	21.00	53
20	21.00	61

16	18.00	54
17	18.75	59
18	24.00	51
19	16.00	45
20	16.50	31
21	22.50	44
22	14.00	59
23	20.00	65

a. Write the hypotheses.

b. Run the criteria of the pretest checklist (normality [for both variables], linearity, and homoscedasticity) and discuss your findings.

c. Run the bivariate correlation and the scatterplot with regression line and document your findings (r and Sig. [p value]).

d. Write an abstract under 200 words detailing a summary of the study, the bivariate correlation, hypothesis resolution, and implications of your findings.
   • Repeat this exercise using Data Set B.

3. A social scientist and an economist working together want to discover if there is a correlation between income and happiness. The researchers recruit a group of participants and ask them to complete a confidential survey. This self-administered survey asks for the participant's annual income; it also includes the Acme Life Happiness Scale (ALHS), which renders a score between 0 and 100 (0 = very unhappy . . . 100 = very happy).

Codebook—set up SPSS to contain two variables:

• *income* is a continuous variable (annual income in dollars rounded to nearest thousand).

• *alhs* is a continuous variable (Acme Life Happiness Scale).

Data set—enter Data Set A.

Data Set A		
Rec. #	*income*	*alhs*
1	72,000	75
2	101,000	56
3	85,000	72

Data Set B		
Rec. #	*income*	*alhs*
1	42,000	31
2	44,000	62
3	35,000	49

4	42,000	89		4	69,000	28
5	116,000	66		5	41,000	61
6	75,000	73		6	55,000	65
7	60,000	71		7	53,000	64
8	122,000	42		8	66,000	71
9	89,000	55		9	39,000	52
10	91,000	73		10	65,000	69
11	90,000	66		11	67,000	38
12	57,000	71		12	58,000	67
13	22,000	48		13	32,000	47
14	87,000	81		14	50,000	63
15	67,000	88		15	43,000	61
16	25,000	75		16	68,000	77
17	34,000	48		17	74,000	81
18	103,000	96		18	75,000	83
				19	80,000	67
				20	68,000	77
				21	68,000	79

a. Write the hypotheses.

b. Run the criteria of the pretest checklist (normality [for both variables], linearity, and homoscedasticity) and discuss your findings.

c. Run the bivariate correlation and the scatterplot with regression line and document your findings (r and Sig. [p value]).

d. Write an abstract under 200 words detailing a summary of the study, the bivariate correlation, hypothesis resolution, and implications of your findings.

   • Repeat this exercise using Data Set B.

4. A political scientist wants to find out if there is a correlation between listening to a newscast and an individual's mood. This researcher recruits a group of participants and has them listen to a newscast that was recorded earlier that morning. Participants are instructed to listen for as long as they want; when they are done listening, the researcher writes down the listening duration and then

asks each participant to complete the Acme Mood Report (AMR), a self-administered instrument that renders a score between 0 and 100 (0 = very bad mood . . . 100 = very good mood).

Codebook—set up SPSS to contain two variables:

- *minnews* is a continuous variable (number of minutes of news listened to).
- *amr* is a continuous variable (Acme Mood Report).

Data set—enter Data Set A.

Data Set A		
Rec. #	minnews	amr
1	17	74
2	20	70
3	23	50
4	27	68
5	30	54
6	31	57
7	35	63
8	38	69
9	39	59
10	41	54
11	42	58
12	47	57
13	48	51
14	55	40

Data Set B		
Rec. #	minnews	amr
1	48	59
2	24	40
3	39	38
4	59	52
5	51	55
6	33	46
7	44	55
8	40	42
9	62	61
10	39	66

a. Write the hypotheses.
b. Run the criteria of the pretest checklist (normality [for both variables], linearity, and homoscedasticity) and discuss your findings.
c. Run the bivariate correlation and the scatterplot with regression line and document your findings (r and Sig. [p value]).
d. Write an abstract under 200 words detailing a summary of the study, the bivariate correlation, hypothesis resolution, and implications of your findings.
- Repeat this exercise using Data Set B.

5. An educational scientist wants to examine the correlation between years of education and job satisfaction. To address this question, the scientist recruits a group of participants and has each complete a self-administered survey; the first question asks how many years of education the participant has (e.g., 12 = high school diploma, 14 = associate's degree, 16 = bachelor's degree, 18 = master's degree). The remaining questions consist of the Acme Job Satisfaction Index (AJSI), which produces a score between 0 and 60 (0 = very unsatisfied with job . . . 60 = very satisfied with job).

Codebook—set up SPSS to contain two variables:

- *yearsed* is a continuous variable (number of years of education).
- *ajsi* is a continuous variable (Acme Job Satisfaction Index).

Data set—enter Data Set A.

Data Set A		
Rec. #	yearsed	ajsi
1	17	48
2	16	17
3	16	40
4	16	36
5	12	22
6	16	45
7	20	48
8	14	46
9	18	52
10	12	41
11	16	36
12	20	52
13	18	40
14	11	15
15	19	42
16	20	53

Data Set B		
Rec. #	yearsed	ajsi
1	17	37
2	16	40
3	16	34
4	16	35
5	12	30
6	16	42
7	20	44
8	14	42
9	18	26
10	12	38
11	16	40
12	20	49
13	18	27
14	11	41
15	19	45

a. Write the hypotheses.
b. Run the criteria of the pretest checklist (normality [for both variables], linearity, and homoscedasticity) and discuss your findings.
c. Run the bivariate correlation and the scatterplot with regression line and document your findings (*r* and Sig. [*p* value]).
d. Write an abstract under 200 words detailing a summary of the study, the bivariate correlation, hypothesis resolution, and implications of your findings.
  • Repeat this exercise using Data Set B.

6. A dietician wants to discover if there is a correlation between age and number of meals eaten outside the home. The dietician recruits participants and administers a two-question survey: (1) How old are you? and (2) How many times do you eat out (meals not eaten at home) in an average week?

Codebook—the data set contains two variables:
  • *age* is a continuous variable (age of participant).
  • *mealsout* is a continuous variable (number of meals out participant eats per week).

Data set—load *Chapter 08 – Exercise 06 A.sav.*

a. Write the hypotheses.
b. Run the criteria of the pretest checklist (normality [for both variables], linearity, and homoscedasticity) and discuss your findings.
c. Run the bivariate correlation and the scatterplot with regression line and document your findings (*r* and Sig. [*p* value]).
d. Write an abstract under 200 words detailing a summary of the study, the bivariate correlation, hypothesis resolution, and implications of your findings.
  • Repeat this exercise using *Chapter 08 – Exercise 06 B.sav.*

7. A social scientist wants to determine if a person's height might be correlated with his or her sense of self-confidence. To explore this, the scientist recruits a group of participants and gathers two metrics: First the researcher administers the Acme Self-Confidence Instrument (ASCI), a self-administered survey that produces a score between 0 and 50 (0 = very low self-confidence . . . 50 = very high self-confidence). Second, the scientist measures the height of each participant.

Codebook—the data set contains two variables:
  • *height* is a continuous variable (height of participant).
  • *asci* is a continuous variable (Acme Self-Confidence Instrument score).

Data set—load *Chapter 08 – Exercise 07 A.sav.*

a. Write the hypotheses.
b. Run the criteria of the pretest checklist (normality [for both variables], linearity, and homoscedasticity) and discuss your findings.
c. Run the bivariate correlation and the scatterplot with regression line and document your findings (*r* and Sig. [*p* value]).

   d. Write an abstract under 200 words detailing a summary of the study, the bivariate correlation, hypothesis resolution, and implications of your findings.
   - Repeat this exercise using *Chapter 08 – Exercise 07 B.sav.*

8. A sociologist has learned from a prior study that there is a strong positive correlation between time spent playing a video game and the score the player earns on that game (practice makes perfect). Since achieving such proficiency is time-consuming, this sociologist expects that there may be a (negative) correlation between game score and GPA. To determine if there is such an inverse correlation, the sociologist recruits a group of participants to play a popular video game for 15 minutes, at which time the researcher records the score. Participants will also be asked to provide a copy of their most recent transcript.

   Codebook—the data set contains two variables:

   - *score* is a continuous variable (score on video game).
   - *gpa* is a continuous variable (GPA for the term).

   Data set—load *Chapter 08 – Exercise 08 A.sav.*

   a. Write the hypotheses.
   b. Run the criteria of the pretest checklist (normality [for both variables], linearity, and homoscedasticity) and discuss your findings.
   c. Run the bivariate correlation and the scatterplot with regression line and document your findings (*r* and Sig. [*p* value]).
   d. Write an abstract under 200 words detailing a summary of the study, the bivariate correlation, hypothesis resolution, and implications of your findings.
   - Repeat this exercise using *Chapter 08 – Exercise 08 B.sav.*

9. During a staff meeting, members of the English department discussed some of the differences they have observed in students (e.g., demeanor, participation, punctuality, etc.) enrolled in the freshman English course in the morning classes compared with those who attend the same course later in the day. The committee chair extracts a sample of data from the grade database for students who took freshman English over the past year and gathers two variables: time of class and grade earned.

   Codebook—the data set contains two variables:

   - *time* is a continuous variable (time of freshman English class: 800 = 8:00 a.m. . . . 1600 = 4:00 p.m.).
   - *grade* is a continuous variable (grade earned in freshman English class: 0 = F . . . 4 = A).

   Data set—load *Chapter 08 – Exercise 09 A.sav.*

   a. Write the hypotheses.
   b. Run the criteria of the pretest checklist (normality [for both variables], linearity, and homoscedasticity) and discuss your findings.

  c. Run the bivariate correlation and the scatterplot with regression line and document your findings (*r* and Sig. [*p* value]).

  d. Write an abstract under 200 words detailing a summary of the study, the bivariate correlation, hypothesis resolution, and implications of your findings.
   - Repeat this exercise using *Chapter 08 – Exercise 09 B.sav.*

10. A sociologist read an old study asserting that the number of children that an adult has tends to match the number of siblings they grew up with; the data were gathered from adults who were 35 years of age and older. To determine if this finding still holds true, the sociologist recruited a group of individuals who were at least 35 years old and asked each to respond to two questions: (1) How many brothers and sisters did you grow up with? and (2) How many children do you have?

  Codebook—the data set contains two variables:

  - *siblings* is a continuous variable (number of siblings the participant grew up with).
  - *children* is a continuous variable (number of children the participant has).

  Data set—load *Chapter 08 – Exercise 10 A.sav.*

  a. Write the hypotheses.

  b. Run the criteria of the pretest checklist (normality [for both variables], linearity, and homoscedasticity) and discuss your findings.

  c. Run the bivariate correlation and the scatterplot with regression line and document your findings (*r* and Sig. [*p* value]).

  d. Write an abstract under 200 words detailing a summary of the study, the bivariate correlation, hypothesis resolution, and implications of your findings.
   - Repeat this exercise using *Chapter 08 – Exercise 10 B.sav.*

C H A P T E R   9

Chi-Square

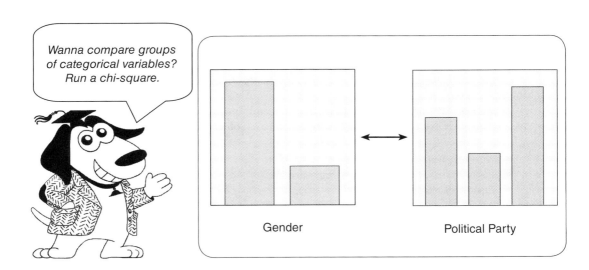

Some people are passionate about aisles, others about window seats.

—Terry Jones

LEARNING OBJECTIVES

Upon completing this chapter, you will be able to:

- Determine when it is appropriate to run a chi-square test
- Identify dichotomous and polychotomous variables
- Verify that the data meet the criteria for running a chi-square test: $n \geq 5$ per cell
- Order a chi-square test: table and bar chart
- Interpret the test results
- Resolve the hypotheses
- Document the results in plain English
- Calculate the % formula

DIGITAL LEARNING RESOURCES

The tutorial video and data sets for this chapter are at **www.sagepub.com/knapp**

- ANOVA test run video (provides details for pretest checklist)
- SPSS files

OVERVIEW

As we have seen, variables can be *continuous*, such as temperature, distance, weight, bank account balance, mood score, height, and grade point average (GPA). Alternatively, variables may be *categorical* (nominal), such as gender, race, religion, blood type, and marital status.

A categorical variable may consist of any number of categories. Variables that contain two categories are *dichotomous* (pronounced *die-cot-uh-muss*), such as

- Gender: female/male
- Voter status: registered/not registered
- Opinion: yes/no
- Attendance: present/absent
- Dwelling: house/apartment
- Grade: pass/fail

A categorical variable that contains more than two categories is *polychotomous* (pronounced *poly-cot-uh-muss*):

- Appointment status: on time/late/canceled/no-show/rescheduled
- Marital status: single/married/separated/divorced/widowed
- Ice cream flavor preference: chocolate/strawberry/vanilla
- Visual aids: none/glasses/contact lenses/surgical correction
- Transportation: train/plane/car/bus/taxi/motorcycle/bicycle/walk
- Blood type: A+/A–/B+/B–/AB+/AB–/O+/O–

The statistical function for comparing categorical variables to each other is the chi-square (*chi* is pronounced *k-eye*), sometimes written as χ^2 (χ is the Greek letter *chi*). Fortunately, the chi-square does not need you to specify how many categories are in each variable; it will derive that as part of the process. Chi-square can efficiently handle a mix of dichotomous and polychotomous variables.

The chi-square organizes the data from each categorical variable into a grid, compares the categories to each other, and produces a p value. If the chi-square produces a p value that is less than α (.05), this indicates that there is a statistically significant difference among the categories; alternatively, a p value greater than α (.05) indicates that no statistically significant differences among the categories exist.

Chi-square can be used to answer questions involving categorical variables, such as, Is *gender* (female/male) correlated with *ice cream preference* (chocolate/strawberry/vanilla)? In other words, do girls and boys tend to select the same ice cream flavors, or are there differences in their preferences? If the p value is less than α (.05), then we would say that there is a statistically significant difference between girls' ice cream preference and boys' ice cream preference (girls like different ice cream flavors from boys). Alternatively, if the p value is greater than the α (.05), then we would say that there is no statistically significant difference between the genders when it comes to ice cream selection (chocolate can be pretty compelling to both genders).

To recap, chi-square can be used to compare categorical variables with the same number of categories in each variable, such as gender (female/male) to opinion (yes/no), which would render a 2 × 2 chi-square table. Chi-square can also analyze categorical variables that have different category counts without having to specify any additional processing parameters, such as gender (female/male) to blood type (A+/A–/B+/B–/AB+/AB–/O+/O–). This chi-square test would produce a 2 × 8 or an 8 × 2 chi-square table, depending on how you choose to load the variables into rows and columns—either way, the analysis would produce equivalent results.

EXAMPLE

A political analyst is seeking to determine if gender is associated with political party affiliation.

RESEARCH QUESTION

Does gender have a bearing on political party affiliation, or are women and men fairly evenly distributed among the political parties?

GROUPS

When it comes to chi-square, it is not so much a matter of *groups* as *categories* within the variables. This inquiry involves two categorical variables: gender, which has two categories, and the party, which has three categories (notice that gender is dichotomous and party is polychotomous):

- Gender: female/male
- Party: Democrat/Republican/Other

PROCEDURE

The researcher will recruit a group of participants and ask each person to complete the following self-administered anonymous survey card:

Please check <u>one</u> answer for each question:

1. What is your gender:
   - ☐ Female
   - ☐ Male

2. What is your political party affiliation:
   - ☐ Democrat
   - ☐ Republican
   - ☐ Other

When completed, please drop this card in the response box.

Thank you for participating in this survey.

HYPOTHESES

H_0: There is no correlation between gender and political party affiliation.

H_1: There is a correlation between gender and political party affiliation.

DATA SET

Use the following data set: *Chapter 09 – Example 01 – Chi-Square.sav.*

This data set contains two categorical variables representing the data gathered from the participants' survey cards: gender (1 = female, 2 = male) and party (1 = Democrat, 2 = Republican, 3 = Other).

PRETEST CHECKLIST

Pretest Checklist Criterion 1—$n \geq 5$ per Cell Minimum

The chi-square will organize the categorical data from the variables into a table. It is easy to anticipate the dimensions of the table simply by multiplying the number of categories in each variable. In this case, gender has two categories (female/male), and party has three categories (Democrat/Republican/Other); hence, the chi-square table will consist of (2 × 3 =) 6 cells (Table 9.1).

Table 9.1	Chi-Square Table Basic Structure for Gender and Party Contains Six Cells		
	Democrat	Republican	Other
Female			
Male			

The pretest checklist rule for chi-square states that each cell should have at least 5 entries; initially, one might anticipate that the total *n* for this study should be 30 (6 cells × 5 per cell = 30). Actually, the total *n* will need to be more than 30, since a total *n* of 30 would presume that participants' responses will fill the six cells evenly (5 per cell). Since this is implausible, we should consider 30 as the *minimum* total *n;* we will require a total *n* of more than 30.

The chi-square report will show these counts for each cell, and hence we will be able to verify these criteria when we inspect the table in the Results section.

TEST RUN

1. From the main screen, click on *Analyze, Descriptive Statistics, Crosstabs . . .* (Figure 9.1); this will bring you to the *Crosstabs* menu (Figure 9.2).

Figure 9.1	Run the Chi-Square Analysis; Click on *Analyze, Descriptive Statistics, Crosstabs . . .*

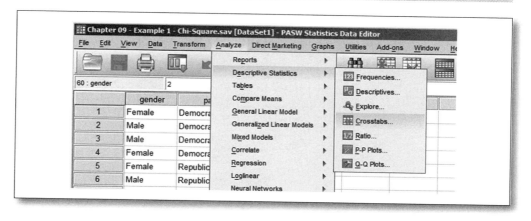

Figure 9.2	Load Variables Into *Row(s)* and *Column(s)* Windows and Check *Display clustered bar charts*

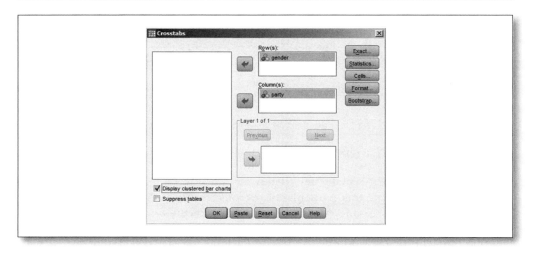

2. On the *Crosstabs* menu, move *gender* from the left window to the *Row(s)* window, and move *party* from the left window to the *Column(s)* window.

3. Check the *Display clustered bar charts* checkbox.

4. Click on the *Statistics . . .* button; this will take you to the *Crosstabs: Statistics* menu (Figure 9.3).

Figure 9.3	*Crosstabs: Statistics* Menu: Check the *Chi-square* Checkbox

5. Check the *Chi-square* checkbox.

6. Click on the *Continue* button. This will take you back to the *Crosstabs* menu.

7. Click the *OK* button, and the chi-square will process.

RESULTS

Finalizing Pretest Criteria

We begin by inspecting the (six) circled cells in the *Crosstabulation* table (Table 9.2) and note that each cell has a count (*n*) of at least 5; hence, the pretest criteria are satisfied.

Next, observe the Sig. (*p*) value in the chi-square tests table (Table 9.3) on the Pearson chi-square row; it indicates a Sig. (*p*) value of .023; since this is less than the specified .05 α level, we conclude that there is a statistically significant difference among genders when it comes to political party affiliation.

Table 9.2   Gender * Political Party Crosstabulation

gender * party Crosstabulation

Count

		party			Total
		Democrat	Republican	Other	
gender	Female	16	9	6	31
	Male	6	18	5	29
Total		22	27	11	60

Table 9.3   Chi-Square Tests Results: Sig. (*p*) = .023

Chi-Square Tests

	Value	df	Asymp. Sig. (2-sided)
Pearson Chi-Square	7.578[a]	2	.023
Likelihood Ratio	7.799	2	.020
Linear-by-Linear Association	2.368	1	.124
N of Valid Cases	60		

a. 0 cells (.0%) have expected count less than 5. The minimum expected count is 5.32.

The *Gender * Political Party Crosstabulation* (Table 9.2) provides clear enough results detailing how many of each gender are affiliated with each political party; even a cursory overview of this table helps us to see that the numbers for females look very different from those of males, which is confirmed by the .023 *p* value (Table 9.3), but to get a more intuitive grasp of these data, inspect the corresponding bar chart (Figure 9.4).

The better you can conceptualize the data, the better prepared you will be to write a cogent Results section detailing your findings. In addition to discussing that the *p* value indicates a statistically significant difference in party affiliation among the genders, the bar chart can help provide additional meaning to the discussion. You may include narrative explaining that the differences detected in this sample show that females tend to be Democrats and males tend to be Republicans, whereas Other seems to attract about the same number of males and females.

HYPOTHESIS RESOLUTION

The chi-square produced a *p* of .023, which is less than the specified .05 α level, which indicates that there is a statistically significant difference between the genders with respect to political party affiliation. As such, we would reject H_0 and not reject H_1.

DOCUMENT RESULTS

According to a survey of 60 adults, we detected a statistically significant difference (*p* = .023, α = .05) in political party affiliation based on gender. Of the 31 females surveyed, most were Democrats (16 Democrats, 9 Republicans, and 6 Other), whereas the 29 men in our sample were predominately Republicans (6 Democrats, 18 Republicans, and 5 Other).

Another way of documenting chi-square results involves discussing percentages. With respect to chi-square, percentages are fairly easy to calculate; just divide the *part* (smaller number) by the *total* (larger number) and multiply by 100 (Table 9.4). Consider this documentation variation (the bracketed portions below are included to clarify the percentage calculations but would not typically be included in the write-up):

> In an effort to discover if gender is associated with political party affiliation, we recruited 60 adults (31 females and 29 males); 52% [16 ÷ 31 = .5161] of the women surveyed identified as Democrats, whereas 62% [18 ÷ 29 = .6207] of men identified as Republicans. Chi-square analysis revealed a statistically significant difference (*p* = .023, α = .05) between genders when it comes to political party affiliation.

GOOD COMMON SENSE

It can be useful to run the chi-square test a second time; try swapping the variables (rows/columns) (Figure 9.2). The statistical results will be the same, but exchanging the

Figure 9.4 Bar Chart for Gender * Political Party

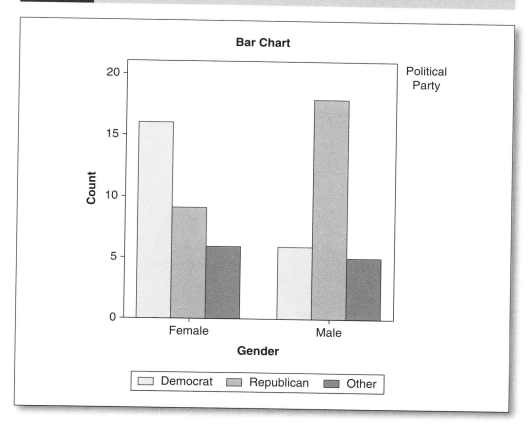

*Table 9.4 % Formula

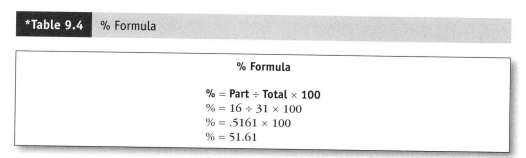

% Formula
% = **Part** ÷ **Total** × **100**
% = 16 ÷ 31 × 100
% = .5161 × 100
% = 51.61

variables in this way will arrange the data differently in the table and bar chart, which may offer an alternate perspective on the results.

You may find it useful to order that the chi-square crosstabulation data be presented using percentages instead of (just) the *n*. To try this, go to the *Crosstabs* menu (Figure 9.2) and click on the *Cells . . .* button. This will take you to the *Crosstabs: Cell Display* menu (Figure 9.5), where you can order percentages for row, column, and total.

| Figure 9.5 | *Crosstabs: Cell Display*—Check *Percentages* |

Occasionally, a continuous variable can be reduced to a categorical variable, thereby facilitating chi-square analyses. For example, age is a continuous variable (ranging from 0–100), but age could be reduced to two categories: 1 = juvenile and 2 = adult. SPSS includes an easy-to-use *Recode* feature that helps automate such processes.

Recoding would leave the continuous variable age as is, but based on the age, we could generate values for a new categorical variable, *AgeClass* (1 = juvenile, 2 = adult), using the following criteria:

If age is less than 18, then *AgeClass* = 1.

If age is 18 or greater, then *AgeClass* = 2.

The procedure for recoding variables in this way is detailed in Chapter 10, specifically the section on recoding.

Key Concepts

- Continuous variables
- Categorical variables
- Chi-square (χ^2)
- Pretest checklist ($n \geq 5$ per cell)
- Overall n actually required
- Crosstabs
- Percentage calculation

Practice Exercises

1. Acme Creamery wants to create advertisements showing boys and girls enjoying Acme Ice Cream; they have consulted with you to discover if boys and girls have the same or different ice cream flavor preferences. You recruit a group of volunteers and gather two pieces of information for each participant using this self-administered survey card:

Ice Cream Preference Survey

Please check <u>one</u> answer for each question:

1. Gender:

   ☐ Female
   ☐ Male

2. What is your favorite ice cream flavor:

   ☐ Chocolate
   ☐ Strawberry
   ☐ Vanilla

Please drop this card in the collection box.

Thank you for participating in our survey.

Codebook—set up SPSS to contain two variables:

- *gender* is a categorical variable (1 = female, 2 = male).
- *icecream* is a categorical variable (1 = chocolate, 2 = strawberry, 3 = vanilla).

Data set—enter Data Set A.

Data Set A				Data Set B		
Rec. #	gender	icecream		Rec. #	gender	icecream
1	1	1		1	1	1
2	2	2		2	2	2
3	2	2		3	1	1
4	1	3		4	1	3
5	2	1		5	2	1
6	1	1		6	2	2
7	1	1		7	1	2
8	2	2		8	1	1
9	1	2		9	1	3
10	1	3		10	2	1
11	2	3		11	1	3
12	2	2		12	1	1
13	2	2		13	1	2
14	1	3		14	1	1
15	1	2		15	2	1
16	2	3		16	2	1
17	2	2		17	2	2
18	2	2		18	1	3
19	1	1		19	1	1
20	1	2		20	2	2
21	2	2		21	1	3
22	2	3		22	2	1
23	1	1		23	1	1
24	1	1		24	2	2
25	2	1		25	2	3
26	1	1		26	2	1
27	1	1		27	1	2
28	1	3		28	2	2
29	1	2		29	2	1
30	2	2		30	1	3
31	2	1		31	2	3
32	2	2		32	2	3
33	1	1		33	1	2

34	2	2
35	2	2
36	2	1
37	2	2
38	2	3
39	1	3
40	1	3
41	1	2
42	1	1
43	2	2
44	2	3
45	1	1
46	1	3
47	2	2
48	2	1

34	2	3
35	2	3
36	1	1
37	1	1
38	2	1
39	1	1
40	1	2
41	1	2
42	2	2
43	2	3
44	2	1
45	1	2
46	1	2

a. Write the hypotheses.

b. Run the criteria of the pretest checklist (n is at least 5 per cell in the Crosstabs) and discuss your findings.

c. Run the chi-square test and document your findings (ns and/or percentages, Sig. [p value]).

d. Write an abstract under 200 words detailing a summary of the study, the chi-square test results, hypothesis resolution, and implications of your findings.

• Repeat this exercise using Data Set B.

2. You notice that some bus riders wear headphones while others do not, but with so many passengers on so many different buses, it is hard to estimate if gender is a factor when it comes to wearing or not wearing headphones. To address this question, you spend the day riding city buses as you unobtrusively record your observations of each passenger on the following data sheet:

Gender	Headphones
☐ F ☐ M	☐ Headphones ☐ No headphones
☐ F ☐ M	☐ Headphones ☐ No headphones
☐ F ☐ M	☐ Headphones ☐ No headphones
☐ F ☐ M	☐ Headphones ☐ No headphones

☐ F ☐ M	☐ Headphones ☐ No headphones
☐ F ☐ M	☐ Headphones ☐ No headphones
☐ F ☐ M	☐ Headphones ☐ No headphones
☐ F ☐ M	☐ Headphones ☐ No headphones
☐ F ☐ M	☐ Headphones ☐ No headphones
☐ F ☐ M	☐ Headphones ☐ No headphones
☐ F ☐ M	☐ Headphones ☐ No headphones

Codebook—set up SPSS to contain two variables:

- *gender* is a categorical variable (1 = female, 2 = male).
- *headphones* is a categorical variable (1 = headphones, 2 = no headphones).

Data set—enter Data Set A.

Data Set A		
Rec. #	gender	headphones
1	1	1
2	1	2
3	2	2
4	1	2
5	1	2
6	2	1
7	1	2
8	2	1
9	1	1
10	2	1
11	1	1
12	2	1
13	2	2
14	2	1
15	2	1
16	2	1

Data Set B		
Rec. #	gender	headphones
1	1	1
2	1	1
3	1	1
4	2	2
5	1	1
6	2	1
7	1	1
8	1	2
9	2	1
10	1	1
11	2	2
12	1	1
13	1	2
14	1	1
15	1	1
16	2	1

17	2	2		17	2	1
18	1	2		18	1	1
19	2	1		19	2	2
20	2	1		20	2	2
21	1	2		21	2	1
22	2	1		22	1	1
23	2	1		23	1	1
24	2	1		24	2	1
25	2	2		25	2	1
26	1	2		26	1	2
27	2	1		27	2	1
28	1	2		28	2	1
29	2	1		29	1	1
30	2	2		30	1	2
31	1	1		31	1	2
32	2	1		32	1	1
33	1	1		33	1	1
34	1	2		34	2	2
35	1	1		35	1	2
36	1	1		36	2	1
37	1	2		37	1	1
				38	2	2
				39	1	1
				40	1	2
				41	1	2
				42	1	1
				43	2	1

a. Write the hypotheses.
b. Run the criteria of the pretest checklist (n is at least 5 per cell in the Crosstabs) and discuss your findings.
c. Run the chi-square test and document your findings (ns and/or percentages, Sig. [p value]).
d. Write an abstract under 200 words detailing a summary of the study, the chi-square test results, hypothesis resolution, and implications of your findings.

   • Repeat this exercise using Data Set B.

3. The clinicians at Anytown Health Clinic want to determine how useful the flu shot is in their community. The researcher approaches patients as they exit the clinic; those who are willing to partake in this study are asked to sign an informed consent document and complete the following card:

Flu Shot Survey

1. Have you had a flu shot this season?

   ☐ Yes

   ☐ No

2. Phone number or e-mail ID: _____.

A member of our staff will contact you in 60 days.

Please drop this card in the collection box.

Thank you for participating in our survey.

> *FOR ADMINISTRATIVE USE ONLY*
>
> ☐ *Got sick with flu*
> ☐ *Did not get sick with flu*

The researcher will contact each participant in 60 days to ask if he or she contracted the flu in the past 60 days and mark the bottom of each card accordingly.

Codebook—set up SPSS to contain two variables:

- *flushot* is a categorical variable (1 = had flu shot, 2 = did not have flu shot).
- *flusick* is a categorical variable (1 = got sick with flu, 2 = did not get sick with flu).

Data set—enter Data Set A.

Data Set A		
Rec. #	flushot	flusick
1	2	2
2	1	1

Data Set B		
Rec. #	flushot	flusick
1	1	1
2	2	1

3	2	1
4	2	2
5	1	2
6	1	2
7	1	1
8	1	2
9	1	2
10	1	1
11	2	1
12	2	2
13	2	1
14	2	2
15	2	2
16	1	1
17	1	1
18	2	1
19	2	1
20	2	1
21	2	1
22	1	2
23	1	2
24	2	1
25	2	1
26	2	2
27	1	2
28	2	1
29	2	2
30	2	1

3	2	1
4	2	1
5	2	1
6	2	2
7	1	2
8	2	1
9	1	1
10	2	1
11	2	1
12	2	2
13	2	1
14	1	2
15	1	2
16	1	2
17	2	1
18	2	1
19	2	1
20	1	2
21	1	1
22	1	2
23	2	2
24	1	1
25	2	2
26	2	1
27	2	1
28	2	1
29	2	2
30	1	2
31	1	2
32	2	1
33	2	2
34	1	2
35	1	1
36	1	2

a. Write the hypotheses.

b. Run the criteria of the pretest checklist (n is at least 5 per cell in the Crosstabs) and discuss your findings.

c. Run the chi-square test and document your findings (ns and/or percentages, Sig. [p value]).

d. Write an abstract under 200 words detailing a summary of the study, the chi-square test results, hypothesis resolution, and implications of your findings.

- Repeat this exercise using Data Set B.

4. The administrative staff of Acme College wants to tune the availability of student resources (e.g., website content, library hours, support staffing, etc.) to better fit the needs of students. You have been asked to determine if the degree students are working on (bachelor's vs. master's) is associated with the type of learning (in classroom vs. remote learning) students have opted for; you are given a sample drawn from the student enrollment database to analyze.

Codebook—set up SPSS to contain two variables:

- *degree* is a categorical variable (1 = bachelor's, 2 = master's).
- *location* is a categorical variable (1 = in classroom, 2 = remote learning).

Data set—enter Data Set A.

Data Set A				Data Set B		
Rec. #	*degree*	*location*		*Rec. #*	*degree*	*location*
1	1	1		1	1	2
2	2	1		2	2	1
3	2	2		3	1	1
4	2	2		4	2	1
5	1	1		5	1	2
6	1	1		6	1	2
7	2	1		7	1	2
8	2	2		8	1	2
9	1	1		9	2	2
10	1	1		10	2	1
11	1	2		11	2	2
12	1	2		12	1	1

13	1	1
14	1	1
15	2	1
16	2	2
17	2	1
18	1	1
19	2	2
20	2	2
21	2	2
22	2	2
23	1	1
24	1	2
25	1	1
26	2	2
27	1	1
28	1	1
29	1	2
30	1	1
31	2	1
32	2	2
33	1	2
34	2	2
35	1	2
36	1	2

13	1	1
14	1	1
15	1	1
16	2	2
17	1	1
18	2	2
19	1	2
20	2	2
21	1	2
22	2	1
23	1	2
24	2	2
25	1	1
26	1	1
27	1	2
28	1	1
29	1	1
30	1	1
31	2	1
32	2	2
33	2	2
34	1	1

a. Write the hypotheses.
b. Run the criteria of the pretest checklist (n is at least 5 per cell in the Crosstabs) and discuss your findings.
c. Run the chi-square test and document your findings (ns and/or percentages, Sig. [p value]).

d. Write an abstract under 200 words detailing a summary of the study, the chi-square test results, hypothesis resolution, and implications of your findings.

- Repeat this exercise using Data Set B.

5. To determine if *how* data are gathered has any bearing on responses to a question involving substance abuse (*Have you ever used an illegal drug?*), you recruit willing participants and randomly assign them to one of three groups: Those in Group 1 will be asked the question via face-to-face interview, those in Group 2 will respond using a standard pencil-and-paper mail-in survey, and those in Group 3 will be directed to an online survey; no names or identifying information will be gathered.

Codebook—set up SPSS to contain two variables:

- *media* is a categorical variable (1 = face-to-face interview, 2 = mail-in survey, 3 = online survey).
- *drug* is a categorical variable (1 = yes, 2 = no).

Data set—enter Data Set A.

Data Set A		
Rec. #	media	drug
1	2	1
2	3	2
3	3	1
4	2	2
5	3	1
6	2	2
7	1	2
8	3	1
9	1	2
10	3	2
11	3	1
12	2	2
13	3	2
14	2	1
15	3	2
16	2	1
17	1	2
18	3	2

Data Set B		
Rec. #	media	drug
1	1	2
2	1	1
3	1	2
4	2	1
5	3	2
6	3	1
7	2	2
8	1	2
9	3	2
10	2	1
11	3	1
12	3	1
13	3	1
14	1	1
15	2	1
16	3	1
17	1	2
18	2	1

19	2	2		19	1	1
20	1	2		20	3	2
21	1	2		21	3	1
22	2	2		22	2	1
23	2	2		23	2	2
24	3	1		24	3	2
25	1	2		25	3	2
26	2	1		26	3	1
27	3	1		27	2	1
28	1	2		28	1	2
29	1	2		29	1	2
30	2	2		30	1	1
31	1	1		31	2	2
32	1	1		32	1	2
33	2	2		33	1	2
34	1	1		34	2	1
35	2	1		35	3	1
36	1	1		36	2	1
37	3	2		37	3	2
38	2	2		38	1	2
39	2	2		39	3	1
40	3	2		40	2	1
41	2	2		41	2	1
42	1	2		42	2	1
43	1	1		43	1	1
44	3	2		44	2	1
45	2	2		45	3	1
46	1	2		46	1	1
				47	1	2
				48	2	2
				49	2	2
				50	3	1
				51	1	2
				52	2	1
				53	1	2

a. Write the hypotheses.

b. Run the criteria of the pretest checklist (n is at least 5 per cell in the Crosstabs) and discuss your findings.

c. Run the chi-square test and document your findings (ns and/or percentages, Sig. [p value]).

d. Write an abstract under 200 words detailing a summary of the study, the chi-square test results, hypothesis resolution, and implications of your findings.

  • Repeat this exercise using Data Set B.

6. In an effort to better accommodate students, Acme University wants to find out if students pursuing different degrees (bachelor's/master's/doctorate) have the same or different preferences when it comes to class time (day/night). To determine this, you are commissioned to administer the following survey to a sample of the students currently enrolled.

Course Schedule Preference Survey

Please check <u>one</u> answer for each question:

1. When do you prefer to take the majority of your courses?

   ☐ Day (8:00 a.m.–5:00 p.m.)

   ☐ Night (5:00 p.m.–10:00 p.m.)

2. What degree are you currently working on?

   ☐ Bachelor's

   ☐ Master's

   ☐ Doctorate

Please drop this card in the collection box.

Thank you for participating in our survey.

Codebook—the data set contains two variables:

  • *time* is a categorical variable (1 = day, 2 = night).
  • *degree* is a categorical variable (1 = bachelor's, 2 = master's, 3 = doctorate).

Data set—load *Chapter 09 – Exercise 06 A.sav*.

a. Write the hypotheses.

b. Run the criteria of the pretest checklist (n is at least 5 per cell in the Crosstabs) and discuss your findings.

c. Run the chi-square test and document your findings (*ns* and/or percentages, Sig. [*p* value]).

d. Write an abstract under 200 words detailing a summary of the study, the chi-square test results, hypothesis resolution, and implications of your findings.

- Repeat this exercise using *Chapter 09 – Exercise 06 B.sav.*

7. A political scientist expects that how a person votes (or does not vote) may be associated with his or her age. To investigate this, the scientist gathers a convenience sample, asking voluntary participants to anonymously complete the following card:

Voter Survey

Please check <u>one</u> answer for each question:

1. How old are you?

   ☐ 18–35

   ☐ 36–64

   ☐ 65 and older

2. How did you vote in the last election?

   ☐ I voted in person at a polling precinct.

   ☐ I voted by mail.

   ☐ I did not vote.

Please drop this card in the collection box.

Thank you for participating in our survey.

Codebook—The data set contains two variables:

- *age* is a categorical variable (1 = 18–35, 2 = 36–64, 3 = 65 and older).
- *vote* is a categorical variable (1 = vote in person, 2 = vote by mail, 3 = not vote).

Data set—load *Chapter 09 – Exercise 07 A.sav.*

a. Write the hypotheses.

b. Run the criteria of the pretest checklist (*n* is at least 5 per cell in the Crosstabs) and discuss your findings.

c. Run the chi-square test and document your findings (*ns* and/or percentages, Sig. [*p* value]).

d. Write an abstract under 200 words detailing a summary of the study, the chi-square test results, hypothesis resolution, and implications of your findings.

- Repeat this exercise using *Chapter 09 – Exercise 07 B.sav.*

8. The Acme Veterinary Science Center wants to find out if its three dog foods appeal to all dogs equally or if breed is a factor in a dog's food preference. Per the research criteria specified, you use quota sampling to recruit 90 pets: 30 Cocker Spaniels, 30 Beagles, and 30 Keeshonds. Owners are asked not to feed their pets for 4 hours prior to the test. Each dog is tested individually; the dog is placed 5 feet (1.5 meters) away from three clear bowls of dog food, all with equal weights. On cue, the leash is removed and the dog is free to eat from any bowl(s). After dismissing each participant, you weigh the bowls; the lightest bowl wins (meaning that the dog ate the most food from that bowl). In case of a tie, the winning bowl is the one that the dog went to first.

Codebook—the data set contains two variables:

- *dog* is a categorical variable (1 = Cocker Spaniel, 2 = Beagle, 3 = Keeshond).
- *food* is a categorical variable (1 = Food A, 2 = Food B, 3 = Food C).

Data set—load *Chapter 09 – Exercise 08 A.sav.*

a. Write the hypotheses.
b. Run the criteria of the pretest checklist (*n* is at least 5 per cell in the Crosstabs) and discuss your findings.
c. Run the chi-square test and document your findings (*n*s and/or percentages, Sig. [*p* value]).
d. Write an abstract under 200 words detailing a summary of the study, the chi-square test results, hypothesis resolution, and implications of your findings.

- Repeat this exercise using *Chapter 09 – Exercise 08 B.sav.*

9. Each year, the Department of Education in Anytown publishes a report of college-bound high school seniors. You have been recruited to compare data gathered from seniors at the Acme Academy, a local private school, with seniors at Anytown High School, a public institution.

Codebook—the data set contains two variables:

- *school* is a categorical variable (1 = Acme Academy, 2 = Anytown High School).
- *college* is a categorical variable (1 = not attending university, 2 = attending university).

Data set—load *Chapter 09 – Exercise 09 A.sav.*

a. Write the hypotheses.
b. Run the criteria of the pretest checklist (*n* is at least 5 per cell in the Crosstabs) and discuss your findings.

c. Run the chi-square test and document your findings (*ns* and/or percentages, Sig. [*p* value]).

d. Write an abstract under 200 words detailing a summary of the study, the chi-square test results, hypothesis resolution, and implications of your findings.

- Repeat this exercise using *Chapter 09 – Exercise 09 B.sav.*

10. A political analyst is conducting a survey aimed at tuning campaign messages; the question of interest is, "Do women and men tend to vote the same or differently when it comes to electing the mayor?" The analyst gathered responses from willing participants using self-administered survey cards:

Voter Survey–City Mayor

Please check <u>one</u> answer for each question:

1. What is your gender?

☐ Female

☐ Male

2. Who will you vote for?

☐ Smith

☐ Jones

☐ Undecided

Please drop this card in the collection box.

Thank you for participating in our survey.

Codebook—the data set contains two variables:

- *gender* is a categorical variable (1 = female, 2 = male).
- *vote* is a categorical variable (1 = Smith, 2 = Jones, 3 = undecided).

Data set—load *Chapter 09 – Exercise 10 A.sav.*

a. Write the hypotheses.

b. Run the criteria of the pretest checklist (*n* is at least 5 per cell in the Crosstabs) and discuss your findings.

c. Run the chi-square test and document your findings (*ns* and/or percentages, Sig. [*p* value]).

d. Write an abstract under 200 words detailing a summary of the study, the chi-square test results, hypothesis resolution, and implications of your findings.

- Repeat this exercise using *Chapter 09 – Exercise 10 B.sav.*

PART III

Data Handling

Supplemental SPSS Operations

Here are a few more tricks you can train SPSS to do.

- Generating Random Numbers
- Sort Cases
- Select Cases
- Recoding
- Importing Data
- Syntax

Never trust a computer you can't throw out a window.

—Steve Wozniak

LEARNING OBJECTIVES

Upon completing this chapter, you will be able to:

- Perform extended SPSS operations to enhance your capabilities, versatility, and data-processing efficiency
- Generate a list of random numbers to your specifications
- Perform single and multilevel sorting
- Select cases using multiple criteria
- Recode variables
- Import data from external sources: Excel and ASCII files
- Comprehend how to generate SPSS Syntax code automatically using the Paste function
- Understand how to customize SPSS Syntax code
- Save, load, and execute SPSS Syntax code
- Practice safe data storage protocols

DIGITAL LEARNING RESOURCES

The data sets for this chapter are at **www.sagepub.com/knapp**

- SPSS data files
- SPSS Syntax file
- Excel file
- ASCII file

OVERVIEW

The data sets that have been provided thus far has been crafted to work as is in the SPSS environment, but as you become more statistically proficient, your research curiosity and scientific creative thinking are likely to further develop. You may want to analyze data of your own, examine data from other non-SPSS sources, or run more elaborate statistical analyses. This chapter explains some of the most useful supplemental SPSS features and functions to help you work more productively.

GENERATING RANDOM NUMBERS

In Chapter 2, the "Simple Random Sampling" section discussed the need to randomly select 30 individuals from a sample frame of 1,000 potential participants. Flipping a coin to make these selections is clearly out of the question for this task; instead, we can use SPSS to generate this list of random numbers:

1. On the Variable View screen, create a numeric variable to contain the random numbers that we will have SPSS generate; we will call it *randnum* (Figure 10.1).

Figure 10.1 Create a Numeric Variable (*randnum*) to Contain the Random Numbers

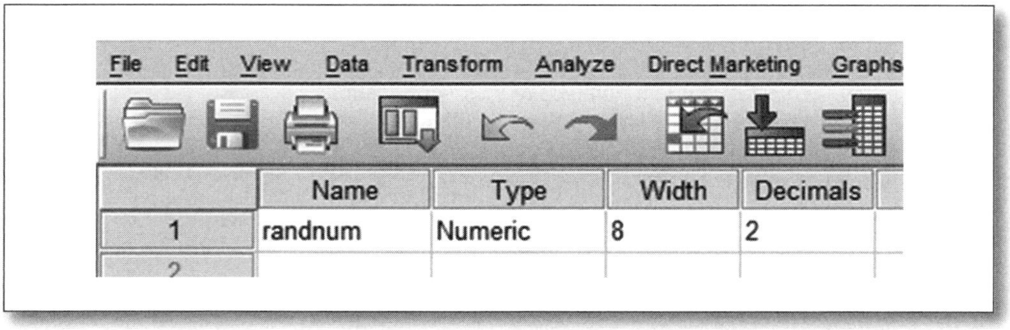

2. Switch to the Data View screen and put a 0 (or any number) in the *randnum* column at record 30 (Figure 10.2).

Figure 10.2 Enter Any Number at Record 30 for *randnum* (So SPSS Will Know How Long the List Should Be)

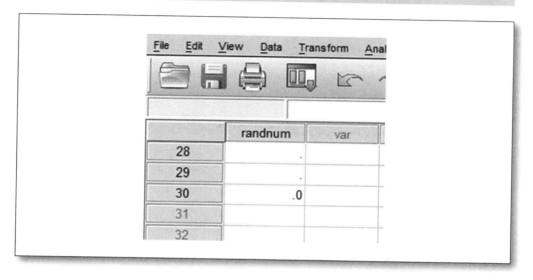

3. Click on *Transform/Compute Variable* . . . (Figure 10.3). This will take you to the *Compute Variable* menu.

Figure 10.3 Click on *Transform/Compute Variables* . . .

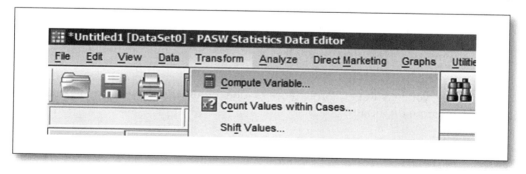

4. On the *Compute Variable* menu, in the *Target Variable* window, enter *randnum*; in the *Numeric Expression* window, enter *rnd(rv.uniform(1, 1000))* (Figure 10.4).

This tells SPSS to place the random values in the *randnum* variable. Now to demystify the *rnd(rv.uniform(1,1000))* expression:

- *rnd* means round the result to the nearest integer; if you wanted the random numbers to include decimal digits, you could enter *rv.uniform(1,1000)*.
- *rv.uniform* means "random values, uniform," wherein each number has an equal chance of being selected.
- *(1,1000)* specifies the minimum and maximum values.

Figure 10.4	On the *Compute Variable* Menu, in the *Target Variable* Window, Enter *randnum;* in the *Numeric Expression* Window, Enter *rnd(rv.uniform(1,1000))*

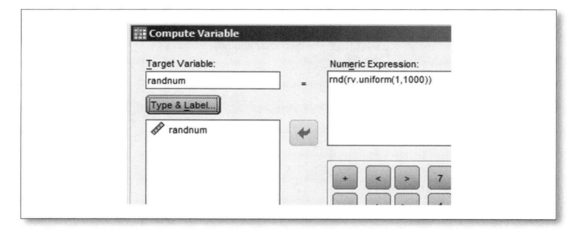

5. Click on the *OK* button. If you are then asked if you wish to *Change existing variable?,* click on the *OK* button.

6. The Data View screen should now show 30 random numbers in the *randnum* column (Figure 10.5).

NOTE: Naturally, your results will produce a different set of random numbers.

The random number generator does not keep track of repeats among these numbers; hence, you may want to order more random numbers than you actually need so that you can ignore duplicates.

SORT CASES

As you have probably noticed, the order of the data on the Data View screen has no effect on the statistical outcomes, but at times you may find it useful to inflict some order on the data. In data processing, the term *sort* is akin to *alphabetizing;* you can

Figure 10.5 Data View Screen With Resulting Random Numbers for *randnum*

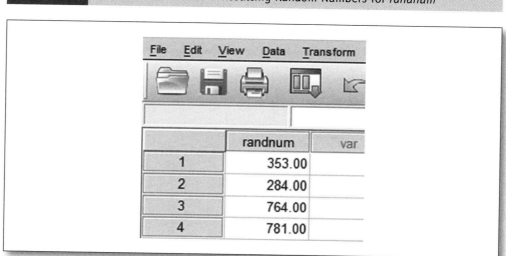

sort the data to help you make sense of them. You might be interested in those who scored highest or lowest on a particular variable to better conceptualize the data set; inflicting such order may help you identify patterns or trends within the data set that may not have been evident otherwise—you can then follow your curiosity with additional statistical tests.

SPSS supports multilevel sorting. This means that you could specify the first level to sort by name and the second level to sort by age (you can specify as many levels as you need). So if two or more people have the same name, the system would then look to age to finalize the sorting sequence (Table 10.1).

Table 10.1 Data Sorted by Name (Level 1) and Then by Age (level 2)

name	age
Abbey	15
Brett	12
Brett	27
Brett	38
Charles	19

The default is to sort the variable at each level in *ascending* order (from lowest to highest); alternatively, you can specify that you want to sort in *descending* order (from highest to lowest). For example, if you specify that Level 1 is *name ascending* and Level 2 is *age descending*, the system will sort the data with names from A to Z, but if there is a tie at Level 1 (name), it will subsort those records by age, from highest to lowest (Table 10.2).

Table 10.2	Data Sorted Ascending by Name (Level 1), Then Descending by Age (Level 2)

name	age
Abbey	15
Brett	38
Brett	27
Brett	12
Charles	19

1. Load the following data file: *Chapter 10 – Example 01 – Sort, Select, Recode.sav.* This data set contains bowling league information. Notice that initially, the records are in no particular order.

   Codebook—the data set contains five variables:
   - *name* is a string variable.
   - *gender* is a categorical variable (1 = female, 2 = male).
   - *age* is a continuous variable.
   - *bowlavg* is the bowler's average score to date.
   - *team* is a categorical variable (1 = Strike Force, 2 = Lane Surfers, 3 = 7-10 Squad, 4 = Pinbots, 5 = Bowled Over, 6 = The Pin Boys).

2. Suppose you want to identify the top bowler in each team; this would involve a two-level sort:

   Level 1:   *team* (ascending)

   Level 2:   *bowlavg* (descending)

3. Click on *Data/Sort Cases . . .* (Figure 10.6). This will take you to the *Sort Cases* menu (Figure 10.7).

4. On the *Sort Cases* menu (Figure 10.7), move *team* from the left window to the *Sort by* window, and click on *Ascending*.

5. Move *bowlavg* from the left window to the *Sort by* window and click on *Descending*.

Figure 10.6 To Sort Data, Click on *Data/Sort Cases* . . .

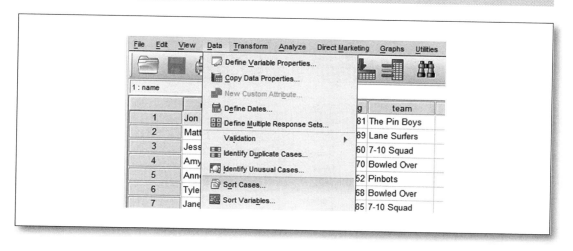

6. Notice that once a variable is in the *Sort by* window, you can click on a variable to drag it up and down the list, thereby altering the sorting levels. You can also change the *Sort Order* for a variable by clicking on the variable, then selecting *Ascending* or *Descending*.

7. Click on *OK*, and the system will sort the cases.

8. Observe the order of the data on the Data View screen (Figure 10.8).

Figure 10.7 *Sort Cases* Menu Indicates a Two-Level Sort: First by *team* (in Ascending Order), Then by *bowlavg* (in Descending Order)

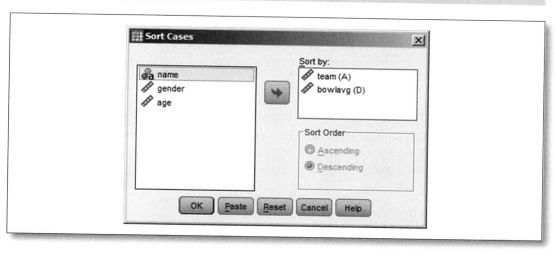

| Figure 10.8 | Data View Screen Showing Labels (Not Values) |

	name	gender	age	bowlavg	team
1	Justin	Male	26	196	Strike Force
2	Megan	Female	23	156	Strike Force
3	Arlene	Female	28	148	Strike Force
4	Jay	Male	28	142	Strike Force
5	Matt	Male	26	189	Lane Surfers
6	Kate	Female	16	166	Lane Surfers
7	Sam	Male	41	156	Lane Surfers
8	Anne A.	Female	16	148	Lane Surfers
9	Jane	Female	27	185	7-10 Squad
10	Jessica	Female	27	160	7-10 Squad

Notice that the data are grouped by *team,* then by highest to lowest bowling average (*bowlavg*), but the teams are not arranged alphabetically. This is because *team* is not really a string (alphanumeric) variable like *name; team* is actually a numeric variable, with labels assigned. If you click on the *Value Labels* icon, you will see *team* switch to the numeric values for that variable (Figure 10.9), which will show that the sort actually did work as ordered—per the codebook, the label "Strike Force" is coded as 1, "Lane Surfers" is coded as 2, and so on.

Feel free to sort the data other ways and observe the resulting sequences.

SELECT CASES

In prior chapters, we have used the *Select Cases* (icon) to run the pretest checklist for various statistical tests, which has enabled us to process statistics for one group at a time. The *Select Cases* function is also capable of isolating data using more complex selection criteria.

For example, you may wish to perform statistical analyses only on members of the bowling league who are (1) females and (2) have a bowling average of 120 or higher.

1. Load the following data file: *Chapter 10 – Example 01 – Sort, Select, Recode.sav.*

2. Click on the *Select Cases* icon.

Figure 10.9 Data View Screen Showing Values (Not Labels)

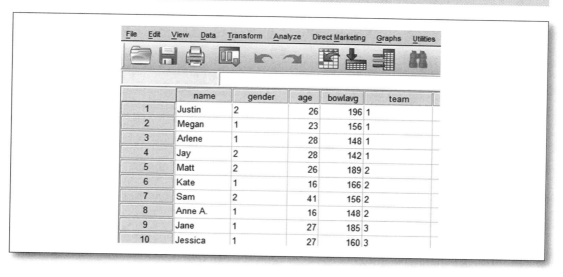

3. In the *Select* group, click on the *If condition is satisfied* button.

4. Click on the *If* . . . button. This will take you to the *Select Cases: If* menu; in the large box at the top, enter the following selection criteria: *gender = 1 and bowlavg >= 120* (Figure 10.10). Note: These criteria include gender = 1 since the gender variable has the following labels assigned to it: 1 = female, 2 = male.

Figure 10.10 *Select If* Menu, Specifying Two Selection Criteria

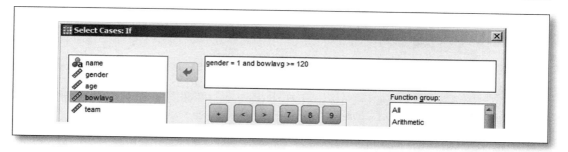

5. Click on the *Continue* button; this will take you back to the *Select Cases* menu.

6. Click on the *OK* button.

7. Go to the Data View screen.

8. Notice that all records are slashed out except for the *females with bowling averages that are at least 120*. Now you can proceed with whatever statistical analysis you wish to perform on the selected (not slashed-out) records.

Try some other case selection criteria and observe which records are affected on the Data View screen:

- team > 2 and team <= 5 and bowlavg > 150
- team = 3 or team = 5
- name < "G"
- name > "A" and name < "F"
- age >= 17 and age < 31 and bowlavg < 170

You have probably surmised some of the coding syntax from the examples above; just to clarify a few things:

- Single and compound *and/or* logic is supported.
- Commonly used logical relationships are symbolized as
    - < less than
    - > greater than
    - = equal to
    - <= less than or equal to
    - >= greater than or equal to

- Although the system does support *not* logic, negative logic can be confusing; try to build your selection criteria using *and/or* parameters.
- When your selection criteria involve string variables, be sure to wrap quotation marks around your parameter(s) (e.g., *name < "G"*); otherwise, the processor will think you are referring to a variable (*G*).

RECODING

Occasionally, you may wish to change the way a variable is presented in a data set. For example, in the current database, age is a continuous variable that ranges from 16 to 41, but suppose you wanted to use a *t* test to compare bowling averages of minors versus adults; you would need a categorical variable to designate which group (minor vs. adult) each record belonged to based on age. This is accomplished via *recoding*. We will leave *age* (a continuous variable) intact, but we can use the *recode* function to create the new variable, *age2* (a categorical variable), which will be based on age using the following (two) criteria:

- If age < 18, then *age2* = 1.
- If age >= 18, then *age2* = 2.

Remember: ">=" notation is computer language for "greater than or equal to." After the *recode* function generates the values for *age2*, we will assign the following value labels to *age2* to provide clarity:

- 1 = "Minor"
- 2 = "Adult"

1. Load the following data file: *Chapter 10 – Example 01 – Sort, Select, Recode.sav*.
2. Click on *Transform/Recode into Different Variables . . .* (Figure 10.11).

Figure 10.11 To Begin Recoding, Click on *Transform/Recode into Different Variables . . . .*

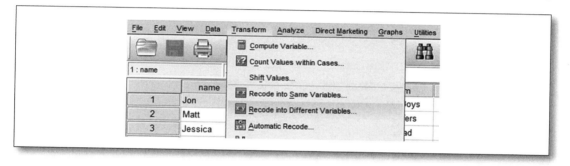

3. On the *Recode into Different Variables* menu, move *age* from the left window into the *Numeric Variable* —≫ *Output Variable* window (Figure 10.12).
4. Enter *age2* in the *Output Variable, Name* box.
5. Click on the *Change* button.

Figure 10.12 *Recode into Different Variables* Menu

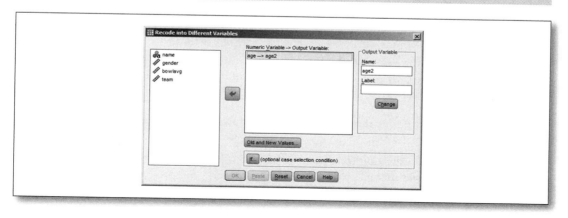

6. So far, you have indicated that the (continuous) variable *age* will be recoded into the new (categorical) variable *age2*. Now you need to indicate how *age* will be recoded into *age2*. Click on the *Old and New Values* . . . button.

7. Notice that there are variety of recoding options; we will use a simple method. In the *Old Value* area, select *Range,* and enter *1 through 17* (Figure 10.13). In the *New Value* area, select *Value* and enter *1*. Then click on the *Add* button.

This tells the processor to look for *age,* and for any record with an age between 1 and 17 (inclusive), write a 1 in that record in the *age2* variable (and do not change the contents of the age variable).

Figure 10.13 | *Recode into Different Variables: Old and New Values* Menu, Recoding Ages 1–17 to *age2* as 1

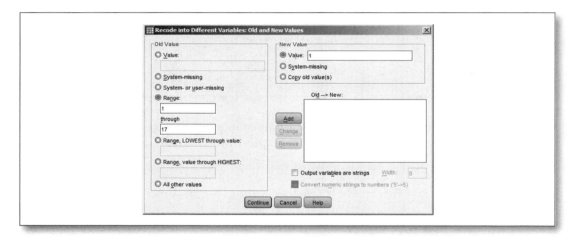

---

8. In the *Old Value* area, select *Range,* and enter *18 through 99*. In the *New Value* area, select *Value* and enter *2*. Then click on the *Add* button (Figure 10.14).

This tells the processor to look for *age,* and for any record with an age between 18 and 99 (inclusive), write a 2 in that record in the *age2* variable (and do not change the contents of the age variable).

9. At this point, the Old → New window shows the recoding criteria (Figure 10.15).

10. Click on the *Continue* button; this will return you to the *Recode into Different Variables* menu.

11. Click on the *OK* button, and the recoding will process.

Figure 10.14	*Recode into Different Variables: Old and New Values* Menu, Recoding Ages 18–99 to *age2* as 2

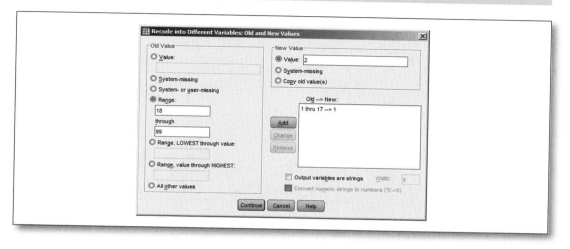

Figure 10.15	Excerpt From *Recode into Different Variables: Old and New Values* Menu: Criteria Used to Recode *age* to *age2*

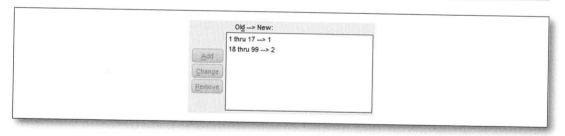

12. Go to the Data View screen, and notice that the new variable *age2* is populated appropriately based on the age for each record.

13. To finalize the process, go to the Variable View screen and specify the corresponding *Value Labels* for *age2* (1 = minor, 2 = adult) (Figure 10.16).

In this example, notice that we opted to *Recode into Different Variables . . .* as opposed to *Recode into Same Variables . . . .* This choice preserved the original (continuous) age variable, so that we could perform further analyses on it. Had we used *Recode into Same Variables . . . ,* each original age would have been overwritten with 1s and 2s as we specified (signifying minors and adults); you would not be able to get back to the original age(s). In addition, if an error had occurred during the recoding process, the age variable itself would have been altered, and hence it would not

| Figure 10.16 | Assign *Value Labels* to *age2* (1 = Minor, 2 = Adult) |

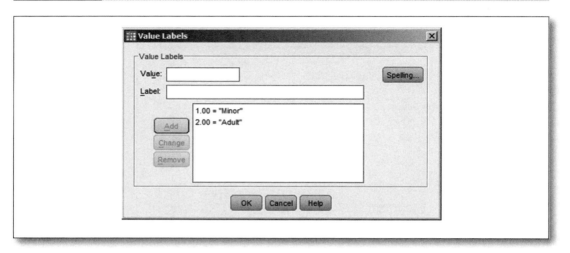

be possible to retry the recoding procedure. A reasonable rule of thumb is this: *Recode all you want, but always keep your source data intact.*

IMPORTING DATA

So far, all data used have been prepared to operate properly in SPSS, but, as you might expect, there is a world of worthy data not necessarily in SPSS format. When the data are only available on paper, naturally you will have to enter the data manually. Fortunately, more and more data are available in a digital form; even if the data are not in SPSS format, SPSS is equipped with some fairly versatile data import features designed to promptly load non-SPSS data into the SPSS environment for processing.

The two most common forms of non-SPSS data are Microsoft Excel and ASCII (pronounced *ask-key*) files; once you see how to import data from these two sources, you should be able to reason your way through importing other data formats.

The import data feature in SPSS tends to vary somewhat from version to version. If there is a discrepancy between the instructions in this section and how your version of SPSS operates, then consult the *Help* menu in your software and search for *import* or *import data.*

Importing Excel Data

The Excel worksheet in this example contains 101 rows; the first row contains the variable name for each column (*ID, Age, Score*), followed by 100 records, each with three variables (columns):

1. *ID* is a string variable consisting of six letters and numbers.

2. *Age* is a numeric variable consisting of two digits.

3. *Score* is a numeric variable consisting of two digits.

The first row of the Excel file that you will be importing has the variable names at the top of each column; this will be useful when it comes to the import process. If these names were not present, you could still proceed with the import, but you would need a codebook to know how to label the variables after the file has been imported.

1. Click on *File/Open/Data* . . . (Figure 10.17). This will take you to the *Open File* menu (Figure 10.18).

Figure 10.17   To Begin the Import Process, Click on *File/Open/Data* . . .

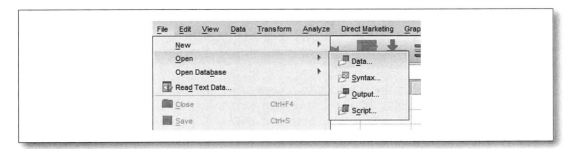

2. On the *Open Data* menu (Figure 10.18) for *Files of type*, select *Excel;* this will narrow the file list to Excel worksheets only.

Figure 10.18   *Open Data* Menu: For *Files of type*, Select *Excel;* for *File name*, Select *Chapter 10 – Example 02 – Excel Data.xls*

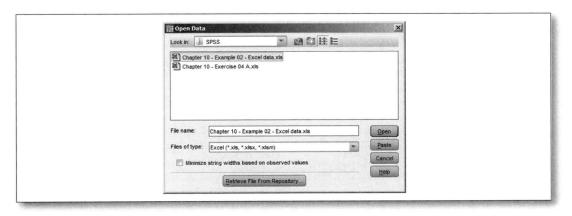

3. In the large file list window, select *Chapter 10 – Example 02 – Excel Data.xls* and click on the *Open* button. This will take you to the *Open Excel Data Source* menu (Figure 10.19).

Figure 10.19   *Opening Excel Data Source* Menu

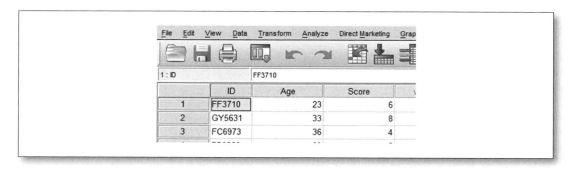

4. In this case, in the *Opening Excel Data Source* menu (Figure 10.19), the defaults are correct: Since the Excel worksheet has the variable names at the top of each column, the corresponding checkbox (*Read variable names from the first row of data*) is checked. If the variable names are not included as the first row in the Excel sheet, then uncheck that box.

5. The input utility also identified the worksheet and cells involved correctly: *Sheet1 [A1:C101]*. Click on the *OK* button.

6. SPSS will process the import; notice that the system loaded the Excel file and the variable names have been assigned accordingly (Figure 10.20).

Figure 10.20   Data View Screen After Excel File Import

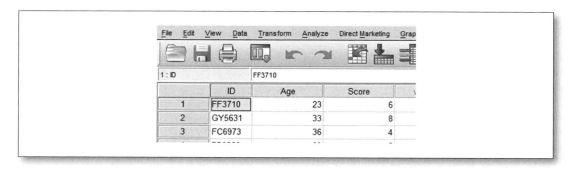

7. To further verify that the import worked properly, switch to the Variable View screen (Figure 10.21). Notice that *ID* has been brought in as a string variable since it contains alphanumeric characters, and age and score have been correctly configured as numeric variables.

Figure 10.21 Variable View Screen After Excel file Import

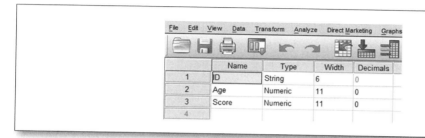

8. You can now proceed with statistical analyses. When you are ready to save the file, the system will write it out as an SPSS file unless you specify otherwise.

Importing ASCII Data

ASCII stands for *American Standard Code for Information Interchange;* it is basically a generic, plain text file, not associated with any particular software package. ASCII file names typically have a *.txt* (text) or, less often, an *.asc* (ASCII) suffix (e.g., *Experiment18. txt, DistrictA.asc*). The data in such files are traditionally arranged with one record per row; the variables within each row are usually separated by a *delimiter* character, such as a comma or other symbol (Figure 10.22). Alternatively, some files do not use delimiters to separate variables; instead, they use a fixed number of characters per variable, producing columns of data padded with spaces (Figure 10.23).

Figure 10.22 Comma-Delimited ASCII Data

```
ID,Age,Score
DE7015,72,5
LP4964,35,6
PF9120,51,6
HC4109,49,10
EH8610,66,3
RV3966,31,3
JZ4866,61,8
```

Figure 10.23 Fixed-Column ASCII Data

```
ID         Age      Score
DE7015     72       5
LP4964     35       6
PF9120     51       6
HC4109     49       10
EH8610     66       3
RV3966     31       3
JZ4866     61       8
```

Since delimited files are more common, this example will involve a comma-delimited ASCII file.

1. Click on *File/Open/Data* . . . (Figure 10.24). This will take you to the *Open File* menu (Figure 10.24).

Figure 10.24 To Begin Import Process, Click on *File/Open/Data* . . .

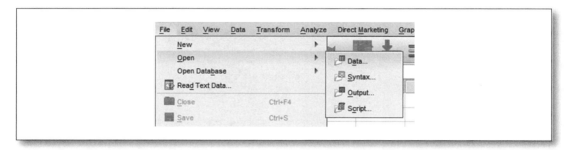

---

2. In the *Open Data* menu (Figure 10.25) for *Files of type,* select *Text;* this will narrow the file list. If the file name has a suffix other than .txt, then at the *Files of type* option, select *All files*.

3. In the large file list window, select *Chapter 10 – Example 03 – Comma delimited data.txt* and click on the *Open* button. This will take you to the *Text Import Wizard – Step 1 of 6* menu (Figure 10.26).

Figure 10.25 *Open Data* Menu: For *Files of type,* Select *Text;* for *File name,* Select *Chapter 10 – Example 03 – Comma Delimited Data.txt*

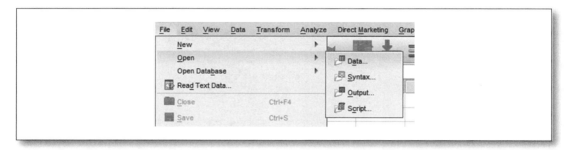

Figure 10.26 *Text Import Wizard – Step 1 of 6* Menu

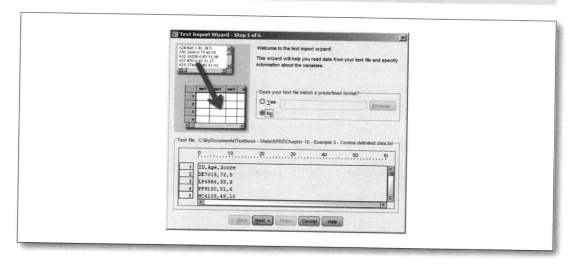

4. In the *Text Import Wizard – Step 1 of 6* menu, click on the *Next* > button. This will take you to the *Text Import Wizard – Step 2 of 6* menu (Figure 10.27).

Figure 10.27 *Text Import Wizard – Step 2 of 6* Menu

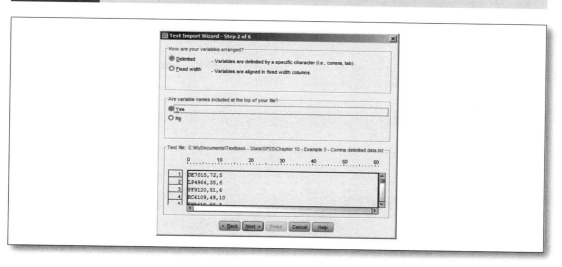

5. In the *Text Import Wizard – Step 2 of 6* menu, since this is a comma-delimited data set, for the *How are your variables arranged?* question, select *Delimited*.

For the *Are variables names included at the top of your file?* question, select *Yes*. Then, click on the *Next >* button; this will take you to the *Text Import Wizard – Step 3 of 6* menu.

6. In the *Text Import Wizard – Steps 3 – 5* menus, the defaults are all appropriate. Click on the *Next >* button for each of these menus until you reach the *Text Import Wizard – Step 6 of 6* menu.

7. In the *Text Import Wizard – Step 6 of 6* menu, click on the *Finish* button.

8. SPSS will process the import; notice that the system loaded the ASCII comma-delimited text file, with the variable names assigned accordingly (Figure 10.28).

Figure 10.28   Data View Screen After Text File Import

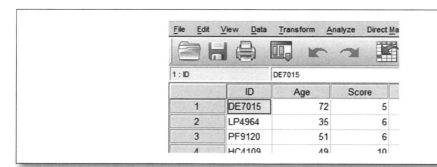

9. To further verify that the import worked properly, switch to the Variable View screen (Figure 10.29). Notice that ID has been brought in as a string variable since it contains alphanumeric characters, and age and score have been correctly configured as numeric variables.

Figure 10.29   Variable View Screen After Text File Import

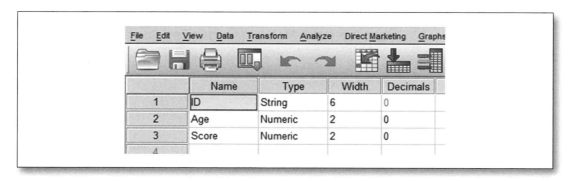

10. You can now proceed with statistical analyses. When you are ready to save the file, the system will write it out as an SPSS file unless you specify otherwise

 If the data that you are importing contain categorical variables coded as numbers (e.g., 1 = yes, 2 = no), it would be to your advantage to gather as much codebook information as you can, so you can create the appropriate data labels for each such variable.

SYNTAX

First, a bit of history: SPSS was initially developed and implemented long, long ago, in the dark ages of computing, before mankind had discovered the ability to point and click. In those days, the only way to communicate with SPSS was to type in commands and parameters using the SPSS Syntax language. Despite the advent of elegant menu systems, the SPSS Syntax language is still alive and well, lurking silently in the background of every SPSS menu and beyond. End of history lesson.

So far, we have used the SPSS menu system to run analyses, which is optimal for procedures that you intend to run only once, but in cases where you will be running the same analyses repeatedly on a data set over time, it is possible to record and save your series of menu selections and parameter settings so you can rerun the entire analysis without having to click your way through multiple menus.

The good news is, you do not have to learn the entire SPSS Syntax programming language to use it; you can use the *Paste* function to generate these programs for you. Here is how it works:

1. Load the following file: *Chapter 10 – Exercise 04 – Syntax.sav* (this data set may look familiar; it is a copy of *Chapter 06 – Example 01 – ANOVA.sav*).

2. Order the traditional descriptive statistics with a histogram for the variable *score*, BUT instead of clicking on the *OK* button at the end to execute the analysis, click on the *Paste* button. It will initially seem as if nothing happened (but keep reading).

NOTE: For more details on this procedure, please refer to Chapter 4 ("SPSS—Descriptive Statistics: Continuous Variables (Age)"); see the star (★) icon on page **71**, but instead of age, process the score variable.

3. Whereas clicking on the *OK* button runs the analysis, clicking on the *Paste* button instead produces the block of code shown in Figure 10.30, which is the programmed equivalence for producing the summary statistics and histogram with a normal curve that you specified via the menus:

4. To run this block of code, click on *Run/All* (Figure 10.30), and it will process as if you had clicked on the *OK* button.

5. When working with larger Syntax programs, you may choose to run only a section of the code—in that case, highlight the lines of code that you want to execute, then click on the *Selection* icon (the triangle icon just to the right of the binoculars icon).

| **Figure 10.30** | Variable View Screen After Text File Import |

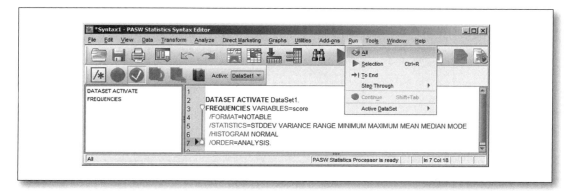

Each time you click on the *Paste* button on a menu, SPSS will assess the parameters that you specified on the menu involved, convert that to SPSS Syntax code, and add it to the *bottom* of the accumulating Syntax file—essentially, you are building a program one block of code at a time.

When you save the Syntax code, it will be assigned the *.sps* suffix to the file name; you have probably already noticed that SPSS data files have the *.sav* file name suffix.

To better comprehend the power and convenience of using SPSS Syntax programs, imagine that you are involved in a long-term study wherein data are collected regularly, and each week, you need to run an ANOVA report. If you opted for an SPSS Syntax program to carry out your tests, you could use the following three-step procedure:

1. Load *Chapter 10 – Example 04 – Syntax.sav* (if it is not already loaded).

2. Load *Chapter 10 – Example 04 – Syntax.sps* (this is the Syntax program).

3. In the Syntax editor window, click on *Run/All*.

This SPSS Syntax program, which was derived using the *Paste* function, automatically carries out all tests, specifying each parameter along the way to run the three-group ANOVA, as opposed to manually going to multiple menus and entering all corresponding parameters to carry out the following steps (note that Steps 1–6 pertain to the pretest checklist):

1. Select *group 1*.

2. Run a histogram with a normal curve for *score*.

3. Select *group 2*.

4. Run a histogram with a normal curve for *score.*

5. Select *group 3.*

6. Run a histogram with a normal curve for *score.*

7. Select all *groups.*

8. Run an ANOVA specifying that the *factor* is *group* and the *dependent list* is *score,* with a homogeneity of variance test, descriptive statistics, and a Tukey post hoc test.

Take a moment to scroll through the Syntax file—examine the code. Notice the comments; these comments are manually entered into the Syntax file by the user to help make the code more readable. It is good practice to use comments at the top of the program to identify who wrote the program, the version of the program, the data file that it is associated with, and a brief synopsis of what the program does. If you want to better appreciate the value of comments, try deleting them and see how readable the code looks; it becomes less comprehensible and, in turn, less maintainable.

There are a few further points regarding the use of comments:

- The processor will ignore everything after the word *comment* until it encounters a period, so be sure to put a period at the end of each comment. Without the period at the end of the comment, the processor will ignore all further code until a period is encountered.
- Comments do not slow down the processing; the system simply ignores them. As a rule, comments help to make your programs clearer to you, making the code easier to comprehend and, thereby, maintain and edit.
- You can also use as many blank lines as you want to separate blocks of code; this will help you see where one procedure ends and the next begins, which can help with debugging.

The SPSS Syntax language is a fully developed programming language that extends well beyond the blocks of code that you can generate by clicking on the *Paste* button and the *comment* function. Most but not all menus in SPSS contain the *Paste* button; hence, if you opt for the SPSS Syntax language to run your jobs, occasionally you may need to do some manual coding.

For a more comprehensive list of the commands and functions available in the SPSS Syntax language, search the SPSS Help menu for *Syntax.*

GOOD COMMON SENSE

It is good practice to save an unedited *master copy* of your source data sets (e.g., *Filename[MASTER].sav*) and only work on a copy of the file (e.g., *Filename[WORK].sav*).

Even for the most careful person, data loss or data corruption is just an accidental key-stroke away.

Try to avoid deleting records; a better practice is to use *Select Cases* to rule them out of the analyses.

If you have source data (e.g., survey cards, written records, recordings, etc.), keep them intact and stored in a secured fashion. Do not destroy or discard source media just because the information has been entered into a database; you may need to refer to such materials over the course of your investigation (e.g., to resolve discrepancies, verify that some anomalous data are coded properly, etc.). Occasionally, such references to source materials take place during the analytic process as outliers, and other reasonably questionable data begin to emerge in reports or in visual inspection of the coded data.

All hardware fails at some point; therefore, it is good practice to keep secured/encrypted up-to-date backups of data files in at least two safe locations (e.g., a copy at home and another copy at work), unless your research protocol prohibits this. The rational for *two* sites is to offer additional protection against unforeseen adverse events at a site (e.g., fire, water damage, natural disaster, theft, electrical problems, etc.).

Some research protocols specify how long the research team is required to retain the source data (e.g., surveys, field notes, recordings, etc.). The time frame may range from days to years. The research protocol may also indicate how such data are to be disposed of on the specified expiration date (e.g., shredding, purging media, transfer to a secured storage site, etc.) so as to facilitate participant confidentiality. As a responsible researcher, be sure you fully understand and adhere to these protocols.

Key Concepts

- Generating random numbers
- Sorting cases
  - Ascending
  - Descending
- Selecting cases
- Recoding
- Importing data
- Syntax
  - Paste
  - Manual edits
- Master file
- Work file
- Data handling
- Data storage
- Data disposal

Practice Exercises

1. You have been given a data set reflecting the baseline test results of a group of people administered a pretest prior to a training.

   Data set—load *Chapter 10 – Exercise 01.sav.*

   Codebook—the data set contains three variables:

   - *name* is a string variable (participant's name).
   - *score* is a continuous variable (participant's pretest score).
   - *skill* is a categorical variable (1 = novice, 2 = intermediate, 3 = expert).

      a. Sort the data alphabetically by *name.*
      b. Sort the data from highest to lowest *score;* in cases where the *score* is a tie, subsort alphabetically by *name.*

2. You have been given a sample frame with record numbers ranging from 852 through 5723; the research team wants to gather a 2% sample (*n* = 97). Use SPSS to generate this list of random numbers.

3. You have been requested to compute statistics using only certain records within a data set.

   Data set—load *Chapter 10 – Exercise 03.sav* (this is the same data set as *Chapter 10 – Exercise 01.sav*).

   Codebook—the data set contains three variables:

   - *name* is a string variable (participant's name).
   - *score* is a continuous variable (participant's pretest score).
   - *skill* is a categorical variable (1 = novice, 2 = intermediate, 3 = expert).

   Compute descriptive statistics and histograms with a normal curve for *score* for:

   a. participants with a *skill* level that is intermediate.
   b. participants with a *score* between 20 and 65.

4. You have been given two non-SPSS data sets to import into SPSS and process:

   a. Data set—import the Excel file: *Chapter 10 – Exercise 04 A.xls* into SPSS.

NOTE: The import utility does not know what value labels are involved in the (categorical) group variable; it will just bring in the 1s and 2s.

   Codebook—the data set contains two variables:

   - *group* is a categorical variable (1 = control, 2 = treatment).
   - *score* is a continuous variable (participant's score).

   Compute a *t* test on *score* using *group* as the grouping variable.

b. Data set—import the ASCII file: *Chapter 10 – Exercise 04 B.txt* into SPSS.

   Codebook—the data set contains three variables:
   - *ID* is a numeric variable (the participant's ID).
   - *pretest* is a continuous variable (pretest score).
   - *posttest* is a continuous variable (posttest score).

Compute a paired *t* test using *pretest* and *posttest*.

5. Prior to a training, those who enrolled were given a pretest to determine their baseline knowledge of the subject. Those who scored 75 or higher on a pretest will be issued a *pass* and will be excused from the training session.

   Data set—load *Chapter 10 – Exercise 05.sav* (this is the same data set as *Chapter 10 – Exercise 01.sav*).

   Codebook—the data set contains three variables:
   - *name* is a string variable (participant's name).
   - *score* is a continuous variable (participant's pretest score).
   - *skill* is a categorical variable (1 = novice, 2 = intermediate, 3 = expert).
     a. Use the *Recode* function to create a new variable (based on *score*) that identifies those who passed and those who failed.
     b. Run a *t* test comparing the scores of those who passed with those who failed.

6. Acme Research Labs gathers data on an ongoing basis; you have been asked to automate the analytic process for a data set that is updated each week.

   Data set—load *Chapter 10 – Exercise 06.sav*.

   Codebook—the data set contains four variables:
   - *id* is a string variable (participant's ID).
   - *reading* is a continuous variable (reading score).
   - *writing* is a continuous variable (writing score).
   - *math* is a continuous variable (math score).
     a. Use the *Paste* function to create an SPSS Syntax file that performs the following operations:
   - Performs a multilevel sort:
     1. *reading* (ascending)
     2. *writing* (descending)
     3. *math* (ascending)
   - Runs descriptive statistics with histograms and normal curves for *reading* and *math*
     b. Save the SPSS Syntax file as *Weekly Report – 3 Subject Test.sps* (this SPSS Syntax file will be used in Exercise 7).

7. Open the SPSS Syntax file created in Exercise 6 (*Weekly Report – 3 Subject Test.sps*) and (manually) add in comments detailing:
   - Appropriate header information (name of source data set, name of programmer, version number, and summary of what this SPSS Syntax program does)
   - Notes explaining what each block of code does

8. Explain what is meant by a *master file* and the rationale for safely preserving it.

9. Explain what is meant by a *work file* and the rationale for performing analyses on it.

10. Data safety and confidentiality are essential in the realm of research and analysis. Discuss the rationale and techniques for appropriate data handling, data storage, and data disposal.

Solutions to Odd-Numbered Exercises

C H A P T E R   1

Research Principles

(1a) Will 30 minutes of square dancing, 5 days a week, help to reduce pediatric weight?

(1b) This would be a two-group study. The control group would have recess as usual with no structured activities; the kids can do whatever they want (except participate in the square dancing). The experimental group would participate in the square dancing.

(1c) The briefing sheet that would be distributed to teachers would instruct each teacher to go through his or her roll list and flip a coin one time for each student: Heads assigns the student to the square dancing, and tails assigns the student to have regular recess.

(1d) H_0: Aerobic square dancing 30 minutes a day, 5 days a week facilitates no weight loss among elementary school students.

H_1: Aerobic square dancing 30 minutes a day, 5 days a week facilitates weight loss among elementary school students.

(1e) At the conclusion of the study, the school nurse will weigh each student. The statistician will compare the weights of those who participated in the aerobic square dancing against those who had regular recess. If there is no statistically significant difference between the weights of these two groups, then we would accept H_0; otherwise, we would reject H_0 in favor of H_1.

(3a) Will placing a security camera on cashiers reduce cash shortages?

(3b) This will be a two-group study. The control group will have no cameras installed. The experimental group will have a camera installed focused on each cashier, and all cashiers will be notified that their actions are now being recorded.

(3c) The name of each of the 10 stores will be written on a chip and placed into a bag. The bag will be sealed, shaken, and then opened; a staff member will reach into the bag and, without looking, withdraw five chips. The stores indicated on these five chips will constitute the experimental group; the other five stores will constitute the control group. [NOTE: Since this is a two-group design, one could have simply used the coin-flip method; the chip selection is one potential alternative to consider when there are more than two groups, as will be the case in Chapter 6.]

(3d) H_0: Video recording will have no effect on cashier balances.

H_1: Video recording will reduce cashier losses.

(3e) The statistician will gather data from all 10 stores and compare cash register losses from the stores with no cameras to the stores with cameras. If there is no statistically significant difference between the cash losses of these two groups, then we would accept H_0; otherwise, we would reject H_0 in favor of H_1.

(5a) Will entering on-time employees in a weekly *get out of Friday free* lottery reduce morning lateness?

(5b) Two of the four buildings should participate in the *get out of Friday free* lottery—these sites will serve as the experimental groups. The other two should continue business as usual, serving as the control groups.

(5c) A staff member writes the name or address of each of the four buildings on four identical cards and places them in a box. Without looking, the staff member draws two cards out of the box, one at a time. These two cards will constitute the experimental groups; the other two will serve as the control groups.

(5d) H_0: Rewarding on-time arrivals with the chance to win a free day off will have no effect on lateness.

H_1: Rewarding on-time arrivals with the chance to win a free day off will reduce lateness.

(5e) After running this lottery program for a month, the statistician will gather and analyze the time cards from each of the four buildings and compare the minutes late from those in the two buildings that had no day-off lottery (in the control groups) with those who did participate in the day-off lottery (in the experimental group). If there is no significant difference in the minutes late, comparing the employees in the control group with those in the experimental group, then we would accept H_0; otherwise, we would reject H_0, in favor of H_1.

(7a) Does singing 1 hour a day improve memory?

(7b) Members in the control group will sit quietly for an hour and then take a memory test. Those in the experimental group will sing well-known songs for 1 hour (karaoke style) and then take the memory test.

(7c) Professor Madrigal will recruit 30 participants for this experiment. Prior to the arrival of the first participant, the professor flipped a coin (heads for control group, tails for experimental group)—the coin flip rendered tails, and hence the first participant who shows up will be assigned to the experimental group. Each remaining subject would be assigned to the control or experimental group on an alternating basis, upon arrival, thereby keeping the groups balanced.

(7d) H_0: Singing has no effect on memory.

H_1: Singing enhances memory.

(7e) Upon the departure of the last subject, the professor compares the memory test scores of those in the control group with those in the experimental group. If there is no statistically significant difference in the scores, then this supports H_0; otherwise, the professor would reject H_0 in that the data support H_1.

(9a) Do flashcards help students memorize the multiplication table?

(9b) Members in the experimental group will each be issued a set of 100 flashcards $(1 \times 1 \ldots 10 \times 10)$ and will be instructed to work with them for 30 minutes a day for 1 month. Members in the control group will use the usual multiplication teaching method (only). Members of both groups will be tested once a week; they will be given 10 minutes to answer 100 multiplication problems $(1 \times 1 = \underline{\quad} \ldots 10 \times 10 = \underline{\quad})$.

(9c) Ms. Fractal calls each student to the front of the room one at a time; she holds up a coin and asks the student to guess heads or tails. She then flips a coin; if the student guessed correctly, then that student is assigned to the experimental group and given a set of multiplication flashcards; otherwise, the student is assigned to the control group and receives no flashcards.

(9d) H_0: Flashcards do not help students learn the multiplication table.

H_1: Flashcards help students learn the multiplication table.

(9e) Ms. Fract al will grade the tests. If the experimental group's overall score is statistically significantly higher than the control group's score, then she would reject the null hypothesis (H_0), in favor of the experimental hypothesis (H_1); otherwise, the findings suggest support for the null hypothesis (H_0).

CHAPTER 2

Sampling

(1a) In terms of time, gathering a sample of an entire population could take weeks, months, or possibly years depending on the size of the population, geographical area involved, and complexity of the data to be gathered. The point of research is to get the answer to a meaningful question, presumably to solve a problem or improve a situation. Such answers can be expedited by sampling, as opposed to gathering data on the entire population. Attempting to sample the entire population would be so time-consuming that by the time you had acquired your full data set, the nature of the initial problem may have changed substantially, thereby making your findings virtually irrelevant.

(1b) No matter what method of gathering data one uses (e.g., in-person surveys, phone surveys, postal/e-mail contact, experimental designs, tests, etc.), costs are involved. When it comes to data collection, subject participation fees are customary, data collection teams need to be paid, and there are administrative costs involved (photocopying, office space, equipment, office supplies, etc.). Considering the volume of individuals that would be involved in studying an entire population, the costs would be prohibitive.

(1c) Beyond the lengthy time and exorbitant costs that would be involved in studying an entire population, it is seldom feasible to gather data on so many people. The population may span a broad geographical region, requiring lengthy travel among the research staff. Within a population, one would likely encounter a variety of languages; it may not be possible to translate verbal or written instructions to attain a full population sample. In addition, some studies may involve experiments that can be administered only at a special facility; it would be impossible to arrange a round-trip commute for every member of a population to that facility to participate.

(1d) Extrapolation involves working diligently to gather a representative sample in sufficient quantities to facilitate stable statistical processing. If the data gathered constitute a representative sample, then one could (more) confidently extrapolate the findings to (better) comprehend the overall population from which it was drawn; this is also known as external validity.

(3a) The population is the entire student body currently enrolled (e.g., 22,000 students).

(3b) The sample frame is the available list of students currently enrolled (e.g., 16,000 students).

(3c) Fortunately, the list of participants in the sample frame was already numbered from 1 to 16,000. I would want to gather data on 2% of the sample frame (16,000 × .02 = 320); I would use SPSS to generate 320 random numbers between 1 and 16,000—this list would indicate which students in the sample frame to recruit. Actually, I would probably generate more than 320 random numbers just in case SPSS produces some duplicates.

(3d) I would build (and test) an online survey. Next, I would send an e-mail to each of the 320 students in the sample set; the e-mail would concisely explain the nature of the study and courteously request that they voluntarily click on the link to the online survey.

(5a) The population is all of the people who enter the library.

(5b) The sample frame consists of those who enter the Reference Room.

(5c) I would approach each person accessing the reference section throughout the day and ask if they would be willing to spend a few minutes answering some simple questions about how they use the library.

(5d) I would use a clipboard with a prepared questionnaire. To satisfy the strata (children/adults), the first question would be, "How old are you?"

(7a) I wouldn't want to bother people who are walking someplace or who are engaged in conversations with friends/family, so I would approach people waiting in line (for food or an attraction) since they'd probably be a bit bored just waiting in line.

(7b) I would ask them their first name, just to be friendly, and then tell them that I work for Acme Research Firm (I'd point to my badge) and tell them that I'm gathering some information about how much money they intend to spend today and ask them if they wouldn't mind estimating that amount for me. Whether they choose to respond or not, I'd thank them.

(9a) I would ride the bus starting at 8:00 a.m. At first I'd approach anyone. If they consented to talk to me, I would begin by asking them their age. Once I'd hit my quota for a group (50 minors, 100 adults), I'd stop approaching that group and proceed with the other group. When I'd gathered all 150 surveys, I'd stop the sampling process completely and move on to the analysis (off the bus).

(9b) I would approach potential participants, identify myself as a staff member of the Acme Bus Company (I'd point to my badge), and ask the person if I could ask them a few questions about their impressions of their bus riding experience(s). I would record their responses on a clipboard, which would contain the printed survey. The first question I would ask is "What is your age?" which I would record on the survey form; if they didn't want to tell me their age, I would ask "Are you 18 or over?" unless it was obvious that the person was clearly either a child or an adult. This way I could keep a running count of how many minors and how many adults I had surveyed.

C H A P T E R 3

Working in SPSS

(1)

enrolled

		Value	Count	Percent
Standard Attributes	Position	1		
	Label	Are you currently enrolled in school?		
	Type	Numeric		
	Format	F8		
	Measurement	Nominal		
	Role	Input		
Valid Values	1	Yes	4	80.0%
	2	No	1	20.0%

units

		Value
Standard Attributes	Position	2
	Label	How many units are you taking?
	Type	Numeric
	Format	F8
	Measurement	Scale
	Role	Input
N	Valid	5
	Missing	0
Central Tendency and Dispersion	Mean	9.20
	Standard Deviation	6.261
	Percentile 25	6.00
	Percentile 50	12.00
	Percentile 75	12.00

gpa

		Value
Standard Attributes	Position	3
	Label	What is your overall GPA?
	Type	Numeric
	Format	F8.2
	Measurement	Scale
	Role	Input
N	Valid	5
	Missing	0
Central Tendency and Dispersion	Mean	3.1400
	Standard Deviation	.49704
	Percentile 25	2.8000
	Percentile 50	2.9000
	Percentile 75	3.6400

(3)

degree

		Value	Count	Percent
Standard Attributes	Position	1		
	Label	What is the highest degree you've completed?		
	Type	Numeric		
	Format	F8		
	Measurement	Nominal		
	Role	Input		
Valid Values	1	Associate's	1	20.0%
	2	Bachelor's	2	40.0%
	3	Master's	2	40.0%
	4	Doctorate	0	.0%

pretest

		Value
Standard Attributes	Position	2
	Label	What was your pretest score?
	Type	Numeric
	Format	F8
	Measurement	Scale
	Role	Input
N	Valid	5
	Missing	0
Central Tendency and Dispersion	Mean	27.20
	Standard Deviation	3.701
	Percentile 25	25.00
	Percentile 50	28.00
	Percentile 75	30.00

posttest

		Value
Standard Attributes	Position	3
	Label	What was your posttest score?
	Type	Numeric
	Format	F8
	Measurement	Scale
	Role	Input
N	Valid	5
	Missing	0
Central Tendency and Dispersion	Mean	39.00
	Standard Deviation	8.000
	Percentile 25	34.00
	Percentile 50	38.00
	Percentile 5	46.00

pretest

		Value
Standard Attributes	Position	2
	Label	What was your pretest score?
	Type	Numeric
	Format	F8
	Measurement	Scale
	Role	Input
N	Valid	5
	Missing	0
Central Tendency and Dispersion	Mean	27.20
	Standard Deviation	3.701
	Percentile 25	25.00
	Percentile 50	28.00
	Percentile 75	30.00

(5)

first_initial

		Value	Count	Percent
Standard Attributes	Position	1		
	Label	What is the first initial of your first name?		
	Type	String		
	Format	A1		
	Measurement	Nominal		
	Role	Input		
Valid Values	D		1	20.0%
	J		1	20.0%
	P		1	20.0%
	T		1	20.0%
	V		1	20.0%

last_name

		Value	Count	Percent
Standard Attributes	Position	2		
	Label	What is your last name?		
	Type	String		
	Format	A25		
	Measurement	Nominal		
	Role	Input		
Valid Values	Freeman		1	20.0%
	Gower		1	20.0%
	Jones		1	20.0%
	Rexx		1	20.0%
	Smith		1	20.0%

siblings

		Value
Standard Attributes	Position	3
	Label	How many siblings do you have?
	Type	Numeric
	Format	F8
	Measurement	Scale
	Role	Input
N	Valid	5
	Missing	0
Central Tendency and Dispersion	Mean	1.60
	Standard Deviation	1.140
	Percentile 25	1.00
	Percentile 50	2.00
	Percentile 75	2.00

adopted

		Value	Count	Percent
Standard Attributes	Position	4		
	Label	Are you adopted?		
	Type	Numeric		
	Format	F8		
	Measurement	Nominal		
	Role	Input		
Valid Values	1	Yes	1	20.0%
	2	No	4	80.0%

(7)

passport

		Value	Count	Percent
Standard Attributes	Position	1		
	Label	Do you have a passport?		
	Type	Numeric		
	Format	F8		
	Measurement	Nominal		
	Role	Input		
Valid Values	1	Yes	2	40.0%
	2	No	3	60.0%
	3	Decline to answer	0	.0%

fired

		Value	Count	Percent
Standard Attributes	Position	2		
	Label	Have you ever been fired from a job?		
	Type	Numeric		
	Format	F8		
	Measurement	Nominal		
	Role	Input		
Valid Values	1	Yes	1	20.0%
	2	No	3	60.0%
	3	Decline to answer	1	20.0%

er

		Value	Count	Percent
Standard Attributes	Position	3		
	Label	Have you ever been treated in an emergency room?		
	Type	Numeric		
	Format	F8		
	Measurement	Nominal		
	Role	Input		
Valid Values	1	Yes	2	40.0%
	2	No	3	60.0%
	3	Decline to answer	0	.0%

dob

		Value
Standard Attributes	Position	4
	Label	What is your birth date?
	Type	Numeric
	Format	ADATE10
	Measurement	Scale
	Role	Input
N	Valid	5
	Missing	0
Central Tendency and Dispersion	Mean	8/21/1965
	Standard Deviation	280683:12:07.445
	Percentile 25	1/23/1936
	Percentile 50	6/07/1974
	Percentile 75	3/01/1987

(9)

blood_type

		Value	Count	Percent
Standard Attributes	Position	1		
	Label	What is your blood type?		
	Type	Numeric		
	Format	F8		
	Measurement	Nominal		
	Role	Input		
Valid Values	1	A-	1	20.0%
	2	A+	0	.0%
	3	B-	0	.0%
	4	B+	1	20.0%
	5	AB-	0	.0%
	6	AB+	1	20.0%
	7	O-	1	20.0%
	8	O+	0	.0%
	9	Don't know	1	20.0%

Gender

		Value	Count	Percent
Standard Attributes	Position	2		
	Label	What is your gender?		
	Type	Numeric		
	Format	F8		
	Measurement	Nominal		
	Role	Input		
Valid Values	1	Female	2	40.0%
	2	Male	3	60.0%

prior_donor

		Value	Count	Percent
Standard Attributes	Position	3		
	Label	Have you ever donated blood before?		
	Type	Numeric		
	Format	F8		
	Measurement	Nominal		
	Role	Input		
Valid Values	1	Yes	2	40.0%
	2	No	3	60.0%

CHAPTER 4

Descriptive Statistics

(1a)

Statistics

siblings

N	Valid	41
	Missing	0
Mean		1.54
Median		1.00
Mode		1
Std. Deviation		.951
Variance		.905
Range		4
Minimum		0
Maximum		4

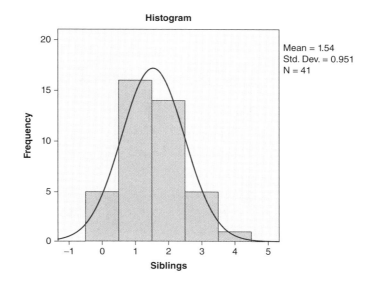

(1b)

class

		Frequency	Percent	Valid Percent	Cumulative Percent
Valid	Prof. Lamm	20	48.8	48.8	48.8
	Prof. Milner	21	51.2	51.2	100.0
	Total	41	100.0	100.0	

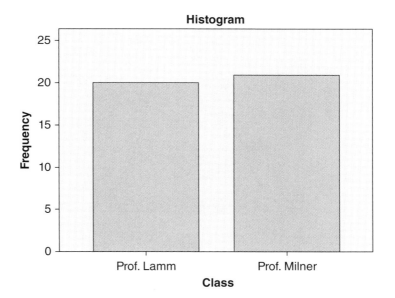

(1c)

Statistics

siblings

N	Valid	20
	Missing	0
Mean		1.35
Median		1.00
Mode		1[a]
Std. Deviation		.813
Variance		.661
Range		3
Minimum		0
Maximum		3

a. Multiple modes exist. The smallest value is shown

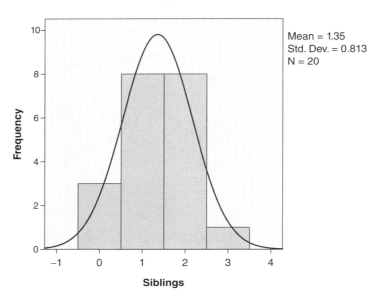

Histogram

(1d)

Statistics

siblings

N	Valid	21
	Missing	0
Mean		1.71
Median		2.00
Mode		1
Std. Deviation		1.056
Variance		1.114
Range		4
Minimum		0
Maximum		4

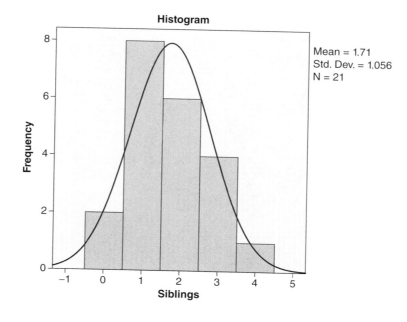

Histogram

Mean = 1.71
Std. Dev. = 1.056
N = 21

(3a)

Statistics

spelling

N	Valid	22
	Missing	0
Mean		16.23
Median		16.00
Mode		16
Std. Deviation		2.308
Variance		5.327
Range		8
Minimum		12
Maximum		20

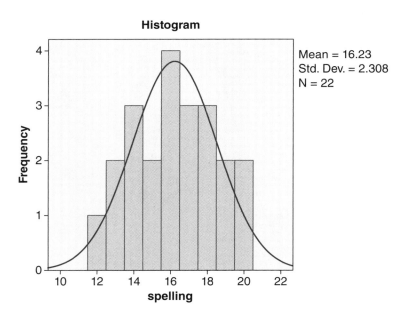

Histogram

Mean = 16.23
Std. Dev. = 2.308
N = 22

(3b)

Statistics

looker

N	Valid	22
	Missing	0

looker

		Frequency	Percent	Valid Percent	Cumulative Percent
Valid	Looks at keyboard	15	68.2	68.2	68.2
	Doesn't look at keyboard	7	31.8	31.8	100.0
	Total	22	100.0	100.0	

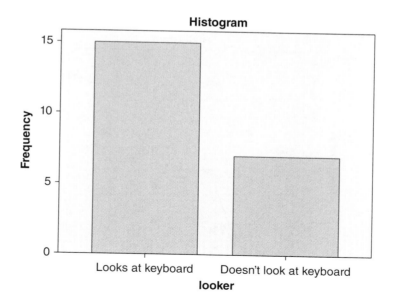

(3c)

Statistics

spelling

N	Valid	15
	Missing	0
Mean		15.60
Median		16.00
Mode		16
Std. Deviation		1.765
Variance		3.114
Range		6
Minimum		12
Maximum		18

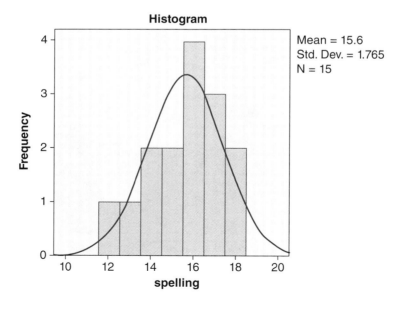

Mean = 15.6
Std. Dev. = 1.765
N = 15

(3d)

Statistics

spelling

N	Valid	7
	Missing	0
Mean		17.57
Median		19.00
Mode		19[a]
Std. Deviation		2.878
Variance		8.286
Range		7
Minimum		13
Maximum		20

a. Multiple modes exist. The smallest value is shown

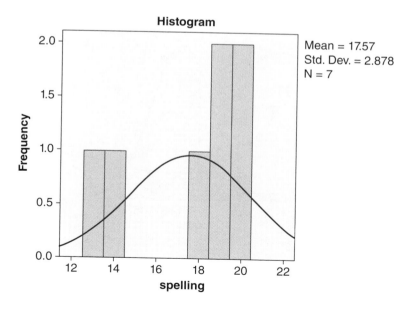

Histogram

Mean = 17.57
Std. Dev. = 2.878
N = 7

(5a)

Statistics

units

N	Valid	40
	Missing	0
Mean		11.85
Median		12.00
Mode		12
Std. Deviation		2.348
Variance		5.515
Range		9
Minimum		6
Maximum		15

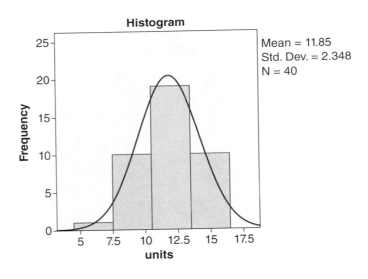

Histogram

Mean = 11.85
Std. Dev. = 2.348
N = 40

(5b)

degree

		Frequency	Percent	Valid Percent	Cumulative Percent
Valid	Bachelor's	31	77.5	77.5	77.5
	Master's	7	17.5	17.5	95.0
	Doctorate	2	5.0	5.0	100.0
	Total	40	100.0	100.0	

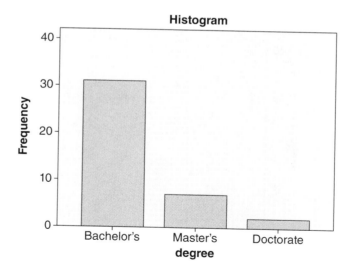

(5c)

Statistics

units

N	Valid	31
	Missing	0
Mean		12.10
Median		12.00
Mode		12
Std. Deviation		2.119
Variance		4.490
Range		6
Minimum		9
Maximum		15

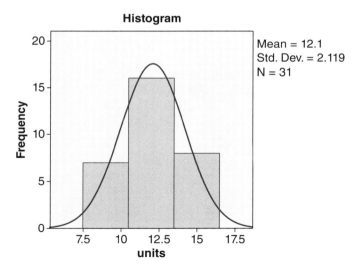

Histogram

Mean = 12.1
Std. Dev. = 2.119
N = 31

(5d)

Statistics

units

N	Valid	7
	Missing	0
Mean		10.29
Median		9.00
Mode		9
Std. Deviation		2.928
Variance		8.571
Range		9
Minimum		6
Maximum		15

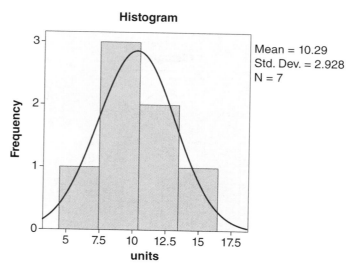

Histogram

Mean = 10.29
Std. Dev. = 2.928
N = 7

(5e)

Statistics

units

N	Valid	2
	Missing	0
Mean		13.50
Median		13.50
Mode		12[a]
Std. Deviation		2.121
Variance		4.500
Range		3
Minimum		12
Maximum		15

a. Multiple modes exist. The smallest value is shown

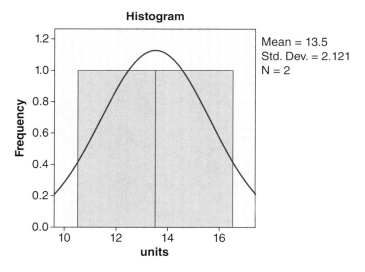

(7a)

Statistics

emails

N	Valid	173
	Missing	0
Mean		169.77
Median		168.00
Mode		170
Std. Deviation		33.078
Variance		1094.164
Range		166
Minimum		109
Maximum		275

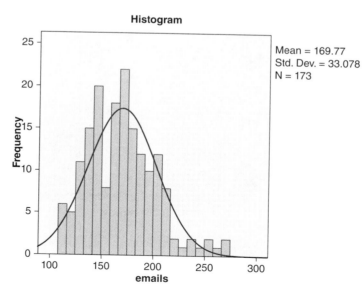

Histogram

Mean = 169.77
Std. Dev. = 33.078
N = 173

(7b)

employ

		Frequency	Percent	Valid Percent	Cumulative Percent
Valid	Full-time	85	49.1	49.1	49.1
	Part-time	39	22.5	22.5	71.7
	Unemployed	49	28.3	28.3	100.0
	Total	173	100.0	100.0	

(7c)

Statistics

emails

N	Valid	85
	Missing	0
Mean		153.71
Median		153.00
Mode		137[a]
Std. Deviation		23.294
Variance		542.615
Range		91
Minimum		109
Maximum		200

a. Multiple modes exist. The smallest value is shown

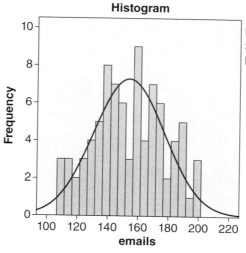

(7d)

Statistics

emails

N	Valid	39
	Missing	0
Mean		166.77
Median		168.00
Mode		129[a]
Std. Deviation		24.330
Variance		591.972
Range		89
Minimum		129
Maximum		218

a. Multiple modes exist. The smallest
value is shown

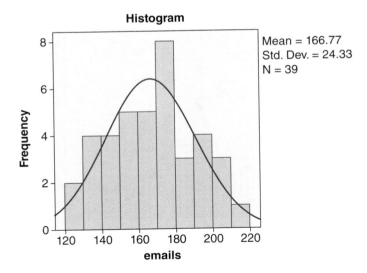

Histogram

Mean = 166.77
Std. Dev. = 24.33
N = 39

(7e)

Statistics

emails

N	Valid	49
	Missing	0
Mean		200.04
Median		204.00
Mode		175[a]
Std. Deviation		33.209
Variance		1102.832
Range		139
Minimum		136
Maximum		275

a. Multiple modes exist. The smallest value
is shown

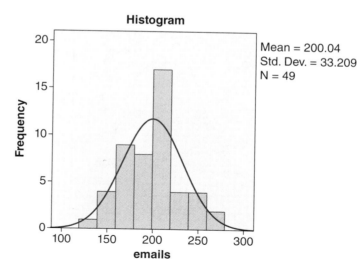

Histogram

Mean = 200.04
Std. Dev. = 33.209
N = 49

(9a)

Statistics

nsatisfy

N	Valid	336
	Missing	0
Mean		72.78
Median		74.00
Mode		82
Std. Deviation		11.154
Variance		124.421
Range		56
Minimum		42
Maximum		98

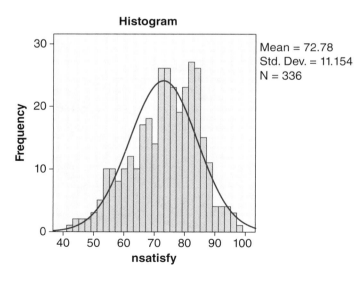

Histogram

Mean = 72.78
Std. Dev. = 11.154
N = 336

(9b)

ward

		Frequency	Percent	Valid Percent	Cumulative Percent
Valid	2 patients per nurse	162	48.2	48.2	48.2
	4 patients per nurse	174	51.8	51.8	100.0
	Total	336	100.0	100.0	

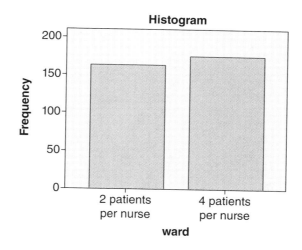

(9c)

Statistics

nsatisfy

N	Valid	162
	Missing	0
Mean		79.84
Median		80.00
Mode		82
Std. Deviation		7.049
Variance		49.688
Range		35
Minimum		63
Maximum		98

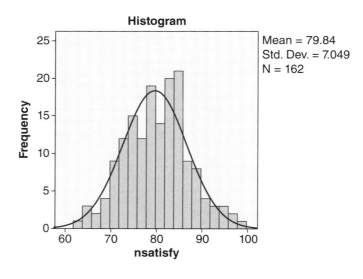

Histogram

Mean = 79.84
Std. Dev. = 7.049
N = 162

(9d)

Statistics

nsatisfy

N	Valid	174
	Missing	0
Mean		66.21
Median		66.00
Mode		65[a]
Std. Deviation		10.229
Variance		104.642
Range		46
Minimum		42
Maximum		88

a. Multiple modes exist. The smallest

value is shown

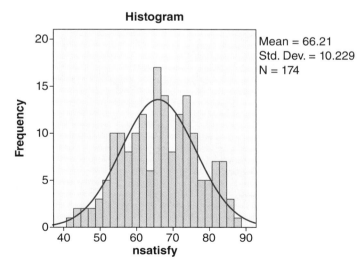

Histogram

Mean = 66.21
Std. Dev. = 10.229
N = 174

CHAPTER 5

t Test

1. Data Set A

(1a) H_0: Practicing meditation for 30 minutes a day, 3 days a week for 2 weeks has no effect on resting pulse rate.

H_1: Practicing meditation for 30 minutes a day, 3 days a week for 2 weeks affects resting pulse rate.

(1b) Histograms with normal curve plots show a normal distribution of *pulse* for both groups, as shown in the two figures below; hence, the pretest criterion of normality is satisfied.

Normal distribution for *pulse* in Group 1 (no meditation)

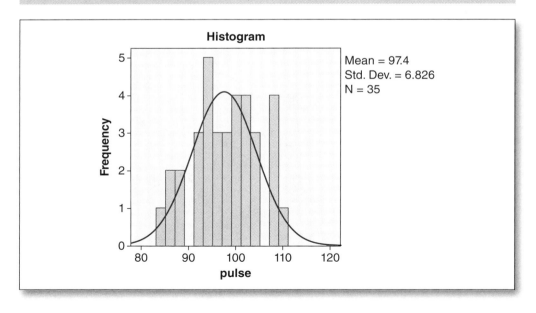

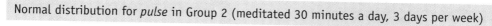

Normal distribution for *pulse* in Group 2 (meditated 30 minutes a day, 3 days per week)

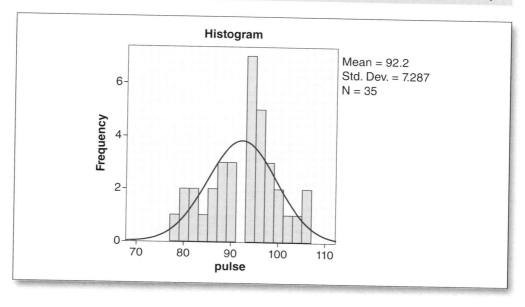

Histogram

Mean = 92.2
Std. Dev. = 7.287
N = 35

Test of Homogeneity of Variances

pulse

Levene Statistic	df1	df2	Sig.
.089	1	68	.766

The homogeneity of variance score shows a significance (*p*) of .766; since this is greater than the α level of .05, this suggests that there is no statistically significant difference between the variances of the two groups; hence, this pretest criterion passes.

The *n* for each group, as shown in the Descriptives table below, is 35 for each group; since the *n*s are greater than 30, this criterion passes also.

(1c) The *t* test revealed the following:

Descriptives

pulse

	N	Mean	Std. Deviation	Std. Error	95% Confidence Interval for Mean		Minimum	Maximum
					Lower Bound	Upper Bound		
No meditation	35	97.40	6.826	1.154	95.06	99.74	84	109
Meditates 30 minutes	35	92.20	7.287	1.232	89.70	94.70	78	105
Total	70	94.80	7.483	.894	93.02	96.58	78	109

ANOVA

pulse

	Sum of Squares	df	Mean Square	F	Sig.
Between Groups	473.200	1	473.200	9.492	.003
Within Groups	3390.000	68	49.853		
Total	3863.200	69			

The mean pulse rate for Group 1 (no meditation) is 97.40, whereas the mean pulse rate for Group 2 (meditated 30 minutes, 3 days per week) is 92.20. This 5.2-point difference is statistically significant since the significance (p) is .003 (which is less than the .05 α level).

(1d)   This study analyzed the effects that meditation had on resting pulse rates. The subjects were randomly assigned to one of two groups: the group that did not meditate and the other group that meditated for 30 minutes on Monday, Wednesday, and Friday for 2 weeks. Results revealed a mean resting pulse rate of 97.40 for those who did not meditate and 92.20 for those who meditated. Using a .05 α level, the p value of .003 suggests that meditation facilitates a significant reduction in resting pulse rate; hence, we reject H_0. These findings suggest support for H_1—specifically, that practicing meditation for 30 minutes a day, 3 days a week for 2 weeks affected the mean resting pulse rate among these participants.

1. Data Set B

   (1a) H_0: Practicing meditation for 30 minutes a day, 3 days a week for 2 weeks has no effect on resting pulse rate.

   H_1: Practicing meditation for 30 minutes a day, 3 days a week for 2 weeks affects resting pulse rate.

   (1b)   Histograms with normal curve plots show a normal distribution of *pulse* for both groups, as shown in the two figures below; hence, the pretest criterion of normality is satisfied.

The homogeneity of variance score for *pulse* shows a significance (p) of .576; since this is greater than the α level of .05, this suggests that there is no statistically significant difference between the variances of the two groups; hence, this pretest criterion passes.

The n criterion is satisfied as both groups have an n of more than 30 (see Descriptives table below).

Normal distribution for *pulse* in Group 1 (no meditation)

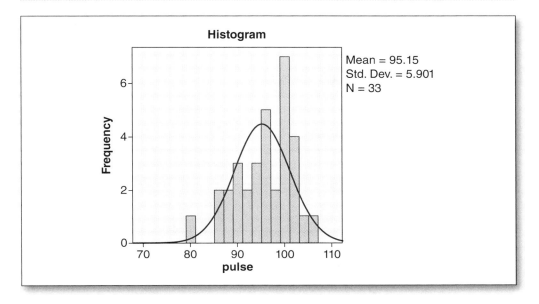

Mean = 95.15
Std. Dev. = 5.901
N = 33

Normal distribution for *pulse* in Group 2 (meditated 30 minutes a day, 3 days per week)

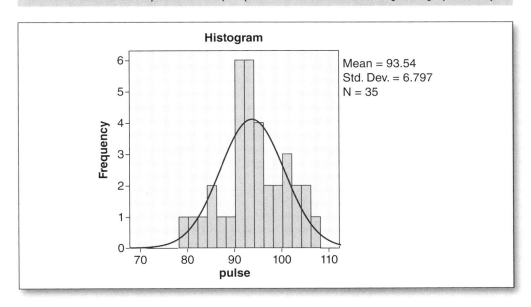

Mean = 93.54
Std. Dev. = 6.797
N = 35

Test of Homogeneity of Variances

Pulse

Levene Statistic	df1	df2	Sig.
.317	1	66	.576

(1c) The *t* test revealed the following:

Descriptives

Pulse

	N	Mean	Std. Deviation	Std. Error	95% Confidence Interval for Mean		Minimum	Maximum
					Lower Bound	Upper Bound		
No meditation	33	95.15	5.901	1.027	93.06	97.24	80	105
Meditates 30 minutes	35	93.54	6.797	1.149	91.21	95.88	79	107
Total	68	94.32	6.382	.774	92.78	95.87	79	107

ANOVA

pulse

	Sum of Squares	df	Mean Square	F	Sig.
Between Groups	43.954	1	43.954	1.080	.302
Within Groups	2684.928	66	40.681		
Total	2728.882	67			

The mean pulse rate for Group 1 (no meditation) is 95.15, whereas the mean pulse rate for Group 2 (meditated 30 minutes, 3 days per week) is 93.54. Even though the mean pulse rate for the meditation group is 1.61 points lower than the control group, this difference is not considered statistically significant since the significance (*p*) is .302 (which is greater than the .05 α level).

(1d) This study analyzed the effects that meditation had on resting pulse rates. The participants were randomly assigned to two groups: those who did not meditate and those who meditated for 30 minutes on Monday, Wednesday, and Friday for 2 weeks. Results revealed a mean resting pulse rate of 95.15 for those who did not meditate and 93.54 for those who did meditate. This study showed a 1.61 reduction in the pulse rate of those who meditated, but since the *p* value of .302 is greater than the .05 α level, we would conclude that this difference is not statistically significant; hence, we do not reject H_0. For the subjects studied, meditation did not significantly affect resting pulse rate (we would reject H_1).

3. Data Set A

(3a) H_0: The Acme reading lamp is no different from regular room lighting when it comes to reading speed.

   H_1: The Acme reading lamp facilitates faster reading speed than regular room lighting.

(3b) Histograms with normal curve plots show a normal distribution of *seconds* for both groups, as shown in the two figures below; hence, the pretest criterion of normality is satisfied.

Normal distribution for *seconds* in Group 1 (room lighting)

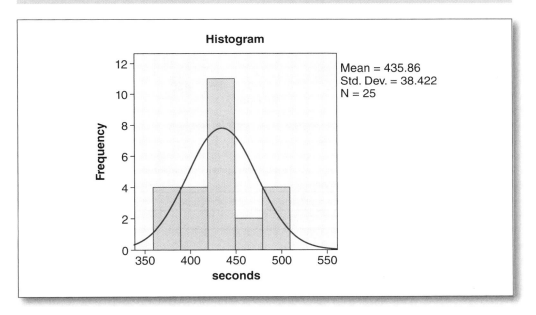

The homogeneity of variance score for *seconds* shows a significance (*p*) of .643; since this is greater than the α level of .05, this suggests that there is no statistically significant difference between the variances of the two groups; hence, this pretest criterion passes.

The room lighting group had an *n* of 25, and the Acme lamp group had an *n* of 28 (see Descriptives table below); these figures are close to the minimal quota of 30 per group. The findings of the *t* test would be more robust if the *n*s were slightly higher for these groups.

Normal distribution for *seconds* in Group 2 (Acme reading lamp)

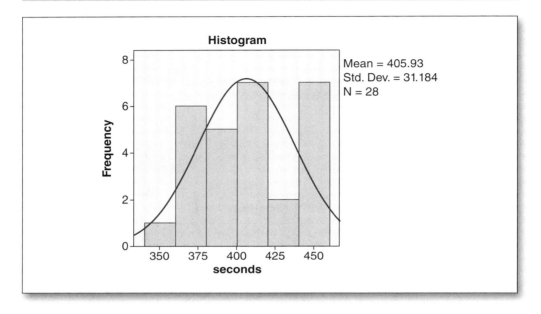

Test of Homogeneity of Variances

seconds

Levene Statistic	df1	df2	Sig.
.217	1	51	.643

(3c) The *t* test revealed the following:

Descriptives

seconds

	N	Mean	Std. Deviation	Std. Error	95% Confidence Interval for Mean		Minimum	Maximum
					Lower Bound	Upper Bound		
Room lighting	25	435.86	38.422	7.684	420.00	451.72	374	509
Acme lamp	28	405.93	31.184	5.893	393.84	418.02	357	455
Total	53	420.05	37.601	5.165	409.68	430.41	357	509

ANOVA

Seconds

	Sum of Squares	df	Mean Square	F	Sig.
Between Groups	11835.678	1	11835.678	9.785	.003
Within Groups	61685.335	51	1209.516		
Total	73521.012	52			

The mean read time (seconds) rate for Group 1 (room lighting) is 436 seconds (rounded), whereas the mean read time for Group 2 (Acme reading lamp) is 406 seconds (rounded). This 30-second difference is statistically significant since the significance (p) is .003 (which is less than the .05 α level).

(3d) This study analyzed the effects that the Acme reading lamp had on reading speed. The 53 subjects were randomly assigned to one of two groups; one group read a 1,000-word essay using regular room lighting, and the other group read the same essay using the new Acme reading lamp. Results revealed that on average, those who read using the Acme reading lamp completed the essay 30 seconds earlier than those who used regular room lighting (406 seconds vs. 436 seconds, respectively). Using a .05 α level, the p value of .003 suggests that the Acme reading lamp facilitates prompter reading speeds; hence, we reject H_0. These findings suggest support for H_1—specifically, that the Acme reading lamp enhances reading rates.

3. Data Set B

(3a) H_0: The Acme reading lamp is no different from regular room lighting when it comes to reading speed.

H_1: The Acme reading lamp facilitates faster reading speed than regular room lighting.

(3b) Histograms with normal curve plots show a normal distribution of *seconds* for both groups, as shown in the two figures below; hence, the pretest criterion of normality is satisfied.

The homogeneity of variance score for *seconds* shows a significance (p) of .380; since this is greater than the α level of .05, this suggests that there is no statistically significant difference between the variances of the two groups; hence, this pretest criterion passes.

The n for each group is 25 (see Descriptives table below), which is close to the minimal quota of 30 per group. The findings of the t test would be more robust if the ns were slightly higher.

Normal distribution for *seconds* in Group 1 (room lighting)

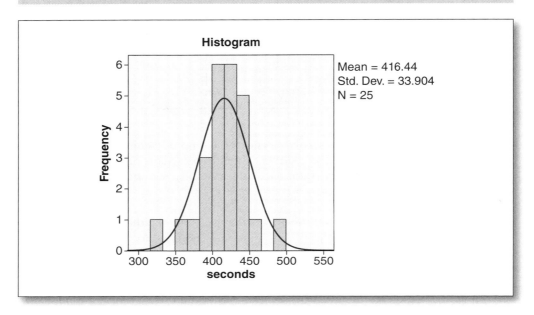

Normal distribution for *seconds* in Group 2 (Acme reading lamp)

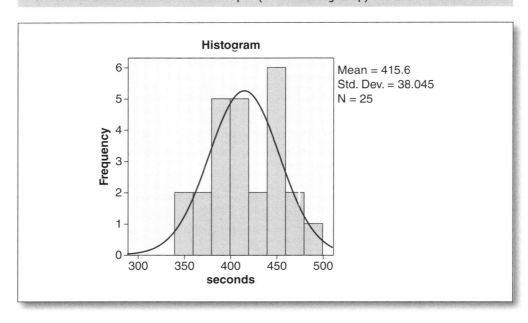

Test of Homogeneity of Variances

seconds

Levene Statistic	df1	df2	Sig.
.785	1	48	.380

(3c) The *t* test revealed the following:

Descriptives

seconds

	N	Mean	Std. Deviation	Std. Error	95% Confidence Interval for Mean		Minimum	Maximum
					Lower Bound	Upper Bound		
Room lighting	25	416.44	33.904	6.781	402.44	430.44	331	489
Acme lamp	25	415.60	38.045	7.609	399.90	431.30	344	481
Total	50	416.02	35.667	5.044	405.88	426.16	331	489

ANOVA

seconds

	Sum of Squares	df	Mean Square	F	Sig.
Between Groups	8.820	1	8.820	.007	.935
Within Groups	62326.160	48	1298.462		
Total	62334.980	49			

The mean read time (seconds) rate for Group 1 (room lighting) is 416.44 seconds, whereas the mean read time for Group 2 (Acme reading lamp) is 415.60 seconds. This .84-second difference is statistically insignificant since the significance (*p*) is .935 (which is greater than the .05 α level).

(3d) This study analyzed the effects that the Acme reading lamp had on reading speed. The 50 subjects were randomly assigned to one of two groups; half read a 1,000-word essay using regular room lighting, and the other half read the same essay using the new Acme reading lamp. Results revealed that on average, those who read using the Acme reading lamp completed the essay about 1 second (.86 seconds) earlier than those who used regular room lighting (415.60 seconds vs. 416.44 seconds, respectively). Using a .05 α level, the p value of .935 suggests that the Acme reading lamp does not facilitate significantly prompter reading speeds; hence, we do not reject H_0, but we do reject H_1. The claim that the Acme Company made, that this lamp increases reading speed, is not supported by these findings.

5. Data Set A

(5a) H$_0$: Classical music has no effect on problem-solving skills.

H$_1$: Classical music enhances problem-solving skills.

(5b) Histograms with normal curve plots show a normal distribution of *seconds* for both groups, as shown in the two figures below; hence, the pretest criterion of normality is satisfied.

Normal distribution for *seconds* in Group 1 (no music)

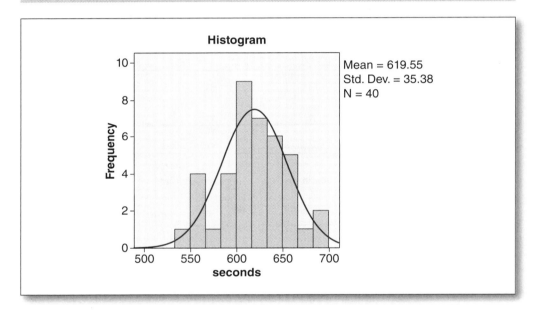

The homogeneity of variance score for *seconds* shows a significance (*p*) of .095; since this is greater than the α level of .05, this suggests that there is no statistically significant difference between the variances of the two groups; hence, this pretest criterion passes.

The *n* for each group is 40 (see Descriptives table below), which satisfies the 30 per group minimum criterion.

Normal distribution for *seconds* in Group 2 (music at 30 dB)

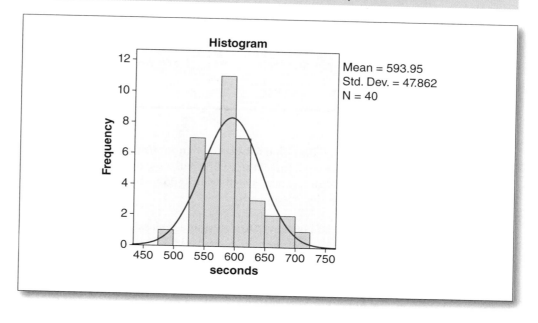

Test of Homogeneity of Variances

Seconds

Levene Statistic	df1	df2	Sig.
2.861	1	78	.095

(5c) The *t* test revealed the following:

Descriptives

seconds

	N	Mean	Std. Deviation	Std. Error	95% Confidence Interval for Mean		Minimum	Maximum
					Lower Bound	Upper Bound		
No music	40	619.55	35.380	5.594	608.23	630.86	541	690
Music at 30 dB	40	593.95	47.862	7.568	578.64	609.26	497	707
Total	80	606.75	43.758	4.892	597.01	616.49	497	707

ANOVA

Seconds

	Sum of Squares	df	Mean Square	F	Sig.
Between Groups	13105.152	1	13105.152	7.399	.008
Within Groups	138161.213	78	1771.298		
Total	151266.366	79			

The mean puzzle completion time for Group 1 (no music) is 620 seconds (rounded), whereas the subjects in Group 2 (music at 30 dB) had a mean completion of 594 seconds (rounded). This 26-second difference is statistically significant since the significance (p) is .008 (which is less than the .05 α level).

(5d) This experiment was designed to determine if classical music facilitates problem solving. We recruited 80 subjects; half were randomly assigned to solve a 100-piece jigsaw puzzle in a silent room, and the other half solved the same puzzle in a room with soft classical music playing (at 30 dB). Those in the music group solved the puzzle an average of 26 seconds faster than those who worked in silence (594 seconds vs. 620 seconds). Using a .05 α level, the p value of .008 suggests that this is a statistically significant difference; hence, we reject H_0. These findings support H_1—that classical music facilitates problem solving.

5. Data Set B

(5a) H_0: Classical music has no effect on problem-solving skills.

   H_1: Classical music enhances problem-solving skills.

(5b) Histograms with normal curve plots show a normal distribution of *seconds* for both groups, as shown in the two figures below; hence, the pretest criterion of normality is satisfied.

The homogeneity of variance score for *seconds* shows a significance (p) of .235; since this is greater than the α level of .05, this suggests that there is no statistically significant difference between the variances of the two groups; hence, this pretest criterion passes.

The n for each group is over 30: 43 for the no music and 39 for music at 30 dB (see Descriptives table below), which satisfies the 30 per group minimum criterion.

Normal distribution for *seconds* in Group 1 (no music)

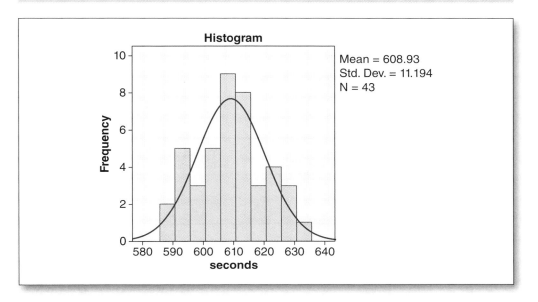

Normal distribution for *seconds* in Group 2 (music at 30 dB)

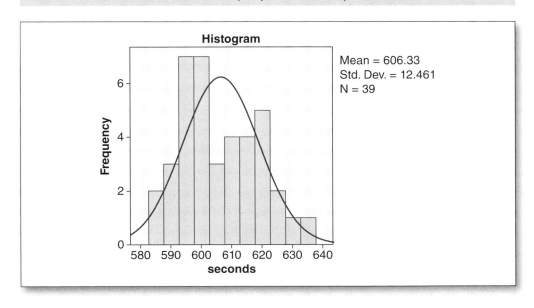

Test of Homogeneity of Variances

seconds

Levene Statistic	df1	df2	Sig.
1.430	1	80	.235

(5c) The *t* test revealed the following:

Descriptives

seconds

	N	Mean	Std. Deviation	Std. Error	95% Confidence Interval for Mean		Minimum	Maximum
					Lower Bound	Upper Bound		
No music	43	608.93	11.194	1.707	605.49	612.38	588	635
Music at 30 dB	39	606.33	12.461	1.995	602.29	610.37	585	637
Total	82	607.70	11.812	1.304	605.10	610.29	585	637

ANOVA

Seconds

	Sum of Squares	df	Mean Square	F	Sig.
Between Groups	137.921	1	137.921	.988	.323
Within Groups	11163.457	80	139.543		
Total	11301.378	81			

The mean puzzle completion time for Group 1 (no music) is 609 seconds (rounded), whereas the subjects in Group 2 (music at 30 dB) had a mean puzzle completion time of 606 seconds (rounded). This difference is statistically insignificant since the significance (*p*) is .323 (which is greater than the .05 α level).

(5d) This experiment was designed to determine if classical music aids in problem solving. We recruited 82 participants and randomly assigned them to one of two groups: those who assembled a 100-piece jigsaw puzzle in a silent room and those who assembled the same puzzle in a room with soft classical music playing (at 30 dB). On average, participants in the music group completed the puzzle 2.6 seconds faster than those who worked in silence (606.33 seconds vs. 608.93 seconds), but using a .05 α level, the *p* value of .323 suggests that this difference is not statistically significant; hence, we do not reject H_0 but reject H_1. For those tested, it appears that classical music is not a substantial factor when it comes to problem solving.

7. Data Set A

   (7a) H_0: Light therapy has no effect on depression.

   H_1: Light therapy is effective in reducing depression.

   (7b) Histograms with normal curve plots show a normal distribution of *mood* for both groups, as shown in the two figures below; hence, the pretest criterion of normality is satisfied.

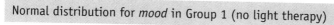

Normal distribution for *mood* in Group 1 (no light therapy)

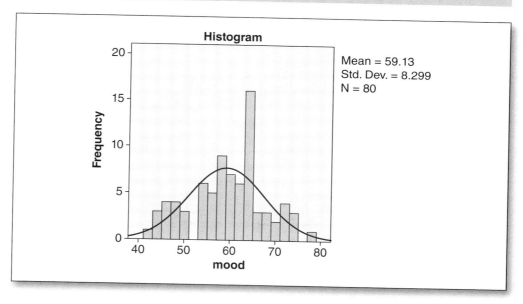

The homogeneity of variance score for *mood* shows a significance (*p*) of .194; since this is greater than the α level of .05, this suggests that there is no statistically significant difference between the variances of the two groups; hence, this pretest criterion passes.

The *n* for each group is 80, which satisfies the 30 per group minimum criterion (see Descriptives table below).

Normal distribution for *mood* in Group 2 (light therapy: even days)

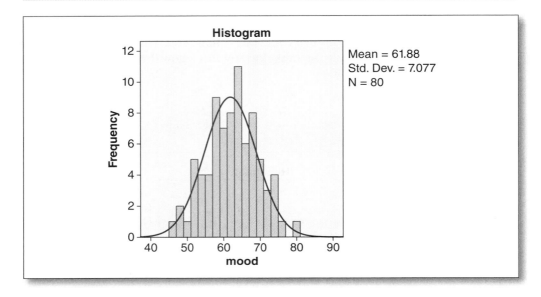

Test of Homogeneity of Variances

mood

Levene Statistic	df1	df2	Sig.
1.700	1	158	.194

(7c) The *t* test revealed the following:

Descriptives

mood

	N	Mean	Std. Deviation	Std. Error	95% Confidence Interval for Mean		Minimum	Maximum
					Lower Bound	Upper Bound		
No light therapy	80	59.13	8.299	.928	57.28	60.97	42	77
Light therapy: even days	80	61.88	7.077	.791	60.30	63.45	46	79
Total	160	60.50	7.811	.617	59.28	61.72	42	79

ANOVA

mood

	Sum of Squares	df	Mean Square	F	Sig.
Between Groups	302.500	1	302.500	5.086	.025
Within Groups	9397.500	158	59.478		
Total	9700.000	159			

The mean mood level for those in the light therapy group was 61.88, which is 2.75 points higher than the mean score of those in the control group (59.13). In light of the significance (p) score of .025 (which is less than the .05 α level), this difference is considered statistically significant.

(7d) To determine if light therapy is a viable supplement to treating depression, 160 subjects diagnosed with depression were randomly assigned to one of two groups: Half received 1 hour of light therapy every other day for a month; the other half received no light therapy. After 30 days, all participants completed the Acme Mood Scale, a 10-question survey that renders a score from 1 to 100 (1 = extremely bad mood . . . 100 = extremely good mood). Those who received light therapy showed a small but statistically significant improvement in mood; light therapy participants had an average mood score of 61.88, which is 2.75 points higher than those who did not have the light therapy, who scored an average of 59.13 on the mood test. Using a .05 α level, the p value of .025 suggests that this difference is statistically significant; hence, we reject H_0. For those tested, it appears that light therapy provided some relief from depressive symptoms, hence supporting H_1.

7. Data Set B

(7a) H_0: Light therapy has no effect on depression.

H_1: Light therapy is effective in reducing depression.

(7b) Despite the spike in the histogram for the no light therapy group (the tall bar at around 42), the histograms with normal curve plots show a normal distribution of *mood* for both groups, as shown in the two figures below; hence, the pretest criterion of normality is satisfied.

The homogeneity of variance score for *mood* shows a significance (p) of .731; since this is greater than the α level of .05, this suggests that there is no statistically significant difference between the variances of the two groups; hence, this pretest criterion passes.

The n for the groups are 48 and 56 (see Descriptives table below); these figures exceed the 30 per group minimum criterion.

Normal distribution for *mood* in Group 1 (no light therapy)

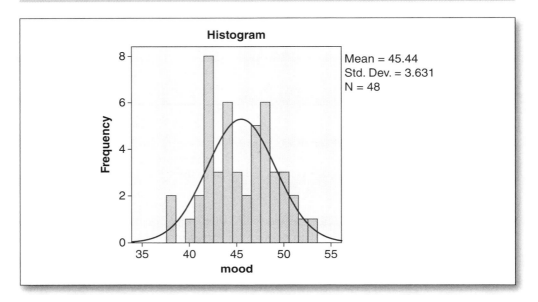

Normal distribution for *mood* in Group 2 (light therapy: even days)

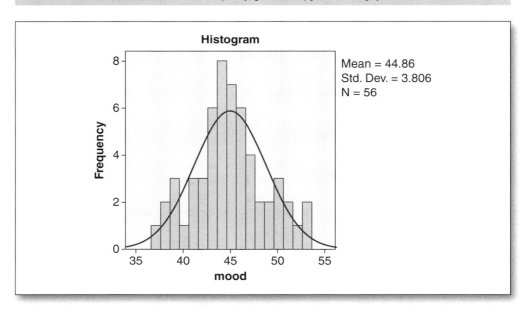

Test of Homogeneity of Variances

mood

Levene Statistic	df1	df2	Sig.
.119	1	102	.731

(7c) The *t* test revealed the following:

Descriptives

Mood

	N	Mean	Std. Deviation	Std. Error	95% Confidence Interval for Mean		Minimum	Maximum
					Lower Bound	Upper Bound		
No light therapy	48	45.44	3.631	.524	44.38	46.49	38	53
Light therapy: even days	56	44.86	3.806	.509	43.84	45.88	37	53
Total	104	45.13	3.720	.365	44.40	45.85	37	53

ANOVA

Mood

	Sum of Squares	df	Mean Square	F	Sig.
Between Groups	8.705	1	8.705	.627	.430
Within Groups	1416.670	102	13.889		
Total	1425.375	103			

The mean mood level for those in the control group (no light therapy) was 45.44, whereas those in the treatment group (light therapy: even days) had a mean mood level of 44.86. Unexpectedly, the mood level for those who received no light therapy was .58 points higher than that of those who did, but since the significance (p) is .430 (which is greater than the .05 α level), this difference is not considered statistically significant.

(7d) To determine if light therapy is a viable supplement to treating depressed individuals, 104 participants with a diagnosis of depression were randomly assigned to one of two groups: In addition to their regular care, 56 subjects received light therapy for 1 hour every other day; the other 48 participants received none. After 30 days, all participants completed the Acme Mood Scale, a 10-question survey that renders a score from 1 to 100 (1 = extremely bad mood . . . 100 = extremely good mood). Contrary to expectations, on average, those in the light therapy group scored 44.86, about a half point (.58) lower than those who had no light therapy, who had an average mood score of 45.44. Using a .05 α level, the *p* value of .430 suggests that this difference is not statistically significant; hence, we do not reject H₀, but we do reject H₁. For those tested, it appears that light therapy did not have a significant impact on their mood.

9. Data Set A

(9a) H₀: Tending to a plant has no effect on depressive mood.

H₁: Tending to a plant reduces depressive mood.

(9b) Despite the few low-score outliers shown in the histogram for Group 2, the histograms with normal curve plots show a normal distribution of the *depress* variable for both groups, as shown in the two figures below; hence, the pretest criterion of normality is satisfied.

Normal distribution for *depress* in Group 1 (no plant)

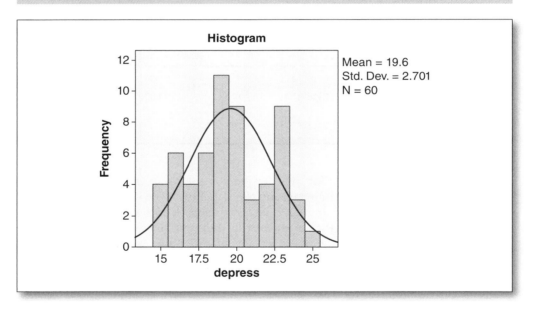

The homogeneity of variance score for *mood* shows a significance (*p*) of .060; since this is greater than the a level of .05, this suggests that there is no statistically significant difference between the variances of the two groups; hence, this pretest criterion passes.

The *n* for each group is 60 (see Descriptives table below), which satisfies the 30 per group minimum criterion.

Normal distribution for *depress* in Group 2 (bamboo)

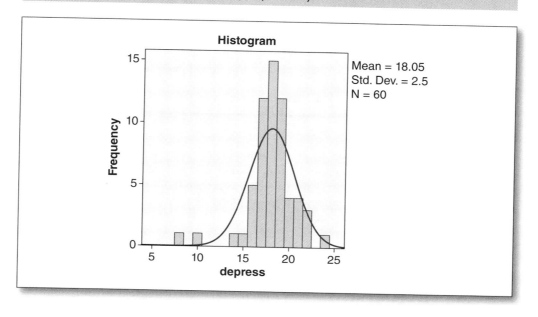

Histogram

Mean = 18.05
Std. Dev. = 2.5
N = 60

Test of Homogeneity of Variances
depress

Levene Statistic	df1	df2	Sig.
3.615	1	118	.060

(9c) The *t* test revealed the following:

Descriptives

depress

	N	Mean	Std. Deviation	Std. Error	95% Confidence Interval for Mean		Minimum	Maximum
					Lower Bound	Upper Bound		
No plant	60	19.60	2.701	.349	18.90	20.30	15	25
Bamboo	60	18.05	2.500	.323	17.40	18.70	8	24
Total	120	18.83	2.706	.247	18.34	19.31	8	25

ANOVA

depress

	Sum of Squares	df	Mean Square	F	Sig.
Between Groups	72.075	1	72.075	10.641	.001
Within Groups	799.250	118	6.773		
Total	871.325	119			

The mean depression level for those in the control group (no plant) was 19.60, whereas those in the treatment group (bamboo) had a mean depression level of 18.05. Since the significance (p) is .001 (which is less than the .05 α level), the 1.55-point mood improvement in those who were given plants is considered statistically significant. As such, we would reject H_0 in favor of H_1.

(9d) We hypothesized that empowering nursing home residents with an opportunity to provide nurturance would help to reduce depression. To test this hypothesis, 120 residents were randomly assigned to one of two groups: The 60 people in the treatment group were each given a small bamboo plant to tend to along with a card providing care instructions; the 60 members of the control group were given no plant. After 90 days, we administered the Acme Depression Scale (1 = low depression . . . 100 = high depression) to members of both groups. We found that those who were given the bamboo plant scored an average of 18.05; their depression level was 1.55 points lower than those in the control group, who had an average depression score of 19.60. This improvement in depression, although small, produced a statistically significant p value of .001, using a .05 α level; hence, we rejected H_0. For those involved in this study, it appears that having a plant reduced depression, thereby supporting H_1.

9. Data Set B

(9a) H_0: Tending to a plant has no effect on depressive mood.

H_1: Tending to a plant reduces depressive mood.

(9b) The histograms with normal curve plots show a normal distribution of the *depress* variable for both groups, as shown in the two figures below; hence, the pretest criterion of normality is satisfied.

The homogeneity of variance score for *mood* shows a significance (p) of .156; since this is greater than the α level of .05, this suggests that there is no statistically significant difference between the variances of the two groups; hence, this pretest criterion passes.

The n for the no-plant group is 58, and the n for the bamboo group is 51 (see Descriptives table below). These ns exceed the 30 per group minimum criterion.

Normal distribution for *depress* in Group 1 (no plant)

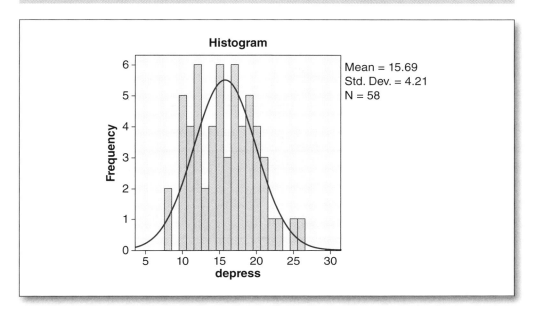

Normal distribution for *depress* in Group 2 (bamboo)

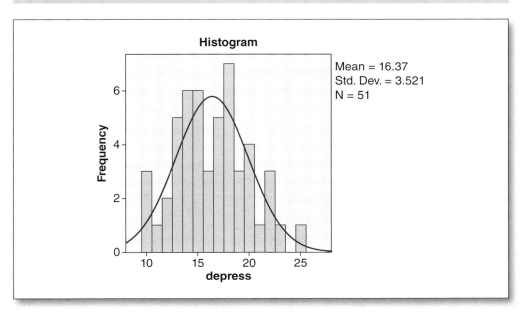

Test of Homogeneity of Variances

depress

Levene Statistic	df1	df2	Sig.
2.039	1	107	.156

(9c) The *t* test revealed the following:

Descriptives

depress

	N	Mean	Std. Deviation	Std. Error	95% Confidence Interval for Mean Lower Bound	95% Confidence Interval for Mean Upper Bound	Minimum	Maximum
No plant	58	15.69	4.210	.553	14.58	16.80	8	26
Bamboo	51	16.37	3.521	.493	15.38	17.36	10	25
Total	109	16.01	3.900	.374	15.27	16.75	8	26

ANOVA

depress

	Sum of Squares	df	Mean Square	F	Sig.
Between Groups	12.655	1	12.655	.831	.364
Within Groups	1630.335	107	15.237		
Total	1642.991	108			

The mean depression level for those in the control group (no plant) was 15.69, whereas those in the treatment group (bamboo) had a mean depression level of 16.37. Even though the mean depression score for those who received the bamboo plant was .68 points higher than those in the control group, ultimately, this difference is not statistically significant since the significance (*p*) is .364 (which is greater than the .05 α level). As such, we would not reject H_0, but we would reject H_1.

(9d) We hypothesized that empowering nursing home residents with an opportunity to provide nurturance would help to reduce depression. To test this hypothesis, 109 residents were randomly assigned to one of two groups: 51 of the residents were given a small bamboo plant to tend to along with a card providing care instructions; the remaining 58 residents received no plant. After 90 days, we administered the Acme Depression Scale (1 = low depression . . . 100 = high depression) to members of both groups; we found that on average, those who were given no plant were less depressed (15.69) than those who were given the bamboo plant (16.37), but in light of the *p* value of .364, using a .05 α level, this .68-point difference in the average depression scores is not considered statistically significant. Accordingly, we did not reject H_0.

ANOVA

1. Data Set A

(1a) H_0: Practicing meditation has no effect on resting pulse rate.

H_1: Practicing meditation for 30 minutes a day, 3 days a week for 2 weeks affects resting pulse rate.

H_2: Practicing meditation for 30 minutes a day, 6 days a week for 2 weeks affects resting pulse rate.

(1b) Histograms with normal curve plots show a normal distribution of *pulse* for the groups, as shown in the three figures below; hence, the pretest criterion of normality is satisfied.

Normal distribution for *pulse* in Group 1 (no meditation)

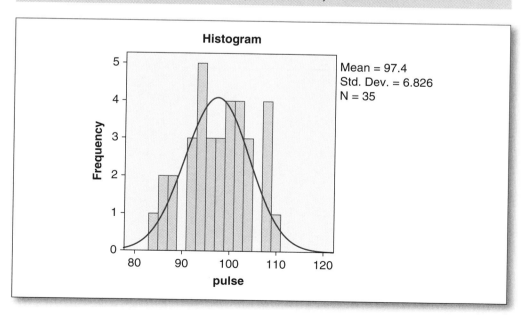

Normal distribution for *pulse* in Group 2 (meditated 30 minutes a day, 3 days per week)

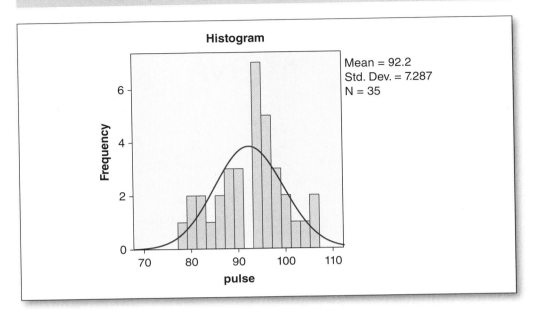

Normal distribution for *pulse* in Group 3 (meditated 30 minutes a day, 6 days per week)

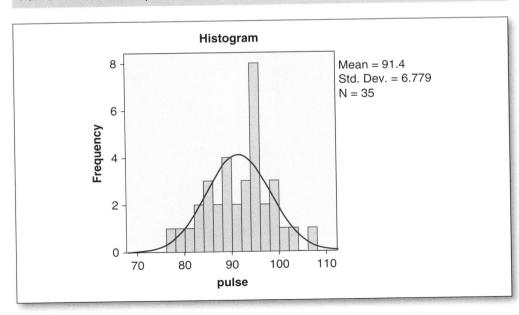

Test of Homogeneity of Variances

pulse

Levene Statistic	df1	df2	Sig.
.083	2	102	.920

The homogeneity of variance score shows a significance (p) of .920; since this is greater than the α level of .05, this suggests that there is no statistically significant difference among the variances of the three groups; hence, this pretest criterion passes.

The n for each group, as shown in the Descriptives table below, is 35 for each group; since the ns are greater than 30, this criterion passes also.

(1c) The ANOVA revealed the following:

Descriptives

pulse

	N	Mean	Std. Deviation	Std. Error	95% Confidence Interval for Mean		Minimum	Maximum
					Lower Bound	Upper Bound		
No meditation	35	97.40	6.826	1.154	95.06	99.74	84	109
Meditates 3 days	35	92.20	7.287	1.232	89.70	94.70	78	105
Meditates 6 days	35	91.40	6.779	1.146	89.07	93.73	77	106
Total	105	93.67	7.400	.722	92.23	95.10	77	109

ANOVA

pulse

	Sum of Squares	df	Mean Square	F	Sig.
Between Groups	742.933	2	371.467	7.651	.001
Within Groups	4952.400	102	48.553		
Total	5695.333	104			

Multiple Comparisons

pulse

Tukey HSD

(I) group	(J) group	Mean Difference (I-J)	Std. Error	Sig.	95% Confidence Interval	
					Lower Bound	Upper Bound
No meditation	Meditates 3 days	5.200*	1.666	.007	1.24	9.16
	Meditates 6 days	6.000*	1.666	.001	2.04	9.96
Meditates 3 days	No meditation	-5.200*	1.666	.007	-9.16	-1.24
	Meditates 6 days	.800	1.666	.881	-3.16	4.76
Meditates 6 days	No meditation	-6.000*	1.666	.001	-9.96	-2.04
	Meditates 3 days	-.800	1.666	.881	-4.76	3.16

*. The mean difference is significant at the 0.05 level.

The Tukey post hoc test was used since the *ns* for each group were the same (35 each).

NOTE: Since the ANOVA test renders results involving multiple comparisons, it may be helpful to organize the findings as shown in the table below. SPSS does not generate this table directly, but you can construct it manually by copying the *group names* and *means* from the Descriptives table, as well as the *p* values from the *Sig.* column in the Multiple Comparisons table.

Groups (μ = resting pulse rate after 2 weeks)	p
μ(No meditation) = 97.40 : μ(Meditation 3× / wk) = 92.20	.007*
μ(No meditation) = 97.40 : μ(Meditation 6× / wk) = 91.40	.001*
μ(Meditation 3× / wk) = 92.20 : μ(Meditation 6× / wk) = 91.40	.881

*Statistically significant difference (α = .05).

Practicing meditation for 2 weeks was effective in statistically significantly reducing resting pulse rate, but there was no statistically significant difference in resting pulse rate when comparing those who meditated for 30 minutes three times a week with those who meditated for 30 minutes six times a week.

On the basis of these findings, we reject H_0, but we do not reject H_1 or H_2.

(1d) This study analyzed the effects that meditation had on resting pulse rates. The subjects were randomly assigned to one of three groups. Members of the control group did not meditate; those in the second group meditated for 30 minutes on Monday, Wednesday and Friday; and members of the third group meditated for 30 minutes Monday through Saturday. After 2 weeks, those who meditated (3×/wk, μ = 92.20; 6×/wk, μ = 91.40) showed a statistically significant reduction (p = .007 and p = .001, respectively) in resting pulse rate compared with those who did not meditate (μ = 97.40) using a .05 α level. We found no statistically significant difference in the resting pulse rates between those who meditated 3 days per week compared with those who meditated 6 days per week (p = .881).

1. Data Set B

(1a) H_0: Practicing meditation has no effect on resting pulse rate.

H_1: Practicing meditation for 30 minutes a day, 3 days a week for 2 weeks affects resting pulse rate.

H_2: Practicing meditation for 30 minutes a day, 6 days a week for 2 weeks affects resting pulse rate.

(1b) Histograms with normal curve plots show a normal distribution of *pulse* for the three groups, as shown in the three figures below; hence, the pretest criterion of normality is satisfied.

Normal distribution for *pulse* in Group 1 (no meditation)

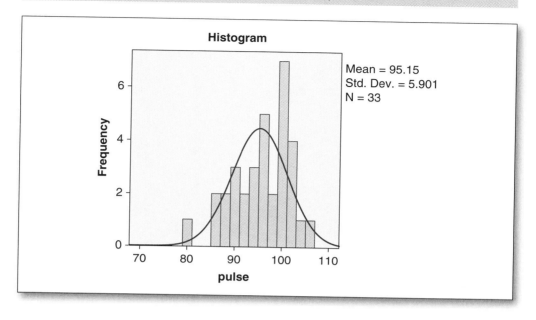

Histogram

Mean = 95.15
Std. Dev. = 5.901
N = 33

Normal distribution for *pulse* in Group 2 (meditated 30 minutes a day, 3 days per week)

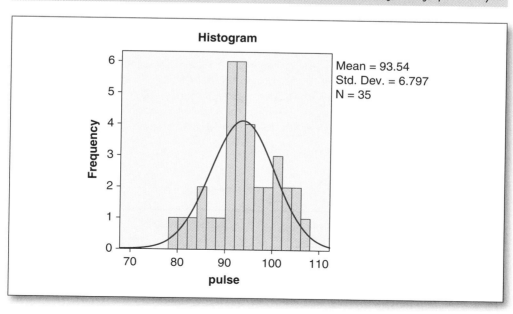

Histogram

Mean = 93.54
Std. Dev. = 6.797
N = 35

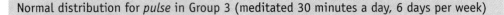

Normal distribution for *pulse* in Group 3 (meditated 30 minutes a day, 6 days per week)

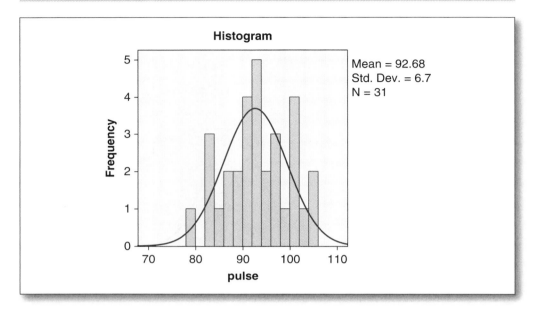

Test of Homogeneity of Variances

pulse

Levene Statistic	df1	df2	Sig.
.241	2	96	.786

The homogeneity of variance score shows a significance (p) of .786; since this is greater than the α level of .05, this suggests that there is no statistically significant difference among the variances of the three groups; hence, this pretest criterion passes.

The *ns* for each group, as shown in the Descriptives table below, are 33, 35, and 31; since the *ns* are greater than 30, this criterion passes also.

(1c) The ANOVA revealed the following:

Descriptives

pulse

	N	Mean	Std. Deviation	Std. Error	95% Confidence Interval for Mean		Minimum	Maximum
					Lower Bound	Upper Bound		
No meditation	33	95.15	5.901	1.027	93.06	97.24	80	105
Meditates 3 days	35	93.54	6.797	1.149	91.21	95.88	79	107
Meditates 6 days	31	92.68	6.700	1.203	90.22	95.14	79	104
Total	99	93.81	6.494	.653	92.51	95.10	79	107

ANOVA

pulse

	Sum of Squares	df	Mean Square	F	Sig.
Between Groups	101.651	2	50.826	1.210	.303
Within Groups	4031.702	96	41.997		
Total	4133.354	98			

Multiple Comparisons

pulse

Sidak

(I) group	(J) group	Mean Difference (I-J)	Std. Error	Sig.	95% Confidence Interval	
					Lower Bound	Upper Bound
No meditation	Meditates 3 days	1.609	1.572	.670	-2.21	5.43
	Meditates 6 days	2.474	1.621	.342	-1.46	6.41
Meditates 3 days	No meditation	-1.609	1.572	.670	-5.43	2.21
	Meditates 6 days	.865	1.598	.931	-3.02	4.75
Meditates 6 days	No meditation	-2.474	1.621	.342	-6.41	1.46
	Meditates 3 days	-.865	1.598	.931	-4.75	3.02

The Sidak post hoc test was used since the ns for each group were not all the same ($ns = 33, 35, 31$).

Groups (μ = resting pulse rate after 2 weeks)	p
μ(No meditation) = 95.15 : μ(Meditation 3× / wk) = 93.54	.670
μ(No meditation) = 95.15 : μ(Meditation 6× / wk) = 92.68	.342
μ(Meditation 3× / wk) = 93.54 : μ(Meditation 6× / wk) = 92.68	.931

Per the table above, practicing meditation for 2 weeks produced no statistically significant reduction in resting pulse rate using a .05 α level.

On the basis of these findings, we would not reject H_0, but we would reject H_1 and H_2.

(1d) This study analyzed the effects that meditation had on resting pulse rates. The subjects were randomly assigned to one of three groups. Members of the control group did not meditate; those in the second group meditated for 30 minutes on Monday, Wednesday, and Friday; and members of the third group meditated for 30 minutes Monday through Saturday. After 2 weeks, resting pulse rates were recorded for each participant. Those who did not meditate had a mean resting pulse rate of 95.15, which was slightly higher than those who meditated (3 days per week: $\mu = 93.54$; 6 days per week: $\mu = 92.68$), but we detected no statistically significant differences among any of the three groups using a .05 α level, suggesting that the meditation schedules tested were not effective in reducing resting pulse rates.

3. Data Set A

(3a) H_0: The Acme reading lamp is no different from any other lighting source when it comes to reading speed.

   H_1: The Acme reading lamp facilitates faster reading speed than regular room lighting.

   H_2: The Acme reading lamp facilitates faster reading speed than a generic reading lamp.

   H_3: The Acme reading lamp facilitates faster reading speed than a flashlight.

(3b) Histograms with normal curve plots show a normal distribution of *seconds* for all groups as shown in the four figures below; hence, the pretest criterion of normality is satisfied.

Normal distribution for *seconds* in Group 1 (room lighting)

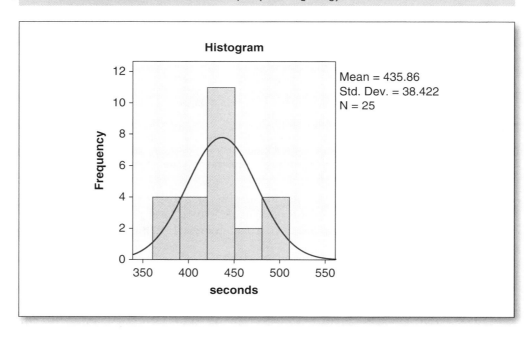

Mean = 435.86
Std. Dev. = 38.422
N = 25

Normal distribution for *seconds* in Group 2 (Acme reading lamp)

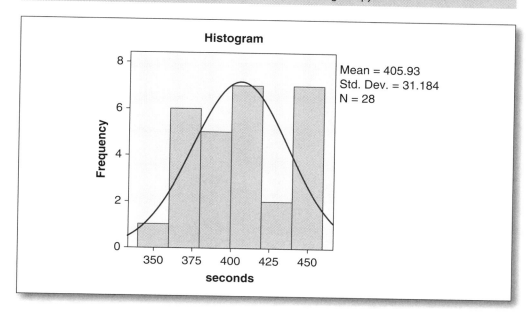

Histogram

Mean = 405.93
Std. Dev. = 31.184
N = 28

Normal distribution for *seconds* in Group 3 (generic reading lamp)

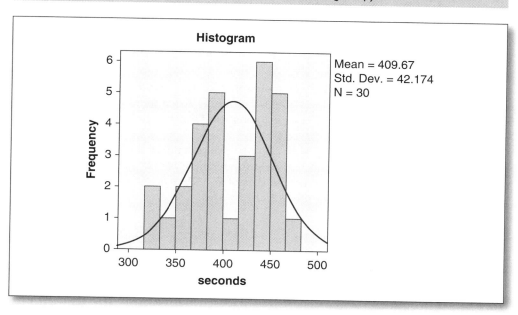

Histogram

Mean = 409.67
Std. Dev. = 42.174
N = 30

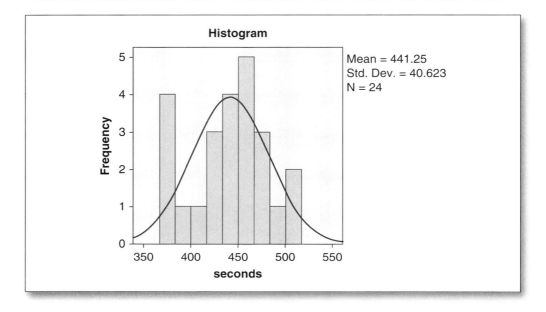

Normal distribution for *seconds* in Group 4 (flashlight)

Test of Homogeneity of Variances

seconds

Levene Statistic	df1	df2	Sig.
1.499	3	103	.219

The homogeneity of variance score for *seconds* shows a significance (p) of .219; since this is greater than the α level of .05, this suggests that there is no statistically significant difference between the variances among the four groups; hence, this pretest criterion passes.

The generic lamp group was the only group that had the minimal n of 30. The room lighting, Acme lighting, and flashlight groups had ns of 25, 28, and 24, respectively (see Descriptives table below). The findings of the ANOVA test would be more robust if the ns were slightly higher for these three groups.

(3c) The ANOVA test revealed the following:

Descriptives

seconds

	N	Mean	Std. Deviation	Std. Error	95% Confidence Interval for Mean		Minimum	Maximum
					Lower Bound	Upper Bound		
Room lighting	25	435.88	38.511	7.702	419.98	451.78	374	509
Acme lamp	28	405.93	31.184	5.893	393.84	418.02	357	455
Generic lamp	30	409.67	42.174	7.700	393.92	425.41	328	470
Flashlight	24	441.25	40.623	8.292	424.10	458.40	368	512
Total	107	421.90	40.851	3.949	414.07	429.73	328	512

ANOVA

seconds

	Sum of Squares	df	Mean Square	F	Sig.
Between Groups	25504.205	3	8501.402	5.784	.001
Within Groups	151385.664	103	1469.764		
Total	176889.869	106			

Multiple Comparisons

seconds

Sidak

(I) group	(J) group	Mean Difference (I-J)	Std. Error	Sig.	95% Confidence Interval	
					Lower Bound	Upper Bound
Room lighting	Acme lamp	29.951*	10.549	.032	1.65	58.25
	Generic lamp	26.213	10.382	.076	-1.64	54.06
	Flashlight	-5.370	10.956	.997	-34.76	24.02
Acme lamp	Room lighting	-29.951*	10.549	.032	-58.25	-1.65
	Generic lamp	-3.738	10.074	.999	-30.76	23.29
	Flashlight	-35.321*	10.665	.008	-63.93	-6.71
Generic lamp	Room lighting	-26.213	10.382	.076	-54.06	1.64
	Acme lamp	3.738	10.074	.999	-23.29	30.76
	Flashlight	-31.583*	10.499	.020	-59.75	-3.42
Flashlight	Room lighting	5.370	10.956	.997	-24.02	34.76
	Acme lamp	35.321*	10.665	.008	6.71	63.93
	Generic lamp	31.583*	10.499	.020	3.42	59.75

*. The mean difference is significant at the 0.05 level.

Groups (μ = reading time in seconds)	p
μ(Room lighting) = 436 : μ(Acme Lamp) = 406	.032*
μ(Room lighting) = 436 : μ(Generic lamp) = 410	.076
μ(Room lighting) = 436 : μ(Flashlight) = 441	.997
μ(Acme lamp) = 406 : μ(Generic lamp) = 410	.999
μ(Acme lamp) = 406 : μ(Flashlight) = 441	.008*
μ(Generic lamp) = 410 : μ(Flashlight) = 441	.020*

Means rounded to nearest second.

*Statistically significant difference (α = .05).

Per the table above, since the mean reading time in the Acme reading lamp group is statistically significantly lower than that of those who read using room lighting and by flashlight, we reject H_0. For the same reason, we would not reject H_1 and H_3. Since there was no statistically significant difference in the reading times from those in the Acme reading lamp group compared with those who used a generic reading lamp, we would reject H_2.

(3d) This study analyzed the effects that the Acme reading lamp had on reading speed compared with other light sources. The 107 participants were randomly assigned to one of four groups. One group read a 1,000-word essay using regular room lighting, the second group read the same essay using the new Acme reading lamp, the third group read using a generic reading lamp, and the fourth group read using a flashlight. Results revealed that on average, those who read using the Acme reading lamp read significantly faster (μ = 406) than those who read using a flashlight (μ = 441, p = .008), or regular room lighting (μ = 436, p = .032), using an α level of .05. Incidentally, those who used a generic reading lamp (μ = 410) finished reading the essay significantly faster than those who read by flashlight (μ = 441, p = .032). We also discovered that those who read using an Acme reading lamp (μ = 406) completed the essay faster than those who used the generic reading lamp (μ = 410), but this difference was not statistically significant (p = .999).

3. Data Set B

(3a) H_0: The Acme reading lamp is no different from any other lighting source when it comes to reading speed.

H_1: The Acme reading lamp facilitates faster reading speed than regular room lighting.

H_2: The Acme reading lamp facilitates faster reading speed than a generic reading lamp.

H_3: The Acme reading lamp facilitates faster reading speed than a flashlight.

(3b) Histograms with normal curve plots show a normal distribution of *seconds* for all groups, as shown in the four figures below; hence, the pretest criterion of normality is satisfied.

Normal distribution for *seconds* in Group 1 (room lighting)

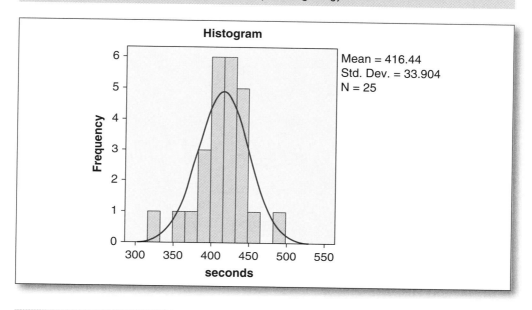

Normal distribution for *seconds* in Group 2 (Acme reading lamp)

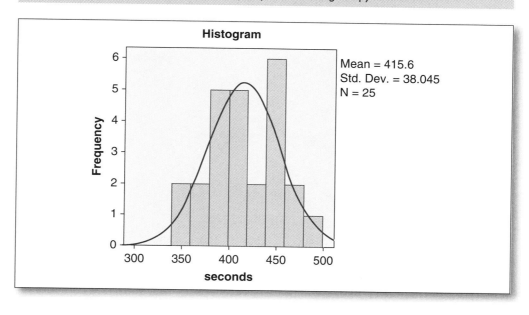

Normal distribution for *seconds* in Group 3 (generic reading lamp)

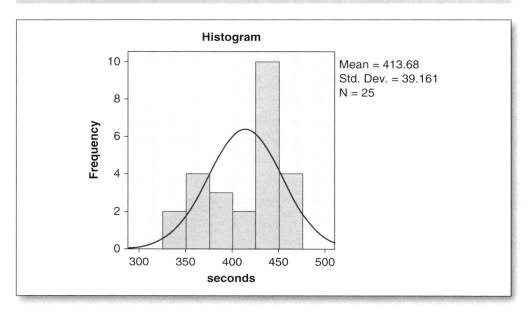

Normal distribution for *seconds* in Group 4 (flashlight)

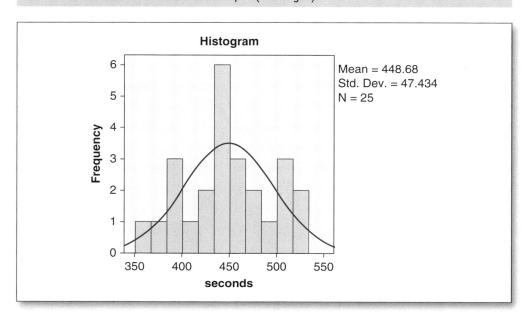

Test of Homogeneity of Variances

seconds

Levene Statistic	df1	df2	Sig.
1.163	3	96	.328

The homogeneity of variance score for *seconds* shows a significance (p) of .328; since this is greater than the α level of .05, this suggests that there is no statistically significant difference between the variances among the four groups; hence, this pretest criterion passes.

The groups each had an n of 25 (see Descriptives table below). The findings of the ANOVA test would be more robust if the ns were at least 30 per group.

(3c) The ANOVA test revealed the following:

Descriptives

seconds

	N	Mean	Std. Deviation	Std. Error	95% Confidence Interval for Mean		Minimum	Maximum
					Lower Bound	Upper Bound		
Room lighting	25	416.44	33.904	6.781	402.44	430.44	331	489
Acme lamp	25	415.60	38.045	7.609	399.90	431.30	344	481
Generic lamp	25	413.68	39.161	7.832	397.52	429.84	338	470
Flashlight	25	448.68	47.434	9.487	429.10	468.26	361	525
Total	100	423.60	41.947	4.195	415.28	431.92	331	525

ANOVA

seconds

	Sum of Squares	df	Mean Square	F	Sig.
Between Groups	21066.960	3	7022.320	4.402	.006
Within Groups	153131.040	96	1595.115		
Total	174198.000	99			

Multiple Comparisons

seconds

Tukey HSD

(I) group	(J) group	Mean Difference (I-J)	Std. Error	Sig.	95% Confidence Interval	
					Lower Bound	Upper Bound
Room lighting	Acme lamp	.840	11.296	1.000	-28.70	30.38
	Generic lamp	2.760	11.296	.995	-26.78	32.30
	Flashlight	-32.240*	11.296	.027	-61.78	-2.70
Acme lamp	Room lighting	-.840	11.296	1.000	-30.38	28.70
	Generic lamp	1.920	11.296	.998	-27.62	31.46
	Flashlight	-33.080*	11.296	.022	-62.62	-3.54
Generic lamp	Room lighting	-2.760	11.296	.995	-32.30	26.78
	Acme lamp	-1.920	11.296	.998	-31.46	27.62
	Flashlight	-35.000*	11.296	.013	-64.54	-5.46
Flashlight	Room lighting	32.240*	11.296	.027	2.70	61.78
	Acme lamp	33.080*	11.296	.022	3.54	62.62
	Generic lamp	35.000*	11.296	.013	5.46	64.54

*. The mean difference is significant at the 0.05 level.

Groups (μ = reading time in seconds)	p
μ(Room lighting) = 416 : μ(Acme Lamp) = 416	1.000
μ(Room lighting) = 416 : μ(Generic lamp) = 414	.995
μ(Room lighting) = 416 : μ(Flashlight) = 449	.027*
μ(Acme lamp) = 416 : μ(Generic lamp) = 414	.998
μ(Acme lamp) = 416 : μ(Flashlight) = 449	.022*
μ(Generic lamp) = 414 : μ(Flashlight) = 449	.013*

Means rounded to nearest second.

*Statistically significant difference (α = .05).

Per the table above, since the mean reading time in the Acme lamp group (μ = 416) is statistically significantly lower than that of those who read using a flashlight (μ = 449, p = .022), based on the .05 α level, we reject H_0. For the same reason, we would not reject H_3.

Since comparing the Acme lamp (μ = 416) with the generic lamp (μ = 414) produced a p value of .998, we see that there is no statistically significant difference between these groups; we would reject H_2.

Comparing the Acme lamp (μ = 416) with room lighting (μ = 416) produced a p value of 1.000; hence, we reject H_1.

In summary, it appears that all lighting facilitated about the same reading speed, except for the flashlight; those who read using a flashlight took (statistically) significantly longer than those in the other three groups.

(3d) This study analyzed the effects that the Acme reading lamp had on reading speed. The 100 participants were randomly assigned to one of four groups. One group read a 1,000-word essay using regular room lighting, the second group read the same essay using the new Acme reading lamp, the third group read using a generic reading lamp, and the fourth group read using a flashlight. There was no statistically significant difference in reading times among those who used the Acme reading lamp ($\mu = 416$), room lighting ($\mu = 416$), or the generic lamp ($\mu = 414$), using an α level of .05. All three of these groups read statistically significantly faster than the fourth group, who read using a flashlight ($\mu = 449$); p values ranged from .013 to .027.

5. Data Set A

(5a) H_0: Classical music does not enhance problem-solving skills.

   H_1: Classical music at 30 dB enhances problem-solving skills.

   H_2: Classical music at 60 dB enhances problem-solving skills.

   H_3: Classical music at 90 dB enhances problem-solving skills.

(5b) Histograms with normal curve plots show a normal distribution of *seconds* for all groups, as shown in the four figures below; hence, the pretest criterion of normality is satisfied.

Normal distribution for *seconds* in Group 1 (no music)

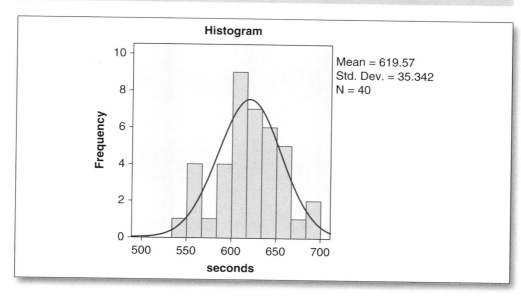

Normal distribution for *seconds* in Group 2 (music at 30 dB)

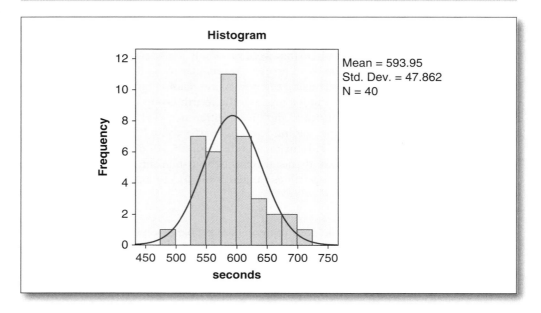

Normal distribution for *seconds* in Group 3 (music at 60 dB)

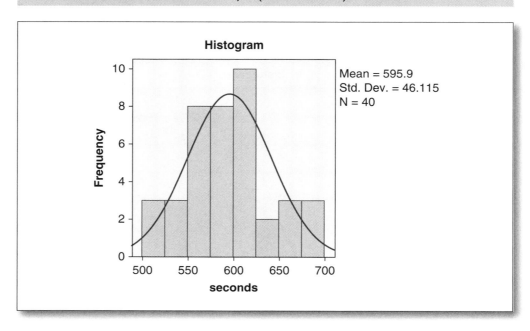

Normal distribution for *seconds* in Group 4 (music at 90 dB)

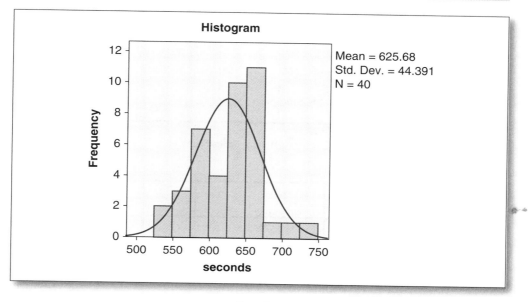

Histogram

Mean = 625.68
Std. Dev. = 44.391
N = 40

Test of Homogeneity of Variances

seconds

Levene Statistic	df1	df2	Sig.
1.195	3	156	.314

The homogeneity of variance score for *seconds* shows a significance (p) of .314; since this is greater than the α level of .05, this suggests that there is no statistically significant difference between the variances among the four groups; hence, this pretest criterion passes.

The n for each group is 40 (see Descriptives table below), which satisfies the 30 per group minimum criterion.

(5c) The ANOVA test revealed the following:

Descriptives

seconds

	N	Mean	Std. Deviation	Std. Error	95% Confidence Interval for Mean Lower Bound	95% Confidence Interval for Mean Upper Bound	Minimum	Maximum
No music	40	619.58	35.342	5.588	608.27	630.88	541	690
Music at 30 dB	40	593.95	47.862	7.568	578.64	609.26	497	707
Music at 60 dB	40	595.90	46.115	7.291	581.15	610.65	505	696
Music at 90 dB	40	625.67	44.391	7.019	611.48	639.87	525	727
Total	160	608.78	45.513	3.598	601.67	615.88	497	727

ANOVA

seconds

	Sum of Squares	df	Mean Square	F	Sig.
Between Groups	31511.850	3	10503.950	5.502	.001
Within Groups	297846.050	156	1909.270		
Total	329357.900	159			

Multiple Comparisons

seconds

Tukey HSD

(I) group	(J) group	Mean Difference (I-J)	Std. Error	Sig.	95% Confidence Interval	
					Lower Bound	Upper Bound
No music	Music at 30 dB	25.625*	9.771	.047	.25	51.00
	Music at 60 dB	23.675	9.771	.077	-1.70	49.05
	Music at 90 dB	-6.100	9.771	.924	-31.47	19.27
Music at 30 dB	No music	-25.625*	9.771	.047	-51.00	-.25
	Music at 60 dB	-1.950	9.771	.997	-27.32	23.42
	Music at 90 dB	-31.725*	9.771	.008	-57.10	-6.35
Music at 60 dB	No music	-23.675	9.771	.077	-49.05	1.70
	Music at 30 dB	1.950	9.771	.997	-23.42	27.32
	Music at 90 dB	-29.775*	9.771	.014	-55.15	-4.40
Music at 90 dB	No music	6.100	9.771	.924	-19.27	31.47
	Music at 30 dB	31.725*	9.771	.008	6.35	57.10
	Music at 60 dB	29.775*	9.771	.014	4.40	55.15

*. The mean difference is significant at the 0.05 level.

Groups (μ = seconds to complete puzzle)	p
μ(No music) = 620 : μ(Music at 30 dB) = 594	.047*
μ(No music) = 620 : μ(Music at 60 dB) = 596	.077
μ(No music) = 620 : μ(Music at 90 dB) = 626	.924
μ(Music at 30 dB) = 594 : μ(Music at 60 dB) = 596	.997
μ(Music at 30 dB) = 594 : μ(Music at 90 dB) = 626	.008*
μ(Music at 60 dB) = 596 : μ(Music at 90 dB) = 626	.014*

Means rounded to nearest second.

*Statistically significant difference (α = .05).

Participants who assembled the puzzle with classical music at 30 dB ($\mu = 594$) completed the puzzle statistically significantly faster than those who had no music ($\mu = 620$) ($p = .047$, $\alpha = .05$).

Based on these findings, the hypotheses would be resolved as such:

Reject H_0 and do not reject H_1 since those who were exposed to classical music at 30 dB solved the puzzle an average of 26 seconds faster than those who worked in silence.

Reject H_2 since there was no statistically significant difference between the mean completion time of those who worked with classical music at 60 dB ($\mu = 596$) compared with those who worked in silence ($\mu = 620$) ($p = .077$, $\alpha = .05$).

Reject H_3 since there was no statistically significant difference between the mean completion time of those who worked with classical music at 90 dB ($\mu = 626$) compared with those who worked in silence ($\mu = 620$) ($p = .924$, $\alpha = .05$).

(5d) This experiment was designed to determine if classical music facilitates problem solving. We recruited 160 people and randomly assigned participants to one of four groups: Members of each group were given a 100-piece jigsaw puzzle to solve. Those in Group 1 worked in silence, and those in Groups 2, 3, and 4 solved the puzzle with classical music playing at different volumes in each group: soft (30 dB), medium (60 dB), and loud (90 dB), respectively. We found that those who listened to the soft classical music (at 30 dB) completed the puzzle (statistically) significantly faster ($\mu = 594$ seconds) than those who worked in silence ($\mu = 620$) ($p = .047$, $\alpha = .05$), but it seems that as the music was played louder, the beneficial effect was lost: Those who listened at a medium volume completed the puzzle in 596 seconds, and those who were exposed to the loud volume took 626 seconds. It seems that while the soft classical music helped to facilitate the problem solving, louder volumes may have been distracting.

5. Data Set B

(5a) H_0: Classical music does not enhance problem-solving skills.

H_1: Classical music at 30 dB enhances problem-solving skills.

H_2: Classical music at 60 dB enhances problem-solving skills.

H_3: Classical music at 90 dB enhances problem-solving skills.

(5b) Histograms with normal curve plots show a normal distribution of *seconds* for all groups, as shown in the four figures below; hence, the pretest criterion of normality is satisfied.

Normal distribution for *seconds* in Group 1 (no music)

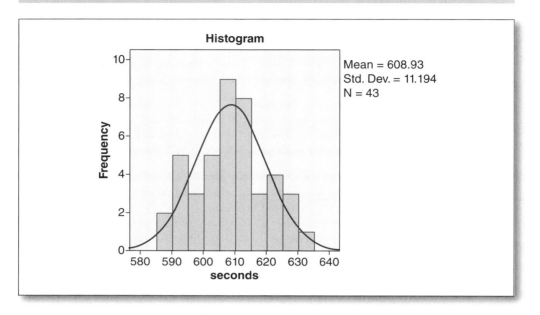

Normal distribution for *seconds* in Group 2 (music at 30 dB)

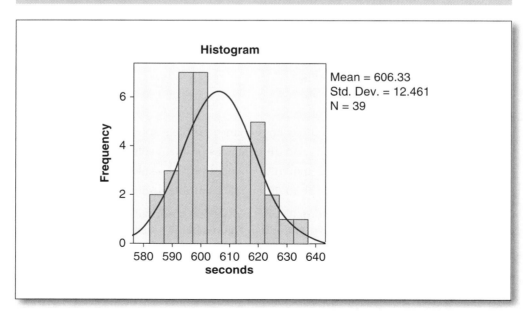

Normal distribution for *seconds* in Group 3 (music at 60 dB)

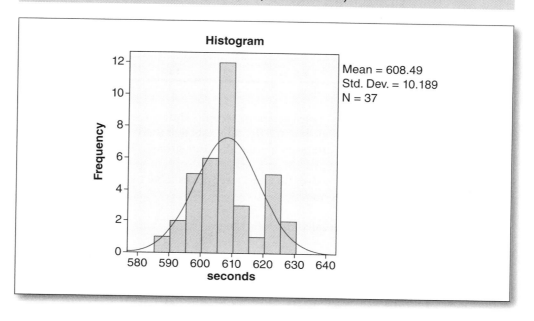

Histogram

Mean = 608.49
Std. Dev. = 10.189
N = 37

Normal distribution for *seconds* in Group 4 (music at 90 dB)

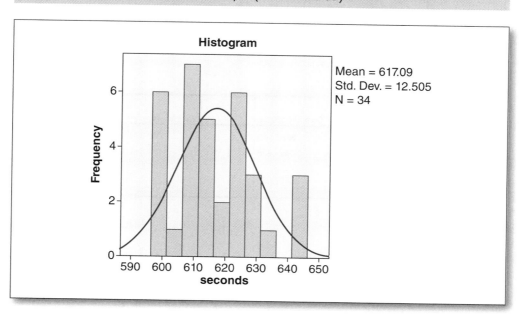

Histogram

Mean = 617.09
Std. Dev. = 12.505
N = 34

Test of Homogeneity of Variances

seconds

Levene Statistic	df1	df2	Sig.
1.279	3	149	.284

The homogeneity of variance score for *seconds* shows a significance (p) of .284; since this is greater than the α level of .05, this suggests that there is no statistically significant difference between the variances among the four groups; hence, this pretest criterion passes.

The *n* for each group is over 30 (see Descriptives table below), which satisfies the 30 per group minimum criterion.

(5c) The ANOVA test revealed the following:

Descriptives

seconds

	N	Mean	Std. Deviation	Std. Error	95% Confidence Interval for Mean		Minimum	Maximum
					Lower Bound	Upper Bound		
No music	43	608.93	11.194	1.707	605.49	612.38	588	635
Music at 30 dB	39	606.33	12.461	1.995	602.29	610.37	585	637
Music at 60 dB	37	608.49	10.189	1.675	605.09	611.88	588	630
Music at 90 dB	34	617.09	12.505	2.145	612.72	621.45	599	644
Total	153	609.97	12.147	.982	608.03	611.91	585	644

ANOVA

seconds

	Sum of Squares	df	Mean Square	F	Sig.
Between Groups	2366.460	3	788.820	5.859	.001
Within Groups	20061.436	149	134.641		
Total	22427.895	152			

Multiple Comparisons

seconds

Sidak

(I) group	(J) group	Mean Difference (I-J)	Std. Error	Sig.	95% Confidence Interval	
					Lower Bound	Upper Bound
No music	Music at 30 dB	2.597	2.566	.895	-4.24	9.44
	Music at 60 dB	.444	2.602	1.000	-6.49	7.38
	Music at 90 dB	-8.158*	2.663	.015	-15.26	-1.06
Music at 30 dB	No music	-2.597	2.566	.895	-9.44	4.24
	Music at 60 dB	-2.153	2.663	.962	-9.25	4.95
	Music at 90 dB	-10.755*	2.723	.001	-18.01	-3.50
Music at 60 dB	No music	-.444	2.602	1.000	-7.38	6.49
	Music at 30 dB	2.153	2.663	.962	-4.95	9.25
	Music at 90 dB	-8.602*	2.757	.013	-15.95	-1.25
Music at 90 dB	No music	8.158*	2.663	.015	1.06	15.26
	Music at 30 dB	10.755*	2.723	.001	3.50	18.01
	Music at 60 dB	8.602*	2.757	.013	1.25	15.95

*. The mean difference is significant at the 0.05 level.

Groups (μ = seconds to complete puzzle)	p
μ(No music) = 609 : μ(Music at 30 dB) = 606	.895
μ(No music) = 609 : μ(Music at 60 dB) = 608	1.000
μ(No music) = 609 : μ(Music at 90 dB) = 617	.015*
μ(Music at 30 dB) = 606 : μ(Music at 60 dB) = 608	.962
μ(Music at 30 dB) = 606 : μ(Music at 90 dB) = 617	.001*
μ(Music at 60 dB) = 608 : μ(Music at 90 dB) = 617	.013*

Means rounded to nearest second.

*Statistically significant difference (α = .05).

There was no statistically significant difference in the participants' time to complete the puzzle among those who worked in silence (μ = 609) compared with those who listened to soft classical music (μ = 606) (p = .895); hence, we reject H_1.

Similarly, there was no statistically significant difference in completion time between those who worked with no music (μ = 609) compared with those who listened to classical music at a medium volume (μ = 608) (p = 1.000); hence, we reject H_2.

Those who listened to loud classical music took (statistically) significantly longer (μ = 617) to complete the puzzle compared with those who worked in silence (μ = 609) (p = .015); hence, we would reject H_0 and H_3.

(5d) This experiment was designed to determine if classical music facilitates problem solving. We recruited 153 subjects and randomly assigned them to one of four groups. Those in Group 1 worked on a 100-piece jigsaw puzzle in silence; those in Groups 2, 3, and 4 solved the same puzzle with classical music playing at different volumes in each group: soft (30 dB), medium (60 dB), and loud (90 dB), respectively. We found no statistically significant difference in puzzle solving time among those who worked in silence ($\mu = 609$ seconds) compared with those who had classical music played at a soft volume ($\mu = 606$, $p = .895$, $\alpha = .05$) or moderate volume ($\mu = 608$, $p = 1.000$, $\alpha = .05$). However, participants who worked on the puzzle while listening to loud classical music (90 dB) took significantly longer ($\mu = 617$) to solve the puzzle compared with those who worked in silence ($\mu = 509$, $p = .015$, $\alpha = .05$), suggesting that classical music has no effect on this sort of problem solving, unless it is played loudly, in which case, the music appears to act as a distraction.

7. Data Set A

   (7a) H_0: Light therapy has no effect on depression.

      H_1: Light therapy given every other day is effective in reducing depression.

      H_2: Light therapy given daily is effective in reducing depression.

   (7b) Histograms with normal curve plots show a normal distribution of *mood* for all groups as shown in the three figures below; hence, the pretest criterion of normality is satisfied.

Normal distribution for *mood* in Group 1 (no light therapy)

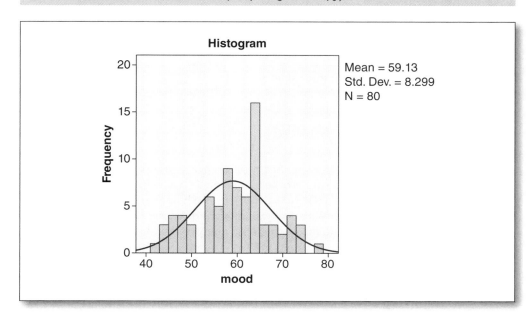

Normal distribution for *mood* in Group 2 (light therapy: even days)

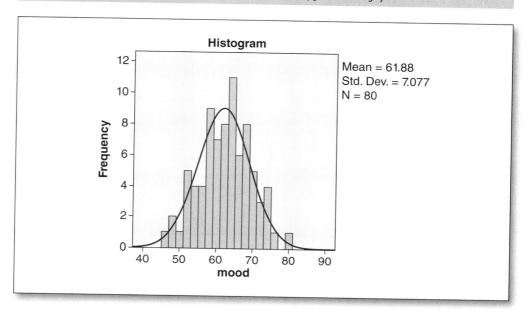

Normal distribution for *mood* in Group 3 (light therapy: every day)

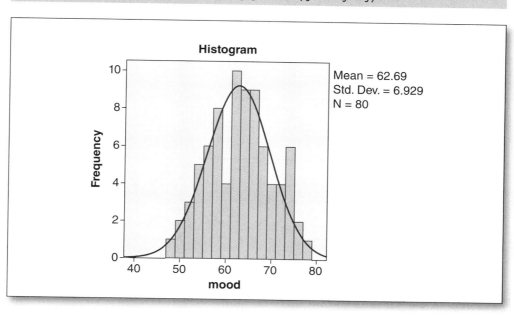

Test of Homogeneity of Variances

mood

Levene Statistic	df1	df2	Sig.
1.409	2	2	.2
		37	46

The homogeneity of variance score for *mood* shows a significance (*p*) of .246; since this is greater than the α level of .05, this suggests that there is no statistically significant difference between the variances of the three groups; hence, this pretest criterion passes.

The *n* for each group is 80, which satisfies the 30 per group minimum criterion (see Descriptives table below).

(7c) The ANOVA test revealed the following:

Descriptives

mood

	N	Mean	Std. Deviation	Std. Error	95% Confidence Interval for Mean		Minimum	Maximum
					Lower Bound	Upper Bound		
No light therapy	80	59.13	8.299	.928	57.28	60.97	42	77
Light therapy: even days	80	61.88	7.077	.791	60.30	63.45	46	79
Light therapy: every day	80	62.69	6.929	.775	61.15	64.23	48	78
Total	240	61.23	7.585	.490	60.26	62.19	42	79

ANOVA

mood

	Sum of Squares	df	Mean Square	F	Sig.
Between Groups	557.708	2	278.854	5.010	.007
Within Groups	13190.688	237	55.657		
Total	13748.396	239			

Multiple Comparisons

mood

Tukey HSD

(I) group	(J) group	Mean Difference (I-J)	Std. Error	Sig.	95% Confidence Interval	
					Lower Bound	Upper Bound
No light therapy	Light therapy: even days	-2.750	1.180	.053	-5.53	.03
	Light therapy: every day	-3.563*	1.180	.008	-6.34	-.78
Light therapy: even days	No light therapy	2.750	1.180	.053	-.03	5.53
	Light therapy: every day	-.813	1.180	.770	-3.59	1.97
Light therapy: every day	No light therapy	3.563*	1.180	.008	.78	6.34
	Light therapy: even days	.813	1.180	.770	-1.97	3.59

*. The mean difference is significant at the 0.05 level.

Groups (μ = mood)	p
μ(No light th.) = 59.1 : μ(Light th. even days) = 61.9	.053
μ(No light th.) = 59.1 : μ(Light th. every day) = 62.7	.008*
μ(Light th. even days) = 61.9 : μ(Light th. every day) = 62.7	.770

Means rounded to one decimal digit.

*Statistically significant difference (α = .05).

After 1 month of treatment, participants who received light therapy for 1 hour a day scored an average of 62.7 on a mood test compared with 59.1 among those who had no light therapy; this 3.6-point difference in their scores is statistically significant (p = .008, α = .05). Those who received 1 hour of light therapy every other day showed a better mood score (61.9) than those who received no light therapy, but the improvement is not considered statistically significant (p = .053) using the .05 α level. Incidentally, comparing the mean mood score of those who received light therapy for every-other-day use (61.9) and daily use (62.7) revealed no statistically significant difference between these two groups (p = .770, α = .05).

H_0: Light therapy has no effect on mood.

H_1: Light therapy given every other day enhances mood.

H_2: Light therapy given daily enhances mood.

Comparing the mood score from those who received no light therapy (μ = 59.1) with those who received light therapy daily (μ = 62.7) produced a statistically significant difference (p = .008); since this is less than the specified α level of .05, we reject H_0.

Since there is no statistically significant difference (p = .053) between receiving no light therapy (μ = 59.1) and receiving light therapy every other day (μ = 61.9), we reject H_1.

Comparing the mood level of those who received no light therapy (μ = 59.1) with those who received light therapy daily (μ = 62.7) renders a statistically significant difference (p = .008, α = .05); hence, we do not reject H_2.

(7d) To determine if light therapy is a viable supplement to treating depression, 240 subjects diagnosed with depression were randomly assigned to one of three groups: The control group received no light therapy, the second group received 1 hour of light therapy every other day for a month, and the third group received light therapy for 1 hour every day for a month. After 30 days, all participants completed the Acme Mood Scale, a 10-question survey that renders a score from 1 to 100 (1 = extremely bad mood . . . 100 = extremely good mood). The group average scores on the mood test were similar among the two light therapy groups: 61.9 for the every-other-day group and 62.7 for the daily group. Although these differences were not statistically significantly different from each other ($p = .770$, $\alpha = .05$), only the group that received light therapy on a daily basis ($\mu = 62.7$) showed a statistically significant improvement in mood compared with those who received no light therapy ($\mu = 59.1$) ($p = .008$, $\alpha = .05$).

7. Data Set B

(7a) H_0: Light therapy has no effect on depression.

H_1: Light therapy given every other day is effective in reducing depression.

H_2: Light therapy given daily is effective in reducing depression.

(7b) Histograms with normal curve plots show a normal distribution of *mood* for all groups per the three figures below; hence, the pretest criterion of normality is satisfied.

Normal distribution for *mood* in Group 1 (no light therapy)

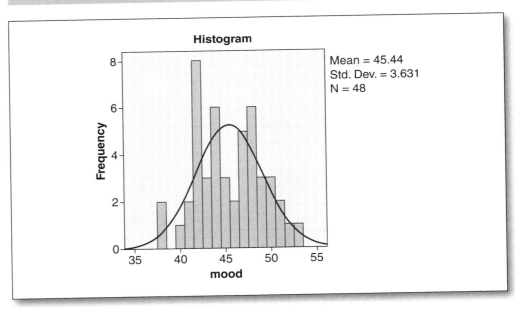

Normal distribution for *mood* in Group 2 (light therapy: even days)

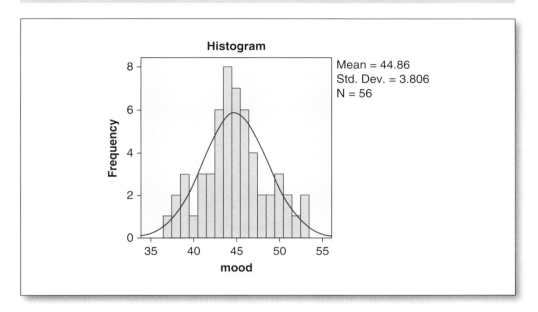

Normal distribution for *mood* in Group 3 (light therapy: every day)

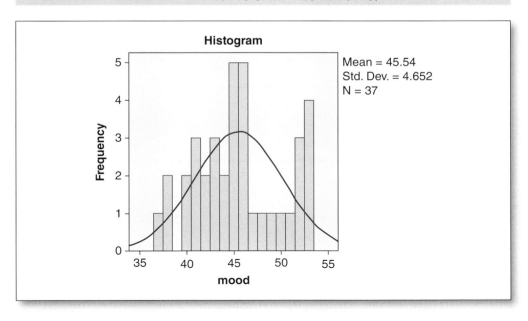

Test of Homogeneity of Variances

mood

Levene Statistic	df1	df2	Sig.
1.352	2	138	.262

The homogeneity of variance score for *mood* shows a significance (*p*) of .262; since this is greater than the α level of .05, this suggests that there is no statistically significant difference between the variances among the three groups; hence, this pretest criterion passes.

The *n*s for these groups are 48, 56, and 37, which satisfies the 30 per group minimum criterion (see Descriptives table below).

(7c) The ANOVA test revealed the following:

Descriptives

mood

	N	Mean	Std. Deviation	Std. Error	95% Confidence Interval for Mean		Min.	Max.
					Lower Bound	Upper Bound		
No light therapy	48	45.44	3.631	.524	44.38	46.49	38	53
Light therapy: even days	56	44.86	3.806	.509	43.84	45.88	37	53
Light therapy: every day	37	45.54	4.652	.765	43.99	47.09	37	53
Total	141	45.23	3.972	.335	44.57	45.90	37	53

ANOVA

mood

	Sum of Squares	df	Mean Square	F	Sig.
Between Groups	13.418	2	6.709	.422	.657
Within Groups	2195.859	138	15.912		
Total	2209.277	140			

Multiple Comparisons

mood
Sidak

(I) group	(J) group	Mean Difference (I-J)	Std. Error	Sig.	95% Confidence Interval	
					Lower Bound	Upper Bound
No light therapy	Light therapy: even days	.580	.785	.843	-1.32	2.48
	Light therapy: every day	-.103	.873	.999	-2.21	2.01
Light therapy: even days	No light therapy	-.580	.785	.843	-2.48	1.32
	Light therapy: every day	-.683	.845	.805	-2.73	1.36
Light therapy: every day	No light therapy	.103	.873	.999	-2.01	2.21
	Light therapy: even days	.683	.845	.805	-1.36	2.73

Groups (μ = mood)	p
μ(No light th.) = 45.44 : μ(Light th. even days) = 44.86	.843
μ(No light th.) = 45.44 : μ(Light th. every day) = 45.54	.999
μ(Light th. even days) = 44.86 : μ(Light th. every day) = 45.54	.805

After 1 month of treatment, participants who received light therapy for 1 hour a day scored an average of 45.54 on a mood test, those who had light therapy every other day scored an average of 44.86, and those who had no light therapy had an average score of 45.44. The ANOVA table reports a Sig. (p) value of .657, which is greater than the .05 α level, indicating that there are no statistically significant differences among the groups. This is confirmed by the Sig. column in the Multiple Comparisons table, wherein the p values range from .805 to .999, which is well above the .05 α level. Hence, we can conclude that for this sample, the light therapy protocol produced no statistically significant improvement in mood.

H_0: Light therapy has no effect on mood.

H_1: Light therapy given every other day enhances mood.

H_2: Light therapy given daily enhances mood.

The Sig. (p) level in the ANOVA table is .657; since this is greater than the .05 α level, this tells us that there are no statistically significant differences among the groups involved; hence, we would not reject H_0.

Those who had light therapy every other day had a mean mood score of 44.86, and those who had no light therapy had a mean mood score of 45.44, which renders a p value of .843. Since the p value is greater than the α level of .05, we rule that there is no statistically significant difference between these groups; light therapy given every other day does not enhance mood; hence, we reject H_1.

Those who had light therapy daily had a mean mood score of 45.54, and those who had no light therapy had a mean mood score of 45.44, which renders a p value of .999. Since the p value is greater than the α level of .05, we rule that there is no statistically significant difference between these groups; light therapy given every day does not enhance mood; hence, we reject H_2.

(7d) To determine if light therapy is a viable supplement to treating depression, 141 subjects diagnosed with depression were randomly assigned to one of three groups: The control group received no light therapy, the second group received 1 hour of light therapy every other day for a month, and the third group received light therapy for 1 hour every day for a month. After 30 days, all participants completed the Acme Mood Scale, a 10-question survey that renders a score from 1 to 100 (1 = extremely bad mood . . . 100 = extremely good mood). The group average scores on the mood test were similar: 45.44 for those who received no light therapy, 44.86 for those who had light therapy every other day, and 45.54 for those who had light therapy daily. The p values among these three groups ranged from .805 to .999; using an α level of .05, we conclude that this schedule of light therapy did not produce a statistically significant improvement in mood for these participants.

9. Data Set A

(9a) H_0: Tending to a plant has no effect on depressive mood.

H_1: Tending to a bamboo plant reduces depressive mood.

H_2: Tending to a cactus plant reduces depressive mood.

(9b) Despite the few low-score outliers shown in the histogram for Group 2, the histograms with normal curve plots exhibit a normal distribution of the *depress* variable for all groups as shown in the three figures below; hence, the pretest criterion of normality is satisfied.

Normal distribution for *depress* in Group 1 (no plant)

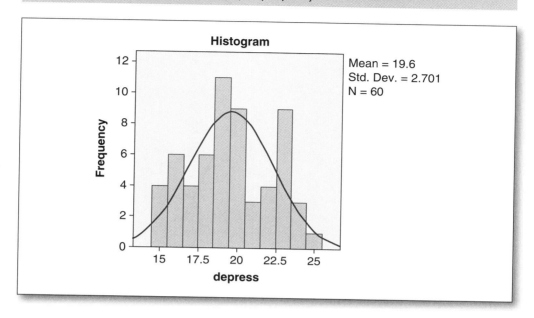

Histogram

Mean = 19.6
Std. Dev. = 2.701
N = 60

Normal distribution for *depress* in Group 2 (bamboo)

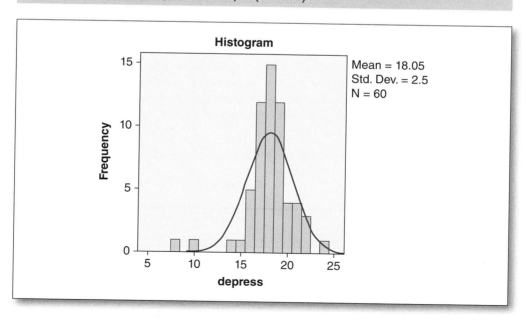

Histogram

Mean = 18.05
Std. Dev. = 2.5
N = 60

Normal distribution for *depress* in Group 3 (cactus)

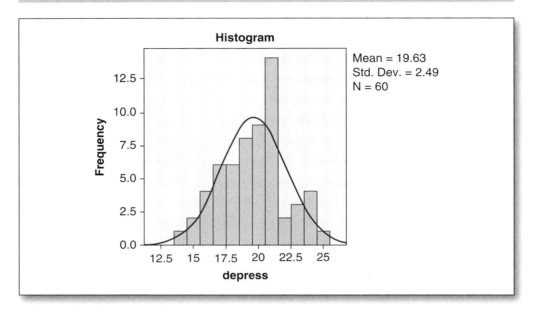

Histogram

Mean = 19.63
Std. Dev. = 2.49
N = 60

Test of Homogeneity of Variances

depress

Levene Statistic	df1	df2	Sig.
2.037	2	177	.133

The homogeneity of variance score for *mood* shows a significance (*p*) of .133; since this is greater than the α level of .05, this suggests that there is no statistically significant difference between the variances among the three groups; hence, this pretest criterion passes.

The *n* for each group is 60 (see Descriptives table below), which satisfies the 30 per group minimum criterion.

(9c) The ANOVA test revealed the following:

Descriptives

depress

	N	Mean	Std. Deviation	Std. Error	95% Confidence Interval for Mean		Minimum	Maximum
					Lower Bound	Upper Bound		
No plant	60	19.60	2.701	.349	18.90	20.30	15	25
Bamboo	60	18.05	2.500	.323	17.40	18.70	8	24
Cactus	60	19.63	2.490	.322	18.99	20.28	14	25
Total	180	19.09	2.657	.198	18.70	19.49	8	25

ANOVA

Depress

	Sum of Squares	df	Mean Square	F	Sig.
Between Groups	98.211	2	49.106	7.459	.001
Within Groups	1165.183	177	6.583		
Total	1263.394	179			

Multiple Comparisons

depress

Tukey HSD

(I) group	(J) group	Mean Difference (I-J)	Std. Error	Sig.	95% Confidence Interval	
					Lower Bound	Upper Bound
No plant	Bamboo	1.550*	.468	.003	.44	2.66
	Cactus	-.033	.468	.997	-1.14	1.07
Bamboo	No plant	-1.550*	.468	.003	-2.66	-.44
	Cactus	-1.583*	.468	.003	-2.69	-.48
Cactus	No plant	.033	.468	.997	-1.07	1.14
	Bamboo	1.583*	.468	.003	.48	2.69

*. The mean difference is significant at the 0.05 level.

Groups (μ = depression)	p
μ(No plant) = 19.60 : μ(Bamboo) = 18.05	.003*
μ(No plant) = 19.60 : μ(Cactus) = 19.63	.997
μ(Bamboo) = 18.05 : μ(Cactus) = 19.63	.003*

*Statistically significant difference (α = .05).

There is no statistically significant difference in the average scores between those who received no plant (μ = 19.60) and those who received a cactus (μ = 19.63) (p = .997, α = .05). The mean depression score for those who received a bamboo plant (μ = 18.05) was statistically significantly lower than the scores for those who received no plant (p = .003) and those who received a cactus (p = .003).

H_0: Tending to a plant has no effect on depressive mood.

H_1: Tending to a bamboo plant reduces depressive mood.

H_2: Tending to a cactus plant reduces depressive mood.

Since those in the bamboo group had a statistically significantly lower depression score than those who received no plant, we would reject H_0; by that same reasoning, we would not reject H_1.

There was no statistically significant difference between the depression score for the group that received no plant and the group that received a cactus; in summary, tending to a cactus did not reduce depression, and hence we would reject H_2.

(9d) We hypothesized that empowering nursing home residents with an opportunity to provide nurturance would help reduce depression. To test this hypothesis, 180 residents were randomly assigned to one of three groups: Those in Group 1 served as the control group and were given no plant; Group 2 members were given a small bamboo plant, and those in Group 3 were given a small cactus. After 90 days, we administered the Acme Depression Scale (1 = low depression . . . 100 = high depression) to members of all three groups. Participants in the bamboo group scored an average of 18.05, which was statistically significantly lower than the no-plant group ($\mu = 19.60$, $p = .003$) and the cactus group ($\mu = 19.63$, $p = .003$) using a .05 α level. The cactus group had a slightly higher mean depression score ($\mu = 19.63$) compared with those who received no plant ($\mu = 19.60$), but this was not a statistically significant difference ($p = .997$). This suggests that tending to a plant has the potential to reduce depression in nursing home residents, but the cactus, which requires very little tending, did not provide the desired effect, whereas the bamboo, which required more monitoring and watering, did.

9. Data Set B

(9a) H_0: Tending to a plant has no effect on depressive mood.

H_1: Tending to a bamboo plant reduces depressive mood.

H_2: Tending to a cactus plant reduces depressive mood.

(9b) The histograms with normal curve plots exhibit a normal distribution of the *depress* variable for all groups, as shown in the three figures below; hence, the pretest criterion of normality is satisfied.

Normal distribution for *depress* in Group 1 (no plant)

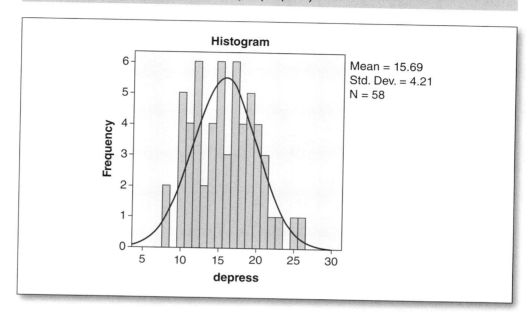

Normal distribution for *depress* in Group 2 (bamboo)

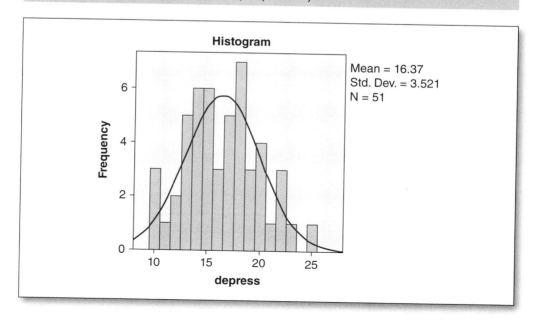

Normal distribution for *depress* in Group 3 (cactus)

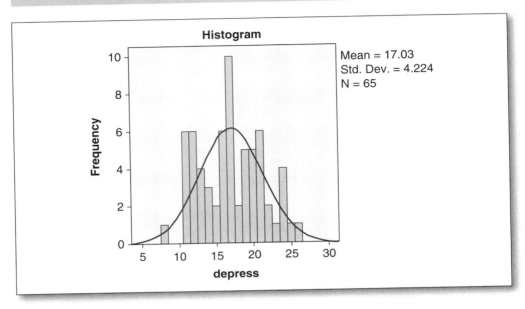

Test of Homogeneity of Variances

depress

Levene Statistic	df1	df2	Sig.
1.108	2	171	.333

The homogeneity of variance score for *mood* shows a significance (*p*) of .333; since this is greater than the α level of .05, this suggests that there is no statistically significant difference variances among the three groups; hence, this pretest criterion passes.

The *ns* for the groups are 58, 51, and 65 (see Descriptives table below), which satisfies the 30 per group minimum criterion.

(9c) The ANOVA test revealed the following:

Descriptives

depress

	N	Mean	Std. Deviation	Std. Error	95% Confidence Interval for Mean Lower Bound	95% Confidence Interval for Mean Upper Bound	Minimum	Maximum
No plant	58	15.69	4.210	.553	14.58	16.80	8	26
Bamboo	51	16.37	3.521	.493	15.38	17.36	10	25
Cactus	65	17.03	4.224	.524	15.98	18.08	8	26
Total	174	16.39	4.043	.306	15.79	17.00	8	26

ANOVA

depress

	Sum of Squares	df	Mean Square	F	Sig.
Between Groups	55.151	2	27.576	1.701	.186
Within Groups	2772.274	171	16.212		
Total	2827.425	173			

Multiple Comparisons

depress

Sidak

(I) group	(J) group	Mean Difference (I-J)	Std. Error	Sig.	95% Confidence Interval	
					Lower Bound	Upper Bound
No plant	Bamboo	-.683	.773	.760	-2.55	1.18
	Cactus	-1.341	.727	.188	-3.09	.41
Bamboo	No plant	.683	.773	.760	-1.18	2.55
	Cactus	-.658	.753	.766	-2.47	1.16
Cactus	No plant	1.341	.727	.188	-.41	3.09
	Bamboo	.658	.753	.766	-1.16	2.47

Groups (μ = depression)	p
μ(No plant) = 15.69 : μ(Bamboo) = 16.37	.760
μ(No plant) = 15.69 : μ(Cactus) = 17.03	.188
μ(Bamboo) = 16.37 : μ(Cactus) = 17.03	.766

Inspection of the Sig. (*p*) figure in the ANOVA table (*p* = .186, which is greater than the .05 α level) tells us that there are no statistically significant differences detected in the *depression* scores among any of the groups.

Upon reviewing the comparisons presented in the Multiple Comparisons table, we see that this finding is confirmed: The *p* level for each pair of depression scores is greater than the specified .05 α level, and hence there are no statistically significant differences among any of the groups, as shown in the table above.

H_0: Tending to a plant has no effect on depressive mood.

H_1: Tending to a bamboo plant reduces depressive mood.

H_2: Tending to a cactus plant reduces depressive mood.

Since there are no statistically significant differences between the mean depression score of those who received no plant and those who received any plant, we would not reject H_0.

There was no statistically significant difference between the depression score for the group that received no plant and the group that received a bamboo plant; apparently, tending to a bamboo did not significantly reduce depression, and hence we would reject H_1.

There was no statistically significant difference between the depression score for the group that received no plant and the group that received a cactus; in summary, tending to a cactus did not significantly reduce depression, and hence we would reject H_2.

(9d)   We hypothesized that empowering nursing home residents with an opportunity to provide nurturance would help to reduce depression. To test this hypothesis, 174 residents were randomly assigned to one of three groups: Those in Group 1 served as the control group and were given no plant; Group 2 members were given a small bamboo plant to tend to along with a card providing care instructions, and those in Group 3 were given a small cactus along with a card providing care instructions. After 90 days, we administered the Acme Depression Scale (1 = low depression . . . 100 = high depression) to members of both groups. We found that those who were given the cactus scored an average of 17.03, those who were given a bamboo plant had an average score of 16.37, and those who were given no plant scored an average of 15.69; using a .05 α level, we found no statistically significant differences among any of these groups (p ranged from .188 to .766). We found that these plants were not helpful in reducing depression among these nursing home residents.

Paired *t* Test

1. Data Set A

(1a) H_0: Acme Monster spray has no effect on children's monster anxiety.

H_1: Acme Monster spray reduces children's monster anxiety.

(1b) After computing the difference between the pretest score and posttest score (*diff = posttest – pretest*), a histogram with normal curve was plotted for this difference (*diff*). The graph below presents a symmetrical (bell-shaped) normal curve for *diff*, thus satisfying this criterion.

Posttest – pretest (*diff*) renders a normal curve

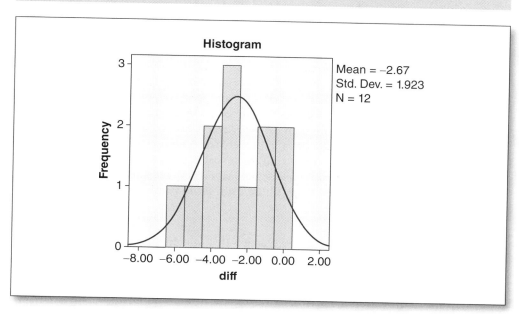

(1c) The paired *t* test revealed the following:

Paired Samples Statistics

		Mean	N	Std. Deviation	Std. Error Mean
Pair 1	pretest	6.75	12	1.485	.429
	posttest	4.08	12	1.443	.417

Paired Samples Test

		Paired Differences							
				Std.	95% Confidence Interval of the Difference				
		Mean	Std. Deviation	Error Mean	Lower	Upper	t	df	Sig. (2-tailed)
Pair 1	pretest - posttest	2.667	1.923	.555	1.445	3.888	4.804	11	.001

Prior to using the Monster Spray, the children's mean anxiety level was 6.75; after using the spray, that level dropped to 4.08. This 2.67-point reduction in reported anxiety is statistically significant since the *p* value of .001 is less than the specified α level of .05. On the basis of these findings, we would reject H_0 but not reject H_1.

(1d) To help children rest easier at night, 12 children were asked to rate their bedtime anxiety due to fear of nighttime monsters on a 1 to 10 scale (1 = not afraid at all . . . 10 = very afraid), and then Acme Monster Spray, an inert sweet-smelling mist, was administered by their parents, after which children were asked to rate their anxiety level. Upon spraying, children reported a 2.67-point average drop in anxiety (6.75 before spraying, down to 4.08 after spraying). Paired *t* test analysis revealed this change to be statistically significant (*p* = .001) using a .05 α level, suggesting that the (placebo) effect of this spray may help children rest more comfortably.

1. Data Set B

(1a) H_0: Acme Monster spray has no effect on children's monster anxiety.

H_1: Acme Monster spray reduces children's monster anxiety.

(1b) After computing the difference between the pretest score and posttest score (*diff = posttest – pretest*), a histogram with a normal curve was plotted for this difference (*diff*). The graph below presents a symmetrical (bell-shaped) normal curve for *diff,* thus satisfying this criterion.

Posttest – pretest (*diff*) renders a normal curve

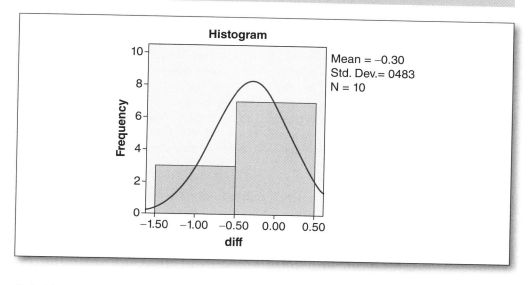

Histogram

Mean = −0.30
Std. Dev.= 0483
N = 10

(1c) The paired *t* test revealed the following:

Paired Samples Statistics

		Mean	N	Std. Deviation	Std. Error Mean
Pair 1	pretest	5.70	10	1.947	.616
	posttest	5.40	10	2.066	.653

Paired Samples Test

		Paired Differences							
					95% Confidence Interval of the Difference				
		Mean	Std. Deviation	Std. Error Mean	Lower	Upper	t	df	Sig. (2-tailed)
Pair 1	pretest - posttest	.300	.483	.153	−.046	.646	1.964	9	.081

Prior to using the Monster Spray, the children's mean anxiety level was 5.70; after using the spray, that level dropped to 5.40. This .30-point reduction in reported anxiety is not statistically significant since the *p* value of .081 is greater than the specified α level of .05. On the basis of these findings, we would not reject H_0 but reject H_1.

(1d) To help children rest easier at night, 10 children were asked to rate their bedtime anxiety due to fear of nighttime monsters on a 1 to 10 scale (1 = not afraid at all . . . 10 = very afraid), and then Acme Monster Spray, an inert sweet-smelling mist, was administered by their parents, after which children were asked to rate their anxiety level. Upon spraying, children reported a .30-point average drop in anxiety (5.70 before spraying, down to 5.40 after spraying). Paired *t* test analysis revealed a *p* level of .081; using a .05 α level, this suggests that this difference in scores is not statistically significant; hence, parents will need to find a different way to console their children at nighttime.

3. Data Set A

(1a) H_0: Students do not significantly improve their spelling skills over the course of a month.

  H_1: Students improve their spelling skills over the course of a month.

(1b) After computing the difference between the pretest score and posttest score (*diff* = *posttest – pretest*), a histogram with a normal curve was plotted for this difference (*diff*). The graph below presents a symmetrical (bell-shaped) normal curve for *diff,* thus satisfying this criterion.

Posttest – pretest (*diff*) renders a normal curve

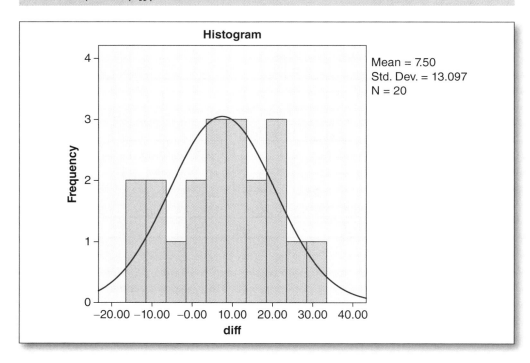

(1c) The paired t test revealed the following:

Paired Samples Statistics

		Mean	N	Std. Deviation	Std. Error Mean
Pair 1	pretest	62.05	20	9.041	2.022
	posttest	69.55	20	9.478	2.119

Paired Samples Test

		Paired Differences							
					95% Confidence Interval of the Difference				
		Mean	Std. Deviation	Std. Error Mean	Lower	Upper	t	df	Sig. (2-tailed)
Pair 1	pretest - posttest	-7.500	13.097	2.929	-13.629	-1.371	-2.561	19	.019

At the start of the month, students were administered a 100-word spelling test to find out how many words on the prescribed spelling list for that month students could already spell correctly. Students spelled an average of 62.05 words correctly on this pretest. At the end of the month, students were readministered this 100-word test and spelled an average of 69.55 words correctly. The 7.5-point increase in score constitutes a statistically significant improvement since the p level is .019, which is less than the specified α level of .05. On the basis of these findings, we would reject H_0 but not reject H_1.

(1d) To assess if students substantially advance their spelling proficiency on a monthly basis, students were given a 100-word spelling test at the beginning of the month; after studying 25 words per week from the list, students took the same 100-word test 30 days later. At the end of the month, students spelled an average of 69.55 of the words correctly compared with 62.05 at the beginning of the month. Using an α level of .05, this 7.5-point improvement in score was found to be statistically significant ($p = .019$).

3. Data Set B

(1a) H_0: Students do not significantly improve their spelling skills over the course of a month.

H_1: Students improve their spelling skills over the course of a month.

(1b) After computing the difference between the pretest score and posttest score (*diff = posttest – pretest*), a histogram with a normal curve was plotted for this difference (*diff*). The graph below presents a symmetrical (bell-shaped) normal curve for *diff,* thus satisfying this criterion.

Posttest – pretest (*diff*) renders a normal curve

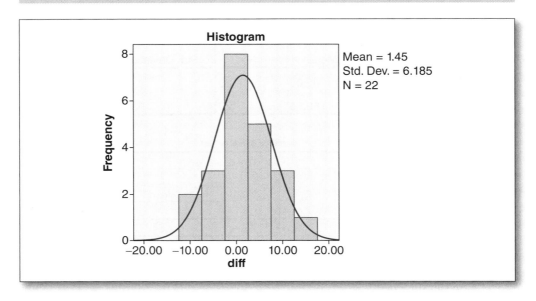

(1c) The paired *t* test revealed the following:

Paired Samples Statistics

		Mean	N	Std. Deviation	Std. Error Mean
Pair 1	pretest	86.14	22	4.201	.896
	posttest	87.59	22	4.469	.953

Paired Samples Test

		Paired Differences							
					95% Confidence Interval of the Difference				
		Mean	Std. Deviation	Std. Error Mean	Lower	Upper	t	df	Sig. (2-tailed)
Pair 1	pretest - posttest	−1.455	6.185	1.319	−4.197	1.288	−1.103	21	.283

At the start of the month, students were administered a 100-word spelling test to find out how many words on the prescribed spelling list for that month students could already spell correctly. Students spelled an average of 86.14 words correctly on this pretest. At the end of the month, students were readministered this 100-word test and spelled an average of 87.59 words correctly. The 1.45-point increase in score is not a statistically significant improvement since the p level is .283, which is greater than the specified α level of .05. On the basis of these findings, we would not reject H_0 but reject H_1.

(1d)   To find out if students substantially advance their spelling proficiency on a monthly basis, students were given a 100-word spelling test at the beginning of the month; after studying 25 words per week from the list, students took the same 100-word test 30 days later. At the end of the month, students spelled an average of 87.59 of the words correctly compared with 86.14 at the beginning of the month. Using an α level of .05, this 1.45-point improvement in score is not statistically significant ($p = .283$).

5. Data Set A

(1a) H_0: A 15-minute individual session with a bowling coach has no effect on bowling scores.

H_1: A 15-minute individual session with a bowling coach enhances bowling scores.

(1b)   After computing the difference between the pretest score and posttest score ($diff = posttest - pretest$), a histogram with a normal curve was plotted for this difference ($diff$). The graph below presents a symmetrical (bell-shaped) normal curve for $diff$, thus satisfying this criterion.

Posttest – Pretest (*diff*) renders a normal curve

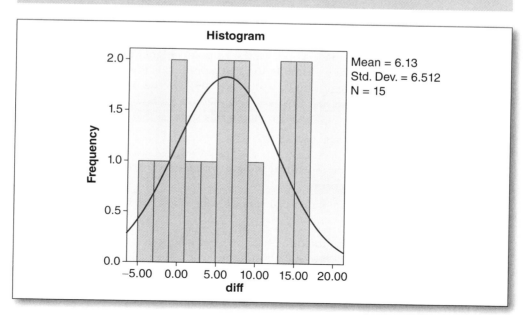

(1c) The paired t test revealed the following:

Paired Samples Statistics

		Mean	N	Std. Deviation	Std. Error Mean
Pair 1	pretest	151.60	15	15.459	3.991
	posttest	157.73	15	13.936	3.598

Paired Samples Test

		Paired Differences							
					95% Confidence Interval of the Difference				
		Mean	Std. Deviation	Std. Error Mean	Lower	Upper	t	df	Sig. (2-tailed)
Pair 1	pretest - posttest	−6.133	6.512	1.681	−9.740	−2.527	−3.648	14	.003

Fifteen students bowled an initial game and scored a mean of 151.60, and then a coach provided 15 minutes of instructions based on observations made during the students' first game. Students' mean score in the second game was 157.73. This 6.13-point increase produced a p level of .003; since this is less than the α level of .05, this is considered a statistically significant difference. On the basis of these findings, we would reject H_0 but not reject H_1.

(1d) To assess the effectiveness of short-term coaching, 15 students bowled one game with a coach observing unobtrusively. Next, the coach provided 15 minutes of individual coaching, after which each student bowled a second game. On average, scores were 6.13 points higher in the second game (157.73, up from 151.60 in the first game). This finding is considered statistically significant (p = .003, α = .05). On the basis of these findings, we will continue to use this coaching method for bowling, and we will be evaluating the utility of providing this style of coaching for other sports.

5. Data Set B

(1a) H_0: A 15-minute individual session with a bowling coach has no effect on bowling scores.

H_1: A 15-minute individual session with a bowling coach enhances bowling scores.

(1b) After computing the difference between the pretest score and posttest score (*diff* = *posttest – pretest*), a histogram with a normal curve was plotted for this difference (*diff*). The graph below presents a symmetrical (bell-shaped) normal curve for *diff*, thus satisfying this criterion.

Posttest – pretest (*diff*) renders a normal curve

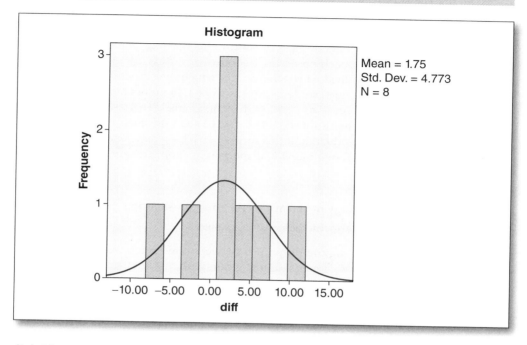

Histogram

Mean = 1.75
Std. Dev. = 4.773
N = 8

(1c) The paired *t* test revealed the following:

Paired Samples Statistics

		Mean	N	Std. Deviation	Std. Error Mean
Pair 1	pretest	72.50	8	3.742	1.323
	posttest	74.25	8	3.919	1.386

Paired Samples Test

		Paired Differences							
				Std.	95% Confidence Interval of the Difference				
		Mean	Std. Deviation	Error Mean	Lower	Upper	t	df	Sig. (2-tailed)
Pair 1	pretest - posttest	-1.750	4.773	1.688	-5.741	2.241	-1.037	7	.334

Eight students bowled an initial game and scored a mean of 72.50, and then a coach provided 15 minutes of instructions based on observations made during the students' first game. Students' mean score in the second game was 74.25. This 1.75-point increase produced a *p* level of .334; since this is greater than the α level of .05, this is not considered a statistically significant difference. On the basis of these findings, we would not reject H_0 but reject H_1.

(1d) To assess the effectiveness of short-term coaching, eight students bowled one game with a coach observing unobtrusively. Next, the coach provided 15 minutes of individual coaching, after which the students bowled a second game. On average, students' scores were 1.75 points higher in their second game (74.25, up from 72.50 in their first game). This finding is not considered statistically significant ($p = .334$, $\alpha = .05$). On the basis of these findings, we are considering evaluating if this form of coaching may provide more promising results for different individual sports (e.g., golf, archery, weight training).

7. Data Set A

(1a) H_0: Acme allergy medicine has no effect on sneezing.

H_1: Acme allergy medicine reduces sneezing.

(1b) After computing the difference between the pretest score and posttest score (*diff* = *posttest* − *pretest*), a histogram with a normal curve was plotted for this difference (*diff*). The graph below presents a symmetrical (bell-shaped) normal curve for *diff*, thus satisfying this criterion.

Posttest − pretest (*diff*) renders a normal curve

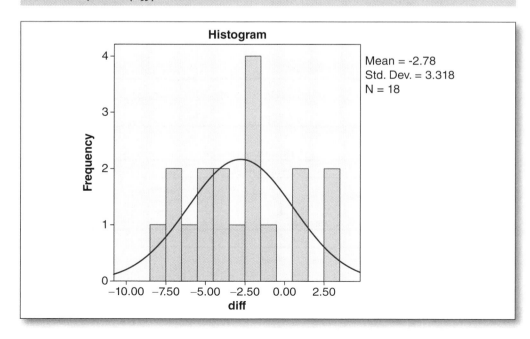

(1c) The paired t test revealed the following:

Paired Samples Statistics

		Mean	N	Std. Deviation	Std. Error Mean
Pair 1	pretest	15.39	18	3.274	.772
	posttest	12.61	18	3.165	.746

Paired Samples Test

		Paired Differences							
				Std.	95% Confidence Interval of the Difference				
		Mean	Std. Deviation	Error Mean	Lower	Upper	t	df	Sig. (2-tailed)
Pair 1	pretest - posttest	2.778	3.318	.782	1.128	4.428	3.552	17	.002

Eighteen people who were experiencing allergy symptoms were recruited and asked to count their total number of sneezes for a day. The next day, they took the Acme allergy medicine as directed and counted their total number of sneezes for that (second) day. This resulted in an average of 2.778 fewer sneezes (an average of 15.39 on the first day and 12.61 on the second day). Using a .05 α level, this difference is considered statistically significant ($p = .002$). As such, we would reject H_0 but not reject H_1.

(1d) To determine if Acme allergy medicine helps reduce sneezing among those experiencing allergy symptoms, 18 participants were recruited and instructed to count their total number of sneezes for 1 day. The next morning, each took the Acme allergy medicine as directed and counted their total sneezes for that day. On average, participants sneezed a total of 15.39 times the day before taking the medication and 12.61 times after taking the medication, an average of 2.778 fewer sneezes, which equates to an 18%* reduction in sneezing. This difference is considered statistically significant ($p = .002$, $\alpha = .05$), suggesting that the medicine provided some allergy symptom relief.

*NOTE: The 18% figure was calculated using the $\Delta\%$ formula on page **165:**

$$\Delta\% = (\text{New} - \text{Old}) \div \text{Old} \times 100.$$

7. Data Set B

(1a) H_0: Acme allergy medicine has no effect on sneezing.

H_1: Acme allergy medicine reduces sneezing.

(1b) After computing the difference between the pretest score and posttest score (*diff* = *posttest* – *pretest*), a histogram with a normal curve was plotted for this difference (*diff*). The graph below presents a symmetrical (bell-shaped) normal curve for *diff*, thus satisfying this criterion.

Posttest – pretest (*diff*) renders a normal curve

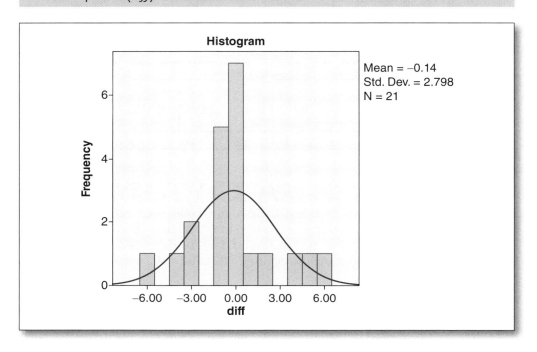

(1c) The paired *t* test revealed the following:

Paired Samples Statistics

		Mean	N	Std. Deviation	Std. Error Mean
Pair 1	pretest	4.10	21	1.640	.358
	posttest	3.95	21	1.830	.399

Paired Samples Test

		Paired Differences							
				Std. Error Mean	95% Confidence Interval of the Difference				
		Mean	Std. Deviation		Lower	Upper	t	df	Sig. (2-tailed)
Pair 1	pretest – posttest	.143	2.798	.611	−1.131	1.416	.234	20	.817

Twenty-one people who were experiencing allergy symptoms were recruited and asked to count their total number of sneezes for a day. The next day, they took the Acme allergy medicine as directed and counted their total number of sneezes for that (second) day. This resulted in an average of .15 fewer sneezes (an average of 4.10 on the first day and 3.95 on the second day). This rendered a *p* of .817; since the *p* value is greater than the designated .05 α level, this difference is not considered statistically significant. As such, we would not reject H_0 but reject H_1.

(1d) To determine if Acme allergy medicine helps reduce sneezing among those experiencing allergy symptoms, 21 participants were recruited and instructed to count their total number of sneezes for 1 day. The next morning, they took the Acme allergy medicine as directed and counted their total sneezes for that day. On average, participants sneezed a total of 4.10 times the day before taking the medication and 3.95 times after taking the medication, amounting to an average of .15 fewer sneezes, which is about a 3.6%* reduction in sneezing. This reduction is not considered statistically significant (*p* = .817, α = .05), suggesting that this medicine was not particularly helpful for these individuals.

*NOTE: The 3.6% figure was calculated using the formula on page **165**:

$$\Delta\% = (\text{New} - \text{Old}) \div \text{Old} \times 100.$$

9. Data Set A

(1a) H_0: Chocolate has no effect on attitude.

   H_1: Chocolate enhances attitude.

(1b) After computing the difference between the pretest score and posttest score (*diff* = *posttest* – *pretest*), a histogram with a normal curve was plotted for this difference (*diff*). The graph below presents a symmetrical (bell-shaped) normal curve for *diff*, thus satisfying this criterion.

Posttest – pretest (*diff*) renders a normal curve

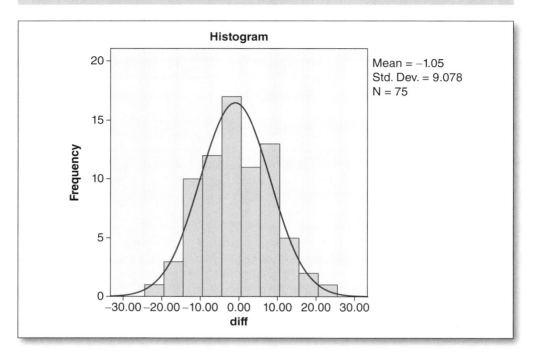

(1c) The paired *t* test revealed the following:

Paired Samples Statistics

		Mean	N	Std. Deviation	Std. Error Mean
Pair 1	pretest	81.91	75	5.707	.659
	posttest	80.85	75	5.897	.681

Paired Samples Test

		Paired Differences							
		Mean	Std. Deviation	Std. Error Mean	95% Confidence Interval of the Difference Lower	Upper	t	df	Sig. (2-tailed)
Pair 1	pretest - posttest	1.053	9.078	1.048	-1.035	3.142	1.005	74	.318

Seventy-five people were recruited to determine if chocolate helps to enhance attitude. We began by administering the Acme Attitude Survey (AAS) (0 = very bad attitude . . . 100 = very good attitude), resulting in a mean score of 81.91. After eating a piece of chocolate fudge cake, participants answered the AAS again; the mean of the results dropped by 1.06 points to 80.85. This change in the AAS score produced a p level of .318, which, using a .05 α level, is not statistically significant. This suggests that the chocolate cake did not make a statistically significant impact on attitude; hence, we would not reject H_0 but reject H_1.

(1d)   To better comprehend the effects that chocolate might have on attitude, 75 participants were recruited; we began by administering the Acme Attitude Survey (AAS), which renders a score ranging from 0 to 100 (0 = very bad attitude . . . 100 = very good attitude). Next, each participant was served a generous slice of chocolate fudge cake. After the cake, participants were asked to complete a second AAS. The pretest revealed a mean attitude score of 81.91; contrary to our expectations, the post-chocolate AAS score dropped an average of 1.06 points, to 80.85, rendering a p value of .318. Using a .05 α level, this drop in the AAS is not considered statistically significant; hence, in this case, chocolate had no impact on mood.

9. Data Set B

(1a) H_0: Chocolate has no effect on attitude.

H_1: Chocolate enhances attitude.

(1b)   After computing the difference between the pretest score and posttest score ($diff = posttest - pretest$), a histogram with a normal curve was plotted for this difference ($diff$). The graph below presents a symmetrical (bell-shaped) normal curve for $diff$, thus satisfying this criterion.

Posttest – pretest (*diff*) renders a normal curve

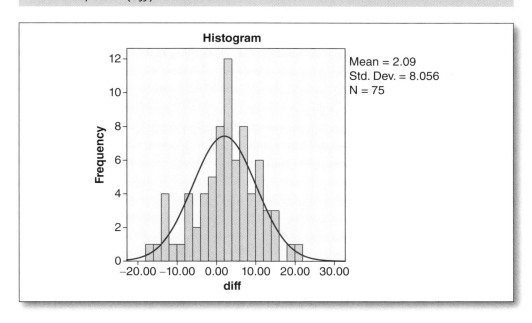

(1c) The paired *t* test revealed the following:

Paired Samples Statistics

		Mean	N	Std. Deviation	Std. Error Mean
Pair 1	pretest	81.17	75	5.869	.678
	posttest	83.27	75	6.267	.724

Paired Samples Test

		Paired Differences							
					95% Confidence Interval of the Difference				
		Mean	Std. Deviation	Std. Error Mean	Lower	Upper	t	df	Sig. (2-tailed)
Pair 1	pretest - posttest	-2.093	8.056	.930	-3.947	-.240	-2.250	74	.027

Seventy-five people were recruited to determine if chocolate helps to enhance attitude. We began by administering the Acme Attitude Survey (AAS) (0 = very bad attitude . . . 100 = very good attitude), resulting in an average score of 81.17. After eating a piece of chocolate fudge cake, participants answered the AAS again; the mean results rose by 2.10 points to 83.27. This change in the AAS score produced a *p* level of .027, which, using a .05 α level, is considered statistically significant. This suggests that the chocolate cake made a statistically significant impact on attitude; hence, we would reject H_0 but not reject H_1.

(1d) To better comprehend the effects that chocolate might have on attitude, 75 participants were recruited; we began by administering the Acme Attitude Survey (AAS), which renders a score ranging from 0 to 100 (0 = very bad attitude . . . 100 = very good attitude). After collecting the AAS forms, each participant was served a generous slice of chocolate fudge cake. After the cake, participants were asked to complete a second AAS. The pretest revealed a mean attitude score of 81.17, and after dining on the chocolate cake, the mean AAS score went up an average of 2.10 points, to 83.27. These figures rendered a *p* value of .027. Using a .05 α level, this increase in the AAS score suggests that chocolate may help to enhance attitude.

C H A P T E R 8

Correlation and Regression

1. Data Set A

    (1a) H_0: There is no significant correlation between hours of walking and weight loss.

          H_1: There is a significant correlation between hours of walking and weight loss.

    (1b) Histograms with normal curve plots show a normal distribution for *walkhrs* and *wtloss* as shown in the two figures below; hence, the pretest criterion of normality is satisfied.

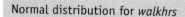

Normal distribution for *walkhrs*	Normal distribution for *wtloss*

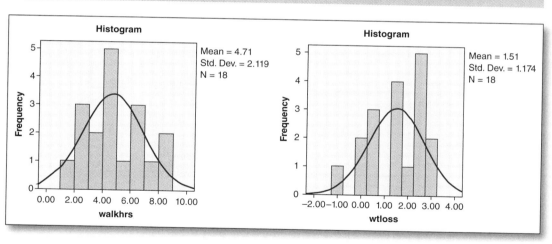

The scatterplot below shows that the straight regression line reasonably fits the field of points, and hence the criterion of linearity is satisfied. The scatterplot also shows that the points are primarily clustered toward the center of the regression line with substantially fewer points toward the ends, and hence the criterion of homoscedasticity is satisfied.

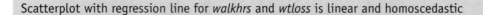

Scatterplot with regression line for *walkhrs* and *wtloss* is linear and homoscedastic

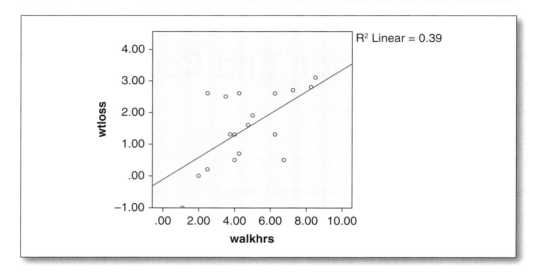

(1c) The correlations table below shows a positive correlation (r = .624) between *walkhrs* and *wtloss; p* = .006, which is less than the specified .05 α level, indicating that this is a statistically significant correlation.

Correlations

		walkhrs	wtloss
walkhrs	Pearson Correlation	1	.624**
	Sig. (2-tailed)		.006
	N	18	18
wtloss	Pearson Correlation	.624**	1
	Sig. (2-tailed)	.006	
	N	18	18

**. Correlation is significant at the 0.01 level (2-tailed).

(1d) In a study examining the effects of brisk walking on weight loss, 18 adults were recruited and instructed to walk as many days of the week as possible for as long as they could. The researcher gathered each participant's daily walking time, as well as his or her weight at the beginning and end of the week, and found a positive, statistically significant correlation between the amount of walking time and the amount of weight lost ($r = .624$, $p = .006$; $\alpha = .05$). In other words, on the whole, the more the participants walked, the more weight they lost. These findings suggest that moderate daily exercise may be effective in facilitating weight loss. As such, we reject H_0 but do not reject H_1.

NOTE: You might also inspect the descriptive statistics for *walkhrs* and *wtloss* and consider including the supplement in your findings: "Participants averaged 4.7 hours of walking per week and had an average weight loss of 1.5 pounds."

1. Data Set B

(1a) H_0: There is no significant correlation between hours of walking and weight loss.

H_1: There is a significant correlation between hours of walking and weight loss.

(1b) Histograms with normal curve plots show a normal distribution for *walkhrs* and *wtloss,* as shown in the two figures below; hence, the pretest criterion of normality is satisfied.

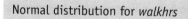

Normal distribution for *walkhrs*　　　Normal distribution for *wtloss*

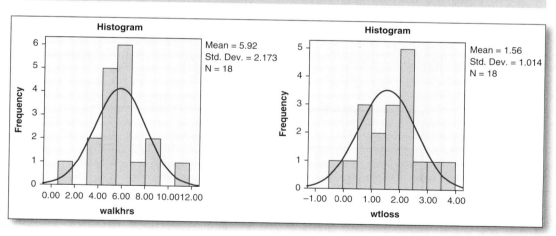

The scatterplot below shows that the straight regression line reasonably fits the field of points, and hence the criterion of linearity is satisfied. The scatterplot also shows that the points are primarily clustered toward the center of the regression line

with substantially fewer points toward the ends, and hence the criterion of homoscedasticity is satisfied.

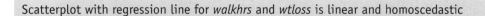

Scatterplot with regression line for *walkhrs* and *wtloss* is linear and homoscedastic

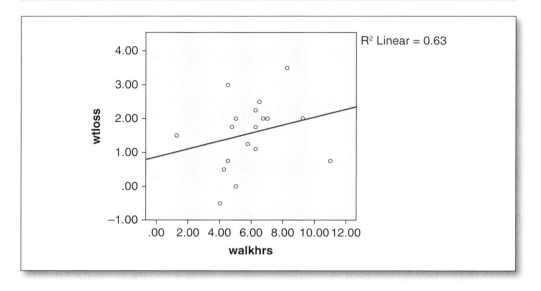

(1c) The correlations table below shows a positive correlation ($r = .250$) between
walkhrs and *wtloss,* but since $p = .317$, which is greater than the specified .05
α level, this indicates that this is not a statistically significant correlation.

Correlations

		walkhrs	wtloss
walkhrs	Pearson Correlation	1	.250
	Sig. (2-tailed)		.317
	N	18	18
wtloss	Pearson Correlation	.250	1
	Sig. (2-tailed)	.317	
	N	18	18

(1d) In a study examining the effects of brisk walking on weight loss, 18 adults were recruited and instructed to walk as many days of the week as possible for as long as they could. The researcher gathered each participant's daily walking time, as well as his or her weight at the beginning and end of the week, and found a positive correlation between the amount of walking time and the amount of weight lost ($r = .250$). Although the participants experienced some weight loss in this study, the correlation between walking and weight loss was not statistically significant ($p = .317$; $\alpha = .05$). As such, we do not reject H_0 but reject H_1.

NOTE: You might also inspect the descriptive statistics for *walkhrs* and *wtloss* and consider including the following supplement in your findings: "Participants averaged 5.9 hours of walking per week and had an average weight loss of 1.5 pounds."

3. Data Set A

(3a) H_0: There is no significant correlation between income and happiness.

H_1: There is a significant correlation between income and happiness.

(3b) Histograms with normal curve plots show a normal distribution for *income* and *alhs*, as shown in the two figures below; hence, the pretest criterion of normality is satisfied.

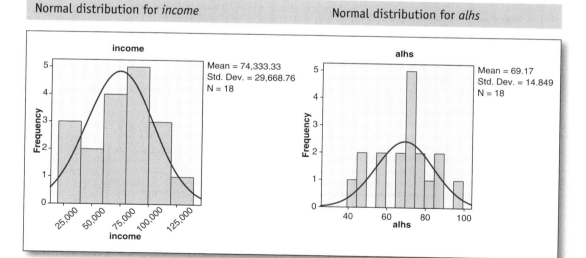

The scatterplot below shows that the straight regression line reasonably fits the field of points, and hence the criterion of linearity is satisfied. The scatterplot also shows that the points are primarily clustered toward the center of the regression line with substantially fewer points toward the ends, and hence the criterion of homoscedasticity is satisfied.

Scatterplot with regression line for *income* and *alhs* is linear and homoscedastic

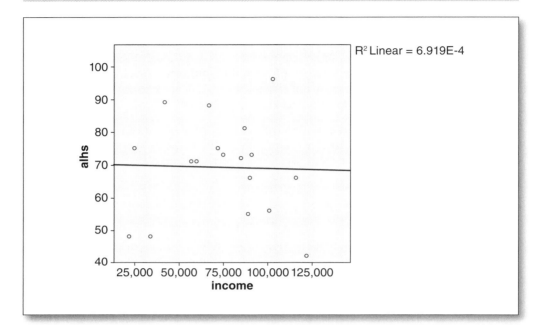

(3c)   The correlations table below shows a negative correlation ($r = -.026$) between *income* and *alhs,* but because $p = .917$, which is greater than the specified .05 α level, this is not a statistically significant correlation, as illustrated in the above scatterplot; note the flatness of the regression line along with the distance of the points from the regression line.

Correlations

		income	alhs
income	Pearson Correlation	1	-.026
	Sig. (2-tailed)		.917
	N	18	18
alhs	Pearson Correlation	-.026	1
	Sig. (2-tailed)	.917	
	N	18	18

(3d) In a study exploring the relationship between money and happiness, 18 adults were recruited and given a self-administered survey that asked their annual income; the survey also included the Acme Life Happiness Scale (ALHS), a 10-question survey that renders a score from 0 to 100 (0 = very unhappy . . . 100 = very happy). Our findings revealed a slight negative correlation ($r = -.026$), meaning that earning more money was slightly associated with less happiness, but this (negative) correlation was not statistically significant ($p = .917$; $\alpha = .05$). As such, we do not reject H_0 but reject H_1.

3. Data Set B

(3a) H_0: There is no significant correlation between income and happiness.

  H_1: There is a significant correlation between income and happiness.

(3b) Histograms with normal curve plots show a normal distribution for *income* and *alhs,* as shown in the two figures below; hence, the pretest criterion of normality is satisfied.

Normal distribution for *income*   Normal distribution for *alhs*

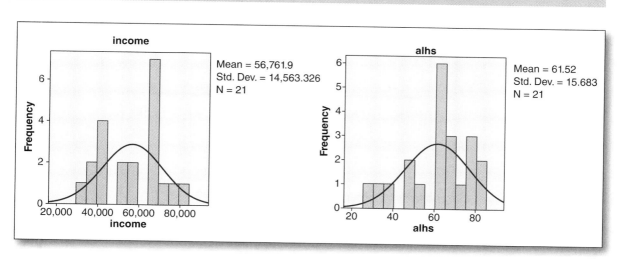

The scatterplot below shows that the straight regression line reasonably fits the field of points, and hence the criterion of linearity is satisfied. The scatterplot also shows that the points are primarily clustered toward the center of the regression line with substantially fewer points toward the ends, and hence the criterion of homoscedasticity is satisfied.

Scatterplot with regression line for *income* and *alhs* is linear and homoscedastic

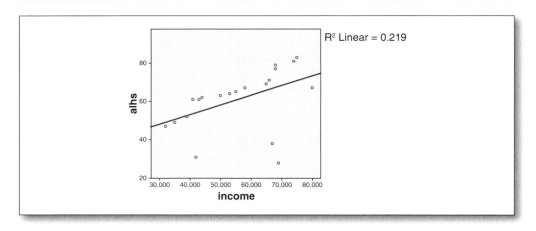

(3c) The correlations table below shows a negative correlation ($r = .468$) between income alhs; since $p = .032$, is less than the specified .05 α level, this indicates that this is a statistically significant correlation.

Correlations

		income	alhs
income	Pearson Correlation	1	.468*
	Sig. (2-tailed)		.032
	N	21	21
alhs	Pearson Correlation	.468*	1
	Sig. (2-tailed)	.032	
	N	21	21

*. Correlation is significant at the 0.05 level (2-tailed).

(3d) In a study exploring the relationship between money and happiness, 21 adults were recruited and given a self-administered survey that asked their annual income; the survey also included the Acme Life Happiness Scale (ALHS), a 10-question survey that renders a score from 0 to 100 (0 = very unhappy . . . 100 = very happy). Our findings revealed a positive correlation ($r = .468$), meaning that earning more money was associated with higher levels of happiness; this (positive) correlation was found to be statistically significant ($p = .032$; $\alpha = .05$). As such, we reject H_0 but do not reject H_1.

5. Data Set A

(5a) H_0: There is no significant correlation between years of education and job satisfaction.

H_1: There is a significant correlation between years of education and job satisfaction.

(5b) Histograms with normal curve plots show a normal distribution for *yearsed* and *ajsi,* as shown in the two figures below; hence, the pretest criterion of normality is satisfied.

Normal distribution for *yearsed*   Normal distribution for *ajsi*

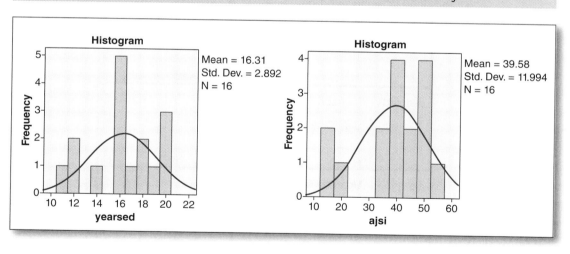

The scatterplot below shows that the straight regression line reasonably fits the field of points, and hence the criterion of linearity is satisfied. The scatterplot also shows that the points are primarily clustered toward the center of the regression line with substantially fewer points toward the ends, and hence the criterion of homoscedasticity is satisfied.

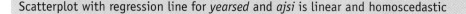

Scatterplot with regression line for *yearsed* and *ajsi* is linear and homoscedastic

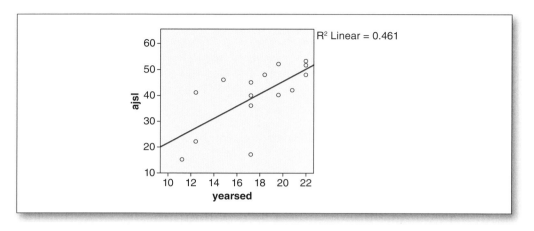

(5c) The correlations table below shows a positive correlation ($r = .679$) between *income* and *ajsi; p = .004*, which is less than the specified .05 α level, indicating that this is a statistically significant correlation, as illustrated in the scatterplot above; note the positive slope of the regression line and that most of the points are clustered fairly close to the regression line.

Correlations

		yearsed	ajsi
yearsed	Pearson Correlation	1	.679**
	Sig. (2-tailed)		.004
	N	16	16
ajsi	Pearson Correlation	.679**	1
	Sig. (2-tailed)	.004	
	N	16	16

**. Correlation is significant at the 0.01 level (2-tailed).

(5d) To assess the possible correlation between years of education and job satisfaction, 16 adults were recruited and given a self-administered survey that asked how many years of education they had; the survey also included the

Acme Job Satisfaction Inventory (AJSI), a six-question survey that renders a score from 0 to 60 (0 = very dissatisfied with one's job . . . 60 = very satisfied). The participant's education level ranged from 11th grade through master's degree. Our findings revealed a relatively strong positive correlation ($r = .679$), suggesting that those with more education tended to get more satisfaction from their jobs; this correlation was statistically significant ($p = .004$; $\alpha = .05$). As such, we reject H_0 but do not reject H_1.

5. Data Set B

(5a) H_0: There is no significant correlation between years of education and job satisfaction.

H_1: There is a significant correlation between years of education and job satisfaction.

(5b) Histograms with normal curve plots show a normal distribution for *yearsed* and *ajsi,* as shown in the two figures below; hence, the pretest criterion of normality is satisfied.

Normal distribution for *yearsed*   Normal distribution for *alhs*

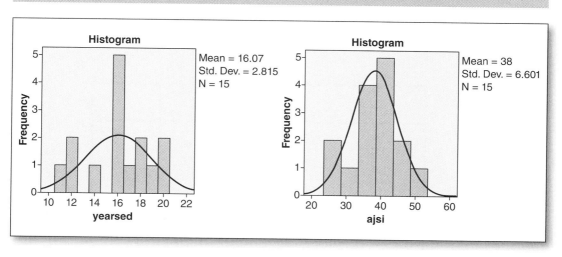

The scatterplot below shows that the straight regression line reasonably fits the field of points, and hence the criterion of linearity is satisfied. The scatterplot also shows that the points are primarily clustered toward the center of the regression line with substantially fewer points toward the ends, and hence the criterion of homoscedasticity is satisfied.

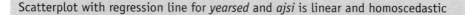

Scatterplot with regression line for *yearsed* and *ajsi* is linear and homoscedastic

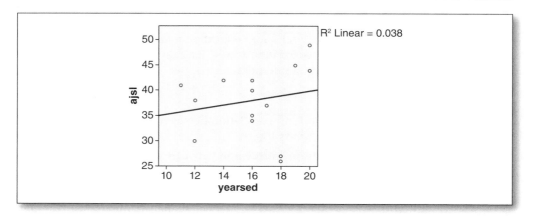

(5c) The correlations table below shows a relatively small positive correlation ($r = .196$) between *income* and *ajsi;* however, $p = .484$, which is greater than the specified .05 α level, indicating that this is not a statistically significant correlation, as illustrated in the scatterplot above; note the slight positive slope of the regression line and that most of the points are clustered fairly far from the regression line.

Correlations

		yearsed	ajsi
yearsed	Pearson Correlation	1	.196
	Sig. (2-tailed)		.484
	N	15	15
ajsi	Pearson Correlation	.196	1
	Sig. (2-tailed)	.484	
	N	15	15

(5d) To assess the possible correlation between years of education and job satisfaction, 15 adults were recruited and given a self-administered survey that asked how many years of education they had; the survey also included the Acme Job Satisfaction Inventory (AJSI), a six-question survey that renders a score from 0 to 60 (0 = very dissatisfied with one's job . . . 60 = very satisfied). The participant's education level ranged from 11th grade through master's degree. Our findings revealed a relatively mild positive correlation ($r = .196$), suggesting that those with more education tended to get somewhat more satisfaction from their jobs, but this correlation was not statistically significant ($p = .484$; $\alpha = .05$). As such, we do not reject H_0 but reject H_1.

7. Data Set A

   (7a) H_0: There is no significant correlation between height and self-confidence.

   H_1: There is a significant correlation between height and self-confidence.

   (7b) Histograms with normal curve plots show a normal distribution for *height* and *asci*, as shown in the two figures below; hence, the pretest criterion of normality is satisfied.

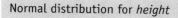

Normal distribution for *height*   Normal distribution for *asci*

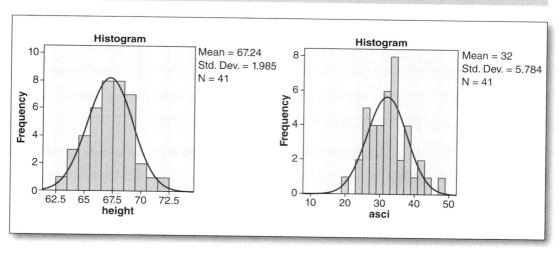

The scatterplot below shows that the straight regression line reasonably fits the field of points, and hence the criterion of linearity is satisfied. The scatterplot also shows that the points are primarily clustered toward the center of the regression line with substantially fewer points toward the ends, and hence the criterion of homoscedasticity is satisfied.

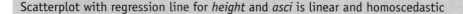

Scatterplot with regression line for *height* and *asci* is linear and homoscedastic

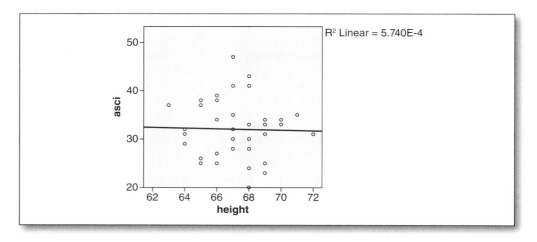

(7c) The correlations table below shows a relatively small negative correlation ($r = -.024$) between *height* and *asci*; $p = .882$, which is greater than the specified .05 α level, indicating that this is not a statistically significant correlation, as illustrated in the above scatterplot; note the relative flatness of the regression line and that most of the points are clustered fairly far from the regression line.

Correlations

		height	asci
Height	Pearson Correlation	1	−.024
	Sig. (2-tailed)		.882
	N	41	41
asci	Pearson Correlation	−.024	1
	Sig. (2-tailed)	.882	
	N	41	41

(7d) To evaluate the possible correlation between height and self-confidence, 41 adults were recruited and given a self-administered survey that asked them to indicate their height; the survey also included the Acme Self-Confidence

Index (ASCI), a 10-question survey that renders a score from 0 to 50 (0 = very low self-confidence . . . 50 = very high self-confidence). Our findings indicated a slight negative correlation between the variables ($r = -.024$), suggesting that taller people were slightly less self-confident than shorter people. Further analysis revealed that this correlation is not statistically significant ($p = .882$; $\alpha = .05$). As such, we do not reject H_0 but reject H_1.

7. Data Set B

(7a) H_0: There is no significant correlation between height and self-confidence.

H_1: There is a significant correlation between height and self-confidence.

(7b) Histograms with normal curve plots show a normal distribution for *height* and *asci,* as shown in the two figures below; hence, the pretest criterion of normality is satisfied.

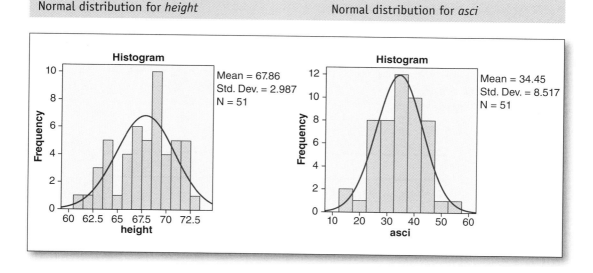

The scatterplot below shows that the straight regression line reasonably fits the field of points, and hence the criterion of linearity is satisfied. The scatterplot also shows that the points are primarily clustered toward the center of the regression line with substantially fewer points toward the ends, and hence the criterion of homoscedasticity is satisfied.

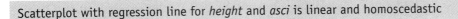
Scatterplot with regression line for *height* and *asci* is linear and homoscedastic

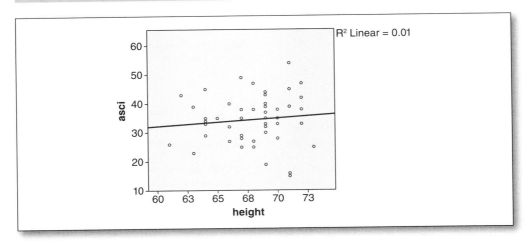

(7c) The correlations table below shows a relatively small positive correlation (r = .098) between *height* and *asci;* however, p = .492, which is greater than the specified .05 α level, indicating that this is not a statistically significant correlation, as illustrated in the above scatterplot; note the relative flatness of the regression line and that most of the points are clustered fairly far from the regression line.

Correlations

		height	asci
height	Pearson Correlation	1	.098
	Sig. (2-tailed)		.492
	N	51	51
asci	Pearson Correlation	.098	1
	Sig. (2-tailed)	.492	
	N	51	51

(7d) To evaluate the possible correlation between height and self-confidence, 51 adults were recruited and given a self-administered survey that asked their height; the survey also included the Acme Self-Confidence Index (ASCI), a

10-question survey that renders a score from 0 to 50 (0 = very low self-confidence . . . 50 = very high self-confidence). Our findings suggest that although there was a slight positive correlation between the variables ($r = .098$), implying that taller people tend to have more self-confidence than shorter people, it was determined that this correlation is not statistically significant ($p = .492$; $\alpha = .05$). As such, we do not reject H_0 but reject H_1.

9. Data Set A

(9a) H_0: There is no significant correlation between class time and freshman English grade.

H_1: There is a significant correlation between class time and freshman English grade.

(9b) Histograms with normal curve plots show a normal distribution for *time* and *grade,* as shown in the two figures below; hence, the pretest criterion of normality is satisfied.

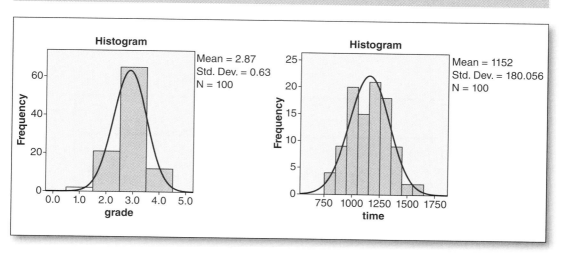

Normal distribution for *grade*

Normal distribution for *time*

The scatterplot below shows that the straight regression line reasonably fits the field of points, and hence the criterion of linearity is satisfied. The scatterplot also shows that the points are primarily clustered toward the center of the regression line with substantially fewer points toward the ends, and hence the criterion of homoscedasticity is satisfied.

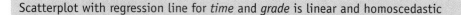

Scatterplot with regression line for *time* and *grade* is linear and homoscedastic

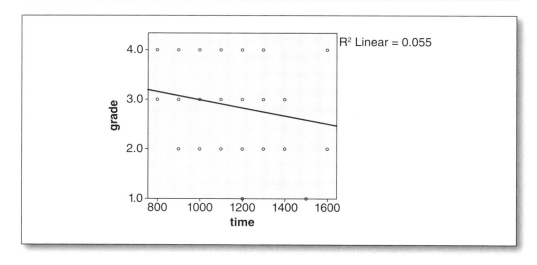

(9c) The correlations table below shows a relatively small negative correlation ($r = -.234$) between *time* and *grade; p* = .019, which is less than the specified .05 α level, indicating that this is a statistically significant correlation, as illustrated in the above scatterplot; note the negative slope of the regression line.

Correlations

		time	grade
time	Pearson Correlation	1	-.234*
	Sig. (2-tailed)		.019
	N	100	100
grade	Pearson Correlation	-.234*	1
	Sig. (2-tailed)	.019	
	N	100	100

*. Correlation is significant at the 0.05 level (2-tailed).

(9d) To evaluate the possible correlation between the time of day that students have their freshman English course and the associated grade, 100 students were surveyed and asked to present their transcript indicating the grade they received in freshman English; the transcript also indicated the day and time that the course met. Our findings revealed a negative correlation ($r = -.234$) between time of day and the grade received, suggesting that students enrolled in earlier classes outperformed those who took the same course later in the day. This correlation was determined to be statistically significant ($p = .019$, $\alpha = .05$). As such, we reject H_0 but do not reject H_1.

9. Data Set B

(9a) H_0: There is no significant correlation between class time and freshman English grade.

H_1: There is a significant correlation between class time and freshman English grade.

(9b) Histograms with normal curve plots show a normal distribution for *time* and *grade,* as shown in the two figures below; hence, the pretest criterion of normality is satisfied.

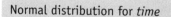

Normal distribution for *time*   Normal distribution for *grade*

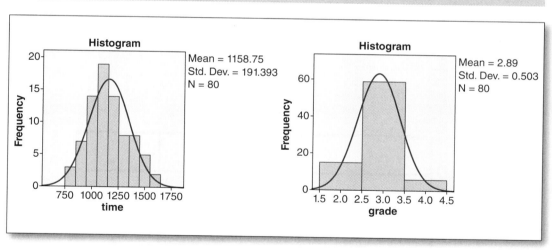

The scatterplot below shows that the straight regression line reasonably fits the field of points, and hence the criterion of linearity is satisfied. The scatterplot also shows that the points are primarily clustered toward the center of the regression line with substantially fewer points toward the ends, and hence the criterion of homoscedasticity is satisfied.

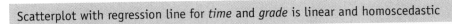

Scatterplot with regression line for *time* and *grade* is linear and homoscedastic

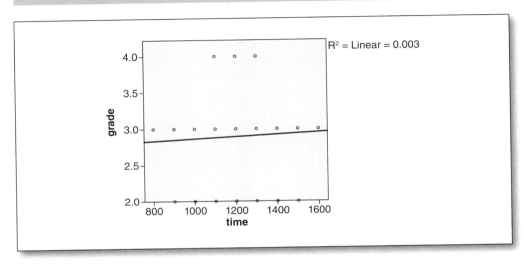

(9c) The correlations table below shows a relatively small positive correlation ($r = .056$) between *time* and *grade*; however, $p = .619$, which is greater than the specified .05 α level, indicating that this is not a statistically significant correlation, as illustrated in the above scatterplot; note the slight positive slope of the regression line.

Correlations

		time	grade
time	Pearson Correlation	1	.056
	Sig. (2-tailed)		.619
	N	80	80
grade	Pearson Correlation	.056	1
	Sig. (2-tailed)	.619	
	N	80	80

(9d) To evaluate the possible correlation between the time of day that students have their freshman English course and the associated grade, 80 students were surveyed and asked to present their transcript indicating the grade they received in freshman English; the transcript also indicated the day and time that the course met. Our findings revealed a slight positive correlation ($r = .056$) between time of day and the grade received, suggesting that students enrolled in classes held later in the day outperformed those who took the same course earlier in the day; however, this correlation was not statistically significant ($p = .619$, $\alpha = .05$). As such, we do not reject H_0 but reject H_1.

C H A P T E R   9

Chi-Square

1. Data Set A

(1a) H_0: There is no significant difference in ice cream preference in terms of gender.

H_1: There is a significant difference in ice cream preference in terms of gender.

(1b) Per the Crosstabulation table below, each cell contains an n of at least 5; hence, the pretest criterion is satisfied.

gender * icecream Crosstabulation

Count

		icecream			
		Chocolate	Strawberry	Vanilla	Total
gender	Female	11	5	7	23
	Male	5	15	5	25
Total		16	20	12	48

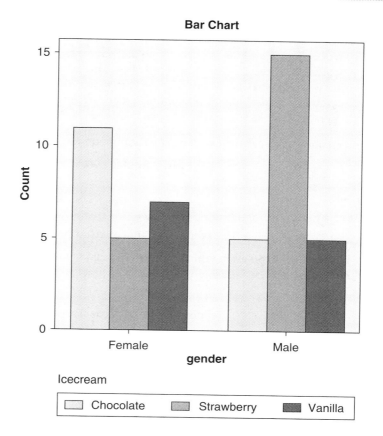

Bar Chart

Icecream
☐ Chocolate   ▨ Strawberry   ▦ Vanilla

(1c) The Chi-Square Tests table below shows a Sig. (*p*) value of .023, which is less than the specified .05 α level, indicating that there is a statistically significant difference among genders when it comes to ice cream preference.

Chi-Square Tests

	Value	df	Asymp. Sig. (2-sided)
Pearson Chi-Square	7.513[a]	2	.023
Likelihood Ratio	7.790	2	.020
Linear-by-Linear Association	.616	1	.433
N of Valid Cases	48		

a. 0 cells (.0%) have expected count less than 5. The minimum expected count is 5.75.

(1d) To determine if gender is associated with ice cream flavor preference, 48 participants (23 females, 25 males) were individually asked to identify which flavor of ice cream they prefer: chocolate, strawberry, or vanilla. Among the females, 11 of the 23 (48%*) selected chocolate, whereas 15 of the 25 (60%*) male participants favored strawberry. Our χ^2 (chi-square) findings revealed that there was a statistically significant difference in flavor preference with respect to gender ($p = .023$, $\alpha = .05$). As such, we reject H_0 but do not reject H_1.

X+Y

*NOTE: The percentages were calculated using the formula on page **207**:

$$\% = \textbf{Part} \div \textbf{Total} \times \textbf{100}.$$

1. Data Set B

(1a) H_0: There is no significant difference in ice cream preference in terms of gender.

H_1: There is a significant difference in ice cream preference in terms of gender.

(1b) Per the Crosstabulation table below, each cell contains an n of at least 5; hence, the pretest criterion is satisfied.

gender * icecream Crosstabulation

Count

| | | icecream | | | Total |
		Chocolate	Strawberry	Vanilla	
gender	Female	10	8	6	24
	Male	9	7	6	22
Total		19	15	12	46

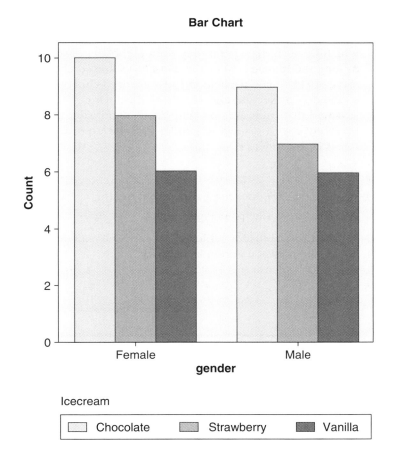

Bar Chart

(1c) The Chi-Square Tests table below shows a Sig. (p) value of .984, which is greater than the specified .05 α level, indicating that there is no statistically significant difference among genders when it comes to ice cream preference.

Chi-Square Tests

	Value	df	Asymp. Sig. (2-sided)
Pearson Chi-Square	.032[a]	2	.984
Likelihood Ratio	.032	2	.984
Linear-by-Linear Association	.016	1	.900
N of Valid Cases	46		

a. 0 cells (.0%) have expected count less than 5. The minimum expected count is 5.74.

(1d) To determine if gender is associated with ice cream flavor preference, 46 participants (24 females, 22 males) were individually asked to identify which flavor of ice cream they prefer: chocolate, strawberry, or vanilla. Among the females, 10 of the 24 (42%) selected chocolate; similarly, 9 of the 22 (41%) male participants also favored chocolate. Both genders ranked strawberry as second and vanilla as third. Our χ^2 (chi-square) findings revealed that there was no statistically significant difference in flavor preference with respect to gender ($p = .984$, $\alpha = .05$). As such, we do not reject H_0 but reject H_1.

3. Data Set A

(3a) H_0: The flu shot does not help prevent the flu.

H_1: The flu shot helps prevent the flu.

(3b) Per the Crosstabulation table below, each cell contains an n of at least 5; hence, the pretest criterion is satisfied.

flushot * flusick Crosstabulation

Count

		flusick		Total
		Got sick with flu	Did not get sick with flu	
flushot	Had flu shot	5	7	12
	Did not have flu shot	11	7	18
Total		16	14	30

Bar Chart

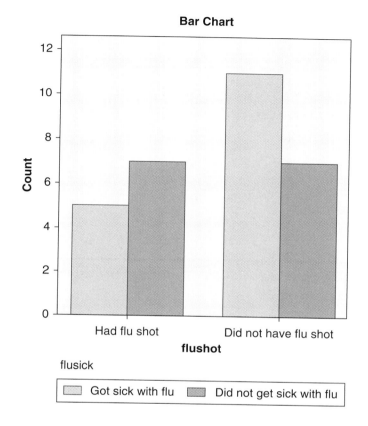

flusick

Got sick with flu   Did not get sick with flu

(3c) The Chi-Square Tests table below shows a Sig. (*p*) value of .296, which is greater than the specified .05 α level, indicating that there is no statistically significant difference in flu sickness comparing those who got a flu shot with those who did not.

Chi-Square Tests

	Value	df	Asymp. Sig. (2-sided)	Exact Sig. (2-sided)	Exact Sig. (1-sided)
Pearson Chi-Square	1.094[a]	1	.296		
Continuity Correction[b]	.452	1	.501		
Likelihood Ratio	1.098	1	.295		
Fisher's Exact Test				.457	.251
Linear-by-Linear Association	1.057	1	.304		
N of Valid Cases	30				

a. 0 cells (.0%) have expected count less than 5. The minimum expected count is 5.60.

b. Computed only for a 2x2 table

(3d) To determine if there were significantly fewer cases of flu among those who had a flu shot compared with those who did not, we analyzed the health status of 30 participants. Sixty days after recruiting participants, our researcher contacted each one to find out of they had contracted the flu. We found that 12 had gotten flu shots and 18 had not. Among those who got the flu shot, 41% reported that they had gotten sick with the flu compared with 61% among those who did not get a flu shot. Even though there were proportionally fewer cases of flu among those who had a flu shot, chi-square analysis indicates that this difference is not statistically significant ($p = .296$, $\alpha = .05$). As such, we do not reject H_0 but reject H_1.

3. Data Set B

(3a) H_0: The flu shot does not help prevent the flu.

H_1: The flu shot helps prevent the flu.

(3b) Per the Crosstabulation table below, each cell contains an n of at least 5; hence, the pretest criterion is satisfied.

flushot * flusick Crosstabulation

Count

		flusick		Total
		Got sick with flu	Did not get sick with flu	
flushot	Had flu shot	5	10	15
	Did not have flu shot	15	6	21
Total		20	16	36

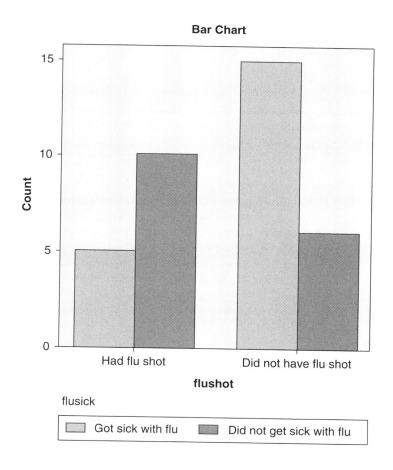

Bar Chart

(3c) The Chi-Square Tests table below shows a Sig. (p) value of .023, which is less than the specified .05 α level, indicating that there is a statistically significant difference in flu sickness comparing those who got a flu shot with those who did not.

Chi-Square Tests

	Value	df	Asymp. Sig. (2-sided)	Exact Sig. (2-sided)	Exact Sig. (1-sided)
Pearson Chi-Square	5.143[a]	1	.023		
Continuity Correction[b]	3.716	1	.054		
Likelihood Ratio	5.238	1	.022		
Fisher's Exact Test				.041	.026
Linear-by-Linear Association	5.000	1	.025		
N of Valid Cases	36				

a. 0 cells (.0%) have expected count less than 5. The minimum expected count is 6.67.

b. Computed only for a 2x2 table

(3d) To determine if there were significantly fewer cases of flu among those who had a flu shot compared with those who did not, we analyzed the health status of 36 participants. Sixty days after recruiting participants, our researcher contacted each one to find out of they had contracted the flu. We found that 15 had gotten flu shots, and 21 had not. Among those who got the flu shot, 33% reported that they had gotten sick with the flu compared with 71% among those who did not get a flu shot. Chi-square analysis indicates that this difference is statistically significant ($p = .023$, $\alpha = .05$). As such, we reject H_0 but do not reject H_1.

5. Data Set A

(5a) H_0: Responses are the same across media (face-to-face interview, mail-in survey, online survey) when it comes to asking about substance abuse.

H_1: Responses vary significantly across media (face-to-face interview, mail-in survey, online survey) when it comes to asking about substance abuse.

(5b) Per the Crosstabulation table below, each cell contains an n of at least 5; hence, the pretest criterion is satisfied.

media * drugs Crosstabulation

Count

		drugs		Total
		Yes	No	
media	Face-to-face interview	5	10	15
	Mail-in survey	5	12	17
	On-line survey	6	8	14
Total		16	30	46

Bar Chart

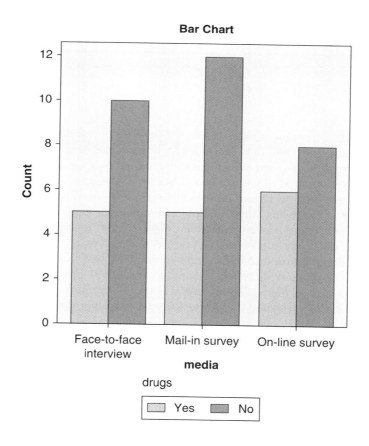

(5c) The Chi-Square Tests table below shows a Sig. (p) value of .729, which is greater than the specified .05 α level, indicating that there is no statistically significant difference in responses across the three media tested: face-to-face interview, mail-in survey, and online survey.

Chi-Square Tests

	Value	df	Asymp. Sig. (2-sided)
Pearson Chi-Square	.632[a]	2	.729
Likelihood Ratio	.626	2	.731
Linear-by-Linear Association	.270	1	.603
N of Valid Cases	46		

a. 1 cells (16.7%) have expected count less than 5. The minimum expected count is 4.87.

(5d) To determine if media make a difference in responses when it comes to inquiries regarding illegal substance use, we recruited 46 subjects and asked each to respond to one question: "Have you ever used illegal drugs?" However, our method of inquiry varied. Subjects were randomly assigned to one of three groups: The 15 participants in Group 1 were asked the question via a face-to-face interview, the 17 people assigned to Group 2 responded via standard pencil-and-paper mail-in survey, and the 14 in Group 3 were directed to an online survey website. The results revealed that 33% of those who were asked the question face-to-face replied that they had used illegal drugs (at least once) compared with 29% in the mail-in group and 43% in the online group. Although there is some response variability among these media, chi-square analysis revealed that these differences are not statistically significant ($p = .729$, $\alpha = .05$). Hence, we do not reject H_0 but do reject H_1.

5. Data Set B

(5a) H_0: Responses are the same across media (face-to-face interview, mail-in survey, online survey) when it comes to asking about substance abuse.

H_1: Responses vary across media (face-to-face interview, mail-in survey, online survey) when it comes to asking about substance abuse.

(5b) Per the Crosstabulation table below, each cell contains an n of at least 5; hence, the pretest criterion is satisfied.

media * drugs Crosstabulation

Count

		drugs		
		Yes	No	Total
media	Face-to-face interview	6	12	18
	Mail-in survey	13	5	18
	On-line survey	11	6	17
Total		30	23	53

Bar Chart

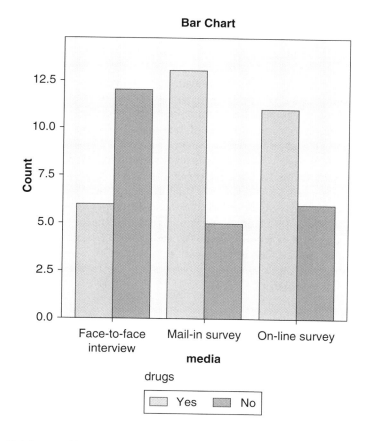

(5c) The Chi-Square Tests table below shows a Sig. (p) value of .045, which is less than the specified .05 α level, indicating that there is a statistically significant difference in responses across the three media tested: face-to-face interview, mail-in survey, and online survey.

Chi-Square Tests

	Value	df	Asymp. Sig. (2-sided)
Pearson Chi-Square	6.210[a]	2	.045
Likelihood Ratio	6.287	2	.043
Linear-by-Linear Association	3.537	1	.060
N of Valid Cases	53		

a. 0 cells (.0%) have expected count less than 5. The minimum expected count is 7.38.

(5d) To determine if media make a difference in responses when it comes to inquiries regarding illegal substance use, we recruited 53 subjects and asked each to respond to one question: "Have you ever used illegal drugs?" However, our method of inquiry varied. Subjects were randomly assigned to one of three groups: The 18 participants in Group 1 were asked the question via a face-to-face interview, the 18 people assigned to Group 2 responded via standard pencil-and-paper mail-in survey, and the 17 in Group 3 were directed to an online survey website. The results revealed that 33% of those who were asked the question face-to-face replied that they had used illegal drugs (at least once) compared with 72% in the mail-in group and 64% in the online group. Chi-square analysis revealed that these differences are statistically significant ($p = .045$, $\alpha = .05$). Hence, we would reject H_0 but not reject H_1. These findings suggest that when it comes to sensitive issues, participants who are interviewed face-to-face seem to "sanitize" or alter their responses to reveal less negative disclosure than those responding by less identifiable means (mail-in/online surveys).

7. Data Set A

(7a) H_0: Age is not associated with voting practices.

H_1: Age is associated with voting practices.

(7b) Per the Crosstabulation table below, each cell contains an n of at least 5; hence, the pretest criterion is satisfied.

age * vote Crosstabulation

Count

		vote			Total
		Vote in person	Vote by mail	Not vote	
age	18-35	6	14	6	26
	36-64	11	28	19	58
	65 -older	9	16	8	33
Total		26	58	33	117

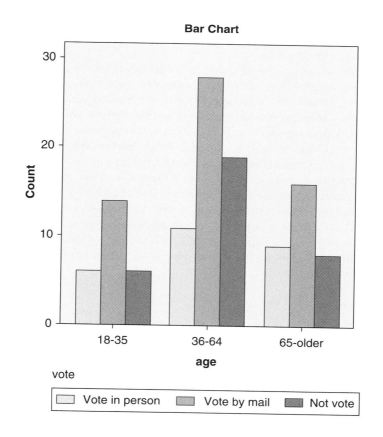

Bar Chart

(7c) The Chi-Square Tests table below shows a Sig. (*p*) value of .802, which is greater than the specified .05 α level, indicating that there is no statistically significant difference in voting practices across age groups.

Chi-Square Tests

	Value	df	Asymp. Sig. (2-sided)
Pearson Chi-Square	1.640[a]	4	.802
Likelihood Ratio	1.630	4	.803
Linear-by-Linear Association	.068	1	.794
N of Valid Cases	117		

a. 0 cells (.0%) have expected count less than 5. The minimum expected count is 5.78.

(7d) To determine if voting practices vary significantly across age groups, we surveyed a total of 117 participants spanning three age groups—26 were 18 to 35, 58 were 36 to 64, and 33 were 65 or older—and asked each about how they voted in the last election: voted in person, voted by mail, or did not vote. The majority of those surveyed in each category indicated they voted by mail: 54% in the 18 to 35 group and 48% in each of the other two groups. In-person voting ranged from 23% in the 18 to 35 group to 19% in the 36 to 64 group. Finally, when it comes to not voting, 36- to 64-year-olds topped the list at 33%, followed by the 65 or older group and the 18 to 35 group: 24% and 23%, respectively. Despite the moderate variability in voting practices observed among these groups, chi-square analysis indicates that these differences are not statistically significant (*p* = .802, α = .05). Hence, we do not reject H_0 but reject H_1. Among these groups, mail-in voting appears to be the preferred option.

7. Data Set B

(7a) H_0: Age is not associated with voting practices.

H_1: Age is associated with voting practices.

(7b) Per the Crosstabulation table below, each cell contains an *n* of at least 5; hence, the pretest criterion is satisfied.

age * vote Crosstabulation

Count

		vote			Total
		Vote in person	Vote by mail	Not vote	
age	18-35	5	8	12	25
	36-64	6	15	5	26
	65 - older	20	16	5	41
Total		31	39	22	92

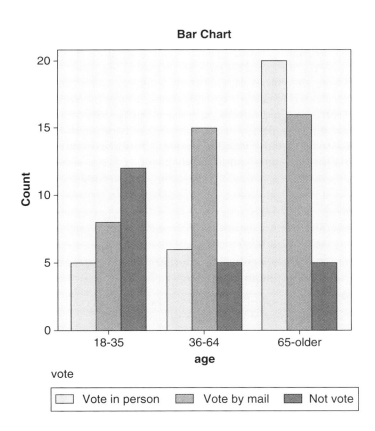

Bar Chart

(7c) The Chi-Square Tests table below shows a Sig. (p) value of .003, which is less than the specified .05 α level, indicating that there is a statistically significant difference in voting practices based on age groups.

Chi-Square Tests

	Value	df	Asymp. Sig. (2-sided)
Pearson Chi-Square	15.871[a]	4	.003
Likelihood Ratio	14.947	4	.005
Linear-by-Linear Association	11.533	1	.001
N of Valid Cases	92		

a. 0 cells (.0%) have expected count less than 5. The minimum expected count is 5.98.

(7d) To determine if voting practices vary significantly across age groups, we surveyed a total of 60 participants spanning three age groups—25 were 18 to 35, 26 were 36 to 64, and 41 were 65 or older—and asked each about how they voted in the last election: voted in person, voted by mail, or did not vote. Each group indicated a different majority: 48% of those in the 18 to 35 group did not vote, 58% of those in the 36 to 64 group voted by mail, and 49% of those 65 or older voted in person. Chi-square analysis revealed that there is a statistically significant difference among age groups when it comes to voting practices ($p = .003$, $\alpha = .05$). Hence, we rejected H_0 but did not reject H_1.

9. Data Set A

(9a) H_0: There is no significant difference in university admissions based on high school (public vs. private).

H_1: There is a significant difference in university admissions based on high school (public vs. private).

(9b) Per the Crosstabulation table below, each cell contains an n of at least 5; hence, the pretest criterion is satisfied.

school * college Crosstabulation

Count

		college		Total
		Not attending university	Attending university	
school	Acme Academy	22	27	49
	Anytown High School	109	116	225
Total		131	143	274

Bar Chart

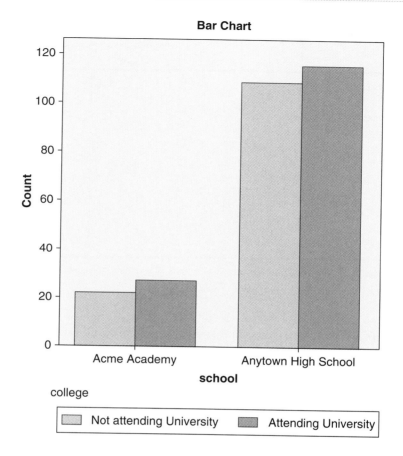

college

| Not attending University | Attending University |

(9c)   The Chi-Square Tests table below shows a Sig. (*p*) value of .652, which is greater than the specified .05 α level, indicating that there is no statistically significant difference in university admissions based on school (public vs. private).

Chi-Square Tests

	Value	df	Asymp. Sig. (2-sided)	Exact Sig. (2-sided)	Exact Sig. (1-sided)
Pearson Chi-Square	.203[a]	1	.652		
Continuity Correction[b]	.086	1	.770		
Likelihood Ratio	.203	1	.652		
Fisher's Exact Test				.753	.386
Linear-by-Linear Association	.202	1	.653		
N of Valid Cases	274				

a. 0 cells (.0%) have expected count less than 5. The minimum expected count is 23.43.

b. Computed only for a 2x2 table

(9d) We evaluated college admission rates from two schools: the Acme Academy, a private school with a graduating class of 49 students, and Anytown High School, a public school with a graduating class of 225 students. We found that 55% of those who graduated from the Acme Academy were admitted to a university compared with 51% of the students who graduated from Anytown High School. In terms of total students, Acme Academy launched 27 students into higher education compared with 116 students from Anytown High School. Despite the variability among these figures, chi-square analysis indicates that the (proportional) difference is not statistically significant ($p = .652$, $\alpha = .05$). Hence, we do not reject H_0 but reject H_1.

9. Data Set B

(9a) H_0: There is no significant difference in university admissions based on high school (public vs. private).

H_1: There is a significant difference in university admissions based on high school (public vs. private).

(9b) Per the Crosstabulation table below, each cell contains an n of at least 5; hence, the pretest criterion is satisfied.

school * college Crosstabulation

Count

		college		Total
		Not attending university	Attending university	
school	Acme Academy	5	28	33
	Anytown High School	72	78	150
Total		77	106	183

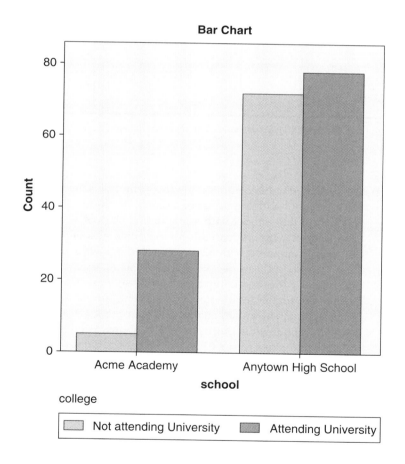

Bar Chart

(9c) The Chi-Square Tests table below shows a Sig. (*p*) value of .001, which is less than the specified .05 α level, indicating that there is a statistically significant difference in university admissions based on school (public vs. private).

Chi-Square Tests

	Value	df	Asymp. Sig. (2-sided)	Exact Sig. (2-sided)	Exact Sig. (1-sided)
Pearson Chi-Square	11.975[a]	1	.001		
Continuity Correction[b]	10.666	1	.001		
Likelihood Ratio	13.301	1	.000		
Fisher's Exact Test				.000	.000
Linear-by-Linear Association	11.910	1	.001		
N of Valid Cases	183				

a. 0 cells (.0%) have expected count less than 5. The minimum expected count is 13.89.

b. Computed only for a 2x2 table

(9d) We evaluated college admission rates from two schools: the Acme Academy, a private school with a graduating class of 33 students, and Anytown High School, a public school with a graduating class of 150 students. We found that 85% of those who graduated from the Acme Academy were admitted to a university compared with 52% of the students who graduated from Anytown High School. In terms of total students, Acme Academy launched 28 students into higher education compared with 78 students from Anytown High School. Despite the higher total number of students admitted to a university from the public school, chi-square analysis indicates that proportionally, the Acme Academy significantly outperformed Anytown High School when it comes to college admissions (*p* = .001, α = .05). Hence, we reject H_0 but do not reject H_1.

Supplemental SPSS Operations

(1a)

Rec.#	name	score	skill
1	Adrian	50	Novice
2	Alex	46	Novice
3	Avery	62	Novice
4	Bailey	71	Intermediate
5	Blaine	88	Expert
6	Blake	22	Novice
7	Bo	70	Intermediate
8	Brett	27	Novice
9	Brook	61	Novice
10	Cameron	67	Novice
11	Cary	37	Novice
12	Casey	59	Novice
13	Chris	12	Novice
14	Corey	44	Novice
15	Dale	48	Novice
16	Daryl	71	Intermediate
17	Dean	84	Intermediate
18	Devin	49	Novice
19	Drew	75	Intermediate
20	Dustin	71	Intermediate

21	Dusty	82	Intermediate
22	Erin	44	Novice
23	Evan	42	Novice
24	Jaden	82	Intermediate
25	Jan	59	Novice
26	Jean	5	Novice
27	Jess	34	Novice
28	Jessie	72	Intermediate
29	Kelly	68	Novice
30	Kerry	17	Novice
31	Kyle	58	Novice
32	Lee	39	Novice
33	Lindsay	73	Intermediate
34	Morgan	82	Intermediate
35	Ray	27	Novice
36	Rene	49	Novice
37	Riley	27	Novice
38	Robin	46	Novice
39	Ryan	2	Novice
40	Sandy	92	Expert
41	Sean	11	Novice
42	Spencer	85	Expert
43	Taylor	22	Novice
44	Toby	58	Novice
45	Val	58	Novice
46	Zane	61	Novice

(1b)

Rec.#	name	score	skill
1	Sandy	92	Expert
2	Blaine	88	Expert
3	Spencer	85	Expert
4	Dean	84	Intermediate
5	Dusty	82	Intermediate
6	Jaden	82	Intermediate
7	Morgan	82	Intermediate
8	Drew	75	Intermediate
9	Lindsay	73	Intermediate
10	Jessie	72	Intermediate
11	Bailey	71	Intermediate
12	Daryl	71	Intermediate
13	Dustin	71	Intermediate
14	Bo	70	Intermediate
15	Kelly	68	Novice
16	Cameron	67	Novice
17	Avery	62	Novice
18	Brook	61	Novice
19	Zane	61	Novice
20	Casey	59	Novice
21	Jan	59	Novice
22	Kyle	58	Novice
23	Toby	58	Novice
24	Val	58	Novice
25	Adrian	50	Novice

26	Devin	49	Novice
27	Rene	49	Novice
28	Dale	48	Novice
29	Alex	46	Novice
30	Robin	46	Novice
31	Corey	44	Novice
32	Erin	44	Novice
33	Evan	42	Novice
34	Lee	39	Novice
35	Cary	37	Novice
36	Jess	34	Novice
37	Brett	27	Novice
38	Ray	27	Novice
39	Riley	27	Novice
40	Blake	22	Novice
41	Taylor	22	Novice
42	Kerry	17	Novice
43	Chris	12	Novice
44	Sean	11	Novice
45	Jean	5	Novice
46	Ryan	2	Novice

(3a)

Statistics

Score

N	Valid	11
	Missing	0
Mean		75.73
Median		73.00
Mode		71[a]
Std. Deviation		5.551
Variance		30.818
Range		14
Minimum		70
Maximum		84

a. Multiple modes exist. The smallest value is shown

Histogram

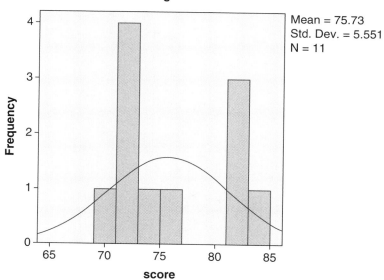

Mean = 75.73
Std. Dev. = 5.551
N = 11

(3b)

Statistics

Score

N	Valid	25
	Missing	0
Mean		45.16
Median		46.00
Mode		27[a]
Std. Deviation		12.957
Variance		167.890
Range		40
Minimum		22
Maximum		62

a. Multiple modes exist. The smallest
value is shown

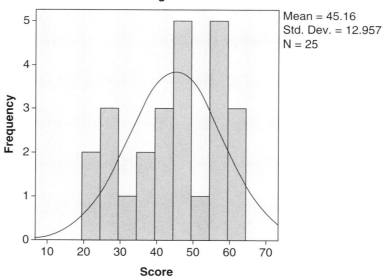

Histogram

Mean = 45.16
Std. Dev. = 12.957
N = 25

(5a)

Rec. #	name	score	skill	passfail
1	Brook	61	Novice	Fail
2	Ray	27	Novice	Fail
3	Spencer	85	Expert	Pass
4	Cary	37	Novice	Fail
5	Morgan	82	Intermediate	Pass
6	Erin	44	Novice	Fail
7	Toby	58	Novice	Fail
8	Zane	61	Novice	Fail
9	Riley	27	Novice	Fail
10	Lee	39	Novice	Fail
11	Corey	44	Novice	Fail
12	Ryan	2	Novice	Fail
13	Drew	75	Intermediate	Pass
14	Jess	34	Novice	Fail
15	Jaden	82	Intermediate	Pass
16	Dustin	71	Intermediate	Fail
17	Bo	70	Intermediate	Fail
18	Val	58	Novice	Fail
19	Blake	22	Novice	Fail
20	Dean	84	Intermediate	Pass
21	Casey	59	Novice	Fail
22	Jessie	72	Intermediate	Fail
23	Chris	12	Novice	Fail
24	Robin	46	Novice	Fail
25	Evan	42	Novice	Fail
26	Jan	59	Novice	Fail
27	Daryl	71	Intermediate	Fail
28	Dale	48	Novice	Fail
29	Devin	49	Novice	Fail

30	Sandy	92	Expert	Pass
31	Avery	62	Novice	Fail
32	Lindsay	73	Intermediate	Fail
33	Rene	49	Novice	Fail
34	Blaine	88	Expert	Pass
35	Kyle	58	Novice	Fail
36	Cameron	67	Novice	Fail
37	Sean	11	Novice	Fail
38	Kerry	17	Novice	Fail
39	Brett	27	Novice	Fail
40	Bailey	71	Intermediate	Fail
41	Jean	5	Novice	Fail
42	Kelly	68	Novice	Fail
43	Taylor	22	Novice	Fail
44	Alex	46	Novice	Fail
45	Adrian	50	Novice	Fail
46	Dusty	82	Intermediate	Pass

(5b)

Descriptives

score

	N	Mean	Std. Deviation	Std. Error	95% Confidence Interval for Mean		Minimum	Maximum
					Lower Bound	Upper Bound		
Failed	38	45.76	20.576	3.338	39.00	52.53	2	73
Passed	8	83.75	4.979	1.760	79.59	87.91	75	92
Total	46	52.37	23.746	3.501	45.32	59.42	2	92

ANOVA

score

	Sum of Squares	df	Mean Square	F	Sig.
Between Groups	9536.349	1	9536.349	26.493	.000
Within Groups	15838.368	44	359.963		
Total	25374.717	45			

(7)

 comment Program: Weekly Report – 3 Subject Test.sps.
 comment Programmed by H Knapp.
 comment Revision 1.2.
 comment Data file: Chapter 10 – Exercise 06.sav.

 comment This program runs the weekly report for the reading, writing, and math scores.
 comment It performs a three-level sort on the data by reading (ascending), by writing (descending), and by math (ascending).
 comment Finally, it runs descriptive statistics with histograms for reading and math scores.
 comment -.
 comment Sort the data using a three-level sort: (1) reading [ascending], (2) writing [descending], (3) math [ascending].

 DATASET ACTIVATE DataSet8.
 SORT CASES BY reading(A) writing(D) math(A).

 comment Run descriptive statistics (mean, median, mode, maximum, minimum, range, standard deviation, and variance) for reading and math; also include histograms with normal curves for those variables.

 FREQUENCIES VARIABLES=reading math
  /FORMAT=NOTABLE
  /STATISTICS=STDDEV VARIANCE RANGE MINIMUM MAXIMUM MEAN MEDIAN MODE
  /HISTOGRAM NORMAL
  /ORDER=ANALYSIS.

 comment end of Syntax file.

(9)

The purpose of a work file is to preserve the source (master) data set in its original form to protect against operator or system errors. Before beginning to work on a data set, it is good practice to make two copies of it: one to save in its original state and another to work on. For example, if the original file is called *Project18.sav,* I would make two copies of the data: *Project18[MASTER].sav* and *Project18[WORK].sav.*

I would work on only the *Project18[WORK].sav* file and store *Project18[MASTER].sav* someplace safe. If somehow the *Project18[WORK].sav* file became altered or corrupted, I could easily create a new *Project18[WORK].sav* work file from the *Project18[MASTER].sav* file.

Index

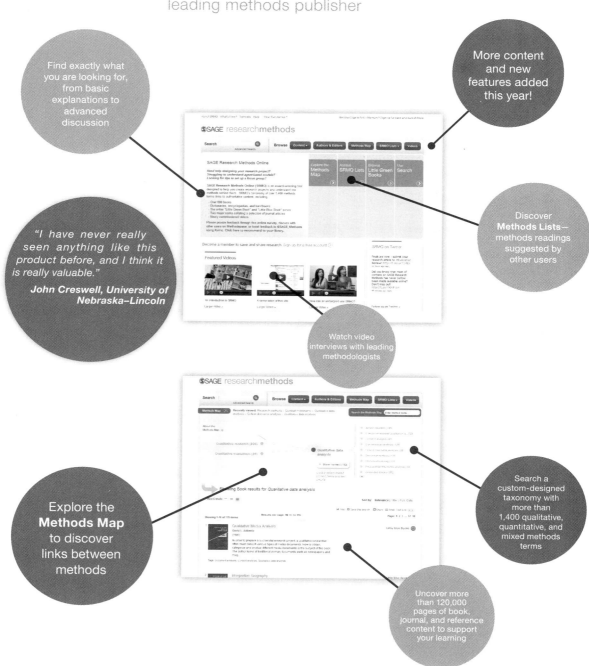

⑤SAGE researchmethods

The essential online tool for researchers from the world's leading methods publisher

Find exactly what you are looking for, from basic explanations to advanced discussion

More content and new features added this year!

"I have never really seen anything like this product before, and I think it is really valuable."

John Creswell, University of Nebraska–Lincoln

Discover **Methods Lists**—methods readings suggested by other users

Watch video interviews with leading methodologists

Explore the **Methods Map** to discover links between methods

Search a custom-designed taxonomy with more than 1,400 qualitative, quantitative, and mixed methods terms

Uncover more than 120,000 pages of book, journal, and reference content to support your learning

Find out more at
www.sageresearchmethods.com